MOSAICS

THIRD EDITION

MOSAICS

FOCUSING ON SENTENCES IN CONTEXT

KIM FLACHMANN

PEARSON
Prentice
Hall

Upper Saddle River, New Jersey 07458

Library of Congress Cataloging-in-Publication Data

Flachmann, Kim.
    Mosaics, focusing on sentences in context / Kim Flachmann.—3rd ed.
        p. cm. — (Mosaics)
    Includes index.
        ISBN 0-13-189358-0
        1. English language—Sentences—Problems, exercises, etc.   2. English
language—Rhetoric—Problems, exercises, etc.   I. Title: Focusing on sentences in context.
    II. Title. III. Mosaics (Upper Saddle River, N.J.)

PE1441.F48 2005
808'.042—dc22

2004050552

Editorial Director: *Leah Jewell*
Senior Acquisitions Editor: *Craig Campanella*
Editorial Assistant: *Joan Polk*
Developmental Editor-in-Chief: *Rochelle Diogenes*
Development Editor: *Marta Tomins*
Media Project Manager: *Christy Schaack*
Marketing Director: *Beth Mejia*
VP/Director of Production and Manufacturing: *Barbara Kittle*
Production Editor: *Maureen Benicasa*
Production Assistant: *Marlene Gassler*
Copyeditor: *Donna Mulder*
Permissions Coordinator: *Ron Fox*
Text Permission Specialist: *Jane Scelta*

Prepress & Manufacturing Manager: *Nick Sklitsis*
Prepress & Manufacturing Buyer: *Ben Smith*
Creative Design Director: *Leslie Osher*
Interior & Cover Designer: *Carmen DiBartolomeo, C2K, Inc.*
Director, Image Resource Center: *Melinda Reo*
Manager, Rights and Permissions: *Zina Arabia*
Manager, Visual Research: *Beth Brenzel*
Image Permission Coordinator: *Robert Farrell*
Cover Art: *Jellybeans, Omni-Photo Communications, Inc.*
Composition: *Interactive Composition Corporation*
Printer/Binder: *Quebecor World Book Services*
Cover Printer: *Phoenix Color Corporation*

This book was set in 11/13 Goudy.

Credits and acknowledgments borrowed from other sources and reproduced, with permission, in this textbook appear on appropriate page within text (or on pages 706–707).

Pearson Education LTD, London
Pearson Education Australia PTY, Limited
Pearson Education Singapore, Pte. Ltd
Pearson Education North Asia Ltd
Pearson Education, Canada, Ltd
Pearson Educación de Mexico, S.A. de C.V.
Pearson Education—Japan
Pearson Education Malaysia, Pte. Ltd
Pearson Education, Upper Saddle River, New Jersey

For
Laura

10 9 8 7 6 5 4 3
ISBN 0-13-189358-0

Brief Contents

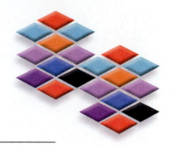

CONTENTS

Experience tells us that students have the best chance of succeeding in college if they learn how to respond productively to the varying academic demands made on them throughout the curriculum. One extremely important part of this process is being able to analyze ideas and think critically about issues in many different subject areas. *Mosaics: Focusing on Sentences in Context* is the first in a series of three books that teach the basic skills essential to all good academic writing. This series illustrates how the companion skills of reading and writing are parts of a larger, interrelated process that moves back and forth through the tasks of prereading and reading, prewriting and writing, and revising and editing. In other words, the *Mosaics* series shows how these skills are integrated at every stage of the writing process.

THE *MOSAICS* SERIES

This third edition of the *Mosaics* series consists of three books, each with a different emphasis: *Focusing on Sentences in Context*, *Focusing on Paragraphs in Context*, and *Focusing on Essays*. The first book highlights sentence structure, the second book paragraph development, and the third the composition of essays. Each book introduces the writing process as a unified whole and asks students to begin writing in the very first chapter. Each volume also moves from personal to more academic writing. The books differ in the length and level of their reading selections, the complexity of their writing assignments, the degree of difficulty of their revising and editing strategies, and the length and level of their student writing samples.

This entire three-book series is based on the following fundamental assumptions:

- Students build confidence in their ability to read and write by reading and writing.
- Students learn best from discovery and experimentation rather than from instruction and abstract discussions.
- Students need to discover their personal writing process.
- Students learn both individually and collaboratively.

- Students profit from studying both professional and student writing.
- Students benefit most from assignments that actually integrate thinking, reading, and writing.
- Students learn how to revise by following clear guidelines.
- Students learn grammar and usage rules by editing their own writing.
- Students must be able to transfer their writing skills to all their college courses.
- Students must think critically and analytically to succeed in college.

HOW THIS BOOK WORKS

Mosaics: Focusing on Sentences in Context teaches students how to write effective sentences. For flexibility and easy reference, this book is divided into four parts:

Part I: The Writing Process
Part II: Writing Effective Sentences
Part III: Paragraphs: Sentences in Context
Part IV: From Reading to Writing

Part I: The Writing Process   All six chapters in Part I demonstrate the cyclical nature of the writing process. They begin with the logistics of getting ready to write and then move systematically through the interlocking stages of the process by following a student essay from prewriting to revising and editing. Part I ends with a quiz that students can take to identify their "Editing Quotient"—their strengths and weaknesses in grammar and mechanics.

Part II: Writing Effective Sentences   Part II, the heart of the instruction in this text, is a complete handbook—including exercises—that covers eight main categories: Sentences, Verbs, Pronouns, Modifiers, Punctuation, Mechanics, Effective Sentences, and Choosing the Right Word. These categories are coordinated with the Editing Checklist that appears throughout this text. The chapters provide at least four types of practice after each grammar concept, moving students systematically from identifying grammar and usage problems to writing their own sentences. Within each chapter, students read professional paragraphs, write their own paragraphs, edit another student's writing, and always edit their own writing. Each unit ends with practical editing exercises that ask students to use the skills they just learned to edit a paragraph written by another student and then edit the paragraph they wrote earlier in the chapter.

Part III: Paragraphs: Sentences in Context   The next section of this text helps students move from writing effective sentences to writing effective paragraphs. It systematically explains how to recognize, write, revise, and edit a paragraph. Then it shows paragraphs at work in both professional and student examples. Part III ends with a series of writing assignments and workshops designed to encourage students to write, revise, and edit a paragraph (or essay) and then reflect on their own writing process.

Part IV: From Reading to Writing   Part IV of this text is a collection of readings arranged by rhetorical mode. Multiple rhetorical strategies are at work in most of these essays, but each is classified according to its primary rhetorical purpose. Each professional essay is preceded by prereading activities that will help students focus on the topic at hand and then is followed by nine questions that move students from literal to analytical thinking skills as they consider the essay's content, purpose, audience, and paragraph structure.

APPENDIXES

The appendixes will help students keep track of their progress in the various skills they are learning throughout this text. References to these appendixes are interspersed throughout the book so that students know when to use them as they study the concepts in each chapter:

Appendix 1: Critical Thinking Log
Appendix 2: Revising and Editing Peer Evaluation Forms
Appendix 3: Editing Quotient Error Chart
Appendix 4: Error Log
Appendix 5: Spelling Log

OVERALL GOAL

Ultimately, each book in the *Mosaics* series portrays writing as a way of thinking and processing information. One by one, these books encourage students to discover how the "mosaics" of their own writing process work together to form a coherent whole. By demonstrating the interrelationship among thinking, reading, and writing on progressively more difficult levels, these books promise to help prepare your students for success in college throughout the curriculum.

UNIQUE FEATURES

Several unique and exciting features separate this book from other basic writing texts:

- It moves students systematically from personal to academic writing.
- It uses both student writing and professional writing as models.
- It demonstrates all aspects of the writing process through student writing.
- It integrates reading and writing throughout the text.
- It teaches revising and editing through student writing.
- It features culturally diverse reading selections that are of high interest to students.
- It teaches rhetorical modes as patterns of thought.
- It helps students discover their own writing process.
- It includes a complete handbook with exercises.
- It offers worksheets for students to chart their progress in reading and writing.

ACKNOWLEDGMENTS

I want to acknowledge the support, encouragement, and sound advice of several people who have helped me through the development of the *Mosaics* series. First, Prentice Hall has provided guidance and inspiration for this project through the wisdom of Craig Campanella, senior acquisitions editor; the insights and vision of Marta Tomins and Harriett Prentiss, development editors; the diligence and clairvoyance of Maureen Benicasa, production editor; the foresight and prudence of Leah Jewell, editorial director; the boundless creative inspiration of Rachel Falk, former marketing manager; the resourceful oversight of Rochelle Diogenes, editor in chief, development; the brilliant leadership of Yolanda de Rooy, President of Humanities and Social Sciences; the hard work and patience of Ron Fox and Jane Scelta, permissions editors; the guidance and fortitude of Donna Mulder, copyeditor; and the common sense and organization of Joan Polk, administrative assistant for developmental English. Also, this book would not be a reality without the insightful persistence of Phil Miller, publisher for modern languages.

I want to give very special thanks to Cheryl Smith, my constant source of inspiration in her role as consultant and advisor for the duration of this project. She was also the co-author of the margin annotations and the co-ordinator of the *Mosaics Instructor's Resource Manuals*. I am also grateful to Rebecca Hewett, Valerie Turner, and Li'i Pearl for their discipline and hard work on the *Instructor's Resource Manuals* for each of the books in the series. And I want to thank Crystal Huddleston, Zandree Stidham, Brooke King, and Anne Elrod for their expertise and assistance.

In addition, I am especially grateful to the following reviewers who have guided me through the development and revision of this book: Lisa Berman, Miami-Dade Community College; Patrick Haas, Glendale Community College; Jeanne Campanelli, American River College; Dianne Gregory, Cape Cod Community College; Clara Wilson-Cook, Southern University at New Orleans; Thomas Beery, Lima Technical College; Jean Petrolle, Columbia College; David Cratty, Cuyahoga Community College; Allison Travis, Butte State College; Suellen Meyer, Meramec Community College; Jill Lahnstein, Cape Fear Community College; Stanley Coberly, West Virginia State University at Parkersville; Jamie Moore, Scottsdale Community College; Nancy Hellner, Mesa Community College; Ruth Hatcher, Washtenaw Community College; Thurmond Whatley, Aiken Technical College; W. David Hall, Columbus State Community College; Marilyn Coffee, Fort Hays State University; Valerie Russell, Valencia Community College; Elizabeth McCall, Gaston College; Sara Safdie, Bellevue Community College; Garrett Flagg, Fayetteville Technical Community College; Irene Gilliam, Tallahassee Community College; and Patricia M. Shade, Merced College.

I also want to express my gratitude to my students, from whom I have learned so much about the writing process, about teaching, and about life itself, and to Cheryl Smith's students, who tested various sections of the books and gave me good ideas for revising them over the past three years. Thanks also to the students who contributed paragraphs and essays to this series: Josh Ellis, Jolene Christie, Mary Minor, Michael Tiede, and numerous others.

Finally, I owe a tremendous personal debt to the people who have lived with this project for the last two years; they are my closest companions and my best advisers: Michael, Christopher, and Laura Flachmann. To Michael, I owe additional thanks for the valuable support and feedback he has given me through the entire process of creating and revising this series.

Kim Flachmann

I

THE WRITING PROCESS

Writing and rewriting are a constant search for what it is one is saying.

—JOHN UPDIKE

The primary goal of this first part of *Mosaics* is to show you how important good sentences are as building blocks to good writing. Clear, effective sentences are the result of clear thinking, and clear thinking will help you get good grades and good jobs. Sentences are the foundation of all of your writing—whether it is a history essay exam, a writing assignment for English, a memo asking for a raise, or an editorial for the newspaper. Your sentences represent you everywhere you go.

WRITING SUCCESSFUL SENTENCES

The fact that a person writes every day makes that person a writer. Whether you make a list of chores to do, e-mail a friend, do your English assignment, or write a note to your manager, you are part of a community of writers. In fact, you *are* a writer.

The more you know about writing sentences, the better you can communicate and get what you want out of life. You should decide what you are trying to say and then state it in the best way possible so that you reach your audience and achieve your purpose. For example, if you want to tell your parents how serious you are about school, you might write, "I am adjusting well to college. I study every day. I hardly go out at all, and I am really serious about school." To a friend, however, you might write the same message with a slightly different slant: "I hope this adjustment period is over soon. I have to study all the time to survive. I have no social life to speak of, and my classes are killing me." Since your purpose is slightly different in these two cases, you choose different words to convey your message.

All writing starts with good sentences. In fact, any piece of writing more formal than a grocery list is usually the result of a series of activities that we call *the writing process*. On the surface, some of these activities may seem to have very little to do with the act of writing itself. But learning to use this process to help you communicate your ideas is part of learning to write well.

YOUR APPROACH TO WRITING

Everyone approaches writing in a different way. At the same time, some general guidelines apply to all writers—students and professionals alike. They include setting aside a time and place for your writing task, gathering the necessary supplies, and thinking of yourself as a writer.

1. ***Set aside a special time for writing, and plan to do nothing else during that time.*** The bills will wait until tomorrow; your car doesn't have to be washed today; your room can be cleaned some other time; and

the dirt on your bike won't turn to concrete overnight. When you first get a writing assignment, a little procrastination is good because it gives your mind time to plan your approach to the task. The trick is to know when to quit procrastinating and get down to work so that you can make your deadline. Don't wait until the day before your paper is due to begin.

2. ***Find a comfortable place with few distractions.*** You need to set up your own place for writing, one that suits your individual needs. Ideally, it should be some place where you will not be distracted or interrupted. Some people work best sitting at a table or desk, while others write best on the floor or on a bed. The particular place doesn't matter, as long as you feel comfortable writing there. Also, some people write best with noise in the background, while others need complete silence. Some snack and wear their favorite jeans while they write, and others sip coffee in their pajamas. Whatever your choices, you need to set up a writing environment that is comfortable for you.

3. ***Gather your supplies before you begin to write.*** Who knows what great idea you might lose while you search for a pen that writes or a disk that's formatted. Gather in advance all the supplies and/or equipment that will bring out your best writing. Some writers use paper and a pen to get started, and others go straight to their computers. One of the big advantages of writing on a computer is that once you type out your ideas, it is easy to change them or move them around. In any case, whatever equipment you choose, make sure it is ready when you want to write.

4. ***Think of yourself as a writer.*** Now that you have a time and place for writing and all the supplies you need, you are ready to learn more about yourself as a writer. Understanding your individual writing habits and taking yourself seriously are extremely important to your growth as a writer. So take a minute now to do Practice 1, and record some of your own preferences when you write.

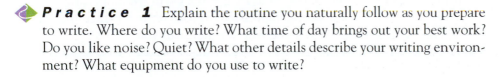 **P r a c t i c e 1**   Explain the routine you naturally follow as you prepare to write. Where do you write? What time of day brings out your best work? Do you like noise? Quiet? What other details describe your writing environment? What equipment do you use to write?

WRITING ASSIGNMENTS

In this text, you will be writing sentences and paragraphs. A **paragraph** is a group of sentences on a single topic. The first line of each paragraph is indented to show that a new topic or subtopic is starting. Although paragraphs vary in length, typical paragraphs average about 100–125 words.

You will get writing assignments of all different lengths in college. They will vary from paragraphs to full essays and research papers. All writing longer than a sentence has a beginning, a middle, and an end.

Here are the parts of a paragraph:

Topic Sentence
Supporting Sentences
Concluding Sentence

No matter what the length, however, all writing is made up of sentences. Successful sentences lead to successful writing—whatever your purpose. So to develop a good writing project of any length, you have to start with individual sentences.

The following writing assignment is typical of what you will be doing throughout this book. You will be working on this assignment over the next five chapters, so you can apply what you are learning about the writing process to a specific assignment. At the same time, you will follow the work of a student named Darryl Jarvis so you can see how he approaches and completes the same assignment. By the end of Chapter 6, you will have an understanding of the entire writing process, which is essential to your success as a writer.

WRITING A PARAGRAPH

Think about your life so far, and recall an incident or event that made you feel a strong emotion, such as happiness, sadness, anger, joy, power, weakness, fear, or pride. It does not have to be a major incident. It can be something as ordinary as going for a walk with a grandparent, losing a favorite toy, fighting with your best friend, or just being 11 or 16 years old—just as long as the event was important enough to have made a lasting impression on you. Write a paragraph explaining this event to someone who was not with you.

UNDERSTANDING THE WRITING PROCESS

Your writing process begins the minute you get a writing assignment. It involves all the mental and physical activities you do, from choosing a subject to turning in a final draft. The main parts of the process are outlined here.

Prewriting

Prewriting refers to any activities that help you explore a subject, generate ideas about it, settle on a specific topic, establish a purpose, and analyze the audience for your assignment. Your mission at this stage is simply to stimulate your thinking.

Writing

When you have generated lots of ideas to work with, you are ready to begin writing. Writing involves expanding your best ideas, organizing your thoughts, and writing a first draft.

Revising

The process of writing is not finished with the first draft. You should always revise your work to make it stronger and better. Revising involves rethinking your content and organization so that your writing says exactly what you want it to. The purpose of your paper should be clear, the main ideas should be supported with details and examples, and the organization should be logical.

Editing

When you have made all the changes that you plan to make in the content of your writing, the final step in the writing process is editing. Read your writing slowly and carefully to find any errors in grammar, punctuation, mechanics, or spelling. Such errors distract your reader from the message you are trying to communicate. Some errors can even cause communication to break down altogether. Editing means cleaning up your draft so that your writing is clear and precise.

◆ *Practice 1*

1. Explain prewriting in your own words.

   _____

2. What does "writing" consist of?

   _____

   _____

3. What is the difference between revising and editing?

   _____

   _____

   _____

PICTURE THE PROCESS

Even though we talk about the stages of writing, writing is actually a cyclical process, which means that at any point you may loop in and out of other stages. In other words, writing is not a lockstep, straight-line activity. A writer does not move among all the stages of the process in a rigid order. The sketch on the next page shows how the stages of the writing process can overlap.

Generally, the writing process moves from prewriting to writing to revising and, finally, to editing. Once you start on a writing project, however, you will loop in and out of the different stages of writing. For example, you may change a word in the very first sentence that you write (revising), think of a new detail to add to a sentence (prewriting), and cross out and rewrite a misspelled word (editing) all in the first two minutes of your writing time.

Although you may approach every writing project in a different way, we hope that in Part I of this text you will settle on a writing process that you follow with each writing task while you find your comfort zone as a writer.

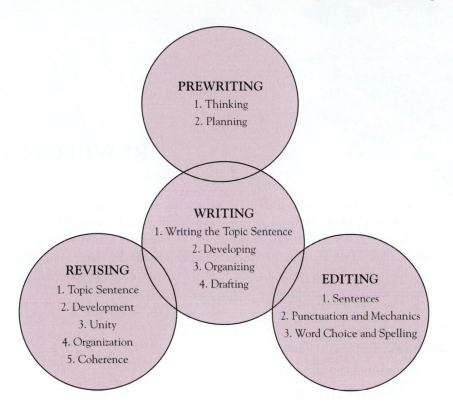

PREWRITING
1. Thinking
2. Planning

WRITING
1. Writing the Topic Sentence
2. Developing
3. Organizing
4. Drafting

REVISING
1. Topic Sentence
2. Development
3. Unity
4. Organization
5. Coherence

EDITING
1. Sentences
2. Punctuation and Mechanics
3. Word Choice and Spelling

◆ *Practice 2*

1. List the two parts of prewriting.

    _____

2. List the four parts of writing.

    _____

3. List the five parts of revising.

    _____

4. List the three parts of editing.

    _____

5. In what ways do the various parts of the writing process overlap?

    _____

3

PREWRITING

Would you be surprised to find out that a number of steps in the writing process have to occur before you can actually put words on paper? All writing tasks involve some sort of **prewriting**—or thinking and planning. The more you know about these two aspects of prewriting the more control you have over your writing process and the more efficient that process will be.

Specifically, prewriting refers to the following activities:

- exploring a subject
- generating ideas about it
- settling on a specific topic
- establishing a purpose
- understanding your audience

We will begin this chapter by looking at activities that many writers use to stimulate their thinking as they approach a writing task.

THINKING

Thinking is always the first stage of any writing project. It's a time to explore your topic and the material you have to work with. The following five activities promise to stimulate your best thoughts: reading, freewriting, brainstorming, clustering, and questioning. You will see how Darryl Jarvis, the student writer, uses each strategy, and then you can try your hand at the strategy yourself.

Reading

A good way to start your thinking and your writing process is to surf the Net or read an article on your topic.

Darryl's Reading   Darryl read the following paragraph from an essay titled "The Sissy" by Tobias Wolff. Wolff describes a fight two sixth-graders get into, which reminded Darryl of some of his own arguments on the playground. He jotted several notes to himself in the margins.

This
reminds
me of a
time I was
attacked
in fourth
grade

This kid is
mad and
serious

His first swing caught me dead on the ear. There was an explosion inside my head, then a continuous rustling sound as of someone crumpling paper. It lasted for days. When he swung again, I turned away and took his fist on the back of my head. He threw punches the way he threw balls, sidearm, with a lot of wrist, but he somehow got his weight behind them before they landed. This one knocked me to my knees. He drew back his foot and kicked me in the stomach. The papers in my bag deadened the blow, but I was stunned by the fact that he had kicked me at all. I saw that his commitment to this fight was absolute.

Ouch!

great
details

Later, Darryl wrote this entry in his writing journal, a notebook he keeps to jot down ideas for writing and reactions to his reading.

I like the way Tobias Wolff talks about this fight. He seems so calm as he writes. Being attacked is really awful. I remember many times when I thought I was going to be in a fight, but I wasn't. Until one time I was chased into the corner of the playground by a big bully. I was really afraid. I thought he was going to destroy me. But then I got the courage to yell at him, and he walked away. He never bothered me again.

Your Reading   Read the following paragraph from "Casa: A Partial Remembrance of a Puerto Rican Childhood," an essay by Judith Ortiz Cofer on page 615, and write your thoughts in the margins as you read.

It was on these rockers that my mother, her sisters, and my grandmother sat on these afternoons of my childhood to tell their stories, teaching each other, and my cousin and me, what it was like to be a woman, more specifically, a Puerto Rican woman. They talked about life on the island and life in *Los Nueva Yores*, their way of referring to the United States from New York City to California—the other place, not home, all the same.

They told real-life stories though, as I later learned, always embellishing them with a little or a lot of dramatic detail. And they told *cuentos,* the morality and cautionary tales told by the women in our family for generations: stories that became a part of my subconscious as I grew up in two worlds, the tropical island and the cold city, and that would later surface in my dreams and in my poetry.

Freewriting

Writing about anything that comes to your mind is the way to freewrite. You should write without stopping for five to ten minutes. Do not worry about grammar or spelling. If you get stuck, repeat an idea or start rhyming words. Just keep writing constantly because the act of writing will actually help you think of other ideas.

Darryl's Freewriting   Darryl wasn't sure if he could freewrite. He had never done anything like this before. But he followed directions and just started in.

My teacher told us to freewrite for a few minutes on anything we want to, but I don't know what to write about. It's hard for me to just sit here and start writing, especially when I have nothing to say. Nothing, nothing, nothing, and still nothing to say. I wonder what all these other people are writing about. Are they writing about their families? Their boyfriends or girlfriends? School? I guess I could write about how my family is proud of me for going to college. I don't know why—it's always been expected. I don't even think I realized college was not an option. I just always knew that after high school came college—no exceptions. I can't imagine not going to college, though. Where else could I learn about freewriting?

Your Freewriting   Try to freewrite following the directions given here.

Brainstorming

Like freewriting, brainstorming draws on free association—letting one thought naturally lead to another. But brainstorming usually takes the form of a list. Write down whatever comes into your mind on a topic—ideas, memories, examples, facts. As with all prewriting strategies, don't worry about grammar or spelling.

Darryl's Brainstorming   Here is Darryl's brainstorming on some of his past memories:

> Alaska—finally away from home
> I could see green everywhere
> started working in the factory
> worked with fish all day long
> spent the evenings with my sister
> earned money for school

Your Brainstorming   Brainstorm about some of your past experiences. If you don't censor yourself and simply list every thought, you may discover something that left a lasting impression on you.

Clustering

Clustering is like brainstorming, but it illustrates how your thoughts are related. To cluster, take a sheet of blank paper, write a key word or phrase in the center of the page, and draw a circle around it. Next write down and circle any related ideas that come to your mind. As you add ideas, draw lines to the thoughts they are related to. Try to keep going for two or three minutes. When you finish, you'll have a map of your ideas that can help you write a good paragraph.

Darryl's Cluster   Here is Darryl's cluster.

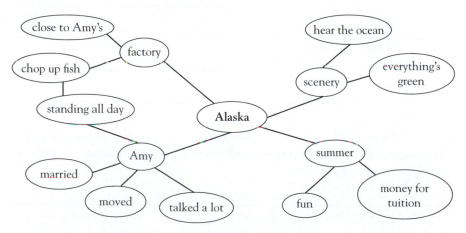

Your Cluster   Write "my past" in the middle of a piece of paper, and draw a cluster of your own personal associations with these words.

Questioning

Journalists use the questions known as the "five *W*s and one *H*"—Who? What? When? Where? Why? and How?—to check that they've covered all the important information in a news story. You can use these same questions to generate ideas on a writing topic.

Darryl's Questions   Here is how Darryl used questioning to generate ideas on his topic:

Who?	Me, Amy, and her husband
What?	My summer job in a fish factory
When?	Last summer
Where?	At my sister's in Alaska
Why?	Because I wanted to see my sister and earn some extra money
How?	By living with my sister and working in the fish factory

Your Questions   Answer these six questions about an event that left a lasting impression on your life: Who? What? When? Where? Why? How?

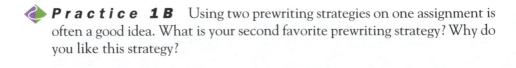 *Practice   1A*   Now that you have been introduced to several prewriting strategies, which is your favorite? Why do you like it best?

_____

_____

_____

Practice   1B   Using two prewriting strategies on one assignment is often a good idea. What is your second favorite prewriting strategy? Why do you like this strategy?

_____

_____

_____

_____

PLANNING

Writing a paragraph takes not only thinking but also planning. You need to decide on your subject, purpose, and audience. These decisions will, in turn, affect all the rest of the decisions you make about your writing assignment.

Subject

A paragraph focuses on a single subject or topic. So your first decision concerns your **subject:** What are you going to write about? Sometimes your topic is given to you—for example, your history instructor may assign a paper on the causes of the Civil War. But other times, you choose your own topic. In such cases, choosing a subject that interests you is the best approach. You will have more to say, and you will enjoy writing much more if you know something about your topic.

Purpose

Your **purpose** is your reason for writing. Your purpose could be to explore your feelings on a topic (*to do personal writing*), to tell a friend about something funny that happened to you (*to entertain*), to explain something or share information (*to inform*), or to convince others of your position on a controversial issue (*to persuade*). Whatever your purpose, deciding on it in advance makes writing your paragraph much easier.

Audience

Your **audience** is made up of the people who will read your writing. The more you know about your audience, the more likely you are to accomplish your purpose. The audience for writing in college is usually your instructor or your classmates, who represent what is called a "general audience"—people with an average amount of knowledge on most subjects. A general audience is the group to aim for in all your writing unless you are given other instructions.

Darryl's Plans   Darryl made the following decisions before beginning to write about his past:

Subject:	my summer in Alaska
Purpose:	personal—to reflect on something in my past that has made a lasting impression on me
Audience:	general—I want people who read this to think about a similar experience and remember how important it is to them

Your Plans   Identify the subject, purpose, and audience of the paragraph you will write on your past experience.

Subject: _____

Purpose: _____

Audience: _____

WRITING

The writing phase is made up of several steps that lead you to your first draft. At this point, you have been given a topic (a memorable experience) and worked through many different prewriting techniques with that subject. You have also produced a number of ideas and decided on a purpose and an audience.

In this chapter, you will learn how to write a topic sentence for your paragraph. Then you will add some specific, concrete details and put your ideas in a logical order. Finally, you will be ready to write your paragraph. The rest of this chapter will guide you through your first draft, which you will then revise and edit in Chapters 5 and 6. Again, you will be working alongside Darryl, who is learning about the writing process with you.

WRITING THE TOPIC SENTENCE

The decisions you made about subject, purpose, and audience will lead you quite naturally to your topic sentence. The **topic sentence** of a paragraph is its controlling idea, the sentence that tells what the paragraph is about. A typical paragraph consists of a topic sentence and details that support the topic sentence. Although a topic sentence can be the first or last sentence in a paragraph, it usually functions better as the first sentence.

A topic sentence has two parts—a topic and a statement about that topic. The topic should be limited enough that it can be developed in a paragraph.

Topic	Limited Topic	Statement
Reading	Leisure reading	can improve your grades.
Politics	Politics in the United States	is difficult to follow.
Sports	Watching sports events	is a relaxing pastime for many people.
Anger	Hate crimes	are tearing our community apart.

◆ **P r a c t i c e   1 A**   Limit the following topics. Then develop them into statements that could be topic sentences.

Topic	Limited Topic	Statement
1. The environment	_____	_____
2. Work	_____	_____
3. Malls	_____	_____
4. Writing	_____	_____
5. Summer	_____	_____

◆ **P r a c t i c e   1 B**   Complete the following topic sentences. Make sure they are general enough to be developed into a paragraph, but not too general.

1. The Internet _____.

2. _____ is the best vacation spot.

3. Becoming a lawyer _____.

4. Cars _____.

5. _____ is a rough and tough macho sport.

◆ **P r a c t i c e   1 C**   Write topic sentences for the following paragraphs.

1. _____

First, people need to look at what different colleges have to offer in the field they think they might pursue. Then they should look into different scholarship or financial aid packages that might help them pay for college. Location is also something people should consider, and, if possible, they should visit schools they might attend. A lot of decisions need to be made before choosing the school that's just right.

2. _____

We fought for years while we were growing up. I often denied even having a sister. She was only two years older, and we went to the same school, but I just said, "No, I am not related to that person." I don't remember why we disliked each other so much. Now she has moved to Connecticut with her husband, and we talk to each other all the time. It's as if we were always friends. The distance makes it easier, I guess. I hate to think about what would happen if we lived in the same city again.

3. _____

It's what I've wanted to be since I was little. I believe there are too many defense lawyers out there, so I prefer the District Attorney's office. I think I can make a big difference by prosecuting defendants. I'm not saying there is anything wrong with defense attorneys; it's just not the job for me. I just couldn't look at myself in the mirror if I got a guilty person off. So I'll try to be the best and fairest prosecutor I can be.

Darryl's Topic Sentence   Darryl writes a sentence that he believes will represent his whole paragraph. It introduces the beginning of his summer.

Limited Topic	Statement
I landed	in Alaska last summer.

Your Topic Sentence   Write a topic sentence that can serve as the controlling idea for your paragraph.

Limited Topic	Statement
_____	_____

DEVELOPING

After you write a topic sentence, you are ready to add specific details that will make up the rest of your paragraph. These must be concrete, supporting details and examples that are directly related to your topic. Concrete words refer to anything you can see, hear, touch, smell, or taste, such as *dogs, tractors, fire, relatives, car, alarm,* and *popcorn.* Concrete words make writing come alive because they help us picture what the writer is talking about.

P r a c t i c e   2   For each of the following topic sentences, list five details and/or examples to develop them.

1. E-mail is the best way to keep in contact with friends who live far away.

   _____

   _____

   _____

   _____

   _____

2. Jokes are a good way to brighten someone's day.

   _____

   _____

   _____

   _____

   _____

3. Weddings are a day to celebrate.

   _____

   _____

   _____

   _____

   _____

4. Swimming is a good way to work every muscle in the body.

   _____

   _____

   _____

_____

_____

5. Vegetarians need to follow a special diet in order to receive the nutrients
    their bodies need.

    _____

    _____

    _____

    _____

Darryl's Development   To come up with concrete details and examples
that will support his topic sentence, Darryl goes back to the cluster he did
during his planning stage. Then, to generate more ideas, he uses the questioning technique.

Who?	me and my sister Amy
What?	away from mom and dad
	ocean and green mountains
	new job—stand all day long
	talking with Amy
	earned money for college
When?	last summer
	evenings with Amy
Where?	Alaska
	in a fish factory
	in my sister's house
Why?	to be on my own
	to be with my sister
	to earn some money for college
	to get out of my hometown for a while
How?	being responsible without parents
	spending time with my sister

Your Development   Choose one of the prewriting activities, and use it to generate more specific details and examples about your topic sentence.

ORGANIZING

At this point, you are moving smoothly through the writing process. You have tried several prewriting strategies. You have determined your subject, purpose, and audience, and you have written your topic sentence. You have also thought of additional details, examples, and facts to develop your topic sentence. Now you are ready to organize your ideas. How do they fit together logically? What should come first? What next?

A working outline is the best way to see how your ideas work together. All your ideas should support your topic sentence and be related to each other. With a working outline, you can visually check to see if the supporting ideas are related to the topic sentence or if any idea is not connected to the others.

For example, if you are describing your car, you can help the reader follow your train of thought by describing the exterior design first, then the interior, and, finally, its performance. In other words, you move from the outside to the inside and then under the hood. This is much better than hopping around from the color of the car to the stereo system to the gas mileage and back outside to the tires. An outline lets you see how your ideas are arranged.

Sometimes the most logical order is according to time. Stories are organized in a time sequence: *The spy was given his assignment. That evening, he flew to Paris, where he met with a secret agent from the Kremlin*, and so on. Time order is also important in giving directions: *First pour 2 cups of milk into a bowl. Add the pudding mix. Then beat with a wire whisk for two minutes. Pour the pudding into individual cups and refrigerate.*

If you are providing facts and reasons as supporting details, the logical organization may be from least important to most important. That way, your most important point will be in your reader's mind at the end of your paragraph. You could also put the most important point first to pull in your reader at the beginning.

 Practice 3   Put the following groups of sentences into logical order in a rough outline. Then write a topic sentence for each group.

1. **Topic Sentence:** _____

Go back inside and find a vase that is big enough to fit all the flowers you have cut and picked.

First, put on gardening gloves.

Cut the stems long enough to fit in the vase.

Grab scissors, and make sure they are sharp.

Fill the vase with lukewarm water, not too hot or too cold.

Go out in your yard and cut all the flowers that you like.

Finally, put the flowers where everyone can see and enjoy them.

Arrange the flowers in the vase.

2. **Topic Sentence:** _____

On the left of my car is a door that opens into the backyard. We keep the garden tools here.

Next to the door to the house are the air-hockey table and bicycles.

My car is located in half of a two-car garage.

To the right of my car is the door to the house, where we keep the recycling boxes.

3. **Topic Sentence:** _____

My parents and I don't get to talk often enough, so this is perfect for us.

I especially love it when we have family days together.

We go to the beach, to the mountains, or into the city.

I don't get to spend too much time with them.

My favorite is going to the beach because we seem to do a lot of talking there.

Darryl's Organization   Darryl decides to organize his paragraph from the least important part of his summer to the most important part. He first talks about the scenery in Alaska. Then he plans to describe his summer job (working in a fish canning factory, chopping up fish). He wants to end by talking about his sister, Amy. He outlines his ideas in this order and then lists as many concrete details as he can under each category.

General: I went to Alaska last summer.

 Least Important: Scenery

  Specific Details: green mountains

        hear the ocean

More Important:	Job
Specific Details:	fish canning factory
	stand all day
	chop up fish
	everywhere I looked there was fish
Most Important:	Amy
Specific Details:	her nice, comfortable house
	house six blocks from work
	moved to Alaska two years ago
	we talked every night
Concluding Thoughts:	that was my summer
Specific Details:	working in a fish place was fun for me
	beautiful scenery
	became closer to Amy
	had a lot of fun

Your Organization   What is the best way for you to organize your ideas about your past experience? Why do you think this order will be best?

DRAFTING

Drafting is writing your thoughts on paper. At this point, you have completed your prewriting activities, written a topic sentence, developed supporting details, and decided how you will organize these details. Now you are ready to write a draft of your paragraph in complete sentences—no more lists and outlines. At this stage, don't worry too much about grammar or spelling. You'll deal with those details when you edit your writing.

Darryl's First Draft   Darryl tries to get down all his ideas in his first draft.

> I went to Alaska last summer. I was glad to finally be away from Mom and Dad for a while. I looked around. Everything was green. I could here the ocean. I was really glad to see my sister, Amy. I only had one day before I started my new job. I just walked to and from work. My new job was in a factory. I had to stand up all day, I had to chop up fish as fast as possable. My friend back home worked in a sardine factory. Every night, I would go home to my sister's house. She just lived about

six blocks away from the factory. Since my sister Amy got married. I hardly ever see her. She moved to Alaska right after her wedding. But we made up for lost time last summer. We talked every night. It was great. So that was my summer. Working in a fish canning factory may not sound exotic. It was for me. A river rafting guide sounds exotic. I earned enough money too pay for my tuition. I also became very close to my sister. We spent so much time together. I had fun.

Your First Draft   Write a draft of your paragraph about a memorable experience.

_____

_____

_____

_____

_____

_____

_____

_____

_____

5

REVISING

Revising your writing means working with it until it says exactly what you want it to say in the best way possible. Revising is changing words and phrases in your writing until you are sure you have communicated your message clearly to your audience. Revision involves both *content* (what you are trying to say) and *form* (how you deliver your message). When you revise, you should look closely at the five main elements that are listed below in the Revising Checklist.

An important part of revising is working with others. This *collaborative work* might be in groups, in pairs, with a tutor, or with a friend. Asking someone to read your writing is always a good idea when you are working toward a final draft. Your readers can let you know which parts of your paragraph are most effective. They can also tell you if any sentences are confusing, if you need more supporting details, or if the information could be organized in some clearer way.

REVISING CHECKLIST

TOPIC SENTENCE
✔ Does the topic sentence convey the paragraph's controlling idea?
✔ Does the topic sentence appear as the first or last sentence of the paragraph?

DEVELOPMENT
✔ Does the paragraph contain *specific* details that support the topic sentence?
✔ Does the paragraph include *enough* details to explain the topic sentence fully?

UNITY
✔ Do all the sentences in the paragraph support the topic sentence?

ORGANIZATION
✔ Is the paragraph organized logically?

COHERENCE
✔ Do the sentences move smoothly and logically from one to the next?

Let's look at these questions one by one.

Topic Sentence

✔ Does the topic sentence convey the paragraph's controlling idea?
✔ Does the topic sentence appear as the first or last sentence of the paragraph?

As you learned in Chapter 4, every paragraph should have a topic sentence that states the paragraph's main idea. This sentence gives direction to the rest of the paragraph. It consists of two parts: a limited topic and a statement about that topic. Generally, the topic sentence is the first sentence in a paragraph.

Practice 1A   Revise the underlined topic sentences of the following paragraphs so that they introduce all the details and ideas in their paragraphs.

1. <u>My friends tried to discourage me from going to college</u>. I like to learn, and I love my classes. My professors are great, and they are all interesting and unique individuals. The professors make the classes fun and not boring like some I've had in the past. All of my classes I find easy because I'm putting myself into them, and I'm not fooling around. I like the campus too. It's really nice and easy to get around because all of the facilities are close. I actually look forward to going to school every day.

   Revised Topic Sentence: _____

   _____

2. <u>It is hard to make a living by painting</u>. First, I make sure I have all the supplies I need. I check to make sure I have the right kind of paper and the right brushes. Then I need to get a bowl full of lukewarm water. Hot

water and cold water will break down the brushes, and then the brushes will be unusable. I also have to make sure I have a towel or paper towels because I have to wipe off the water and paint once I'm finished with a particular color. Finally, I can decide what I'm going to paint. Sometimes I have a plan, but most of the time, I will just place my brush on the paper and let my imagination take over.

Revised Topic Sentence: _____

_____

3. <u>Not many people believe in horoscopes</u>. But I like to learn what the sun and the moon have to do with a person's moods and how the signs of the zodiac interact with one another. The moon phases are what fascinate me the most. The phases of the moon affect each sign in a different way and at different times. I also find it fascinating how a horoscope can be so closely related to what I do every day. I always read it every night before I go to bed so I can see how the prediction matches the day I had.

Revised Topic Sentence: _____

_____

◆ **P r a c t i c e   1 B**   Write a topic sentence for each of the following paragraphs.

1. _____

I feel as if I have given a part of myself to someone, and I always get lost in what I do. I put so much of myself into volunteering that it gives me a feeling of self-worth. I love both working with elderly people and help-less animals. I believe that the animals can tell that someone is there helping them. I also think that volunteering makes elderly people feel better about themselves because it shows them that someone cares.

2. _____

As I look out the tent door, I see the ground covered in dew from the night before, and the smell of pine is everywhere. I can hear the birds chirping as the sun begins to rise. I step out into the crisp summer air and realize how refreshing and clean mountain air can be. I turn in a circle slowly and see the mountains in the distance with a bit of snow on the tops. I walk over to the fire pit and light a fire for the relaxing day that lies ahead.

3. _____

If you go to a college in one state and your girlfriend or boyfriend goes to school in a different state, staying together can be a challenge. No matter how strong the feelings you have for each other, being apart can be lonely. Eventually, one person meets someone who is very interesting. The two might start out being friends, but the friendship may develop into more than that. Before long, the long-distance relationship is stressed to the breaking point.

Darryl's Revision   When Darryl looks back at his topic sentence, he realizes it does not accurately introduce what he talks about in his paragraph. His topic sentence only tells readers that he went to Alaska, not that he was on his own in a new place with his sister.

> **Topic Sentence:**   I went to Alaska last summer.

He decides to expand his topic sentence so that it introduces all the details that will follow in his paragraph:

> **Revised Topic Sentence:**   **When** I went to Alaska last summer, **I was relieved to be on my own to work and happy to be with my sister.**

He feels that this topic sentence introduces the general idea of his summer with Amy and will let him talk about what he did while visiting his sister.

Your Revision   With these guidelines in mind, revise your topic sentence.

Your Topic Sentence:

_____

_____

Your Revised Topic Sentence:

_____

_____

Development

> ✔ Does the paragraph contain *specific* details that support the topic sentence?
>
> ✔ Does the paragraph include *enough* details to explain the topic sentence fully?

Details are the building blocks of a paragraph. The details in your paragraph should be as specific as possible, and you should provide enough details to support your topic sentence. If you keep both of these guidelines in mind, you will develop your paragraphs adequately and specifically.

How can you know if your details are specific enough? What is a specific detail, as opposed to a general detail? Look at the following examples, and see how they move from general to specific and from abstract to concrete. As you learned in Chapter 4, concrete words refer to items you can see, hear, touch, smell, or taste. Abstract words, on the other hand, refer to ideas and concepts like *companionship* and *shelter*.

companionship (general, abstract)
> animal
>> dog
>>> golden retriever
>>>> friendly golden retriever
>>>>> friendly golden retriever named Portia (specific, concrete)

shelter (general, abstract)
> apartment
>> one-bedroom apartment
>>> one-bedroom apartment with a swimming pool and rec room
>>>> one-bedroom apartment with a swimming pool and rec room near campus
>>>>> one-bedroom apartment with a swimming pool and rec room near campus for $500 per month (specific, concrete)

◆ *P r a c t i c e   2 A*   Underline the most specific word or phrase in each group.

1. newspaper, crossword puzzle, advertising, The Sunday Sun, articles
2. animals, cat, fur, Persian cat, domestic animal
3. department stores, shopping mall, food court, hot dog on a stick, food
4. sports, home run, baseball, plays, team
5. entertainment center, surround sound, living room, home, Bose speakers

P r a c t i c e   2 B   Fill in the blanks so that each sequence moves from general and abstract to specific and concrete.

1. homework

    _____

    _____

    _____

2. _____

    love

    _____

    _____

3. nature

    _____

    _____

    _____

4. _____

    _____

    _____

    contact lenses

5. _____

_____

picture frame

_____

Darryl's Revision   When Darryl looks at his first draft, he realizes that he can make his details much more specific and concrete. Here are three sentences that he revises (with concrete details in bold type):

Revised: Everything was green, **especially the lush mountains and open fields.**

Revised: My new job was in a **fish canning** factory.

Revised: Every night, I would go home to my sister's **small white house, which was always neat and comfortable.**

In addition to providing specific, concrete details, you also need to furnish *enough* details to support the main idea of your paragraph. Without enough details, the main idea of a paragraph is not adequately developed, and you may not be communicating your point.

Practice 3A   List three details that could support each of the following sentences.

1. Boats seem to disappear in the Bermuda Triangle.

_____

_____

_____

2. Limousines are a great way to travel around town.

_____

_____

_____

3. I hope that I have enough money for the trip.

_____

_____

4. Computer hackers can get into any program they want to.

_____

_____

5. Miracles can happen when people believe they can.

_____

_____

Practice 3B   Develop two of the following topic sentences into paragraphs with enough specific details.

1. Soft music is good background music while studying.
2. MTV should provide more music videos.
3. When I rearrange my room, I feel calm.
4. Swordfish are the most wanted sports fish for those who fish.
5. Los Angeles is a top vacation spot for young families.

Darryl's Revision   The sentences in Darryl's paragraph need *more* details and *more specific* details to communicate his message as effectively as possible. He accomplishes this by adding more details about his job in the fish canning factory. He writes about how he was able to talk with his sister every night, and he thinks about how he learned something important by the end of the summer.

> When I went to Alaska last summer, I was relieved to be on my own to work and happy to be with my sister. I was glad to finally be away from Mom and Dad for a while. I looked around. Everything was green,

especially the lush mountains and open fields. I could here the ocean. I was really glad to see my sister, Amy. **She is the reason I went to Alaska.** I only had one day before I started my new job. I just walked to and from work. My new job was in a **fish canning** factory—**Great Northern Packing Company.** I had to stand up all day, I had to chop up fish as fast as possible. **There were lots of new tasks to learn.** My friend back home worked in a sardine factory. Every night, I would go home to my sister's **small white** house, **which was always neat and comfortable.** She just lived about six blocks away from the factory. Since my sister Amy got married. I hardly ever see her. She moved to Alaska right after her wedding. But we made up for lost time last summer. We talked every night. **We talked about everything in our lives.** It was great. So that was my summer. Working in a fish canning factory may not sound exotic. It was for me. A river rafting guide sounds exotic. I earned enough money too pay for my **college** tuition. I also became very close to my sister. We spent so much time together. I had **lots of** fun. **The whole summer taught me something. I was happy and extremely proud of my sister and myself.**

Your Revision   Add more details to your paragraph to make your sentences as interesting as possible.

Unity

> ✔ Do all the sentences in the paragraph support the topic sentence?

A paragraph has **unity** when its topic sentence and supporting details focus on only one idea. All the sentences in the paragraph should relate directly to the paragraph's controlling idea or topic sentence. Information that does not expand on the main idea is not relevant and, therefore, does not belong in the paragraph.

◆ *P r a c t i c e   4 A*   Cross out the three irrelevant sentences in the following paragraph.

My Grandpa was a wonderful man. He was a man who did every-thing he could for his community. He helped build the local mall, which to this day still stands. He also built the movie theatre. I love to watch movies. In addition, he built the drive-in theatre, which still shows movies every summer. He was also the mayor of the town for many years. Mayors have difficult jobs. He was always involved and very active in the community. Volunteer work is an admirable pastime. He will be remembered and loved forever.

P r a c t i c e   4 B   Rewrite the following paragraph, deleting the three irrelevant sentences.

    I believe that adoption is wonderful. Adoption gives a child a chance to live a better life. Adopted parents are required to have a background check on them to prove that they are financially stable and will provide a good home. All people should watch their finances. Children who are adopted are lucky. They are given a home full of love and support. Family life is very important. They may not have been given that opportunity for a better home if it weren't for the decision of the birth parents to give up the child. Putting a child up for adoption is often hard for birth parents, but adoption is often best for the child.

Darryl's Revision   Darryl sees now that some of his supporting sentences are not directly related to his topic sentence. The comments about his friend back home and river rafting guides do not support his topic sentence. If these details were dropped, the revised paragraph would read as follows:

    When I went to Alaska last summer, I was relieved to be on my own to work and happy to be with my sister. I was glad to finally be away from Mom and Dad for a while. I looked around. Everything was green, especially the lush mountains and open fields. I could here the ocean. I was really glad to see my sister, Amy. She is the reason I went to Alaska. I only had one day before I started my new job. I just walked to and from work. My new job was in a fish canning factory—Great Northern Packing Company. I had to stand up all day, I had to chop up fish as fast as possable. There were lots of new tasks to learn. ~~My friend back home worked in a sardine factory.~~ Every night, I would go home to my sister's small white house, which was always neat and comfortable. She just lived about six blocks away from the factory. Since my sister Amy got married. I hardly ever see her. She moved to Alaska right after her wedding. But we made up for lost time last summer. We talked every night. We talked about everything in our lives. It was great. So that was my summer. Working in a fish canning factory may not sound exotic. It was for me. ~~A river rafting guide sounds exotic.~~ I earned enough money too pay for my college tuition. I also became very close to my sister. We spent so much time together. I had lots of fun. The whole summer taught me something. I was happy and extremely proud of my sister and myself.

Your Revision   Read your paragraph carefully, and cross out any irrelevant words, phrases, or sentences.

Organization

> ✔ Is the paragraph organized logically?

How you organize your paragraph depends to a great extent on your topic and your purpose. What are you trying to accomplish? What order will help you accomplish your purpose?

Practice 5A   Reorganize the following sentences so that they are in a logical order.

Many get into cars after they've been drinking at parties, sometimes causing fatal accidents.

They attend parties and don't think about the consequences of drinking.

Binge drinking is a growing problem among college students.

When college students get drunk, they may have unprotected sex.

Some college students have died from alcohol poisoning.

Practice 5B   Reorganize the following sentences so they are in a logical order.

They can recycle and use products wisely on a daily basis.

Pollution in California is a growing problem.

It is affecting people, animals, and the atmosphere.

The earth is being destroyed, and it can't be repaired.

But even individuals can help.

The state is trying to control pollution.

Darryl's Revision   In Chapter 4, Darryl decided that the best way to organize his paragraph was from the least important point to the most important. But now he needs to make sure that every detail is in the right place. He notices a sentence about the distance from Amy's house to his job that is out of order, so he moves the sentence to the part of the paragraph that focuses on Amy's house.

> When I went to Alaska last summer, I was relieved to be on my own to work and happy to be with my sister. I was glad to finally be away from Mom and Dad for a while. I looked around. Everything was green, especially the lush mountains and open fields. I could here the ocean. I was really glad to see my sister, Amy. She is the reason I went to Alaska. I only had one day before I started my new job. ~~I just walked to and from work.~~ My new job was in a fish canning factory— Great Northern Packing Company. I had to stand up all day, I had to chop up fish as fast as possable. There were lots of new tasks to learn. Every night, I would go home to my sister's small white house, which was always neat and comfortable. She just lived about six blocks away from the factory. **I just walked to and from work.** Since my sister Amy got married. I hardly ever see her. She moved to Alaska right after her wedding. But we made up for lost time last summer. We talked every night. We talked about everything in our lives. It was great. So that was my summer. Working in a fish canning factory may not sound exotic. It was for me. I earned enough money too pay for my college tuition. I also became very close to my sister. We spent so much time together. I had lots of fun. The whole summer taught me something. I was happy and extremely proud of my sister and myself.

Your Revision   Look again at the order you chose in Chapter 4: Is it best for accomplishing your purpose? Are all your details in their proper place?

Coherence

> ✔ Do the sentences in the paragraph move smoothly and logically from one to the next?

A **coherent** paragraph is smooth, not choppy, and readers move logically from one thought to the next. They can see a clear relationship between the ideas. In other words, the ideas "cohere," or stick together, to make their point. The most successful technique for making paragraphs coherent is well-chosen transitions.

Transitions

Transitional words and phrases are like bridges or links between your thoughts. They show your readers how one idea is related to another or when you are moving to a new point. Good use of transitions makes your writing smooth rather than choppy.

Choppy: Working in a fish canning factory may not sound exotic. It was for me.

Smooth: Working in a fish canning factory may not sound exotic. **But** it was for me.

Transitions have very specific meanings, so you should take care to use the most logical one.

Confusing: Working in a fish canning factory may not sound exotic. **Meanwhile,** it was for me.

Here is a list of some common transitional words and phrases that will make your writing more coherent. They are listed by meaning.

Some Common Transitions

Addition:	*moreover, further, furthermore, besides, and, and then, likewise, also, nor, too, again, in addition, next, first, second, third, finally, last*
Comparison:	*similarly, likewise, in like manner*
Contrast:	*but, yet, and yet, however, still, nevertheless, on the other hand, on the contrary, after all, in contrast to, at the same time, otherwise*
Emphasis:	*in fact, indeed, to tell the truth, in any event, after all, actually, of course*

Example:	*for example, for instance, in this case*
Time:	*meanwhile, at length, immediately, soon, after a few days, now, in the meantime, afterward, later, then, sometimes, other times, still*
Place:	*here, there, beyond, nearby, opposite, adjacent to, near*
Purpose:	*to this end, for this purpose, with this objective*
Result:	*hence, therefore, accordingly, consequently, thus, as a result, then, so*
Summary:	*to conclude, to sum up, to summarize, in brief, on the whole, in sum, in short, as I have said, in other words, that is*

For more information on transitions, see pages 83–87.

Practice 6A   Using the preceding list for reference, underline any transitions you see in the following paragraphs. Not all transitions are on the list here.

1. One summer I went with my friend Liz to my uncle's cabin. We decided that we would take the ATV around the lake and maybe check out some new terrain. I was ahead of her when we did find an interesting area. I was going as fast as the ATV would let me. But I know I should have been going more slowly because there were huge tree roots sticking up in the middle of nowhere. Finally, the tree roots caught up with me, and my ATV flipped upside down. All I can remember is waking up underneath the ATV with Liz calling my name. I guess I passed out for about five minutes. Luckily I had my helmet on because I could have been badly hurt. Consequently, I did learn a lesson on that journey: slow down when I don't know an area.

2. I once worked for an incompetent manager. As a result, I found my job difficult to deal with. My manager was constantly taking credit for work I had performed, and I became more and more resentful of the way I was treated. The manager refused to give me a raise for my good work, yet she continually received raises in pay based upon my performance. I finally decided enough was enough and walked out the door one day. Afterward, a friend who still worked for the company told me the manager was no longer praised for a job well done.

3. Maintaining a household is difficult when people lead such busy lives. When people are busy with school, work, and extracurricular activities, the last thing on their minds is how long the grass is or whether the laundry has been done. There just isn't enough time in

the day to take care of all the responsibilities. Therefore, the little, but necessary, jobs pile up and become enormous jobs. On the whole, it's better to just keep up with the jobs when they are still small.

Practice 6B Fill in the blanks in the following paragraphs with logical transitions. The list on pages 36–37 can guide you in your choices, but it is not a complete list of all transitions.

1. Watching TV can be addicting. Anytime I turn on the TV, I feel compelled to watch it. It doesn't even matter what's on—I just watch and watch and watch. _____, I get very little accomplished when I turn on the TV. _____ I have to restrain myself from turning the TV on; _____, the TV usually wins. I think I'm just going to have to get rid of the TV.

2. I work two full-time jobs and go to school full-time. _____, I get very little sleep. At the end of each school term, I try to catch up on sleep; _____, because of the two jobs, that doesn't always happen. It's funny. I think people actually get used to living on very little sleep. _____, I think people can train themselves to get by on minimum sleep, which is why I'm still able to function after all these years.

3. Staying in shape is not difficult as long as people choose to work out and eat right. The problem is that most people can't get motivated to exercise and don't want to give up their eating habits. _____, most people don't stay in shape. Once people decide that their health is important, _____, they become motivated and try to stay on a work-out and diet schedule. Once people get past the two- or three-week mark, the schedule is stuck in their routines, and they _____ discover how easy it is to keep on track.

Darryl's Revision When Darryl checks his paragraph for transitions, he decides his writing would be much clearer and smoother if he added more signal words to help the readers. So he adds two more transitions that show the relationship between his ideas and make his paragraph more readable.

> When I went to Alaska last summer, I was relieved to be on my own to work and happy to be with my sister. I was glad to finally be away from Mom and Dad for a while. I looked around. Everything was green, especially the lush mountains and open fields. I could here the ocean. I was really glad to see my sister, Amy. **In fact,** she is the reason I went to Alaska. I only had one day before I started my new job. My new job was in a fish canning factory—Great Northern Packing Company. I had to stand up all day, I had to chop up fish as fast as possable. There were lots of new tasks to learn. Every night, I would go home to my sister's small white house, which was always neat and comfortable. She just lived about six blocks away from the factory. I just walked to and from work. Since my sister Amy got married. I hardly ever see her. She moved to Alaska right after her wedding. But we made up for lost time last summer. We talked every night. We talked about everything in our lives. It was great. So that was my summer. Working in a fish canning factory may not sound exotic. **But** it was for me. I earned enough money too pay for my college tuition. I also became very close to my sister. We spent so much time together. I had lots of fun. **As a result,** the whole summer taught me something. I was happy and extremely proud of my sister and myself.

In addition to *but*, what transitions did Darryl add to his paragraph?

_____

List the meaning of all three transitions in Darryl's paragraph:

1. Transition: _____   Meaning: _____

2. Transition: _____   Meaning: _____

3. Transition: _____   Meaning: _____

Your Revision   Now it's time to make your essay more coherent. Check the transitions in your paragraph. Do you use enough transitions so that your sentences move smoothly and logically from one to the next? Do you use your transitions correctly?

Darryl's Revised Paragraph   After revising his topic sentence, his development, his unity, his organization, and his coherence, Darryl wrote the following revised paragraph. All of his revisions are in bold type.

> **When** I went to Alaska last summer, **I was relieved to be on my own to work and happy to be with my sister.** I was glad to finally be away from Mom and Dad for a while. I looked around. Everything was green, **especially the lush mountains and open fields.** I could here the ocean. I was really glad to see my sister, Amy. **In fact, she is the reason I went to Alaska.** I only had one day before I started my new job. ~~I just walked to and from work.~~ My new job was in a **fish canning** factory— **Great Northern Packing Company.** I had to stand up all day, I had to chop up fish as fast as possable. **There were lots of new tasks to learn.** ~~My friend back home worked in a sardine factory.~~ Every night, I would go home to my sister's **small white** house, **which was always neat and comfortable.** She just lived about six blocks away from the factory. **I just walked to and from work.** Since my sister Amy got married. I hardly ever see her. She moved to Alaska right after her wedding. But we made up for lost time last summer. We talked every night. **We talked about everything in our lives.** It was great. So that was my summer. Working in a fish canning factory may not sound exotic. **But** it was for me. ~~A river rafting guide sounds exotic.~~ I earned enough money too pay for my college tuition. I also became very close to my sister. We spent so much time together. I had **lots of** fun. **As a result, the whole summer taught me something. I was happy and extremely proud of my sister and myself.**

Your Revised Paragraph   Now that you have applied all the revision strategies to your own writing, write your revised paragraph here.

_____

_____

_____

_____

_____

_____

_____

_____

_____

_____

_____

_____

_____

_____

CHAPTER 6

EDITING

After you revise your paragraph, editing it is easy. **Editing** involves finding your grammar, punctuation, mechanics, and spelling errors and correcting them. (**Mechanics** refers to capital letters, numbers, and abbreviations.) The editing choices you make are just as important as your choice of words. They help your reader move from one idea to the next in your writing.

For easy reference, we have divided editing into three categories: sentences, punctuation and mechanics, and word choice and spelling. See the Editing Checklist that follows. This checklist doesn't cover all the grammar and usage problems you may find in your writing, but it focuses on some of the main errors college students make.

EDITING CHECKLIST ✔

SENTENCES
✔ Does each sentence have a main subject and verb?

✔ Do all subjects and verbs agree?

✔ Do all pronouns agree with their nouns?

✔ Are modifiers as close as possible to the words they modify?

PUNCTUATION AND MECHANICS
✔ Are sentences punctuated correctly?

✔ Are words capitalized properly?

WORD CHOICE AND SPELLING
✔ Are words used correctly?

✔ Are words spelled correctly?

YOUR EQ (EDITING QUOTIENT)

Editing is finding and correcting errors in your individual sentences. Because sentence skills are the heart of this book, you might want to start the editing stage by finding your EQ (or editing quotient). Knowing your EQ will tell you which errors you recognize and which errors you need to study. Use Practice 1 to determine your EQ.

Practice 1   **EQ Test** In the following paragraphs, underline and label (a, b, c) the errors you find from the following list. Then list each error by name on the lines below the paragraph. Do not make any corrections. At this time, all you want to do is find the errors. The number of lines represents the number of errors in the paragraph. The first couple of errors are done for you.

abbreviation	fragment	spelling
capitalization	modifier	subject-verb agreement
comma	number	verb form
confused word	pronoun agreement	
end punctuation	run-together sentence	

1. Rambo is my playful dog. ⓐ<u>My dad wanted a big ferocious dog, my mom and I wanted a cute fluffy dog.</u> We decided to get the cute fluffy dog but give it a ferocious name, Rambo. Rambo is 3/4 poodle and 1/4 cocker spaniel. He's the cutest dog. ⓑ<u>With the greatest personality.</u> He has never attacked a person or another animal he is one of the gentlest dogs that I know. He does get an attitude sometimes and won't listen. If you have food. Then he'll love you forever. Rambo loves anybody and will be your best friend forever.

   ⓐ *run-together or end punctuation*
   _____

   ⓑ *fragment*
   _____

   ⓒ _____

   ⓓ _____

2. Jet skiing can be dangerous, as I have learned in the past. I was at a lake one summer day with a few friends. We brought a boat, a couple of jet skis, some water skis, knee boards, and wake boards. Since the jet skis were on the beach and it was getting dark out. One of my friends and I decided that we would take the jet skis to the loading dock. As we were waiting to load them onto the truck, we was just

fooling around and showing off. I guess we got carried away. One thing led to another we were just about going full speed. We were also getting too close to the loading dock. We were doing 360 degree turns and was a little too close to each other when we crashed. My jet ski collided with hers. Both jet skis were wrecked, but we were ok. That experience was scary and it shook us up, but we've both learned to be more careful.

a.) _____

b.) _____

c.) _____

d.) _____

e.) _____

3. Smoking is a dangerous and bad habit. Smoking is know to kill people in many ways, and people know that. But they don't seem to care. The majority of people who smoke are the younger generation, teens, and young adults. Tobacco companies advertising smoking so that it appeals to the young. Younger people are drawn into smoking. Because of peer pressure. They think that it's cool and that everyone will like them because they're "cool." It's not cool it's deadly. Smoking doesn't just kill you; it's also a dirty habit.

a.) _____

b.) _____

c.) _____

d.) _____

4. Credit cards can be deceiving. They are sent out to anyone with a bank account many people can't afford to have a credit card. A person can get a card and use it whenever they spend or buy. A person gets the bill and pays the minimum required. They may even pay it all off if they have the money. When a person is in a situation like this. Life can be very difficult for them. A lot of people get in debt because of credit cards, which is why anyone who is unable to deal with a credit card should not be allowed to have one.

a.) _____

b.) _____

(c.) _____

(d.) _____

(e.) _____

(f.) _____

5. There are many teen idols in children's lives who are not good role models. Looking up to idols, lives can be changed. Idols today are just not what they used to be. They are dressing more daringly. Showing that dressing a certain way is cool. Some are into drugs, violence, and weapons. What does this say to children? It sends a bad message it says that drugs, violence, and weapons are ok.

(a.) _____

(b.) _____

(c.) _____

(d.) _____

6. Migraine Headaches are the worst headaches that people can have. When I get a migraine I feel terrible. First, I see a black dot whenever I blink it grows bigger with each blink. Then, on either the left or right temple, it feels like someone is hammering a nail into my head. Finally, I feel queasy. To get rid of this kind of headache. I usually will lie down in a dark quiet room with a cold compress over my forehead. I take an Advil to help me sleep. When I wake up, I usually feel better, but there is the odd time that the headache will last for days. I hate migraine headaches?

(a.) _____

(b.) _____

(c.) _____

(d.) _____

(e.) _____

7. There are 3 types of eating disorders: anorexia, bulimia, and compulsive eating. Although men and women of all ages are affected by eating disorders. The majority affected are adolescent females. Some situations that contribute to these diseases are low self-esteem, helplessness, and the fear of being fat. Anorexia is caused

by a person starving him or herself those suffering from bulimia will purge. People battling compulsive eating disorder will eat whenever they feel depressed or upset. These disorders are dangerous and are severe ways of battling emotional problems that could possibly lead to death.

(a.) _____

(b.) _____

(c.) _____

(d.) _____

8. An opposite-sex best friend is a friend who acts like a big brother or little sis. These types of friends will tease and joke they will also be their whenever you need help. They will give great advise about the opposite sex, and they will also comfort and offer a shoulder to lean on. Opposite-sex best friends will always except and never judge. Because they understand who there best friends are.

(a.) _____

(b.) _____

(c.) _____

(d.) _____

(e.) _____

(f.) _____

(g.) _____

9. One of my most vivid childhood memories were the day I was introduced to my Mother and Grandmother. Although I was only four years old at the time the image is stuck in my mind like a photograph. I remember being very intimidated and frightened of my mother. Instead of going to my new mom. I first went to my grandmother. But when my new mother spoke to me, it sounded like violins playing. She was very magical she had a calm aura about her. She made me feel as if I were going to be safe, and my frightened feelings went away.

(a.) _____

(b.) _____

c. _____

d. _____

e. _____

f. _____

10. During the summer of 2004. I learned a life lesson. I thought that since I was 18 I was able to do what I wanted so I disobeyed my father and went to a nightclub. I did not come home that night or the next couple of nights. I thought that I was teaching them a lesson, I was actually learning one. Once I ran out of money, clean clothes, and places to stay, I finally realized that I was making a mistake. I went back home. I didn't realize until I was on my own for a few days how difficult daily survival could be. At the time, I was immature and determined to grow up my own way. I now value my parents and the life their helping me lead.

a. _____

b. _____

c. _____

d. _____

◆ *P r a c t i c e   2*   **Answers** Use the following answer key to score your answers to Practice 1.

1. Rambo is my playful dog. ⓐMy dad wanted a big ferocious dog, my mom and I wanted a cute fluffy dog. We decided to get the cute fluffy dog but give it a ferocious name, Rambo. Rambo is 3/4 poodle and 1/4 cocker spaniel. He's the cutest dog. ⓑWith the greatest personality. ⓒHe has never attacked a person or another animal he is one of the gentlest dogs that I know. He does get an attitude sometimes and won't listen. ⓓIf you have food. Then he'll love you forever. Rambo loves anybody and will be your best friend forever.

a. *run-together or end punctuation*

b. *fragment*

c. *run-together or end punctuation*

d. *fragment*

2. Jet skiing can be dangerous, as I have learned in the past. I was at a lake one summer day with a few friends. We brought a boat, a couple of jet skis, some water skis, knee boards, and wake boards. (a)Since the jet skis were on the beach and it was getting dark out. One of my friends and I decided that we would take the jet skis to the loading dock. As we were waiting to load them onto the truck, (b)we was just fooling around and showing off. I guess we got carried away. (c)One thing led to another we were just about going full speed. We were also getting too close to the loading dock. We were doing 360 degree turns and (d)was a little too close to each other when we crashed. My jet ski collided with hers. Both jet skis were wrecked, but we were ok. That experience was scary(e) and it shook us up, but we've both learned to be more careful.

   (a.) *fragment* _____

   (b.) *subject-verb agreement* _____

   (c.) *run-together or end punctuation* _____

   (d.) *subject-verb agreement* _____

   (e.) *comma* _____

3. Smoking is a dangerous and bad habit. Smoking is (a)know to kill people in many ways, and people know that. But they don't seem to care. The majority of people who smoke are the younger generation, teens, and young adults. Tobacco companies (b)advertising smoking so that it appeals to the young. Younger people are drawn into smoking. (c)Because of peer pressure. They think that it's cool and that everyone will like them because they're "cool." (d)It's not cool it's deadly. Smoking doesn't just kill you; it's also a dirty habit.

   (a.) *verb form* _____

   (b.) *verb form* _____

   (c.) *fragment* _____

   (d.) *run-together or end punctuation* _____

4. Credit cards can be deceiving. (a)They are sent out to anyone with a bank account many people can't afford to have a credit card. A person can get a card and use it whenever (b)they spend or buy. A person gets the bill and pays the minimum required. (c)They may even

pay it all off if [d]they have the money. [e]When a person is in a situation like this. Life can be very difficult for [f]them. A lot of people get in debt because of credit cards, which is why anyone who is unable to deal with a credit card should not be allowed to have one.

(a.)   *run-together or end punctuation* _____

(b.)   *pronoun agreement* _____

(c.)   *pronoun agreement* _____

(d.)   *pronoun agreement* _____

(e.)   *fragment* _____

(f.)   *pronoun agreement* _____

5. There are many teen idols in children's lives [a]who are not good role models. [b]Looking up to idols, lives can be changed. Idols today are just not what they used to be. They are dressing more daringly. [c]Showing that dressing a certain way is cool. Some are into drugs, violence, and weapons. What does this say to children? [d]It sends a bad message it says that drugs, violence, and weapons are ok.

(a.)   *modifier error* _____

(b.)   *modifier error* _____

(c.)   *fragment* _____

(d.)   *run-together or end punctuation* _____

6. Migraine [a]Headaches are the worst headaches that people can have. When I get a migraine [b], I feel terrible. [c]First, I see a black dot whenever I blink it grows bigger with each blink. Then, on either the left or right temple, it feels like someone is hammering a nail into my head. Finally, I feel queasy. [d]To get rid of this kind of headache. I usually will lie down in a dark quiet room with a cold compress over my forehead. I take an Advil to help me sleep. When I wake up, I usually feel better, but there is the odd time that the headache will last for days. I hate migraine headaches? [e]

(a.)   *capitalization* _____

(b.)   *comma* _____

(c.)   *run-together or end punctuation* _____

(d.)   *fragment* _____

(e.)   *end punctuation* _____

7.   There are [@]3 types of eating disorders: anorexia, bulimia, and compulsive eating. [ⓑ]<u>Although men and women of all ages are affected by eating disorders</u>. The majority affected are adolescent females. Some situations that contribute to these diseases are low self-esteem, helplessness, and the fear of being fat. [ⓒ]<u>Anorexia is caused by a person starving him or herself those suffering from bulimia will purge</u>. People battling compulsive eating disorder will eat whenever they feel depressed or upset. [ⓓ]<u>These disorders are dangerous and are severe ways of battling emotional problems that could possibly lead to death</u>.

(a.)   *number* _____

(b.)   *fragment* _____

(c.)   *run-together or end punctuation* _____

(d.)   *run-together or end punctuation* _____

8.   An opposite-sex best friend is a friend who acts like a big brother or little [@]<u>sis</u>. [ⓑ]<u>These types of friends will tease and joke they will also be</u> [ⓒ]<u>their</u> whenever you need help. They will give great [ⓓ]<u>advise</u> about the opposite sex, and they will also comfort and offer a shoulder to lean on. Opposite-sex best friends will always [ⓔ]<u>except</u> and never judge. [ⓕ]<u>Because they understand who</u> [ⓖ]<u>there</u> best friends are.

(a.)   *abbreviation* _____

(b.)   *run-together or end punctuation* _____

(c.)   *confused word* _____

(d.)   *confused word* _____

(e.)   *confused word* _____

(f.)   *fragment* _____

(g.)   *confused word* _____

9. ⓐ<u>One</u> of my most vivid childhood memories <u>were</u> the day I was introduced to my ⓑ<u>Mother</u> and ⓒ<u>Grandmother</u>. Although I was only four years old at the time ⓓ<u>,</u> the image is stuck in my mind like a photograph. I remember being very intimidated and frightened by my mother. ⓔ<u>Instead of going to my new mom</u>. I first went to my grandmother. But when my new mother spoke to me, it sounded like violins playing. ⓕ<u>She was very magical she had a calm aura about her</u>. She made me feel as if I were going to be safe, and my frightened feelings went away.

(a.) *subject-verb agreement* _____

(b.) *capitalization* _____

(c.) *capitalization* _____

(d.) *comma* _____

(e.) *fragment* _____

(f.) *run-together or end punctuation* _____

10. ⓐ<u>During the summer of 2004</u>. I learned a life lesson. I thought that since I was 18 I was able to do what I wanted ⓑ<u>,</u> so I disobeyed my father and went to a nightclub. I did not come home that night or the next couple of nights. ⓒ<u>I thought that I was teaching them a lesson, I was actually learning one</u>. Once I ran out of money, clean clothes, and places to stay, I finally realized that I was making a mistake. I went back home. I didn't realize until I was on my own for a few days how difficult daily survival could be. At the time, I was immature and determined to grow up my own way. I now value my parents and the life ⓓ<u>their</u> helping me lead.

(a.) *fragment* _____

(b.) *comma* _____

(c.) *run-together or end punctuation* _____

(d.) *confused word* _____

◆ **P r a c t i c e 3 Find Your EQ** Turn to Appendix 3, and chart the errors you didn't identify. Then record your errors on the second EQ chart, and see what pattern they form.

HOW TO EDIT

Editing is a two-part job: First, you must locate the errors. Then you must know how to correct them. We all make errors in our writing, but part of the writing process is to find and correct these errors before we turn in written work.

Finding Your Errors

Since you can't correct errors until you find them, a major part of editing is proofreading. **Proofreading** is reading to catch your sentence-level errors. If you do not proofread carefully, you will not be able to find and correct the errors that interfere with your message.

When we proofread, we often read what we think we wrote instead of what we actually wrote. The best way to overcome this problem is to read your writing out of logical order. For example, you might read your paragraph backward, starting with the last sentence first. This helps you concentrate on your sentences rather than your ideas.

Another technique is to keep an Error Log, in which you list the mistakes you make. An Error Log is provided for you in Appendix 4. To use this log in proofreading, read your paper for one error at a time. For example, if you often write fragments and run-together sentences, read your paper once to catch fragments and a second time to find run-togethers. Then read it again to find other types of errors.

You can also use grammar-check and spell-check on your computer, which will point out possible grammar and spelling errors and make suggestions for rewording some of your sentences. But they are not foolproof. You need to decide if you want to accept or reject the suggestions the computer makes.

Just as working with others—or collaboration—is important when you revise, it is also important in editing. You might work in groups, in pairs, with a tutor, or with a friend. Having someone read your writing is always a good idea when you are preparing a final draft because that person might find errors that you missed. Collaborative work is built into every chapter in Part II.

When others read your writing, they might want to use the Editing Symbols on the inside back cover to highlight your errors for you. You can then use the page references on the chart to guide you to the part of this textbook that explains how to correct those errors.

Correcting Your Errors

After you find your errors, you need to correct them. Part II of this text will help you do just that. It is a complete handbook. You can use it along with the Editing Symbols on the inside back cover to make sure you follow the conventions of standard written English in your writing.

As you proofread, record your errors in the Error Log and Spelling Log. If you do this regularly as you write, these logs will eventually help you get control of the most common errors in your writing.

Finally, use the Editing Checklist at the beginning of this chapter and on an insert to help you edit your writing. Work with your writing until you can answer *yes* to every question on the checklist.

P r a c t i c e 4   **Using the Handbook**   Using the instruction in Part II, list the page references for the 13 different types of errors you worked with in Practice 1.

abbreviation   page _____

capitalization   page _____

comma   page _____

confused word   page _____

end punctuation   page _____

fragment   page _____

modifier   page _____

number   page _____

pronoun agreement   page _____

run-together sentence   page _____

spelling   page _____

subject-verb agreement   page _____

verb form   page _____

◆ *P r a c t i c e   5*   **Using the Error Log and the Spelling Log** Turn to
Appendixes 4 and 5, and start an Error Log and a Spelling Log of your own
with the errors you didn't identify in Practice 1. For each error, write out
the mistake, the Part II reference, and your correction.

◆ *P r a c t i c e   6*   **Using the Editing Checklist** Use the Editing
Checklist at the beginning of this chapter to edit two of the paragraphs
from Practice 1. Rewrite the entire paragraphs.

Darryl's Editing   When Darryl proofreads his paper for grammar, punctuation, mechanics, and spelling, he finds five errors. He looks them up in
Part II and makes the corrections.

 The first error is a comma splice:

Comma Splice: I had to stand up all day, I had to chop up fish as
              fast as possable.

Darryl realizes that this sentence has too many subjects and verbs without
any linking words or end punctuation between them. He looks up "comma
splice" on page 145 of Part II and corrects the error by putting a coordinating conjunction (*and*) between the two sentences.

Correction: I had to stand up all day, and I had to chop up fish as
              fast as possable.

He also finds a sentence that doesn't sound complete:

Fragment: Since my sister Amy got married.

When he looks up the problem in Part II (page 115), he remembers this
error is called a *fragment*. It is easily corrected by connecting it to another
sentence.

Correction: Since my sister Amy got married, I hardly ever see
              her.

Darryl records these two errors in his Error Log (Appendix 4).

 Next, he checks his paragraph for spelling errors. He is unsure about five
words:

1. I could **here** the ocean
2. as fast as **possable**
3. **There** were lots of new tasks

4. **too** pay for my college tuition

5. **extremely** proud

He uses spell-check and a dictionary and finds out that *possable* is wrong. Are all the rest right? He remembers the chapter on confused words (Chapter 31). He looks up *here*, *there*, and *too* and discovers that *there* is correct but *here* and *too* are not used correctly. So he makes the following corrections:

1. I ~~here~~ **hear** the ocean

2. as fast as ~~possable~~ possible

3. **There** were lots of new tasks **CORRECT**

4. ~~too~~ **to** pay for my college tuition

5. **extremely** proud **CORRECT**

He records these errors in the Spelling Log (Appendix 5).

Darryl's Edited Draft   All five of these errors are corrected in Darryl's edited draft.

When I went to Alaska last summer, I was relieved to be on my own to work and happy to be with my sister. I was glad to finally be away from Mom and Dad for a while. I looked around. Everything was green, especially the lush mountains and open fields. I could **hear** the ocean. I was really glad to see my sister, Amy. In fact, she is the reason I went to Alaska. I only had one day before I started my new job. My new job was in a fish canning factory—Great Northern Packing Company. **I had to stand up all day, and I had to chop up fish as fast as possible.** There were lots of new tasks to learn. Every night, I would go home to my sister's small white house, which was always neat and comfortable. She just lived about six blocks away from the factory. I just walked to and from work. **Since my sister Amy got married, I hardly ever see her.** She moved to Alaska right after her wedding. But we made up for lost time last summer. We talked every night. We talked about everything in our lives. It was great. So that was my summer. Working in a fish canning factory may not sound exotic. But it was for me. I earned enough money

to pay for my college tuition. I also became very close
to my sister. We spent so much time together. I had
lots of fun. As a result, the whole summer taught me
something. I was happy and extremely proud of my
sister and myself.

Your Editing   Proofread the sentences in your paragraph carefully. Use at
least two of the methods from this chapter to help you find the errors you
made in your paragraph. Record your errors and their corrections here.

_____

_____

_____

_____

_____

_____

_____

Your Edited Draft   Now write out a corrected draft of your paragraph.

_____

_____

_____

_____

_____

_____

_____

_____

_____

Review of the Writing Process

Clues for Review

◆ The **writing process** is a series of cyclical tasks that involves prewriting, writing, revising, and editing.

◆ **Prewriting** consists of generating ideas and planning your paragraph.

Thinking: Reading, freewriting, brainstorming, clustering, questioning

Planning: Deciding on a subject, purpose, and audience

◆ **Writing** includes writing a topic sentence, developing your ideas, organizing your paragraph, and writing a draft.

Writing a topic sentence: A limited topic and a statement about that topic

Developing: Making details more specific; adding details and examples

Organizing: Arranging ideas from general to particular, particular to general, chronologically, spatially, or from one extreme to another

Drafting: Writing a first draft

◆ **Revising** means "seeing again" and working with organization and development. Check these features of your paragraph:

Topic sentence

Development

Unity

Organization

Coherence

◆ **Editing** involves proofreading and correcting your grammar, punctuation, mechanics, and spelling errors.

◆ Review *P r a c t i c e 1*

1. What are the four main parts of the writing process?

   _____

2. What is your favorite prewriting activity? Why is it your favorite?

   _____

3. How do you prepare yourself for a writing project?

   _____

   _____

4. Where do you usually do your academic writing? Do you write your first draft on a computer? What time of day do you do your best writing?

   _____

   _____

5. What is the difference between revising and editing?

   _____

   _____

6. What are the five main categories of revising?

   _____

7. Explain editing.

   _____

8. What are the two main phases of editing?

   _____

9. Why are revising and editing so important to the final draft?

    _____

    _____

10. Do you try to get someone to read your writing before you turn it in?

    _____

    Explain your answer.

    _____

    _____

Review P r a c t i c e 2 Write a topic sentence for each of the following subjects. Then develop one topic sentence into a paragraph.

   1. Award ceremonies
   2. Fourth of July
   3. Beautiful colors
   4. Chocolate
   5. Gas stations
   6. My best friend
   7. My future plans
   8. My dream car
   9. Political campaigns
  10. My favorite class

Review P r a c t i c e 3 Revise the paragraph you wrote for Review Practice 2, using the checklist on pages 24–25.

Review P r a c t i c e 4 Edit the paragraph you wrote for Review Practice 2, using the checklist on page 42.

II

WRITING EFFECTIVE SENTENCES

This section consists of an introduction and eight units:

The chapters in each unit start with a checklist, then teach specific sentence skills and provide exercises so you can practice what you have learned. Each chapter also asks you to write and revise your own paragraph and then work with another student to edit each other's writing. At the end of each unit, four unit tests are provided that ask you to apply to sentences and paragraphs what you have practiced in the unit. These tests are followed by a writing assignment that lets you put all these skills to work at the same time.

The Editing Symbols on the inside back cover will give you marks for highlighting errors in your papers. In addition, the Error Log (Appendix 4) and the Spelling Log (Appendix 5) will help you tailor the instruction to your own needs and keep track of your progress.

Introduction: Parts of Speech, Phrases, and Clauses

This section uses very little terminology. But sometimes talking about the language and the way it works is difficult without a shared understanding of certain basic grammar terms. For that reason, your instructor may ask you to study parts of this introduction to review basic grammar—parts of speech, phrases, and clauses. You might also use this introduction for reference.

This section has three parts:

Parts of Speech
Phrases
Clauses

PARTS OF SPEECH

Every sentence is made up of a variety of words that play different roles. Each word, like each part of a coordinated outfit, serves a distinct function. These functions fall into eight categories:

1. Verbs
2. Nouns
3. Pronouns
4. Adjectives
5. Adverbs
6. Prepositions
7. Conjunctions
8. Interjections

Some words, such as *is*, can function in only one way—in this case, as a verb. Other words, however, can serve as different parts of speech depending on how they are used in a sentence. For example, look at the different ways the word *paint* can be used:

Verb: We **paint** our house every five years.
            (*Paint* is a verb here, telling what we do.)

Noun: The **paint** needs two days to dry.
            (*Paint* functions as a noun here, telling what needs two days to dry.)

Adjective: My dog knocked over the **paint** can.
            (*Paint* is an adjective here, modifying the noun *can*.)

Note how the following paragraph by Jo Goodwin Parker uses all eight of the different kinds of words to deliver a message.

But you say to me, there are schools. Yes, there are schools. My children have no extra books, no magazines, no extra pencils, or crayons, or paper and most important of all, they do not have health. They have worms, they have infections, they have pink-eye all summer. They do not sleep well on the floor or with me in my one bed. They do not suffer from hunger, my seventy-eight dollars keeps us alive, but they do suffer from malnutrition. Oh yes, I do remember what I was taught about health in school. It doesn't do much good. In some places there is a surplus commodities program. Not here. The county said it cost too much. There is a school lunch program. But I have two children who will already be damaged by the time they get to school.

Verbs

The **verb** is the most important word in a sentence because every other word depends on it in some way. Verbs tell what's going on in the sentence.

There are three types of verbs: action, linking, and helping. An **action verb** tells what someone or something is doing. A **linking verb** tells what someone or something is, feels, or looks like. Sometimes an action or linking verb has **helping verbs**—words that add information, such as when an action is taking place. A **complete verb** consists of an action or linking verb and all the helping verbs.

Action: The boy **hiked** up the hill.

Action: Jeremy **watches** the birds.

Linking: Myra **looks** lonely.

Linking: I **was** happy to be chosen.

Helping: They **will be** leaving when the job is finished.

Helping: Jennifer **has been** taking piano lessons.

Complete Verb: They **will be leaving** when the job is finished.

Complete Verb: Jennifer **has been taking** piano lessons.

REVIEWING VERBS

Define each of the following types of verbs, and give an example of each.

Action: _____

_____

Linking: _____

_____

Helping: _____

_____

What is a complete verb? Give an example with your definition.

_____

_____

Practice 1 **Identifying** In each of the following sentences, identify the underlined verbs as action (A), linking (L), or helping (H).

1. _____ The baby <u>is</u> asleep.
2. _____ We <u>have</u> looked for the best deal.
3. _____ The outfielder <u>saw</u> the ball coming toward him.
4. _____ Most college students <u>want</u> lower tuition.
5. _____ Geoffrey <u>should have</u> paid for my dinner.
6. _____ The orchestra <u>played</u> music by Bach.
7. _____ He <u>looks</u> happy today.
8. _____ Every Sunday, we <u>give</u> money to charity.
9. _____ This <u>seems</u> like the best choice.
10. _____ Carmen <u>had been</u> swimming for an hour.

◆ *P r a c t i c e 2* **Identifying** Underline the complete verbs in the following sentences. Some sentences have more than one verb.

1. I feed my fish every morning.
2. The banker forgot his money.
3. My favorite restaurant is Steak 'n Shake.
4. This instructor seems strict.
5. I was planning a party this weekend.
6. Janelle feels ignored.
7. My friends had been dancing all night.
8. Mario wished for a new car.
9. Andrea has five dollars.
10. The lady walked to the bench and sat down.

◆ *P r a c t i c e 3* **Identifying** List five complete verbs from the paragraph by Jo Goodwin Parker on page 64.

_____

_____

_____

_____

_____

◆ *P r a c t i c e 4* **Completing** Fill in each blank in the following paragraph with a complete verb.

    Yesterday I (1) _____ to the radio when the disc jockey (2) _____ a new contest. He (3) _____ a music question and said he (4) _____ the tenth caller. I immediately (5) _____ the telephone and (6) _____ for the DJ to answer. The phone (7) _____ several times, and it (8) _____ like I was waiting forever. When he finally (9) _____ my call, I (10) _____ $50 and tickets to an upcoming concert.

Practice 5 **Writing Your Own**

A. Write a sentence of your own for each of the following verbs.

1. were growing _____

2. ran _____

3. looks _____

4. had been singing _____

5. draw _____

B. Write five sentences of your own, and underline all the verbs. Remember that sentences can have more than one verb.

_____

_____

_____

_____

_____

Nouns

People often think of **nouns** as "naming words" because they identify—or name—people (*teacher, Jimmy, brother, clerk*), places (*town, lake, Phoenix*), or things (*flower, car, desk, pants*). Nouns also name ideas (*freedom, liberty*), qualities (*honesty, kindness*), emotions (*sadness, happiness*), and actions (*competition, agreement*). A **common noun** names something general (*singer, hill, water, theater*). A **proper noun** names something specific (*Britney Spears, Grand Canyon, Sprite, McDonald's*).

Hint: To test whether a word is a noun, try putting *a*, *an*, or *the* in front of it:

Nouns: a dog, an apple, the courage
NOT Nouns: a silly, an under, the sing

This test does not work with proper nouns:

NOT a Jeffrey, the Washington

REVIEWING NOUNS

What is a noun?

_____

_____

What is the difference between a common noun and a proper noun? Give an example of each.

Common noun: _____

_____

Proper noun: _____

_____

◆ *P r a c t i c e   6* **Identifying** In each of the following sentences, identify the underlined nouns as common (C) or proper (P).

1. _____ There are many tourists at <u>Niagara Falls</u>.
2. _____ My last <u>girlfriend</u> was a model for Calvin Klein.
3. _____ This is the last gas station before we get to <u>Tulsa</u>.
4. _____ Give me a <u>dollar</u> for lunch.
5. _____ Is Fawn ready for her big <u>date</u>?
6. _____ I can't find my pencil from <u>Disneyland</u>.
7. _____ Jack is having a <u>hamburger</u> for dinner.
8. _____ While I was at the office, I met <u>Michael Jordan</u>.
9. _____ Can you take me to <u>school</u> today?
10. _____ The <u>Beale Library</u> is closed for remodeling.

◆ *P r a c t i c e   7* **Identifying** Underline the nouns in the following sentences. Some sentences have more than one noun.

1. We will be going to San Francisco next week.

2. My coin collection is very important to me.

3. Travis is my nephew.

4. Manuel is going to see a movie this afternoon.

5. The most popular TV show is *The West Wing*.

6. I am tired of this hot weather.

7. My grandma makes the best cookies.

8. The basketball player has broken several records.

9. Steve is writing an essay about *Gulliver's Travels* by Jonathan Swift.

10. Melissa grew up in New York City.

◆ **P r a c t i c e 8 Identifying** List five nouns from the paragraph by Jo Goodwin Parker on page 64.

_____

_____

_____

_____

_____

◆ **P r a c t i c e 9 Completing** Fill in each blank in the following paragraph with a noun.

In the month of (1) _____, I had two vacations planned. The first was a short visit to (2) _____, and the other was a five-day cruise in (3) _____. I had to travel by (4) _____ to get to both places, and I was excited about the (5) _____. My younger (6) _____ was going with me on the first trip, and we hadn't been getting along very well. To make sure there was (7) _____ between us, I brought along some old (8) _____ from our younger days. My mom also gave me (9) _____ that brought back lots of funny memories. By the end of our trip, we had become so close that we vowed to be (10) _____ forever!

◀ **P r a c t i c e   1 0   Writing Your Own**

A. Write a sentence of your own for each of the following nouns.

1. pastor _____

2. Sea World _____

3. strength _____

4. audience _____

5. actions _____

B. Write five sentences of your own, and underline all the nouns. Remember that sentences can have more than one noun.

_____

_____

_____

_____

_____

Pronouns

Pronouns can do anything nouns can do. In fact, **pronouns** can take the place of nouns. Without pronouns, you would find yourself repeating nouns and producing boring sentences. Compare the following sentences, for example:

Matt rode **Matt's** bike to **Matt's** house because **Matt** was late for dinner.
Matt rode **his** bike to **his** house because **he** was late for dinner.

There are many different types of pronouns, but you only need to focus on the following four types for now.

Most Common Pronouns

Personal (refer to people or things)

Singular:	First person:	*I, me, my, mine*
	Second person:	*you, your, yours*
	Third person:	*he, she, it, him, her, hers, his, its*
Plural:	First person:	*we, us, our, ours*
	Second person:	*you, your, yours*
	Third person:	*they, them, their, theirs*

Demonstrative (point out someone or something)

Singular:	*this, that*
Plural:	*these, those*

Relative (introduce a dependent clause)

who, whom, whose, which, that

Indefinite (refer to someone or something general, not specific)

Singular:	*another, anybody, anyone, anything, each, either, everybody, everyone, everything, little, much, neither, nobody, none, no one, nothing, one, other, somebody, someone, something*
Plural:	*both, few, many, others, several*
Either Singular or Plural:	*all, any, more, most, some*

Hint: When any of these words are used with nouns, they are pronouns used as adjectives.

Adjective:	My brother wants to borrow **some money.**
Pronoun:	My brother wants to borrow **some.**
Adjective:	The dog wants **that bone.**
Pronoun:	The dog wants **that.**

REVIEWING PRONOUNS

What is a pronoun?

_____

_____

*Define the four most common types of pronouns, and give two examples
of each.*

Personal: _____

Demonstrative: _____

Relative: _____

Indefinite: _____

Practice 11   **Identifying** In each of the following sentences,
identify the underlined pronouns as personal (P), relative (R), demonstrative (D), or indefinite (I).

1. _____ This drink is <u>his</u>.
2. _____ <u>It</u> doesn't matter what you wear to the game.
3. _____ I think the person <u>who</u> broke the lamp should pay for it.
4. _____ Addie gave me <u>that</u> for my birthday.
5. _____ If <u>anyone</u> could do a better job, please tell me.
6. _____ Jackie is taking <u>her</u> to the doctor.
7. _____ <u>These</u> are my favorite shoes.
8. _____ There is <u>something</u> I have to tell you.
9. _____ I hope <u>that</u> we can meet at the movie.
10. _____ I am donating <u>both</u> to the thrift store.

Practice 12   **Identifying** Underline the pronouns in the following sentences. Some sentences have more than one pronoun.

1. Some of us are not happy with the results.
2. These are not the right answers.
3. I think they are being honest with us.
4. Nobody wants to do the work.

5. Is that the dress I loaned you?
6. If you would just study, everything would be easier for you.
7. It is not my fault that Steve broke his arm.
8. Kari knows who that is.
9. Those were the best appetizers at the party.
10. My sister believes in that theory.

Practice 13 **Identifying** List five pronouns from the paragraph by Jo Goodwin Parker on page 64.

_____

_____

_____

_____

_____

Practice 14 **Completing** In the following paragraph, replace the nouns in parentheses with pronouns.

Anne bought (1) _____ (Anne's) cat when Anne was 12. It was a kitten at the time, and (2) _____ (Anne) couldn't resist its cute face. When (3) _____ (Anne's) friends saw the cat, (4) _____ (Anne's friends) told (5) _____ (Anne) to name (6) _____ (the cat) Marble because (7) _____ (the cat) was so colorful. Anne decided to name the cat Spunky instead because (8) _____ (the cat) had lots of energy. Now Anne is going away to college and (9) _____ (Anne's) cat is going with (10) _____ (Anne).

Practice 15 **Writing Your Own**

A. Write a sentence of your own for each of the following pronouns.

1. anybody _____

2. those _____

3. who _____

4. both _____

5. we _____

B. Write five sentences of your own, and underline the pronouns. Remember that sentences can have more than one pronoun.

_____

_____

_____

_____

_____

Adjectives

Adjectives modify—or describe—nouns or pronouns. Adjectives generally make sentences clear and vivid.

Without Adjectives:	He took candy, a camera, and a backpack to the amusement park.
With Adjectives:	He took **licorice** candy, a **digital** camera, and a **blue** backpack to the amusement park.

REVIEWING ADJECTIVES

What is an adjective?

_____

Give three examples of adjectives.

_____ _____ _____

◆ *P r a c t i c e   1 6* **Identifying** For each of the following sentences, if the underlined word is an adjective, write Adj in the blank.

1. _____ That was an <u>ugly</u> dog.
2. _____ My father is a <u>generous</u> man.
3. _____ Stan tried to <u>scare</u> Jessica.
4. _____ The <u>new</u> student has been very helpful.
5. _____ I met a <u>boy</u> in the library today.
6. _____ The <u>rich</u> man is giving his estate to charity.
7. _____ His <u>proud</u> smile was beautiful.
8. _____ Put the <u>cup</u> in the dishwasher.
9. _____ I need a <u>cold</u> drink.
10. _____ Jeremy's <u>computer</u> has a virus.

◆ *P r a c t i c e   1 7* **Identifying** Underline the adjectives in the following sentences. Some sentences have more than one adjective.

1. The curly hair is full of thick knots.
2. Linda plays concert piano in front of large audiences.
3. The longest novel I have ever read is *Bleak House* by Charles Dickens.
4. I need a good parking place today.
5. It was a cold day in November when we won the big football game.
6. That cheese pizza looks like a great meal.
7. The baby's loud cry is giving me a headache.
8. I need a cup of strong coffee to keep studying.
9. Kevin has to mow the long grass in the backyard.
10. Renee uses a black ballpoint pen to sign her checks.

◆ *P r a c t i c e   1 8* **Identifying** List five adjectives from the paragraph by Jo Goodwin Parker on page 64.

_____

_____

_____

_____

_____

◆ *P r a c t i c e   1 9*   **Completing** Fill in each blank in the following paragraph with an adjective.

Last summer, my brother and I drove to a (1) _____ city in Texas. I have some (2) _____ relatives who live there, and they wanted us to visit. We stayed for a (3) _____ week and talked about (4) _____ things. I took lots of (5) _____ pictures also, because I didn't know when we would be back to see them again. All in all, it was a (6) _____ visit. We enjoyed our (7) _____ conversations, and we learned about our family's (8) _____ history. I promised to write often, and they were (9) _____ to see us leave. On the way home, we felt a little more (10) _____ about our relatives and ourselves.

◆ *P r a c t i c e   2 0*   **Writing Your Own**

A. Write a sentence of your own for each of the following adjectives.

   1. pretty _____

   2. heavy _____

   3. small _____

   4. fourth _____

   5. loud _____

B. Write five sentences of your own, and underline all of the adjectives. Remember that sentences can have more than one adjective.

_____

_____

_____

_____

_____

Adverbs

Adverbs modify—or describe—adjectives, verbs, and other adverbs. They do *not* modify nouns. Adverbs also answer the following questions:

How?	thoughtfully, kindly, briefly, quietly
When?	soon, tomorrow, late, now
Where?	inside, somewhere, everywhere, there
How often?	daily, always, annually, rarely
To what extent?	generally, specifically, exactly, very

Hint: Notice that adverbs often end in *-ly*. That might help you recognize them.

REVIEWING ADVERBS

What is an adverb?

_____

What are the five questions that adverbs answer?

_____   _____   _____   _____   _____

Give one example of an adverb that answers each question.

_____   _____   _____   _____   _____

P r a c t i c e   2 1   **Identifying** For each of the following sentences, if the underlined word is an adverb, write Adv in the blank.

1. _____ He <u>kindly</u> waited for me at the corner.
2. _____ Salma spoke <u>softly</u>, and I couldn't hear her.
3. _____ He was <u>outside</u> when I called her.
4. _____ Henry can <u>hop</u> on one leg.
5. _____ That was <u>very</u> thoughtful of you.
6. _____ Delores was <u>much</u> appreciated for her hard work.
7. _____ The <u>power</u> bill is higher this month than last.

8. _____ Peggy's <u>son</u> is a sweet boy.

9. _____ Meet me <u>tomorrow</u> in the lobby.

10. _____ I read it <u>quickly</u>, so I don't remember what it said.

◆ *Practice 22* **Identifying** Underline the adverbs in the following sentences. Some sentences have more than one adverb.

1. I surely won't be at that party.
2. They almost collided in the hall.
3. Nadia will come by today to wash the car.
4. This is the very last time you will make that mistake.
5. Don't drive too fast.
6. This was quite a good movie.
7. Jennifer quickly ran to the bus stop.
8. Are you absolutely sure you can be here?
9. I suddenly realized that I forgot my homework.
10. We went to the meetings monthly.

◆ *Practice 23* **Identifying** List five adverbs from the paragraph by Jo Goodwin Parker on page 64.

_____

_____

_____

_____

_____

◆ *Practice 24* **Completing** Fill in each blank in the following paragraph with an adverb.

When the grocery store in our small town (1) _____ closed, several people were out of work. It was a (2) _____ sad situation for many people. One family, the Johnsons, (3) _____ found a solution. They opened a new grocery

store with more (4) _____ priced items. They also
(5) _____ employed people from the first store, and they
(6) _____ donated food items for families that were
(7) _____ struggling. The town was (8) _____
grateful for their generous help. The Johnsons were (9)
_____ awarded a key to the city at a big dinner held in
their honor. I know the Johnsons never planned to get so much
recognition, but they (10) _____ deserved it.

◆ P r a c t i c e 2 5 Writing Your Own

A. Write a sentence of your own for each of the following adverbs.

1. often _____

2. rarely _____

3. softly _____

4. too _____

5. yesterday _____

B. Write five sentences of your own, and underline all of the adverbs.
Remember that sentences can have more than one adverb.

_____

_____

_____

_____

_____

Prepositions

Prepositions indicate relationships among the ideas in a sentence.
Something is *up, down, next to, behind, around, near,* or *under* something

else. A preposition is always followed by a noun or a pronoun called the **object of the preposition.** Together, they form a **prepositional phrase.**

Preposition	+	Object	=	Prepositional Phrase
beside	+	the water	=	beside the water
at	+	the meeting	=	at the meeting

Here is a list of some common prepositions.

Common Prepositions

about	beside	into	since
above	between	like	through
across	beyond	near	throughout
after	by	next to	to
against	despite	of	toward
among	down	off	under
around	during	on	until
as	except	on top of	up
at	for	out	upon
before	from	out of	up to
behind	in	outside	with
below	in front of	over	within
beneath	inside	past	without

Hint: *To* + a verb (as in *to go, to come, to feel*) is not a prepositional phrase. It is a verb phrase, which we will deal with later in this unit.

REVIEWING PREPOSITIONS

What is a preposition?

_____

Give two examples of prepositions:

_____   _____

What is a prepositional phrase?

_____

Give two examples of prepositional phrases:

_____   _____

P r a c t i c e   2 6   **Identifying** For each of the following sentences, if the underlined word is a preposition, write P in the blank.

1. _____ The most important papers are <u>on</u> the top.
2. _____ My cousins live <u>around</u> the corner.
3. _____ The fisherman went <u>over</u> his limit of trout.
4. _____ I am hanging a <u>poster</u> of Orlando Bloom in my room.
5. _____ Don't walk <u>behind</u> that building at night.
6. _____ Petra went <u>through</u> the neighborhood with fliers.
7. _____ I have been writing in my <u>diary</u> since I was eight years old.
8. _____ The museum is <u>near</u> the community center.
9. _____ Turn off the <u>radio</u> while I'm studying.
10. _____ Paul flew his plane <u>above</u> the clouds.

P r a c t i c e   2 7   **Identifying** Underline the prepositions in the following sentences. Some sentences have more than one preposition.

1. Before getting out of the car, he noticed a lady in a white hat.
2. The house is on the hill at the end of the windy road.
3. The best hotels in San Diego are beside the ocean.
4. My new computer is in a box by my desk.
5. During the dance, I leaned against the table, and it fell.
6. One of the twins has a birthmark under her knee.
7. The cookie jar is sitting on top of the refrigerator.
8. We forgot about the balloons in the car.
9. My slip is hanging below my skirt.
10. Iris walked through the mall with Becky.

◀ *P r a c t i c e **2 8*** **Identifying** List five prepositions from the paragraph by Jo Goodwin Parker on page 64.

_____

_____

_____

_____

_____

◀ *P r a c t i c e **2 9*** **Completing** Fill in each blank in the following paragraph with a preposition.

Miguel has been walking (1) _____ campus all day, trying to sell tickets to a car wash. He walked (2) _____ me this morning and asked me to buy one. He said he was raising money (3) _____ the chess club because the club members are going (4) _____ Disney World (5) _____ Florida. I don't know how much money they need, but (6) _____ the time of our conversation, they had only $50. The chess club is usually very disorganized and is always (7) _____ money. This year, it has a new president, who went (8) _____ the club's books and found a way to pay its bills. Miguel was the vice president, but he quit because he didn't want to be (9) _____ so much pressure. I think he just wants to graduate (10) _____ next year and needs more time for studying.

◀ *P r a c t i c e **3 0*** **Writing Your Own**

A. Write a sentence of your own for each of the following prepositions.

1. below _____

2. with _____

3. around _____

4. between _____

5. toward _____

B. Write five sentences of your own, and underline the prepositions. Remember that sentences can have more than one preposition.

_____

_____

_____

_____

_____

Conjunctions

Conjunctions connect groups of words. Without conjunctions, most of our writing would be choppy and boring. The two types of conjunctions are easy to remember because their names state their purpose: *Coordinating conjunctions* link equal ideas, and *subordinating conjunctions* make one idea subordinate to—or dependent on—another.

Coordinating conjunctions connect parts of a sentence that are of equal importance or weight. These parts can be **independent clauses,** a group of words with a subject and verb that can stand alone as a sentence (see page 93). There are only seven coordinating conjunctions:

Coordinating Conjunctions

and, but, for, nor, or, so, yet

Coordinating: Isaac wanted to see a movie, **and** I wanted to go to dinner.

Coordinating: I enjoy listening to music, **but** I don't know how to play any instruments.

Subordinating conjunctions join two ideas by making one dependent on the other. The idea introduced by the subordinating conjunction becomes a **dependent clause,** a group of words with a subject and a verb that cannot stand alone as a sentence (see page 93). The other part of the sentence is an independent clause.

Dependent Clause

Subordinating: She will stay **until** the baby falls asleep.

Dependent Clause

Subordinating: **Unless** I am busy, you are welcome to come visit.

Here are some common subordinating conjunctions.

Common Subordinating Conjunctions

after	because	since	until
although	before	so	when
as	even if	so that	whenever
as if	even though	than	where
as long as	how	that	wherever
as soon as	if	though	whether
as though	in order that	unless	while

REVIEWING CONJUNCTIONS

What is a coordinating conjunction?

_____

_____

Name the seven coordinating conjunctions.

_____ _____ _____ _____ _____ _____ _____

What is a subordinating conjunction?

_____

_____

Write a sentence using a subordinating conjunction.

_____

◆ P r a c t i c e 3 1 Identifying In each of the following sentences, identify the underlined conjunction as coordinating (C) or subordinating (S).

1. _____ Alma wanted to be here, <u>yet</u> she had prior commitments.
2. _____ <u>Before</u> you go, sign the guest book.
3. _____ I didn't make cookies, <u>though</u> I knew you would be hungry.
4. _____ <u>As if</u> he could read my mind, he brought me flowers.
5. _____ Chi is allergic to chocolate, <u>so</u> he can't eat that cake.
6. _____ Richard will do that part, <u>unless</u> he gets too busy.
7. _____ <u>While</u> I was waiting, I read an article on computers.
8. _____ <u>Although</u> she's never been there, Cara said Hawaii is beautiful.
9. _____ Gina is a lawyer, <u>and</u> she's working on a big tobacco case.
10. _____ I can make a sandwich, <u>or</u> I can call for pizza.

◆ P r a c t i c e 3 2 Identifying Underline the conjunctions in the following sentences.

1. We all want to go, but there are only 10 tickets left.
2. As long as you're watching him, the baby can play outside.
3. I had a good time, yet I never did see my friends there.
4. When you were at the store, I worked on my essay.
5. I know it's going to be hot today, for the forecast predicted mid-90s.
6. Although it's only June, stores are selling Halloween costumes.
7. We can begin the meeting as soon as Diego arrives.
8. Stephanie will buy the donuts even though she lost her job.
9. I made a special card for Amber, so I hope you will sign it.
10. Whenever you come to town, you should call me.

◆ P r a c t i c e 3 3 Identifying List five conjunctions from the paragraph by Jo Goodwin Parker on page 64.

_____

_____

_____

_____

_____

◆ **P r a c t i c e   3 4   Completing** Fill in each blank in the following paragraph with a conjunction.

Cooking is not fun for me, (1) _____ I have been learning a lot about it. (2) _____ I usually make my boyfriend do the cooking, last night it was my turn. I planned to make a pasta dish, (3) _____ I forgot a couple of things at the store, (4) _____ I decided to make chef salads instead. (5) _____ I was doing the cooking, my boyfriend was surfing on the Internet in the back room. (6) _____ he wasn't paying attention to me, he didn't notice how many times I licked my fingers or dropped things on the floor. I think the salads were just fine, (7) _____ I did notice a cat hair had somehow landed in mine. (8) _____ there was anything strange in my boyfriend's salad, he didn't bring it to my attention. I think he was just glad to have the night off, (9) _____ the next time I have to cook, I will get take-out. (10) _____ I've heard that cooking is an expression of love, I still think it is too much work.

◆ **P r a c t i c e   3 5   Writing Your Own**

A. Write a sentence of your own for each of the following conjunctions.

1. but _____

2. until _____

3. so _____

4. wherever _____

5. as long as _____

B. Write five sentences of your own, and underline the conjunctions.
   Remember that sentences can have more than one conjunction.

_____

_____

_____

_____

_____

Interjections

Interjections are words that express strong emotion, surprise, or disappointment. An interjection is usually followed by an exclamation point or a comma.

Interjection: **Hey!** You're standing on my foot.

Interjection: **Wow,** that was scary!

Other common interjections include *aha, awesome, great, hallelujah, neat, oh, oops, ouch, well, whoa, yeah,* and *yippee.*

REVIEWING INTERJECTIONS

What is an interjection?

_____

_____

Write a sentence using an interjection.

_____

◆ *P r a c t i c e   3 6*   **Identifying** For each of the following sentences, if the underlined word is an interjection, write I in the blank.

1. _____ <u>Ouch</u>, I hit my finger!
2. _____ <u>No</u>! That's the wrong house.

3. _____ <u>Oops</u>, I didn't mean to say that.

4. _____ <u>Thank you</u> for taking me home.

5. _____ I can't believe you made it! <u>Wow</u>!

6. _____ <u>Yes</u>! I got an A on that paper.

7. _____ <u>Please</u> take me to the dance.

8. _____ <u>Can</u> you hand me the salt?

9. _____ The car didn't run out of gas. <u>Thank goodness</u>!

10. _____ <u>Well</u>, I think I can find time.

P r a c t i c e 3 7 Identifying Underline the interjections in the following sentences.

1. My goodness! That was a terrible storm.

2. The boys' team, alas, has beaten the girls' team again.

3. Yeah! We are going to the semifinals!

4. Wow, do you know how much that costs?

5. My mom is paying my tuition! Hallelujah!

6. Man, this is a steep hill.

7. Oh, guess who's having another baby!

8. Hooray! We won a new car.

9. That was a great save! Neat!

10. Hey! Am I the only one who knows how to take out the trash around here?

P r a c t i c e 3 8 Identifying List two interjections from the paragraph by Jo Goodwin Parker on page 64.

_____

_____

P r a c t i c e 3 9 Completing Fill in each blank in the following paragraph with an interjection.

(1) _____, we were almost late for the plane!

(2) _____! We thought it was departing at 11:00 a.m., but

our tickets actually said 9:30 a.m. (3) _____, I can't believe we were that careless. Fortunately, we left for the airport two hours early because we were going to buy lunch there. (4) _____! During the drive, I looked at the ticket and, (5) _____, it said 9:30 a.m. in bold. I can't believe I didn't see it before. (6) _____! We ran and ran through the terminal, and when we got to the gate, they told us there were only two seats left. (7) _____! (8) _____, there were only two of us traveling that day. We found our seats on the plane, and (9) _____, was it stuffy! At least we made it to Denver on time. (10) _____!

◆ Practice 40 Writing Your Own

A. Write a sentence of your own for each of the following interjections.

1. yikes _____

2. wow _____

3. yeah _____

4. ouch _____

5. mercy _____

B. Write five sentences of your own, and underline the interjections.

_____

_____

_____

_____

_____

PHRASES

A **phrase** is a group of words that function together as a unit. Phrases cannot stand alone, however, because they are missing a subject, a verb, or both.

Look at how groups of words function as single units in the following paragraph by Scott Russell Sanders.

I climbed out of the car with a greeting on my lips, but the sky hushed me. From the black bowl of space countless fiery lights shone down, each one a sun or swirl of suns, the whole brilliant host of them enough to strike me dumb. The Milky Way arced overhead, reminding me of froth glimmering on the dark surface of a mountain creek. I know the names of a dozen constellations, but I wasn't thinking in words right then. I was too busy feeling brimful of joy, without need of any props except the universe. The deep night drew my scattered pieces back to the center, stripped away clutter and weight, and set me free.

Phrases come in several varieties. Look at the following examples:

Phrases: the new reality TV show, my best friend (missing verbs)
Phrases: had been working, can jump (missing subjects)
Phrases: without any money, near the bank (missing both)
Phrases: helping other people, to be listening (missing subjects)

Notice that all these groups of words are missing a subject, a verb, or both.

REVIEWING PHRASES

What is a phrase?

_____

_____

Give two examples of phrases.

_____   _____

Practice 41   **Identifying** In each of the following sentences, identify the underlined phrase as missing a subject (S), missing a verb (V), or missing both (B).

1. _____ <u>A new car</u> is parked in my driveway.
2. _____ Jefferson is transferring <u>to a new college</u>.
3. _____ Mabel and Sarah <u>should have been exercising</u> instead of sleeping.
4. _____ <u>A very high ladder</u> was leaning against the wall.
5. _____ We wanted to swim <u>under the bridge</u>.
6. _____ Camilla asked <u>for directions</u> when she was lost.
7. _____ We became friends <u>in this dorm room</u>.
8. _____ I don't know how to find a pet <u>with a good personality</u>.
9. _____ <u>The tired plumber</u> stopped to get some milk on the way home.
10. _____ All of us <u>were willing</u> to help her with her math homework.

Practice 42   **Identifying** Underline the phrases in each sentence. Every sentence has more than one phrase.

1. The Shin family will be vacationing in the mountains for two weeks.
2. Driving home from school, Jack remembered about his wallet on his dresser.
3. During the blackout, no one could find the portable generator.
4. We should have been paying more attention to the time.
5. Tired and exhausted, Maria was thankful when her shift ended.
6. The car sped down the street despite the speed limit signs.
7. Pam and Cecilia have been best friends since they were in elementary school.
8. It was foolish to lie to the instructor.
9. Henrik and I talked for hours sitting underneath the stars.
10. I would have accepted that job offter.

Practice 43   **Identifying** List five phrases from the paragraph by Scott Russell Sanders on page 90.

_____

_____

_____

_____

_____

◀ **P r a c t i c e   4 4   Completing** Fill in each blank in the following paragraph with an appropriate phrase to complete the sentence.

Ever since Sam applied for vacation time at (1) _____, he found that he was very excited about (2) _____. As he walked (3) _____, he heard that his roommate, Tony, also got (4) _____. Sam learned that (5) _____ were coming for a surprise visit and (6) _____ in their apartment. Even though Sam had tried hard to get ahead (7) _____, he knew he was going to have to (8) _____ in order to keep up with his classes. In only three hours, he got most of his homework done (9) _____. Now he has to (10) _____. His friends were arriving today.

◀ **P r a c t i c e   4 5   Writing Your Own**

A. Write a sentence of your own for each of the following phrases.

1. tapes, CDs, and DVDs _____

2. around town _____

3. should have been ready _____

4. the man sitting in the front row _____

5. to qualify for the Olympics _____

B. Write five sentences of your own, and underline all the phrases.

_____

_____

_____

_____

_____

CLAUSES

Like phrases, **clauses** are groups of words. But unlike phrases, a clause always contains a subject and a verb. There are two types of clauses: *independent* and *dependent*.

Let's begin by looking at how some clauses, or subject-and-verb sets, work in a paragraph by Mike Rose:

All the hours in class tend to blend into one long, vague stretch of time. What I remember best, strangely enough, are the two things I couldn't understand and over the years grew to hate: grammar lessons and mathematics. I would sit there watching a teacher draw her long horizontal line and her short, oblique lines and break up sentences and put adjectives here and adverbs there and just not get it, couldn't see the reason for it, turned off to it. I would hide by slumping down in my seat and page through my reader, carried along by the flow of sentences in a story. She would test us, and I would dread that, for I always got Cs and Ds. Mathematics was a bit different. For whatever reasons, I didn't learn early math very well, so when it came time for more complicated operations, I couldn't keep up and started day-dreaming to avoid my inadequacy. This was a strategy I would rely on as I grew older. I fell further and further behind. A memory: The teacher is faceless and seems very far away. The voice is faint and is discussing an equation written on the board. It is raining, and I am watching the streams of water form patterns on the windows.

An **independent clause** contains a subject and a verb and can stand alone and make sense by itself. Every complete sentence must have at least one independent clause.

Independent Clause: Tracy loved to watch sunrises.

Now look at the following group of words. It is a clause because it contains a subject and a verb. But it is a **dependent clause** because it is introduced by a word that makes it dependent, *because*.

Dependent Clause: **Because** Tracy loved to watch sunrises.

This clause cannot stand alone. It must be connected to an independent clause to make sense. Here is one way to complete the dependent clause and form a complete sentence.

Dependent   Independent

Because Tracy loved to watch sunrises, she always woke up early.

Hint: Subordinating conjunctions (such as *since, although, because, while*) and relative pronouns (*who, whom, whose, which, that*) make clauses dependent. (For more information on subordinating conjunctions, see page 84, and on relative pronouns, see page 71.)

REVIEWING CLAUSES

For a group of words to be a clause, it must have a _____

and a _____ .

What is an independent clause?

_____

_____

What is a dependent clause?

_____

_____

Name the two kinds of words that can begin a dependent clause.

_____ _____

Name five subordinating conjunctions.

_____ _____ _____ _____ _____

Name the five relative pronouns.

_____ _____ _____ _____ _____

◆ *P r a c t i c e 4 6* **Identifying** Identify the following clauses as either independent (I) or dependent (D).

1. _____ Karen was late for class.

2. _____ Because her car wouldn't start.

3. _____ What I really don't know.

4. _____ The Grand Canyon is one of the Seven Natural Wonders of the World.

5. _____ I only buy name-brand clothes.

6. _____ When Walt visited me last month.

7. _____ Tirana wears beautiful clothes and is self-confident.

8. _____ Although Angela bought a new computer.

9. _____ The next-door neighbor is ready to go overseas.

10. _____ When they are first born.

◆ *P r a c t i c e 4 7* **Identifying** Underline the clauses in the following sentences, and label them independent (I) or dependent (D). Some sentences have more than one clause.

1. Dawn started playing soccer when she was six years old.

2. His plans had been changed, and he didn't mind.

3. Even though Martin liked roller coasters, he didn't want to try the new one.

4. All of my relatives want to stay forever when they visit me.

5. My brothers and sisters created a company, but they got help from our mom and dad.

6. The coach put the girl back in the game after she rested.

7. Children's books have great pictures in them.

8. The number of homeless people in the United States is growing.

9. Alternative rock music is for people who like a heavy beat.

10. I saw Maia running on the track that is across from the dorms.

◀ *Practice 48* **Identifying** List two independent clauses and three dependent clauses from the paragraph by Mike Rose on page 93.

_____

_____

_____

_____

_____

◀ *Practice 49* **Completing** Make the following dependent clauses into independent clauses by crossing out the subordinating word (either a subordinating conjunction or a relative pronoun).

1. Before I got into the car.
2. The waiter who made $50 in tips every night.
3. Each one of the beautiful gardens that contained fresh herbs and flowers.
4. While my brother stayed in Salem, Oregon, and I lived off the Puget Sound in Washington State.
5. When you can earn a living.
6. After they were 10 years old.
7. The shark that lingered near the boat.
8. Although he bought a Chevy Tahoe.
9. Since I passed my final exam.
10. The party that got out of control.

◀ *Practice 50* **Writing Your Own**

A. Add a dependent clause to the following independent clauses.

1. The cat is sleeping on the sofa.

_____

2. My brother borrowed my computer.

_____

3. This test covers five chapters in our textbook.

    _____

4. I can't come over until after lunch.

    _____

5. The box is filled with candy.

    _____

B. Write five independent clauses. Then add at least one dependent clause to each independent clause.

    _____

    _____

    _____

    _____

    _____

REVIEW

You might want to reread your answers to the questions in all the review boxes before you do the following exercises.

Review P r a c t i c e *1* **Identifying** Use the following abbreviations to label the underlined words in these sentences.

v	Verb	adv	Adverb
n	Noun	prep	Preposition
pro	Pronoun	conj	Conjunction
adj	Adjective	int	Interjection
ph	Phrase	cl	Clause

1. <u>Wow</u>, <u>I</u> can't believe how <u>much</u> <u>those</u> shoes <u>cost</u>!

2. <u>Yesterday</u>, Marisol <u>went</u> <u>to</u> the St. Louis Rams football game.

3. Sammi wanted the <u>newly</u> built house, <u>but</u> he couldn't afford the monthly <u>payments</u>.

4. <u>Whatever class Irulan is taking this semester</u>, she <u>reviews</u> her notes and studies <u>in the library</u> every night.

5. <u>The most unique car of</u> the 1980s was <u>probably</u> the De Lorean.

6. <u>Gee</u>, I didn't know that <u>tomorrow we</u> were having our <u>history</u> test.

7. Zora wants <u>to get a job</u>, so she can <u>pay</u> the bill <u>for</u> her college tuition.

8. Lacie <u>forgot</u> to pay her telephone bill <u>and</u> received a notice from <u>them</u> about <u>late</u> charges.

9. <u>Although I needed to take a math class</u>, I was told <u>by my adviser</u> to take history instead.

10. Last winter was <u>warm</u> and sunny, <u>so</u> it was hard to get <u>into the Christmas mood</u>.

◀ *Review P r a c t i c e 2* **Completing** Fill in each blank in the following paragraph with an appropriate word, phrase, or clause, as indicated.

The most expensive trip I ever took was to (1) _____ (noun) with my best friend, Alex. Halfway through our trip, the car began to make a (2) _____ (adjective) sound. After (3) _____ (clause), we decided to stop at a car repair shop. The mechanic (4) _____ (verb) that I needed a new muffler and a new exhaust pipe. I asked him how much the estimate would be (5) _____ (preposition) him to fix the car, and he replied it would cost over $2,500. (6) _____ (interjection), we couldn't believe how much the estimate was! I bought the car for $1,200, (7) _____ (conjunction) I really didn't want to spend that much to fix it. Still, we needed a way to get back home so I (8) _____ (adverb) told the mechanic to start work on the car. Seven hours later, (9) _____ (pronoun) began to drive home. As we drove into my driveway, smoke began coming (10) _____ (phrase), and I realized that I had been swindled out of $2,500.

◆ *Review P r a c t i c e 3*   **Writing Your Own** Write your own paragraph about your favorite pet. What did you name it? What kind of animal was it?

◆ *Review P r a c t i c e 4*   **Editing Your Writing** Exchange paragraphs from Review Practice 3 with a classmate, and do the following:

1. Circle any words that are used incorrectly.
2. Underline any phrases that do not read smoothly.
3. Put an X in the margin where you find a dependent clause that is not connected to an independent clause.

Then return the paragraph to its writer, and use the information in the introduction to edit your own paragraph. Record your errors on the Error Log in Appendix 4.

SENTENCES

Complete sentences are one of the staples of good writing. But sometimes our thoughts pour out of our heads faster than we can get them all down. As a result, we write sentences that need to be corrected in the editing stage. This is a natural part of writing. Always get your ideas down first, and edit your sentences later.

To help you start editing your writing, we will focus on the following sentence elements:

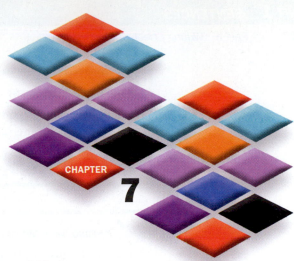

SUBJECTS AND VERBS

 CHECKLIST for Identifying Subjects and Verbs

> ✔ Does each of your sentences contain a subject?
> ✔ Does each of your sentences contain a verb?

A sentence has a message to communicate, but for that message to be meaningful, it must have a subject and a verb. The subject is the topic of the sentence, what the sentence is about. The verb is the sentence's motor. It moves the message forward to its destination. Without these two parts, the sentence is not complete.

Notice how subjects and verbs work together in the following paragraph by Garrison Keillor.

A hydrant was open on Seventh Avenue above 23rd Street last Friday morning, and I stopped on my way east and watched people hop over the water. It was a brilliant spring day. The water was a nice clear creek about three feet wide and ran along the gutter around the northwest corner of the intersection. A gaggle of pedestrians crossing 23rd went *hop hop hop hop hop* over the creek as a few soloists jaywalking Seventh performed at right angles to them, and I got engrossed in the dance. Three feet isn't a long leap for most people, and the ease of it permits a wide range of expression. Some hoppers went a good deal higher than necessary.

In this paragraph, Garrison Keillor describes some unusual observations he made one spring morning. Before continuing in this chapter, take a moment to record some of your own observations. Save your work because you will use it later in the chapter.

WRITING ASSIGNMENT: UNUSUAL OBSERVATIONS

What are some of your funniest observations? Some of your saddest observations? Some of your most memorable observations? Write a paragraph describing one of your most unusual observations. See if you can make it come alive like Keillor does in his paragraph.

REVISING YOUR WRITING

Revise the first draft of your paragraph before you focus on editing. Use the Revising Checklist on pages 24–25 to help you with your revision. Make sure your paragraph has a good topic sentence and is well developed. Then check your paragraph for unity, organization, and coherence.

SUBJECTS

To be complete, every sentence must have a subject. The **subject** tells who or what the sentence is about.

Subject
↓

The **students**   study for their tests.
Computers   solve many problems.

Compound Subjects

When two or more separate words tell what the sentence is about, the sentence has a **compound subject**.

Compound Subject: **Dogs** and **cats** are fun to play with.
Compound Subject: The **cars** and **trucks** were on display.

Hint: Note that *and* is not part of the compound subject.

Unstated Subjects

Sometimes a subject does not actually appear in a sentence but is understood. This occurs in commands and requests. The understood subject is always *you,* meaning either someone specific or anyone in general.

Command:	Move away from the fire.

$\overset{\text{s}}{}$

Unstated Subject:	**(You)** move away from the fire.
Request:	Help me open the jar, please.

$\overset{\text{s}}{}$

Unstated Subject:	**(You)** help me open the jar, please.

Subjects and Prepositional Phrases

The subject of a sentence cannot be part of a prepositional phrase. A **prepositional phrase** is a group of words that begins with a **preposition**, a word such as *in, on, under, after,* or *from.* Here are some examples of prepositional phrases:

in the street	**next to** the wall	**on** the bus	**before** lunch
under the water	**with** Brad	**behind** the car	**instead of** the subway
after work	**into** the boat	**around** the mess	**across** the alley
from the left side	**during** the storm	**for** the children	**at** the intersection

(See page 80 for a more complete list of prepositions.)

If you are looking for the subject of a sentence, first cross out all the prepositional phrases. Then figure out what the sentence is about.

$\qquad\qquad\quad\overset{\text{s}}{}\qquad\overset{\text{s}}{}$

~~During the flood~~, the **men** and **women** helped block the water.

$\qquad\quad\overset{\text{s}}{}$

The **phone** ~~around the corner~~ was working fine.

$\overset{\text{s}}{}$

Some ~~of the water~~ leaked ~~into our boat~~.

REVIEWING SUBJECTS

What is a subject?

_____

What is a compound subject?

_____

_____

What is an unstated subject?

_____

How can you find the subject of a sentence?

_____

_____

◈ **P r a c t i c e   1   Identifying** Cross out the prepositional phrases in each of the following sentences and then underline the subjects.

1. Bob and Jolene got married last weekend.
2. The author was proud of her work.
3. *The Andy Griffith Show* is still my favorite show.
4. Each of the students is responsible for bringing an essay.
5. A popular actor visited our school today.
6. I am getting a better wheelchair in September.
7. Sometimes Lavonne doesn't tell the truth.
8. The boys and girls in the first grade have learned to add and subtract.
9. During the Rosh Hashanah celebrations, my brother will be announcing his engagement.
10. I think that you will make an excellent doctor.

◈ **P r a c t i c e   2   Identifying** Put an X next to the sentence if the underlined portion is not a subject. Cross out the prepositional phrases first.

1. _____ The <u>dogs</u> ate their food.
2. _____ Good musicians practice <u>every day</u>.
3. _____ Manuel was a talented <u>baseball player</u>.
4. _____ After June, <u>I</u> will take a vacation.
5. _____ <u>Every month</u>, Ioana gets money from her parents.
6. _____ The <u>television</u> blared all night.
7. _____ The fountain in the plaza was built by my uncle.
8. _____ <u>Shawna</u> wants an interview with you in the near future.

9. _____ <u>Money</u> doesn't grow on trees.

10. _____ I am <u>applying</u> for a new job.

◆ *P r a c t i c e 3* **Correcting** Correct the errors in Practice 2 by listing the correct subjects here.

_____

_____

_____

_____

_____

◆ *P r a c t i c e 4* **Completing** Fill in each blank in the following sentences with a subject that is not a person's name.

1. _____ took a trip to Hawaii last summer.

2. _____ is a beautiful place in the winter.

3. _____ has been working out every day.

4. _____ is in the shoe department.

5. _____ just finished her medical residency.

6. _____ and _____ have been best friends since kindergarten.

7. Under the umbrella, _____ was staying nice and dry.

8. _____ has a black belt in karate.

9. In two days, _____ will have earned all of his tuition money.

10. Sometimes _____ makes me laugh at myself.

◆ *P r a c t i c e 5* **Writing Your Own**

A. Write a sentence of your own using each of the following nouns as a subject.

1. shirt _____

2. teacher _____

3. courage _____

4. award _____

5. computer _____

B. Write five sentences of your own, and underline the subjects in each sentence.

_____

_____

_____

_____

_____

VERBS

To be complete, a sentence must have a verb as well as a subject. A **verb** tells what the subject is doing or what is happening.

Verb

The students	**study** for their tests.
Computers	**solve** many problems.

Action Verbs

An **action verb** tells what a subject is doing. Some examples of action verbs are *skip, ski, stare, flip, breathe, remember, restate, sigh, cry, decrease, write,* and *pant.*

Action Verb: The lobsters **scurried** across the ocean floor.

Action Verb: The car **swerved** out of the way.

Linking Verbs

A **linking verb** connects the subject to other words in the sentence that say something about it. Linking verbs are also called **state-of-being**

verbs because they do not show action. Rather, they say that something "is" a particular way. The most common linking verb is *be* (*am, are, is, was, were*).

Linking Verb:	The water **is** in the gutter.
Linking Verb:	I **am** worried about the presentation.

Other common linking verbs are *remain*, *act*, *look*, *grow*, and *seem*.

Linking Verb:	The woman **remained** concerned about her clothes.
Linking Verb:	Firefighters **act** proud.
Linking Verb:	The cliff **looks** tall.
Linking Verb:	The stream **grew** wide.
Linking Verb:	Children **seem** happy about going to Six Flags Magic Mountain.

Some words, such as *smell* and *taste*, can be either action verbs or linking verbs.

Action Verb:	I **smell** flowers.
Linking Verb:	This house **smells** like flowers.
Action Verb:	She **tasted** the soup.
Linking Verb:	It **tasted** too salty.

Compound Verbs

Just as a verb can have more than one subject, some subjects can have more than one verb. These are called **compound verbs**.

Compound Verb:	She **skips** and **hops** over the cracks in the sidewalk.
Compound Verb:	He **laughs** when he's happy and **cries** when he's sad.

Hint: A sentence can have both a compound subject and a compound verb.

    s   s   v   v

Men and **women** **avoided** the crowds and **dashed** to their cars.

Helping Verbs

Often the **main verb** (the action verb or linking verb) in a sentence needs help to convey its meaning. **Helping verbs** add information, such as when an action took place. The **complete verb** consists of a main verb and all its helping verbs.

Complete Verb: The snow **will be** <u>gone</u> tomorrow.

Complete Verb: You **might** <u>fall</u> in the ditch.

Complete Verb: We **should have** <u>fixed</u> the faucet.

Complete Verb: City workers **have** <u>checked</u> the stoplights.

Complete Verb: The repair technician **will be** <u>coming</u> to fix the problem.

Complete Verb: You **should** not <u>go</u> outside today.

Hint: Note that *not* isn't part of the helping verb. Similarly, *never, always, only, just,* and *still* are never part of the verb.

Complete Verb: I **have** always <u>liked</u> hot weather.

The most common helping verbs are

be, am, is, are, was, were
have, has, had
do, did

Other common helping verbs are

may, might
can, could
will, would
should, used to, ought to

REVIEWING VERBS

What is a verb?

_____

What is the difference between action and linking verbs?

_____

_____

Give an example of a compound verb.

_____

Give an example of a helping verb.

_____

What is the difference between a subject and a verb?

_____

_____

 **P r a c t i c e   6   Identifying** Underline the complete verbs in each of the following sentences.

1. That book is hard to read.
2. The jurors stayed in the courtroom.
3. Fabio is going to the movies.
4. We waited by the phone and hoped for a call.
5. Martha screamed at the top of her lungs.
6. Until last night, we had never won a game.
7. I cook and eat only healthy foods.
8. Bob and Melissa turned down the wrong street.
9. Every June, we spend a week in the mountains.
10. Ricky was waiting for a ride to work.

P r a c t i c e   7   Identifying Put an X next to the sentence if the underlined portion is not a verb.

1. _____ I <u>gave</u> you my best advice.
2. _____ Gwyneth wrote a <u>paper</u> about *The Tempest*.

3. _____ Next year, I <u>will take</u> piano lessons.

4. _____ Jill just filed her <u>income taxes</u>.

5. _____ The child jumped <u>into the pool</u>.

6. _____ Water <u>is</u> better for you than soft drinks.

7. _____ My father <u>walked</u> to the car and <u>opened</u> the door.

8. _____ Edgar's car is <u>definitely</u> totaled.

9. _____ Doctors and lawyers often have big <u>houses</u>.

10. _____ Abby <u>does</u> not <u>want</u> that cookie.

◆ **P r a c t i c e   8   Correcting** Correct the errors in Practice 7 by listing the correct verbs here.

_____

_____

_____

_____

_____

◆ **P r a c t i c e   9   Completing** Fill in each blank in the following sentences with a verb that makes sense. Avoid using *is*, *are*, *was*, and *were* by themselves.

1. The doctor _____ my forehead.

2. My grandmother _____ me a check for my birthday.

3. We always _____ bottled water on camping trips.

4. They _____ happy soon.

5. My friend _____ jigsaw puzzles.

6. Sometimes college _____ solutions to difficult problems.

7. Most of the time, my uncle _____ the dishes.

8. I _____ n't _____ to leave.

9. We _____ a midnight flight to Las Vegas.

10. I _____ often _____ magazines in bed.

◆ *P r a c t i c e **1 0*****   Writing Your Own**

A. Write a sentence for each of the following verbs, and label the verb as either action or linking.

1. grow _____

2. should have been asking _____

3. appears _____

4. will pay _____

5. has gone _____

B. Write five sentences of your own, and underline the complete verbs in each sentence. Remember that sentences can have more than one complete verb.

_____

_____

_____

_____

_____

CHAPTER REVIEW

You might want to reread your answers to the questions in all the review boxes before you do the following exercises.

◆ *Review P r a c t i c e **1*****   Reading** Refer to the paragraph by Garrison Keillor on page 101 to do the following exercises.

A. List five subjects.

1. _____

2. _____

3. _____

4. _____

5. _____

B. List the five complete verbs that go with the subjects listed in Review Practice 1A.

1. _____

2. _____

3. _____

4. _____

5. _____

◆ *Review* **P r a c t i c e   2** **Identifying** Underline the subjects once and the verbs twice in each of the following sentences.

1. The dogs barked at the door.
2. My neighbor has tropical fish.
3. We watched *The Sopranos* last night.
4. Rocky swam in the lake.
5. Janine and Wallis went to the movies.
6. I ran to the car and unlocked the door.
7. You have been driving all night.
8. Marny is not feeling well today.
9. The TV is fuzzy.
10. They will never see her again.

◆ *Review* **P r a c t i c e   3** **Correcting** List any subjects and verbs you didn't identify correctly in Review Practice 2.

_____

_____

_____

◢ EDITING A STUDENT PARAGRAPH

Following is a paragraph written and revised by Ralph McKensey in response to the writing assignment in this chapter. Read the paragraph, and underline his subjects once and complete verbs twice.

> When I was in sixth grade, I came home from school one day to fire engines in front of my house. Smoke was pouring out of the kitchen window. There was a police car, and I could see my mom and my dog sitting in the back of the car. My mom was holding one hand over her mouth and was petting the dog with her other hand. I ran to my mom as if I was moving in slow motion. It seemed like it took forever to get to the police car. Finally, she put her arms around me and told me that things would be all right. My family and I will never forget that day.

Collaborative Activity

Team up with a partner, and list Ralph's subjects and their verbs in two columns. There are 14 subjects and 15 verbs.

◢ EDITING YOUR OWN PARAGRAPH

Now return to the paragraph you wrote and revised at the beginning of this chapter.

Collaborative Activity

Exchange paragraphs with your partner, and underline the subjects once and the complete verbs twice in your partner's paragraph.

Individual Activity

To complete the writing process, make sure each of your sentences has at least one subject and verb.

CHAPTER **8**

FRAGMENTS

✅ CHECKLIST for Identifying and Correcting Fragments

> ✔ Does each sentence have a subject?
> ✔ Does each sentence have a verb?

One of the most common errors in college writing is the fragment. A fragment is a piece of a sentence that is punctuated as a complete sentence. But it does not express a complete thought. Once you learn how to identify fragments, you can avoid them in your writing.

Notice how all the complete sentences work in the following paragraph by Bailey White.

There is only one paved street in the town, with buildings on only one side of that street. Big oak trees shade the storefronts, and their roots have humped up the sidewalk and crumbled the asphalt of the street. In the middle of the row of buildings is an abandoned municipal garage. It still has its brick walls with the arched openings of doorways and windows, but the roof is gone, and limbs of the oak trees hang over the walls and drop acorns into the Model A Ford roadster that is parked inside, rusting away under a rotten tarpaulin. The other buildings, once hardware stores and drugstores and feed stores, have given over to the peculiar and the exotic.

In this paragraph, Bailey White is recording interesting details about an old town. Before continuing in this chapter, take a moment to record details about your hometown. Save your work because you will use it later in the chapter.

WRITING ASSIGNMENT: HOMETOWN HIGHLIGHTS

What kind of city, town, or rural area were you brought up in? What are some of your most vivid mental pictures of this town? In a paragraph, describe your town's downtown area for someone who has never been there. What are its physical features? What is its general atmosphere? Do you feel that you fit in this town?

REVISING YOUR WRITING

Revise the first draft of your paragraph before you focus on editing. Use the Revising Checklist on pages 24–25 to help you with your revision. Make sure your paragraph has a good topic sentence, is well developed, and is well organized. Then check your paragraph for unity and coherence.

ABOUT FRAGMENTS

A complete sentence must have both a subject and a verb. If one or both are missing or if the subject and verb are introduced by a dependent word, you have only part of a sentence, a **fragment.** Even if it begins with a capital letter and ends with a period, it cannot stand alone and must be corrected in your writing. The five most common types of fragments are explained in this chapter.

Type 1: Afterthought Fragments
He works at the garage. **And the bank.**

Type 2: *-ing* Fragments
Breaking the sidewalk. The oak tree is large and strong.

Type 3: *to* Fragments
Some people have moved. **To live in the heart of town.**

Type 4: Dependent-Clause Fragments
Because there are no malls here. We go to another city to shop.

Type 5: Relative-Clause Fragments

The hardware store is on the corner. **Which is a good location.**

Ways to Correct Fragments

Once you have identified a fragment, you have two options for correcting it. You can connect the fragment to the sentence before or after it or make the fragment into an independent clause.

Correction 1:   *Connect the fragment to the sentence before or after it.*

Correction 2:   *Make the fragment into an independent clause:*

(a) add the missing subject and/or verb, or

(b) drop the subordinating word before the fragment.

We will discuss these corrections for each type of fragment.

REVIEWING FRAGMENTS

What is a sentence fragment?

_____

_____

What are the five types of fragments?

_____   _____

_____   _____

_____

What are the two ways to correct a fragment?

1. _____

2. _____

IDENTIFYING AND CORRECTING FRAGMENTS

The rest of this chapter discusses the five types of fragments and the corrections for each type.

Type 1: Afterthought Fragments

Afterthought fragments occur when you add an idea to a sentence but don't punctuate it correctly.

Fragment: He works at the garage. **And the bank.**

The phrase *And the bank* is punctuated and capitalized as a complete sentence. Because this group of words lacks a verb, however, it is a fragment.

Correction 1:   *Connect the fragment to the sentence before or after it.*

Example: He works at the garage **and** the bank.

Correction 2:   *Make the fragment into an independent clause.*

Example: He works at the garage. **He also works** at the bank.

The first correction connects the fragment to the sentence before it. The second correction makes the fragment an independent clause with its own subject and verb.

REVIEWING AFTERTHOUGHT FRAGMENTS

What is an afterthought fragment?

_____

Give an example of an afterthought fragment.

_____

What are the two ways to correct an afterthought fragment?

1. _____

2. _____

_____

◆ **P r a c t i c e   1   Identifying** Underline the afterthought fragments in each of the following sentences.

1. I applied for a credit card. But was turned down.

2. Tim looked into the room and saw his keys. On the end table. He was very frustrated.

3. Sharla is sleeping in class today because she stayed up late. With her homework.

4. Spring is my favorite time of year because flowers are growing. And blooming.

5. Carlene turned in her paper by the deadline. But received a poor grade.

6. Jerome ate pizza. With anchovies on it. His breath smelled disgusting.

7. Juana sits next to me. In class. And tries to copy my homework.

8. The best books I ever read are *Gulliver's Travels*. And *Lord of the Flies*. *The Slave Dancer* is good too.

9. The boy bumped his head. On the bedpost. And cried loudly until his mother heard him.

10. My air conditioner isn't working. Or blowing out any cold air.

◆ **P r a c t i c e   2   Identifying** Underline the afterthought fragments in the following paragraph.

The best day of my life was July 5, 2004. A Monday. My sister helped me move into my new apartment. On the east side of town. I loved living with my parents, but I felt it was time to move on. When I found this apartment, I knew it was perfect. And just my style. The apartment has a big living room and kitchen. But only one tiny bedroom. While we were moving my stuff, my sister said she was jealous. She had no job. And couldn't move out on her own yet. I almost felt sorry for her. Then I remembered how nice it was to have my own place. And stopped worrying about her.

◆ **P r a c t i c e   3   Correcting** Correct the afterthought fragments in Practice 1 by rewriting them, using both correction methods.

1. _____

2. _____

3. _____

4. _____

5. _____

6. _____

7. _____

8. _____

9. _____

10. _____

P r a c t i c e 4 Correcting Rewrite the paragraph in Practice 2, correcting the fragments.

_____

_____

_____

_____

_____

_____

P r a c t i c e 5 Writing Your Own

A. Write five afterthought fragments of your own, or record five from your papers.

1. _____

2. _____

3. _____

4. _____

5. _____

B. Correct these fragments, using both correction methods.

1. _____

2. _____

3. _____

4. _____

5. _____

Type 2: *-ing* Fragments

Words that end in *-ing* are forms of verbs that cannot be the main verbs in their sentences. For an *-ing* word to function as a verb, it must have a helping verb with it (*be, do,* or *have*; see pages 192–202).

Fragment: **Breaking the sidewalk. The oak tree is large and strong.**

Breaking is not a verb in this sentence because it has no helping verb. Also, this group of words is a fragment because it has no subject.

Correction 1:   *Connect the fragment to the sentence before or after it.*
Example: **Breaking the sidewalk, the oak tree is large and strong.**

Correction 2:   *Make the fragment into an independent clause.*
Example: **The oak tree is breaking the sidewalk. The oak tree is large and strong.**

Hint: When you connect an *-ing* fragment to a sentence, insert a comma between the two sentence parts. You should insert the comma whether the *-ing* part comes at the beginning or the end of the sentence.

The oak tree is large and strong, **breaking the sidewalk.**
Breaking the sidewalk, the oak tree is large and strong.

REVIEWING *-ing* FRAGMENTS

How can you tell if an -ing word is part of a fragment or is a main verb?

_____

_____

Give an example of an -ing fragment.

_____

What are the two ways to correct an -ing fragment?

1. _____

2. _____

_____

What kind of punctuation should you use when you join an -ing fragment to another sentence?

_____

 **P r a c t i c e   6   Identifying** Underline the *-ing* fragments in each of the following sentences.

1. Driving to the store. I wore my seat belt.
2. The boy is coloring. Breaking the crayons in half.
3. Sleeping in the corner. The cat is curled into a ball.
4. Something has leaked on the floor. Making a big mess.
5. I hear soft music in the background. Setting the tone of the movie.
6. Eating a large pastrami sandwich. Nick got a stomach ache.
7. When this term is over, I'm going home. Starting my big vacation.
8. Reading at night. Travis fell asleep on his books.
9. The last time we went to that restaurant, we were unhappy. Waiting 20 minutes for drink refills.
10. Playing in the swimming pool all afternoon. I got a sunburn.

P r a c t i c e 7 Identifying Underline the *-ing* fragments in the following paragraph.

When my brother joined the Navy, he was very excited. Wanting to travel around the world and meet new people. The reality was not so entertaining. He did get to travel, but he wasn't always stationed in exotic places. Lying on the beach or visiting famous landmarks. He also had a pretty boring job. Washing jet planes. Working the graveyard shift. When he was in high school, he was quite rebellious. Making bad choices in friends. He was often in trouble for breaking his curfew and staying out too late. Overall, the Navy was good for him. Forcing him to grow up. Though it wasn't the paid vacation that he expected, it did give him the taste of responsibility that he needed.

P r a c t i c e 8 Correcting Correct the *-ing* fragments in Practice 6 by rewriting them, using both correction methods. Remember to insert a comma when using correction 1.

1. _____

2. _____

3. _____

4. _____

5. _____

6. _____

7. _____

8. _____

9. _____

10. _____

P r a c t i c e 9 Correcting Rewrite the paragraph in Practice 7, correcting the fragments. Remember to insert a comma with correction 1.

_____

_____

_____

_____

_____

◆ *P r a c t i c e 1 0*   **Writing Your Own**

A. Write five *-ing* fragments of your own, or record five from your papers.

1. _____

2. _____

3. _____

4. _____

5. _____

B. Correct these fragments, using both correction methods.

1. _____

2. _____

3. _____

4. _____

5. _____

Type 3: *to* Fragments

When *to* is added to a verb (*to see, to hop, to skip, to jump*), the combination cannot be a main verb in its sentence. As a result, this group of words is often involved in a fragment.

Fragment: Some people have moved. **To live in the heart of town.**

Since *to* + a verb cannot function as the main verb of its sentence, *to live in the heart of town* is a fragment as it is punctuated here.

Correction 1: *Connect the fragment to the sentence before or after it.*

Example: Some people have moved **to live in the heart of town.**

Correction 2: *Make the fragment into an independent clause.*

Example: Some people have moved. **They live in the heart of town.**

Hint: A *to* fragment can also occur at the beginning of a sentence. In this case, insert a comma between the two sentence parts when correcting the fragment.

To live in the heart of town, some people have moved.

REVIEWING *to* FRAGMENTS

What does a to fragment consist of?

_____

Give an example of a to fragment.

_____

What are the two ways to correct a to fragment?

1. _____

2. _____

_____

Practice 11 Identifying Underline the *to* fragments in each of the following sentences.

1. My neighbors drive an expensive car. To look like they are rich.
2. Harry is going with me. To help me buy a car. He is a good negotiator.
3. Breanne makes her own clothes. To save money.
4. To be more prepared for the test. I will devote my weekend to studying.

5. To grow tomatoes in your backyard. You need a big garden area.

6. This is the last time we will call you. To ask you for a donation.

7. To finish wallpapering the living room. My wife will take tomorrow off work.

8. This morning I got up at 5 a.m. To jog around the block before I got in the shower.

9. Mira was getting her nails done. To be in a wedding on Saturday.

10. Put your feet up and relax. To watch this movie with me.

P r a c t i c e   1 2   Identifying Underline the *to* fragments in the following paragraph.

My parents are finally putting in a swimming pool. To keep us from bothering the neighbors. We have been telling them for years that we need a pool, but they always complained about money. To avoid the discussion. Last weekend, my dad learned from a friend about a company that installs swimming pools at a reasonable price. We were so happy. To finally get a pool of our own. The contractor said it would take six to eight weeks. To finish the pool. In the meantime, our back fence has been pulled down. To make room for the big backhoe. It is exciting for my brother and me. To watch the construction. We can't wait to go swimming in our own backyard.

P r a c t i c e   1 3   Correcting Correct the *to* fragments in Practice 11 by rewriting them, using both correction methods.

1. _____

2. _____

3. _____

4. _____

5. _____

6. _____

7. _____

8. _____

9. _____

10. _____

◆ *P r a c t i c e   1 4*   **Correcting** Rewrite the paragraph in Practice 12, correcting the fragments. Rearrange the sentences if necessary. Remember to insert a comma when you add the *to* fragment to the beginning of a sentence.

_____

_____

_____

_____

_____

◆ *P r a c t i c e   1 5*   **Writing Your Own**

A. Write five *to* fragments of your own, or record five from your papers.

1. _____

2. _____

3. _____

4. _____

5. _____

B. Correct these fragments, using both correction methods.

1. _____

2. _____

3. _____

4. _____

5. _____

Type 4: Dependent-Clause Fragments

A group of words that begins with a **subordinating conjunction** (see the list that follows) is called a **dependent clause** and cannot stand alone. Even though it has a subject and a verb, it is a fragment because it depends on an independent clause to complete its meaning. An **independent clause** is a group of words with a subject and a verb that can stand alone. (See pages 93–97 for help with clauses.)

Here is a list of some commonly used subordinating conjunctions that create dependent clauses.

Subordinating Conjunctions

after	because	since	until
although	before	so	when
as	even if	so that	whenever
as if	even though	than	where
as long as	how	that	wherever
as soon as	if	though	whether
as though	in order that	unless	while

Fragment: <u>Because there are no malls here.</u> We go to another city to shop.

This sentence has a subject and a verb, but it is introduced by a subordinating conjunction, *because*. As a result, this sentence is a dependent clause and cannot stand alone.

Correction 1:   *Connect the fragment to the sentence before or after it.*

Example: Because there are no malls here, **we** go to another city to shop.

Correction 2:   *Make the fragment into an independent clause.*

Example: ~~Because~~ There are no malls here. We go to another city to shop.

Hint: If the dependent clause comes first, put a comma between the two parts of the sentence. If the dependent clause comes second, the comma is not necessary.

Because there are no malls here, we go to another city to shop.
We go to another city to shop **because there are no malls here.**

REVIEWING DEPENDENT-CLAUSE FRAGMENTS
....

What is a dependent-clause fragment?

_____

What type of conjunction makes a clause dependent?

_____

What is an independent clause?

_____

Give an example of a dependent-clause fragment.

_____

What are the two ways to correct a dependent-clause fragment?

1. _____

2. _____

_____

◆ **P r a c t i c e 1 6 Identifying** Underline the dependent-clause fragments in each of the following sentences.

1. While my daughter slept. I finished her scrapbook.

2. Although my brother is in my Spanish class. He will not help me with homework.

3. This winter will be very cold. Since this summer was not as warm as usual.

4. Jared will practice basketball every day. Even if he doesn't make the team.

5. As soon as Maury gets here. I'm going home.

6. Nelly can do the video portion of the project. Unless you have a better idea.

7. Before the sun comes up tomorrow. We will be driving through New Mexico.

8. The Dixie Chicks sang "There's Your Trouble." When they gave a concert in our town.

9. My computer speakers went out. While I was listening to a radio show on the Internet.

10. As long as I am in charge. This is the way we should organize the club.

♦ **P r a c t i c e   1 7   Identifying** Underline the dependent-clause fragments in the following paragraph.

> While I was driving through my hometown. I noticed the ice-cream parlor where I used to work. During my high school years, the parlor was a popular hangout. Even though the ice cream was a little overpriced. The owners were Sam and Billy, who let my friends come by to visit with me. Whenever I had to work weekends. Before it was an ice-cream parlor. The building was used as a bank. Everyone in the town was glad to have the parlor instead. So that teenagers had somewhere safe to spend time. Sam and Billy were the best bosses I could have asked for. Although the pay was not very good. I will never forget that job. Because I learned so much about myself.

♦ **P r a c t i c e   1 8   Correcting** Correct the dependent-clause fragments in Practice 16 by rewriting them, using both correction methods.

1. _____

2. _____

3. _____

4. _____

5. _____

6. _____

7. _____

8. _____

9. _____

10. _____

◆ **Practice 19** **Correcting** Rewrite the paragraph in Practice 17, correcting the fragments. When you use correction 1, remember to add a comma if the dependent clause comes first.

_____

_____

_____

_____

_____

◆ **Practice 20** **Writing Your Own**

A. Write five dependent-clause fragments of your own, or record five from your papers.

1. _____

2. _____

3. _____

4. _____

5. _____

B. Correct these fragments, using both correction methods.

1. _____

2. _____

3. _____

4. _____

5. _____

Type 5: Relative-Clause Fragments

A **relative clause** is a dependent clause that begins with a relative pronoun: *who, whom, whose, which,* or *that.* When a relative clause is punctuated as a sentence, the result is a fragment.

Fragment: The hardware store is on the corner. **Which is a good location.**

Which is a good location is a clause fragment that begins with the relative pronoun *which.* This word automatically makes the words that follow it a dependent clause, so they cannot stand alone as a sentence.

Correction 1:   *Connect the fragment to the sentence before or after it.*

Example: The hardware store is on the corner, which is a good location.

Correction 2:   *Make the fragment into an independent clause.*

Example: The hardware store is on the corner. It is a good location.

REVIEWING RELATIVE-CLAUSE FRAGMENTS

How is a relative-clause fragment different from a dependent-clause fragment?

_____

_____

Give an example of a relative-clause fragment.

_____

What are the two ways to correct a relative-clause fragment?

1. _____

2. _____

◆ **P r a c t i c e   2 1   Identifying** Underline the relative-clause fragments in the following sentences.

1. The company president is Mr. Liu. Who always sits with my family at church.
2. My brother is taking the class. That is taught by Dr. Roberts.
3. Those are the neighbors. Whose dogs run loose in the streets.
4. I am taking a trip to Poughkeepsie. Which is in New York.
5. Maureen talked to the woman. Whose car is for sale.
6. You are the one. Whom the committee selected.
7. I just quit smoking. Which was the hardest thing I've ever done.
8. This afternoon, I have a meeting with the dean. Who is in charge of admissions.
9. Dennis works at the restaurant. That is on Elm Street.
10. Laila is going on a date with Jack. Whom she met at the coffeehouse.

◆ **Practice 22** **Identifying** Underline the relative-clause fragments in the following paragraph.

Last year, I celebrated Independence Day with Christine. Whom I met through work. She had a dinner party at her house. Which is on the corner of Fourth Street and Harker Avenue. Christine invited several other people as well. Who brought fireworks and sparklers. The food was great, the company was nice, and the fireworks were entertaining. I met one guy at the party, who drove a beautiful 1965 Mustang. That was fully restored. He was friendly and attractive, but he had a girlfriend. Whose father happened to be the city's mayor. This year, Christine is having another party, and I hope to go.

◆ **Practice 23** **Correcting** Correct the relative-clause fragments in Practice 21 by rewriting them, using both correction methods.

1. _____

2. _____

3. _____

4. _____

5. _____

6. _____

7. _____

8. _____

9. _____

10. _____

◀ *P r a c t i c e   2 4*   **Correcting** Rewrite the paragraph in Practice 22, correcting the fragments.

_____

_____

_____

_____

_____

◀ *P r a c t i c e   2 5*   **Writing Your Own**

A. Write five relative-clause fragments of your own, or record five from your papers.

1. _____

2. _____

3. _____

4. _____

5. _____

B. Correct these fragments, using both correction methods.

1. _____

2. _____

3. _____

4. _____

5. _____

CHAPTER REVIEW

You might want to reread your answers to the questions in all the review boxes before you do the following exercises.

◆ *Review P r a c t i c e 1* **Reading** Refer to the paragraph by Bailey White on page 114 to do the following exercises.

A. Write one of each type of fragment based on White's paragraph:

Afterthought: _____

-*ing* Fragment: _____

to Fragment: _____

Dependent-Clause: _____

Relative-Clause: _____

B. Correct the fragments that you just wrote.

_____

_____

_____

_____

_____

◆ *Review P r a c t i c e 2* **Identifying** Underline the fragments in each of the following sentences.

1. I went to the grocery store. To buy a pound of hamburger.
2. Trying to get the best seats. We arrived at the concert early.
3. Since there was nothing we could do. We decided to go home.

4. Yesterday I spoke with my grandfather. Who is also my best friend.

5. Mrs. Robinson teaches history. And economics.

6. While I was walking to the mailbox. I tripped on my untied shoelaces.

7. Janie got her navel pierced. Thinking that would make her happy.

8. To find the best price on computers. We searched the Internet.

9. The small boy played with the heavy door. And pinched his fingers.

10. We invested in the alarm system. That also comes with a paging service.

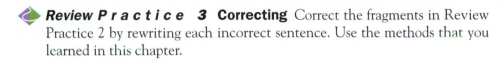 ***Review P r a c t i c e 3* Correcting** Correct the fragments in Review Practice 2 by rewriting each incorrect sentence. Use the methods that you learned in this chapter.

EDITING A STUDENT PARAGRAPH

Following is a paragraph written and revised by Marty Rhodes in response to the writing assignment in this chapter. Read the paragraph, and underline the subjects once and complete verbs twice.

> Our downtown center was just renovated. It has bricks down the center of the street. And lights on the trees all year long. A beautiful sight. I never thought that I would enjoy downtown so much. Every building is also being replastered and repainted. So that the buildings stay in good shape. The bars are now reopening. Downtown is attracting new people. And bringing in a lot of money.

Collaborative Activity

Team up with a partner, and put brackets around the four fragments in Marty's paragraph. Then, working together, use what you have learned in this chapter to correct these errors using both correction methods. Rewrite the paragraph with your corrections.

EDITING YOUR OWN PARAGRAPH

Now return to the paragraph you wrote and revised at the beginning of this chapter. Underline your subjects once and main verbs twice.

Collaborative Activity

Exchange paragraphs with your partner, and put brackets around any fragments that you find in your partner's paragraph. Watch especially for clauses with an implied *that*.

Individual Activity

On the Error Log in Appendix 4, record any fragments that your partner found in your paragraph. To complete the writing process, correct these fragments by rewriting your paragraph.

CHAPTER 9

FUSED SENTENCES AND COMMA SPLICES

✔️ CHECKLIST for Identifying and Correcting Fused Sentences and Comma Splices

> ✔ Are any sentences run together without punctuation?
> ✔ Are any sentences incorrectly joined with only a comma?

When we cram two separate statements into a single sentence without correct punctuation, we create what are called **fused sentences** and **comma splices**. These run-together sentences generally distort our message and cause problems for our readers. In this chapter, you will learn how to identify and avoid these errors in your writing.

Before you study run-together sentences, look at the well-constructed sentences in the following paragraph by Tim O'Brien.

I drank some chocolate milk and then lay down on the sofa in the living room, not really sad, just floating, trying to imagine what it was to be dead. Nothing much came to me. I remember closing my eyes and whispering her name, almost begging, trying to make her come back. "Linda," I said, "please." And then I concentrated. I willed her alive. It was a dream, I suppose, or a daydream, but I made it happen. I saw her coming down the middle of Main Street, all alone. It was nearly dark and the street was deserted, no cars or people, and Linda wore a pink dress and shiny black shoes. I remember sitting down on the curb to watch. All her hair had grown back. The scars and stitches were gone. In the dream, if that's what it was, she was playing a game of some sort, laughing and running up the empty street, kicking a big aluminum water bucket.

In this paragraph, O'Brien is writing about an emotional daydream he once had. Before continuing in this chapter, take a moment to record a time you relied on your imagination. Save your work because you will use it later in the chapter.

WRITING ASSIGNMENT: A FANTASY

Have you ever used your imagination to get you through a tough situation? Have you ever just pretended to be somewhere else? Write a paragraph that describes one time when your imagination worked for you. Give as many details about the situation as you can.

REVISING YOUR WRITING

Revise the first draft of your paragraph before you focus on editing. Use the Revising Checklist on pages 24–25 to help you with your revision. Make sure your paragraph has a good topic sentence, is well developed, and is well organized. Then check your paragraph for unity and coherence.

IDENTIFYING FUSED SENTENCES AND COMMA SPLICES

Whereas a fragment is a piece of a sentence, **fused sentences** and **comma splices** are made up of two sentences written as one. In both cases, the first sentence runs into the next without the proper punctuation between the two.

Fused Sentence: The movie ended I went home.

Comma Splice: The movie ended, I went home.

Both of these sentences incorrectly join two independent clauses. The difference between them is one comma.

A **fused sentence** is two sentences "fused" or jammed together without any punctuation. Look at these examples:

Fused Sentence: I was lying on the sofa I had just eaten lunch.

This example consists of two independent clauses with no punctuation between them:

1. I was lying on the sofa.
2. I had just eaten lunch.

Fused Sentence: I began to think about my brother I felt good.

This example also consists of two independent clauses with no punctuation between them:

1. I began to think about my brother.
2. I felt good.

Like a fused sentence, a **comma splice** incorrectly joins two independent clauses. However, a comma splice puts a comma between the two independent clauses. The only difference between a fused sentence and a comma splice is the comma. Look at the following examples:

Comma Splice: I was lying on the sofa, I had just eaten lunch.

Comma Splice: I began to think about my brother, I felt good.

Both of these sentences consist of two independent clauses. But a comma is not the proper punctuation to separate these two clauses.

REVIEWING FUSED SENTENCES AND COMMA SPLICES

What are the two types of run-together sentences?

_____   _____

What is the difference between them?

_____

_____

◆ *P r a c t i c e   1*   **Identifying** Identify each of the following sentences as either fused (F) or comma splice (CS). Put a slash between the independent clauses that are not joined correctly.

1. _____ Devon wanted to join the swim team he had been practicing all summer.

2. _____ The car stalled in the middle of the road, two men helped push it out of traffic.

3. _____ I don't know why you weren't there, I'm sure you had a good excuse.

4. _____ Henrietta ran quickly to the phone she didn't want to miss the call.

5. _____ Summer is coming, the children are ready for a vacation from school.

6. _____ The team practiced for the tournament, it was three weeks away.

7. _____ The book is on the table it is collecting dust.

8. _____ Journals are on the third floor of the library the copy machines are there too.

9. _____ I like to see movies during my free time the last movie I saw was *Shrek*.

10. _____ Kimber is getting married in August, she has already found her wedding dress.

♦ **P r a c t i c e 2**   **Identifying** In each of the following sentences, put a slash between the independent clauses that are not joined correctly.

1. This class is being taught by Dr. Smith, she is the best professor in the department.

2. I am doing a report on Rudolfo Anaya there are five books about him in our library.

3. We are leaving this morning and should arrive by midafternoon, it is a six-hour drive.

4. Manny's computer has a virus I hope he doesn't send me any e-mail.

5. My grandmother has the prettiest roses in her garden she said they are 80 years old.

6. Olivia called the bank to check on her account, she had more money than she thought.

7. My campus is organizing a drug awareness program, it will be an out-reach for elementary students.

8. We are entering an art contest it is held at the fairgrounds.

9. Yvonne made my favorite dessert it was a chocolate cream pie.

10. The geraniums on the counter are wilting, they need some water.

♦ **P r a c t i c e 3**   **Identifying** Label each run-together sentence in the following paragraph as either fused (F) or comma splice (CS).

(1) _____ My girlfriend and I rented a movie last night it was *Proof of Life*. (2) _____ We ordered a pizza and put on the show, within 15 minutes I was falling asleep. (3) _____ I guess I stayed up too late the night before, there was a big test in my math class. Boy, was I embarrassed when I couldn't stay awake! (4) _____ My girlfriend nudged me about five times, trying to wake me up I just couldn't keep my eyes open. (5) _____ Finally, she gave up and let me sleep, just as the movie was ending, I woke up.

P r a c t i c e   4   Identifying Put a slash between any independent clauses that are not joined correctly.

I went to an antique store yesterday I was looking for an old tricycle. I wanted to put it in the corner of my bedroom, I have the perfect teddy bear to sit on the seat. Unfortunately, the antique store didn't have any tricycles, it did have a little wagon. It was red and just the right size it said "Radio Flyer" on the side in chipped white paint. I talked to the store owner about the price he wanted $50 for it. I told him that was too expensive I didn't want to spend that much money. He wouldn't lower his price, so this weekend I'm going to look at yard sales, maybe I can find something there.

P r a c t i c e   5   Writing Your Own

A. Find five run-together sentences in your writing or in another student's writing.

1. _____

2. _____

3. _____

4. _____

5. _____

B. Write five new run-together sentences of your own.

1. _____

2. _____

3. _____

4. _____

5. _____

CORRECTING FUSED SENTENCES AND COMMA SPLICES

You have four different options for correcting your run-together sentences.

1. Separate the two sentences with a period, and capitalize the next word.
2. Separate the two sentences with a comma, and add a coordinating conjunction (*and, but, for, nor, or, so,* or *yet*).
3. Change one of the sentences into a dependent clause with a subordinating conjunction (such as *if, because, since, after,* or *when*) or a relative pronoun (*who, whom, whose, which,* or *that*).
4. Separate the two sentences with a semicolon.

Correction 1: Use a Period

Separate the two sentences with a period, and capitalize the next word.

I was lying on the sofa**. I** had just eaten lunch.
I began to think about my brother**. I** felt good.

P r a c t i c e   6   Correcting Correct the run-together sentences in Practice 1 by rewriting them, using correction 1.

1. _____

2. _____

3. _____

4. _____

5. _____

6. _____

7. _____

8. _____

9. _____

10. _____

◆ *P r a c t i c e   7*   **Correcting** Correct the run-together sentences in Practice 2, using correction 1.

1. _____

2. _____

3. _____

4. _____

5. _____

6. _____

7. _____

8. _____

9. _____

10. _____

◆ *P r a c t i c e   8*   **Correcting** Correct the run-together sentences in Practice 3 by rewriting the paragraph, using correction 1.

_____

_____

_____

_____

_____

◆ *Practice 9* **Correcting** Correct the run-together sentences in Practice 4 by rewriting the paragraph, using correction 1.

_____

_____

_____

_____

_____

◆ *Practice 10* **Writing Your Own**

A. Correct the five run-together sentences from Practice 5A by rewriting them, using correction 1.

1. _____

2. _____

3. _____

4. _____

5. _____

B. Correct the five run-together sentences from Practice 5B by rewriting them, using correction 1.

1. _____

2. _____

3. _____

4. _____

5. _____

Correction 2: Use a Coordinating Conjunction

Separate the two sentences with a comma, and add a coordinating conjunction (*and, but, for, nor, or, so,* or *yet*).

I was lying on the sofa, **for** I had just eaten lunch.
I began to think about my brother, **so** I felt good.

P r a c t i c e   11   Correcting Correct the run-together sentences in Practice 1 by rewriting them, using correction 2.

1. _____

2. _____

3. _____

4. _____

5. _____

6. _____

7. _____

8. _____

9. _____

10. _____

P r a c t i c e   12   Correcting Correct the run-together sentences in Practice 2, using correction 2.

1. _____

2. _____

3. _____

4. _____

5. _____

6. _____

7. _____

8. _____

9. _____

10. _____

◆ **P r a c t i c e   1 3**   **Correcting** Correct the run-together sentences in Practice 3 by rewriting the paragraph, using correction 2.

_____

_____

_____

_____

_____

◆ **P r a c t i c e   1 4**   **Correcting** Correct the run-together sentences in Practice 4 by rewriting the paragraph, using correction 2.

_____

_____

_____

_____

_____

◆ **P r a c t i c e   1 5**   **Writing Your Own**

A. Correct the five run-together sentences from Practice 5A by rewriting them, using correction 2.

1. _____

2. _____

3. _____

4. _____

5. _____

B. Correct the five run-together sentences from Practice 5B by rewriting them, using correction 2.

1. _____

2. _____

3. _____

4. _____

5. _____

Correction 3: Create a Dependent Clause

Change one of the sentences into a dependent clause with a subordinating conjunction (such as *if, because, since, after,* or *when*) or a relative pronoun (*who, whom, whose, which,* or *that*).

> I was lying on the sofa **because** I had just eaten lunch.
> **Whenever** I began to think about my brother, I felt good.

For a list of subordinating conjunctions, see page 84.

Hint: If you put the dependent clause at the beginning of the sentence, add a comma between the two sentence parts.

> **Because I had just eaten lunch,** I was lying on the sofa.

◆ **P r a c t i c e 1 6** **Correcting** Correct the run-together sentences in Practice 1 by rewriting them, using correction 3.

1. _____

2. _____

3. _____

4. _____

5. _____

6. _____

7. _____

8. _____

9. _____

10. _____

◆ *P r a c t i c e   1 7*   **Correcting** Correct the run-together sentences in Practice 2, using correction 3.

1. _____

2. _____

3. _____

4. _____

5. _____

6. _____

7. _____

8. _____

9. _____

10. _____

Practice 18 **Correcting** Correct the run-together sentences in Practice 3 by rewriting the paragraph, using correction 3.

_____

_____

_____

_____

_____

Practice 19 **Correcting** Correct the run-together sentences in Practice 4 by rewriting the paragraph, using correction 3.

_____

_____

_____

_____

_____

Practice 20 **Writing Your Own**

A. Correct the five run-together sentences from Practice 5A by rewriting them, using correction 3.

1. _____

2. _____

3. _____

4. _____

5. _____

B. Correct the five run-together sentences from Practice 5B by rewriting them, using correction 3.

1. _____

2. _____

3. _____

4. _____

5. _____

Correction 4: Use a Semicolon

Separate the two sentences with a semicolon.

I was lying on the sofa; I had just eaten lunch.
I began to think about my brother; I felt good.

You can also use a **transition,** a word or an expression that indicates how the two parts of the sentence are related, with a semicolon. A transition often makes the sentence smoother. It is preceded by a semicolon and followed by a comma.

I was lying on the sofa; **in fact,** I had just eaten lunch.
I began to think about my brother; **consequently,** I felt good.

Here are some transitions commonly used with semicolons.

Transitions Used with a Semicolon Before and a Comma After

also	for instance	in fact	of course
consequently	furthermore	instead	otherwise
finally	however	meanwhile	similarly
for example	in contrast	nevertheless	therefore

♦ **P r a c t i c e 2 1 Correcting** Correct the run-together sentences in Practice 1 by rewriting them, using correction 4.

1. _____
2. _____
3. _____
4. _____
5. _____
6. _____
7. _____
8. _____
9. _____
10. _____

◆ *P r a c t i c e 2 2*   **Correcting** Correct the run-together sentences in Practice 2, using correction 4.

1. _____
2. _____
3. _____
4. _____
5. _____
6. _____
7. _____
8. _____
9. _____
10. _____

◆ *P r a c t i c e 2 3*   **Correcting** Correct the run-together sentences in Practice 3 by rewriting the paragraph, using correction 4.

_____

_____

_____

_____

_____

◆ **P r a c t i c e 2 4**   **Correcting** Correct the run-together sentences in Practice 4 by rewriting the paragraph, using correction 4.

_____

_____

_____

_____

_____

◆ **P r a c t i c e 2 5**   **Writing Your Own**

A. Correct the five run-together sentences from Practice 5A by rewriting them, using correction 4.

1. _____

2. _____

3. _____

4. _____

5. _____

B. Correct the five run-together sentences from Practice 5B by rewriting them, using correction 4.

1. _____

2. _____

3. _____

4. _____

5. _____

REVIEWING METHODS OF CORRECTING FUSED
SENTENCES AND COMMA SPLICES

What are the four ways to correct a fused sentence or comma splice?

1. _____

2. _____

_____

3. _____

_____

4. _____

Why is correcting fused sentences and comma splices important?

_____

CHAPTER REVIEW

You might want to reread your answers to the questions in all the review boxes before you do the following exercises.

◆ *Review P r a c t i c e   1* **Reading** Refer to the paragraph by Tim O'Brien on page 137 to do the following exercises.

1. Write a fused sentence based on Tim O'Brien's paragraph:

_____

2. Correct the fused sentence that you just wrote using the four correction methods.

Correction 1: _____

Correction 2: _____

Correction 3: _____

Correction 4: _____

3. Write a comma splice based on Tim O'Brien's paragraph:

_____

4. Correct the comma splice that you just wrote using the four correction methods.

Correction 1: _____

Correction 2: _____

Correction 3: _____

Correction 4: _____

♦ *Review* **P r a c t i c e**   **2** **Identifying** Put slashes between the following run-together sentences.

1. My brother wants to go with us we'd better let him, or he'll feel bad.
2. The printer is jammed again that's the second time this month.
3. I hope you remembered to pay the water bill I think it's past due.
4. Tracy left the party last night, she was crying.
5. My memory is failing I can't remember anything anymore.
6. Lend me three dollars, I need to bring cookies to the class party.
7. Simon sits next to me in class, he always takes great notes.
8. The airbag inflated during the accident it broke the driver's nose.
9. My favorite shoes are my white Nike sneakers I wear them every day.
10. If you want to go, you should ask, I can't read your mind.

***Review P r a c t i c e   3* Completing** Correct the run-together sentences in Review Practice 2 by rewriting each incorrect sentence. Use the methods that you learned in this chapter.

EDITING A STUDENT PARAGRAPH

Following is a paragraph written and revised by Melanie Frazier in response to the writing assignment in this chapter. Read the paragraph, and underline each of her independent clauses.

> My imagination has saved my life several times I call on it to get me out of binds all the time. When I am depressed, it finds a way to take me away from the problem that is bothering me. My mom would call this activity day-dreaming, I call it self-defense. Usually, I just start drifting in my mind away from the trouble at hand. I remember one time in my first few weeks of college, I got a paper back in English class with a low grade. To keep myself from crying, I started to drift. I took a journey up into my childhood tree house I stayed up there in my mind for a long time, playing with old toys and talking to my childhood friends. I don't know what happened in class that day, I had a great time remembering.

Collaborative Activity

Team up with a partner, and put slashes between the clauses in the two fused sentences and three comma splices in Melanie's paragraph. Then, working together, use what you have learned in this chapter to correct these errors using all four correction methods. Rewrite the paragraph with your corrections.

EDITING YOUR OWN PARAGRAPH

Now return to the paragraph you wrote and revised at the beginning of this chapter. Underline each of your independent clauses.

Collaborative Activity

Exchange paragraphs with your partner, and put slashes between the clauses in any run-together sentences that you find in your partner's paragraph.

Individual Activity

On the Error Log in Appendix 4, record the run-together sentences that your partner found in your paragraph. To complete the writing process, correct these run-togethers using the four correction methods.

UNIT TESTS

Unit Test 1 Identifying

Underline the subjects once and the verbs twice in the following sentences. Cross out the prepositional phrases first. Then put the fragments in brackets ([ ]), and put a slash (/) between the run-together sentences.

1. Cats and dogs are often treated as children. And part of the family.

2. Carmen was at the public pool, she was meeting Toby there.

3. Hoping it will increase in value. Many people collect old money.

4. When the flowers are in bloom in spring. My grandmother's garden is spectacular.

5. Driving up to Diamond Lake at midnight was a hard task I almost fell asleep at the wheel.

6. Thomas was a fabulous tutor, the university lost him when he became a teacher at Stockdale High.

7. Computers save us a lot of time, they are a good way to organize bills.

8. I went through the old chest. Hoping to find something from my high school days.

9. My mother lives in Sacramento I'm visiting her this weekend.

10. The lawyers were convinced of the jury's decision. After bribing a corrupt juror.

11. The air-pressure gauge was broken she almost panicked underwater when she realized her problem.

12. We visited the Broken Heart. A pub in rural England.

13. To get a better grade. Shelby studied all weekend.

14. If you get a chance, I would like to ask you some questions I have a big decision to make.

15. I didn't get enough sleep last night, now I can't think clearly.

16. I was reading a book about vampires I had nightmares that Dracula was chasing me.

17. People are afraid of the ocean. Because they think that sharks will attack them.

18. Sitting peacefully watching the sunset. She was able to clear her mind.

19. Please carry my books for me, my arm is about to break.

20. During the afternoon that I skipped class. I missed two quizzes and an in-class essay.

Unit Test 2 Correcting

Correct the fragments and run-together sentences in Unit Test 1 by rewriting each incorrect sentence.

Unit Test 3 Identifying

In the following paragraph, cross out the prepositional phrases first. Underline the subjects once and the complete verbs twice. Then put the fragments in brackets ([ ]), and put a slash (/) between the run-together sentences.

Eating fast food is not the healthiest way to go, but it sure is the cheapest. And the best. Places now serve 49-cent tacos, others serve 59-cent hamburgers. Fast-food corporations have ensured that families of four can eat out for less than $10. Which is very cheap. This is appealing to many families then they fall into the fast-food trap. Eating out all the time. Once people become accustomed to eating out cheaply, it's hard to return to making home-cooked meals. Sometimes this can lead to poor health problems often people gain weight. Eating fast food can also cause families to become strangers, they usually don't sit down long enough to talk about what is going on in their lives. Which is very sad. People should take the time to slow down at least once a month. To eat a meal together at home. That way, families can remain connected they will always have one night together. Therefore, families should not get used to eating fast food, then they will never learn good eating habits. They become fast-food junkies for life they will lose valuable time with their family members. Hardly worth it.

Unit Test 4 Correcting

Correct the fragments and run-together sentences in Unit Test 3 by rewriting the paragraph.

UNIT WRITING ASSIGNMENTS

1. What are the people in this picture looking at? Who are they? What has just happened? Use your imagination to fill in the details in this picture. Then explain what's going on here.

2. You have been asked to write a short statement for your English class about a fairly radical change you just made in your life or in your behavior. What did you change? Why did you make this particular change? Explain this adjustment in detail.

3. You have been asked by a friend to recommend a place for her to travel. What is your recommendation? Why do you recommend this place?

4. Describe the atmosphere of the classroom in your English class. Who sets the pace of the instruction in the class? What is the chemistry in the class? How does it compare to other classes? What is your opinion of the classroom atmosphere?

5. Create your own assignment (with the help of your instructor), and write a response to it.

VERBS

UNIT

2

Verbs can do just about anything we ask them to do. Because they have so many forms, they can play lots of different roles in a sentence: The bells *ring* on the hour; voices *rang* through the air; we could hear the clock *ringing* miles away. As you can see from these examples, even small changes, like a single letter, mean something; as a result, verbs make communication more interesting and accurate. But using verbs correctly takes concentration and effort on your part.

In this unit, we will discuss the following aspects of verbs and verb use:

10

REGULAR AND IRREGULAR VERBS

☑ **CHECKLIST for Using Regular and Irregular Verbs**

> ✔ Are regular verbs in their correct forms?
> ✔ Are irregular verbs in their correct forms?

All verbs are either regular or irregular. **Regular verbs** form the past tense and past participle by adding *-d* or *-ed* to the present tense. If a verb does not form its past tense and past participle this way, it is called an **irregular verb.**

Notice how both of these types of verbs work in the following paragraph by Stella Sanfratello.

I will never forget the time in fourth grade when my teacher sternly called me to stand before her desk after I had pleaded ignorance of her instructions one too many times. "I'm tired of hearing you say you don't know what you're supposed to be doing!" she said angrily. "I want you to stop saying 'I didn't know, I didn't know, I didn't know!'" The scolding was intense and continued for several minutes. I recall feeling stunned and confused at her accusation that I had been acting intentionally. I knew it had never occurred to me to do this on purpose or to act maliciously or irresponsibly. Today as an adult, however, I understand my teacher's frustration and the fact that, as a 9-year-old, all I could do was just what I did—stand there helplessly, filled with pain, confusion, and shame.

In this paragraph, author Stella Sanfratello explains how she felt as a deaf child trying to survive in our educational system. Before continuing in this chapter, take a moment to record some of your own childhood memories. Save your work because you will use it later in the chapter.

WRITING ASSIGNMENT: A CHILDHOOD MEMORY

Do you have a vivid childhood memory? What is the memory? What happened? Who was involved? Was the memory a good or bad one? How did the situation make you feel as a child? Do you see the situation differently now that you are older? Write a paragraph describing a vivid childhood memory.

REVISING YOUR WRITING

Now revise the first draft of your paragraph before you focus on editing. Use the Revising Checklist on pages 24–25 to help you with your revision. Make sure your paragraph has a good topic sentence and is well developed. Then check your paragraph for unity, organization, and coherence.

REGULAR VERBS

Here are the principal parts (present, past, and past participle forms) of some regular verbs. They are **regular verbs** because their past tense and past participle end in *-d* or *-ed*. The past participle is the verb form often used with helping verbs like *have*, *has*, or *had*.

Some **Regular** Verbs

PRESENT TENSE	PAST TENSE	PAST PARTICIPLE (USED WITH HELPING WORDS LIKE *HAVE, HAS, HAD*)
listen	*listen**ed***	*listen**ed***
look	*look**ed***	*look**ed***
receive	*receiv**ed***	*receiv**ed***
paint	*paint**ed***	*paint**ed***
call	*call**ed***	*call**ed***

The different forms of a verb tell when something happened—in the *present* (I *walk*) or in the *past* (I *walked*, I *have walked*, I *had walked*).

REVIEWING REGULAR VERBS

What is a regular verb?

_____

_____

Identify three forms of a regular verb.

_____   _____   _____

P r a c t i c e   1   **Identifying**   Underline the regular verbs in each of the following sentences.

1. The old man walked across the street.
2. We recalled happy memories.
3. Henry talked through the lecture.
4. I watched the birds.
5. He asks many questions.
6. The dog barked at the stranger.
7. Samantha burned her arm.
8. The children played all afternoon.
9. I believe in UFOs.
10. You skip down the sidewalk.

P r a c t i c e   2   **Identifying**   Put an X next to the incorrect verb forms in the following chart.

	Present Tense		Past Tense		Past Participle
1.	_____ kicked	_____ kicked		_____ kicked	
2.	_____ jump	_____ jumpt		_____ jumped	
3.	_____ cook	_____ cooked		_____ cooken	
4.	_____ bake	_____ baken		_____ baked	

5. _____ mailed   _____ mailed   _____ mailed

6. _____ played   _____ played   _____ played

7. _____ watch   _____ watched   _____ watchen

8. _____ answer   _____ answered   _____ answerd

9. _____ clean   _____ cleant   _____ cleaned

10. _____ typed   _____ typed   _____ typed

◆ **P r a c t i c e   3   Correcting** List the correct form of each of the incorrect verb forms in Practice 2.

1. _____

2. _____

3. _____

4. _____

5. _____

6. _____

7. _____

8. _____

9. _____

10. _____

◆ **P r a c t i c e   4   Completing** Fill in each blank in the following sentences with a regular verb that makes sense.

1. We _____ to the orchestra.

2. I _____ in that play.

3. Natalie, _____ some flowers out of the garden.

4. They _____ until they cried.

5. I _____ at sad movies.

6. Johnny did _____ for help.

7. The books must have _____ by themselves.

8. The horse _____ over the hedge.

9. The team members have _____ their suitcases to the train station.

10. The workers _____ the wheelbarrow with dirt.

◆ P r a c t i c e 5   Writing Your Own

A. Write a sentence of your own for each of the following verbs.

1. place _____

2. moan _____

3. has tasted _____

4. lift _____

5. have gained _____

B. Write five sentences of your own using regular verbs, and underline the verbs in each sentence.

1. _____

2. _____

3. _____

4. _____

5. _____

IRREGULAR VERBS

Irregular verbs do not form their past tense and past participle with *-d* or *-ed*. That is why they are irregular. Some follow certain patterns (*sing, sang, sung; ring, rang, rung; drink, drank, drunk; shrink, shrank, shrunk*). But the only sure way to know the forms of an irregular verb is to spend time learning them. As you write, you can check a dictionary or the following list.

Irregular Verbs

PRESENT	PAST	PAST PARTICIPLE (USED WITH HELPING WORDS LIKE *HAVE, HAS, HAD*)
am	was	been
are	were	been
be	was	been
bear	bore	borne, born
beat	beat	beaten
begin	began	begun
bend	bent	bent
bid	bid	bid
bind	bound	bound
bite	bit	bitten
blow	blew	blown
break	broke	broken
bring	brought (not *brang*)	brought (not *brung*)
build	built	built
burst	burst (not *bursted*)	burst
buy	bought	bought
choose	chose	chosen
come	came	come
cost	cost (not *costed*)	cost
cut	cut	cut
deal	dealt	dealt

do	did (not *done*)	done
draw	drew	drawn
drink	drank	drunk
drive	drove	driven
eat	ate	eaten
fall	fell	fallen
feed	fed	fed
feel	felt	felt
fight	fought	fought
find	found	found
flee	fled	fled
fly	flew	flown
forget	forgot	forgotten
forgive	forgave	forgiven
freeze	froze	frozen
get	got	got, gotten
go	went	gone
grow	grew	grown
hang[1] (a picture)	hung	hung
has	had	had
have	had	had
hear	heard	heard
hide	hid	hidden
hurt	hurt (not *hurted*)	hurt
is	was	been
know	knew	known
lay	laid	laid
lead	led	led
leave	left	left
lend	lent	lent
lie[2]	lay	lain
lose	lost	lost
meet	met	met
pay	paid	paid

prove	proved	proved, proven
put	put	put
read [rēēd]	read [rĕd]	read [rĕd]
ride	rode	ridden
ring	rang	rung
rise	rose	risen
run	ran	run
say	said	said
see	saw (not *seen*)	seen
set	set	set
shake	shook	shaken
shine[3] (a light)	shone	shone
shrink	shrank	shrunk
sing	sang	sung
sink	sank	sunk
sit	sat	sat
sleep	slept	slept
speak	spoke	spoken
spend	spent	spent
spread	spread	spread
spring	sprang (not *sprung*)	sprung
stand	stood	stood
steal	stole	stolen
stick	stuck	stuck
stink	stank (not *stunk*)	stunk
strike	struck	struck, stricken
strive	strove	striven, strived
swear	swore	sworn
sweep	swept	swept
swell	swelled	swelled, swollen
swim	swam	swum
swing	swung	swung
take	took	taken
teach	taught	taught

tear	*tore*	*torn*
tell	*told*	*told*
think	*thought*	*thought*
throw	*threw*	*thrown*
understand	*understood*	*understood*
wake	*woke*	*woken*
wear	*wore*	*worn*
weave	*wove*	*woven*
win	*won*	*won*
wring	*wrung*	*wrung*
write	*wrote*	*written*

1. *Hang* meaning "execute by hanging" is regular: *hang, hanged, hanged.*
2. *Lie* meaning "tell a lie" is regular: *lie, lied, lied.*
3. *Shine* meaning "brighten by polishing" is regular: *shine, shined, shined.*

REVIEWING IRREGULAR VERBS

What is the difference between regular and irregular verbs?

_____

_____

What is the best way to learn how irregular verbs form their past tense and past participle?

_____

◆ **P r a c t i c e   6   Identifying** Underline the irregular verbs in each of the following sentences.

1. The cat broke your vase.
2. The wind blew all night.
3. You tell the truth.
4. The garbage cans stink.

5. They met once before.
6. The flowers grew in the yard.
7. The children hid behind the house.
8. The criminal fled the scene.
9. I paid the bill.
10. The moon shone brightly.

P r a c t i c e 7   Identifying Put an X next to the incorrect verb forms in the following chart.

Present Tense	**Past Tense**	**Past Participle**
1. _____ shake	_____ shooked	_____ shaken
2. _____ bound	_____ bound	_____ bound
3. _____ am	_____ was	_____ was
4. _____ feed	_____ fed	_____ feded
5. _____ choose	_____ chosen	_____ chosen
6. _____ deal	_____ dealed	_____ dealt
7. _____ pay	_____ payed	_____ paid
8. _____ ring	_____ rang	_____ rang
9. _____ understood	_____ understood	_____ understood
10. _____ get	_____ gotten	_____ gotten

P r a c t i c e 8   Correcting List the correct form of each of the incorrect verb forms in Practice 7.

1. _____

2. _____

3. _____

4. _____

5. _____

6. _____

7. _____

8. _____

9. _____

10. _____

◆ **P r a c t i c e   9**   **Completing** Fill in each blank in the following sentences with an irregular verb that makes sense.

1. We didn't _____ the problem.

2. We had _____ that book before.

3. Every few months, a cable station _____ a James Bond movie marathon.

4. The storm _____ away our garage.

5. Many people _____ their luggage.

6. My foot _____ after I twisted it.

7. My sister will not _____ anything but bottled water.

8. The old man _____ us fishing.

9. Kenneth and Brian _____ Sarah and Jenny to the movies last Friday.

10. My dogs have _____ time in a kennel.

◆ **P r a c t i c e   1 0**   **Writing Your Own**

A. Write a sentence of your own for each of the following irregular verbs.

1. draw _____

2. spread _____

3. fight _____

4. swear _____

5. lay _____

B. Write five sentences of your own using irregular verbs, and underline the verbs in each sentence.

1. _____

2. _____

3. _____

4. _____

5. _____

USING *LIE/LAY* AND *SIT/SET* CORRECTLY

Two pairs of verbs are often used incorrectly—*lie/lay* and *sit/set*.

Lie/Lay

	Present Tense	Past Tense	Past Participle
lie (recline or lie down)	lie	lay	(have, has, had) lain
lay (put or place down)	lay	laid	(have, has, had) laid

The verb *lay* always takes an object. You must lay something down:

Lay down *what?*
Lay down *your books*.

Sit/Set

	Present Tense	Past Tense	Past Participle
sit (get into a seated position)	sit	sat	(have, has, had) sat
set (put or place down)	set	set	(have, has, had) set

Like the verb *lay*, the verb *set* must always have an object. You must set something down:

Set *what?*

Set *the presents* over here.

REVIEWING *Lie/Lay* AND *Sit/Set*

What do lie and lay mean?

_____

What are the principal parts of lie **and** lay?

_____

What do sit and set mean?

_____

What are the principal parts of sit and set?

_____

Which of these verbs always take an object?

_____

 **P r a c t i c e   1 1**   **Identifying** Underline the correct verb in each of the following sentences.

1. Marci has (lay, lain) on the couch for an hour.
2. Will you please (sit, set) down?
3. The dog has (sat, set) his bone on the floor.
4. Yesterday you (lay, laid) the reports on this table.
5. (Lie, Lay) your clothes out on the bed.
6. The shivering man (set, sat) in the hot sun.
7. Eustice has (lain, laid) a beautiful picnic on the grass.
8. He (laid, lay) on the couch and began to snore.
9. That 60-pound dog (set, sat) on my foot.
10. We have (lain, laid) all the cards out on the table.

◆ **P r a c t i c e   1 2**   **Identifying** Put an X next to the sentence if the underlined verb is incorrect.

1. _____ <u>Lie</u> those heavy crates on the ground.
2. _____ I <u>laid</u> back and relaxed while the hairdresser washed my hair.
3. _____ You had <u>sat</u> on a cactus.
4. _____ We had <u>set</u> down in the cool grass.
5. _____ You have <u>lain</u> around the house all day.
6. _____ Please <u>set</u> beside me during the movie.
7. _____ The workers have <u>lay</u> down the concrete.
8. _____ I had <u>sat</u> my purse on the kitchen table.
9. _____ When I'm stressed, I <u>lay</u> on my bed to relax.
10. _____ Will you <u>sit</u> those books on the counter?

◆ **P r a c t i c e   1 3**   **Correcting** Correct the verb errors in Practice 12 by rewriting each incorrect sentence.

1. _____

2. _____

3. _____

4. _____

5. _____

6. _____

7. _____

8. _____

9. _____

10. _____

◆ **P r a c t i c e   1 4**   **Completing** Fill in each blank in the following sentences with a form of *lie/lay* or *sit/set* that makes sense.

1. You have _____ your new suit in a puddle of grape juice.

2. I had _____the hot iron down for only a minute, but it burned my shirt anyway.

3. Sara _____ down in the warm sun and fell asleep.

4. How long did you _____ in the dentist's office?

5. That lazy, overfed cat _____ in the window seat all day and night.

6. Misha gently _____ the antique artifact on the table.

7. Please _____ on the inside so I can have the outside seat.

8. "_____ still while I remove these bandages," said the doctor.

9. Last month we were on vacation, so the newspapers piled up and _____ in the sun for a week.

10. Ouch! I just _____ on a tack.

♦ **P r a c t i c e   1 5**   **Writing Your Own**

A. Write a sentence of your own for each of the following phrases.

1. you just sat _____

2. José had lain _____

3. Mary Ann has set her _____

4. lay out your clothes _____

5. set that _____

B. Write five sentences of your own using *lie, lay, sit,* and *set,* and underline the forms of these verbs in each of your sentences.

1. _____

2. _____

3. _____

4. _____

5. _____

CHAPTER REVIEW

You might want to reread your answers to the questions in all the review boxes before you do the following exercises.

◆ *Review* **P r a c t i c e** *1* **Reading** Refer to the paragraph by Stella Sanfratello on page 160 to do the following exercises.

A. List five regular verbs from Sanfratello's paragraph.

1. _____

2. _____

3. _____

4. _____

5. _____

B. List five irregular verbs from Sanfratello's paragraph.

1. _____

2. _____

3. _____

4. _____

5. _____

◆ *Review* **P r a c t i c e** *2* **Identifying** Underline the incorrect verb forms in each of the following sentences.

1. We drived in the car all night long.
2. He lays down right after he gets home from school.
3. I called you last night, but the phone just ringed.
4. Peter was very supportive, and he said he feeled my pain.
5. Elsa filt up the gas tank yesterday, but it's already empty.
6. The air conditioner broked yesterday.
7. He standed in my front yard and sang to me.

8. When I asked the question, the teacher acted like she never heared me.

9. After Jerry divorced Ruth, she never forgived him.

10. I sat the fork in the sink.

Review P r a c t i c e 3 Correcting Correct the verb errors in Review Practice 2 by rewriting each incorrect sentence.

EDITING A STUDENT PARAGRAPH

Following is a paragraph written and revised by Melba Madison in response to the writing assignment in this chapter. Read the paragraph, and underline each of her complete verbs.

Last year, I walk to the old shed at the edge of my grandmother's backyard. I was determined to either fix the eyesore or tore it down. I begun looking through the old boxes that were inside, and I founded a package of letters. I set down and read them. They was love letters dating back to the early 1900s. The writing was flowery and hard to read, but I eventually begin to make out the words. I set as the sun raised high in the sky. I sat as the sun descended and the moon rose. The letters were from a man whom I had never heard of. He poured his soul out to my grandmother. And then suddenly the letters stop. To this day I often lay down to go to sleep and wonders about that man. Who was he? What happen to him? Why did my grandmother never mention him? I finally decide to leave the shed standing. I couldn't bear to tear down such a memory.

Collaborative Activity

Team up with a partner, and place an X above the 14 verb errors in Melba's paragraph. Then, working together, use what you have learned in this chapter to correct these errors. Rewrite the paragraph with your corrections.

EDITING YOUR OWN PARAGRAPH

Now return to the paragraph you wrote and revised at the beginning of this chapter. Underline each of your verbs.

Collaborative Activity

Exchange paragraphs with your partner, and circle any verb errors that you find in your partner's paragraph.

Individual Activity

On the Error Log in Appendix 4, record any verb errors that your partner found in your paragraph. Then, to complete the writing process, correct these errors by rewriting your paragraph.

CHAPTER 11

VERB TENSE

✓ CHECKLIST for Correcting Tense Problems

> ✔ Are present-tense verbs in the correct form?
> ✔ Are past-tense verbs in the correct form?
> ✔ Are *-ing* verbs used with the correct helping verbs?
> ✔ Are the forms of *be*, *do*, and *have* used correctly?

When we hear the word *verb*, we often think of action. We also know that action occurs in time. We are naturally interested in whether something happened today or yesterday or if it will happen sometime in the future. The time of an action is indicated by the **tense** of a verb, specifically in the ending of a verb or in a helping verb. This chapter discusses the most common errors in using verb tense.

Notice the different tenses and the way they communicate time in the following paragraph by Lansey Namioka.

> Father's approach to English was a scientific one. Since Chinese verbs have no tense, he was fascinated by the way English verbs changed form according to whether they were in the present, past imperfect, perfect, pluperfect, future, or future perfect tense. He was always making diagrams of verbs and their inflections, and he looked for opportunities to show off his mastery of the pluperfect and future perfect tenses, his two favorites. "I shall have finished my project by Monday," he would say smugly.

In this paragraph, author Lansey Namioka explains her father's fascination with English verbs. Before continuing in this chapter, take a moment to record some of your own unique habits or hobbies. Save your work because you will use it later in the chapter.

WRITING ASSIGNMENT: A UNIQUE HOBBY

Do you have a unique habit or hobby? What is it? How do you go about doing it? Why do you do it? How do others see you because of this? Write a paragraph describing a unique hobby or habit of yours.

 REVISING YOUR WRITING

Revise the first draft of your paragraph before you focus on editing. Use the Revising Checklist on pages 24–25 to help you with your revision. Make sure your paragraph has a good topic sentence and is well developed. Then check your paragraph for unity, organization, and coherence.

PRESENT TENSE

One of the most common errors in college writing is reversing the present-tense endings—adding an *-s* where none is needed and omitting the *-s* where it is required. This error causes problems in subject-verb agreement. Make sure you understand this mistake, and then proofread carefully to avoid it in your writing.

Present Tense

Singular		Plural	
INCORRECT	CORRECT	INCORRECT	CORRECT
NOT *I laughs*	*I laugh*	**NOT** *we laughs*	*we laugh*
NOT *you laughs*	*you laugh*	**NOT** *you laughs*	*you laugh*
NOT *he, she, it laugh*	*he, she, it laughs*	**NOT** *they laughs*	*they laugh*

You also need to be able to spot these same errors in sentences.

Incorrect

The black cat climb the tree.

My brother love chocolate.

Correct

The black cat climbs the tree.

My brother loves chocolate.

You speaks beautifully.   **You speak** beautifully.

They sings in the choir.   **They sing** in the choir.

REVIEWING PRESENT-TENSE ERRORS

What is the most common error in using the present tense?

_____

_____

How can you prevent this error?

_____

◆ **P r a c t i c e   1   Identifying** Underline the correct present-tense verbs in each of the following sentences.

1. He (misses, miss) you.
2. The international finance course (is, will be) hard.
3. Janeen (likes, like) bungee jumping at the fair.
4. The cats (runs, run) through the neighborhood.
5. The committee members (votes, vote) on the amendments.
6. The boat (reaches, reach) the harbor at noon.
7. Most people (believes, believe) in justice.
8. The fire hydrant (sprays, spray) water into the air.
9. My friends (thinks, think) a lot of you.
10. They (hopes, hope) for a speedy solution.

◆ **P r a c t i c e   2   Identifying** Put an X next to the sentence if the underlined verb is incorrect.

1. _____ Claude <u>walk</u> his dog in the park every day.
2. _____ They <u>hopes</u> for a miracle.
3. _____ A rabbit's tail <u>bring</u> good luck.
4. _____ The flowers <u>smells</u> nice.

5. _____ The river <u>swell</u> in the spring.

6. _____ My grandparents <u>visit</u> us often.

7. _____ The sun <u>dries</u> grapes into raisins.

8. _____ All the books <u>belongs</u> to the library.

9. _____ Our family <u>travel</u> out of the country every year.

10. _____ You <u>need</u> to be more careful.

◆ **P r a c t i c e   3   Correcting** Correct the verb errors in Practice 2 by rewriting each incorrect sentence.

1. _____

2. _____

3. _____

4. _____

5. _____

6. _____

7. _____

8. _____

9. _____

10. _____

◆ **P r a c t i c e   4   Completing** Fill in each blank in the following sentences with a present-tense verb that makes sense.

1. Every spring, they _____ under the stars.

2. I _____ it when you smile.

3. The pots and pans _____ to be cleaned.

4. The professionals _____ the problem.

5. She _____ whenever he walks by.

6. Will you _____ me a song?

7. This season's new comedies _____ hilarious.

8. Martha _____ once a week.

9. Many people _____ in the supernatural.

10. This jasmine _____ only at night.

◆ **P r a c t i c e 5 Writing Your Own**

A. Write a sentence of your own for each of the following present-tense verbs.

1. graduate _____

2. wastes _____

3. improve _____

4. arrests _____

5. operate _____

B. Write five sentences of your own in the present tense, and underline the verbs in each sentence.

1. _____

2. _____

3. _____

4. _____

5. _____

PAST TENSE

Just as we know that a verb is in the present tense by its ending, we can tell that a verb is in the past tense by its ending. Regular verbs form the past tense by adding *-d* or *-ed*. But some writers forget the ending when they are writing the past tense. Understanding this problem and then proofreading carefully will help you catch this error.

Past Tense

Singular		Plural	
INCORRECT	CORRECT	INCORRECT	CORRECT
NOT I call	I called	**NOT** we call	we called
NOT you call	you called	**NOT** you call	you called
NOT he, she, it call	he, she, it called	**NOT** they call	they called

You also need to be able to spot these same errors in sentences.

Incorrect	Correct
Janet yell the cheer.	**Janet yelled** the cheer.
He wander through the store.	**He wandered** through the store.
Those girls talk too loudly.	**Those girls talked** too loudly.
Yes, **we want** to win the game.	Yes, **we wanted** to win the game.

Reviewing Past-Tense Errors

What is the most common sentence error made with the past tense?

_____

How can you prevent this error?

_____

 P r a c t i c e   6   Identifying Underline the correct past-tense verbs in each of the following sentences.

1. The plane (land, landed) near our house.
2. You (developt, developed) a wonderful presentation.
3. The stars (twinklen, twinkled) in the sky.
4. The children (wanted, will want) water balloons.
5. They (maded, made) a mess throughout the house.
6. Mr. Rocky (teached, taught) us to rock climb.
7. Only a few people (show, showed) up for the party.

8. It (happen, happened) only yesterday.

9. The singers and dancers (performed, perform) a spectacular show.

10. The cars (backed, bact) into each other.

◆ **P r a c t i c e   7   Identifying** Put an X next to the sentence if the underlined past-tense verb is incorrect.

1. _____ Waldo <u>plans</u> the wedding a year ago.

2. _____ They <u>worked</u> very hard on the project.

3. _____ The witches <u>came</u> out on All Hallow's Eve.

4. _____ I <u>burn</u> the meal for tonight's supper.

5. _____ The teacher <u>helps</u> me with this paper yesterday.

6. _____ The neighbor's stereo <u>blares</u> last night.

7. _____ The flag <u>waved</u> in the wind.

8. _____ The politician <u>speaks</u> at the banquet yesterday.

9. _____ Last summer, we <u>drive</u> to Yosemite.

10. _____ Hey! You <u>drink</u> my Pepsi.

◆ **P r a c t i c e   8   Correcting** Correct the verb errors in Practice 7 by rewriting each incorrect sentence.

1. _____

2. _____

3. _____

4. _____

5. _____

6. _____

7. _____

8. _____

9. _____

10. _____

◆ **P r a c t i c e   9   Completing** Fill in each blank in the following sentences with a past-tense verb that makes sense.

1. The baby _____ loudly.

2. The basket weavers _____ many beautiful designs.

3. The meal _____ appetizing.

4. You _____ the wrong question.

5. The Salingers _____ until morning.

6. The firecrackers _____ high in the sky.

7. It _____ me.

8. Oh no! The cat _____ a mouse.

9. These gates _____ only once a year.

10. The thieves _____ into the school.

◆ **P r a c t i c e   1 0   Writing Your Own**

A. Write a sentence of your own for each of the following past-tense verbs.

1. regretted _____

2. swore _____

3. crashed _____

4. wrote _____

5. jumped _____

B. Write five sentences of your own in the past tense, and underline the verbs in each sentence.

1. _____

2. _____

3. _____

4. _____

5. _____

USING HELPING WORDS WITH PAST PARTICIPLES

Helping words are used with the past participle form, *not* with the past-tense form. It is incorrect to use a helping verb (such as *is, was, were, have, has,* or *had*) with the past tense. Make sure you understand how to use helping words with past participles, and then proofread your written work to avoid making these errors.

Incorrect	Correct
They **have drove** to town.	They **have driven** to town.
She **has shook** the shake.	She **has shaken** the shake.
I **have wrote** a book.	I **have written** a book.
We **had took** the test early.	We **had taken** the test early.

REVIEWING ERRORS WITH HELPING WORDS
AND PAST PARTICIPLES

What is the most common sentence error made with past participles?

_____

How can you prevent this error?

_____

 P r a c t i c e   1 1   Identifying Underline the correct helping verbs and their past participles in each of the following sentences.

1. The walls (had shook, had shaken) in the earthquake.
2. Maya (had bitten, had bit) her tongue.
3. The fruit (has fell, has fallen) to the ground.
4. I (have drove, have driven) my mother crazy.
5. The caterpillars (have eaten, have ate) all the leaves on my rose bush.
6. We (have saw, have seen) many strange things.
7. Many of the children (had hidden, had hid) behind the couch.
8. The guests (have went, have gone) home.

9. A cannon (has shotten, has shot) the clown into the air.
10. The outraged citizens (have written, have wrote) a letter to their representative.

♦ **Practice 12** **Identifying** Put an X next to the sentence if the underlined verb is incorrect.

1. _____ They <u>had ridden</u> all the rides.
2. _____ We <u>have grew</u> a garden.
3. _____ My chair <u>had broken</u> before I sat in it.
4. _____ The jeans <u>have tore</u> at the knees.
5. _____ Poor Tom! He <u>has spent</u> all his money.
6. _____ He <u>has drew</u> the pictures in black and white.
7. _____ The children <u>have forgot</u> their coats and gloves.
8. _____ We <u>had begun</u> to see daylight.
9. _____ The ice <u>has froze</u> the fish solid.
10. _____ He <u>has forgave</u> your mean comments.

♦ **Practice 13** **Correcting** Correct the verb errors in Practice 12 by rewriting each incorrect sentence.

1. _____
2. _____
3. _____
4. _____
5. _____
6. _____
7. _____
8. _____
9. _____
10. _____

◆ **P r a c t i c e 1 4**   **Completing** Fill in each blank in the following sentences with a correct past-participle verb that makes sense.

1. The pictures have _____ off the wall.

2. The worker has _____ a break.

3. The attendant has _____ our tickets.

4. The dealer had _____ me a bad hand.

5. Cassidy had _____ her nose all morning.

6. The teacher has _____ the boy many times for his pranks.

7. They have _____ the dinner bell.

8. If we had _____ the answer, we wouldn't have asked the question.

9. The student has _____ to do his best.

10. The gum has _____ under the desk.

◆ **P r a c t i c e 1 5**   **Writing Your Own**

A. Write a sentence of your own for each of the following past-participle verb forms.

1. has known _____

2. had told _____

3. have chosen _____

4. have stolen _____

5. has broken _____

B. Write five sentences of your own using helping verbs and past participles, and underline the complete verbs in each sentence.

1. _____

2. _____

3. _____

4. _____

5. _____

USING *-ing* VERBS CORRECTLY

Verbs ending in *-ing* describe action that is going on or that was going on for a while. To be a complete verb, an *-ing* verb is always used with a helping verb. Two common errors occur with *-ing* verbs:

1. Using *be* or *been* instead of the correct helping verb
2. Using no helping verb at all

Learn the correct forms, and proofread carefully to catch these errors.

Incorrect	Correct
The boys **be going** to the mall.	The boys **are going** to the mall.
	The boys **were going** to the mall.
The boys **been going** to the mall.	The boys **have been going** to the mall.
	The boys **had been going** to the mall.
We **eating** a snack.	We **are eating** a snack.
	We **have been eating** a snack.
	We **were eating** a snack.
	We **had been eating** a snack.

Reviewing *-ing* Verb Errors

What two kinds of errors occur with -ing verbs?

_____

_____

How can you prevent these errors?

_____

◆ **P r a c t i c e 1 6** **Identifying** Underline the correct helping verbs and -*ing* forms in each of the following sentences.

1. Many people (be planning, are planning) the event.
2. Bryn (is going, been going) to Jamaica this holiday.
3. The trinkets (had been sitting, been sitting) on this counter.
4. Those two teams (going, are going) to the playoffs.
5. Ashley (has been finding, has finding) ladybugs in the backyard.
6. The light (been shining, had been shining) all night.
7. Dean (was taking, taking) a swing at the ball.
8. We (have been sitting, have sitting) here for over an hour.
9. Those bikers (are going, be going) too fast.
10. The passengers (telling, are telling) jokes to one another.

◆ **P r a c t i c e 1 7** **Identifying** Put an X next to the sentence if the underlined helping verb or -*ing* form is incorrect.

1. _____ They <u>had been going</u> to college.
2. _____ We <u>running</u> in a race.
3. _____ The roof <u>been raised</u>.
4. _____ The sun <u>was rising</u> over the horizon.
5. _____ The lawn <u>dying</u> in this hot sun.
6. _____ Spiders <u>running</u> up my arm!
7. _____ The motorist <u>is going</u> the wrong way.
8. _____ We <u>be listening</u> very carefully.
9. _____ The clothes <u>be sitting</u> in the dryer.
10. _____ The printer <u>printing</u> out your document now.

◆ **P r a c t i c e 1 8** **Correcting** Correct the verb errors in Practice 17 by rewriting each incorrect sentence.

1. _____

2. _____

3. _____

4. _____

5. _____

6. _____

7. _____

8. _____

9. _____

10. _____

P r a c t i c e 1 9 **Completing** Fill in each blank in the following sentences with a helping verb and *-ing* form that make sense.

1. The crowd _____ for more.

2. I _____ when you called.

3. The wolves _____ at the moon.

4. Many people _____ to the movie.

5. She _____ for a walk to relax.

6. The moths _____ too close to the flame.

7. The photographer _____ still-life photos.

8. That night, we _____ to a professional performer.

9. Your help _____ me out of a lot of trouble.

10. A few weeks ago, I _____ with a friend.

P r a c t i c e 2 0 **Writing Your Own**

A. Write a sentence of your own for each of the following verbs.

1. is leaving _____

2. were cooking _____

3. had been writing _____

4. are feeling _____

5. have been promising _____

B. Write five sentences of your own using *-ing* verb forms, and underline the complete verbs in each sentence.

1. _____

2. _____

3. _____

4. _____

5. _____

PROBLEMS WITH *be*

The verb *be* can cause problems in both the present tense and the past tense. The following chart demonstrates these problems. Learn how to use these forms correctly, and then always proofread your written work carefully to avoid these errors.

The Verb *be*

Present Tense

Singular		Plural	
INCORRECT	CORRECT	INCORRECT	CORRECT
NOT *I be/ain't*	*I **am/am not***	**NOT** *we be/ain't*	*we **are/are not***
NOT *you be/ain't*	*you **are/are not***	**NOT** *you be/ain't*	*you **are/are not***
NOT *he, she, it be/ain't*	*he, she, it **is/is not***	**NOT** *they be/ain't*	*they **are/are not***

Past Tense

Singular		Plural	
INCORRECT	CORRECT	INCORRECT	CORRECT
NOT *I were*	*I **was***	**NOT** *we was*	*we **were***
NOT *you was*	*you **were***	**NOT** *you was*	*you **were***
NOT *he, she, it were*	*he, she, it **was***	**NOT** *they was*	*they **were***

REVIEWING PROBLEMS WITH *be*

What are two common errors made with be?

_____

_____

How can you prevent these errors?

_____

◆ **P r a c t i c e   2 1**   **Identifying** Underline the correct forms of *be* in each of the following sentences.

1. My father (be, is) a taxi driver.
2. They (was, were) very late today.
3. You (aren't, ain't) happy.
4. I (be, was) in the middle of a project when the doorbell rang.
5. It (was, were) a hot day today.
6. That ice cream (be, is) so good.
7. She (is, been) the best person for this assignment.
8. A red signal (be, is) for danger.
9. My favorite novels (been, are) *Emma* and *Pride and Prejudice*.
10. You (was, were) a great host.

◆ **P r a c t i c e   2 2**   **Identifying** Put an X next to the sentence if the underlined form of *be* is incorrect.

1. _____ These balloons <u>be</u> the ones for the party.
2. _____ I <u>ain't</u> going to travel by bus.
3. _____ They <u>was</u> outside in the rain.
4. _____ I <u>am</u> switching phone services.
5. _____ I <u>were</u> the one who broke the stereo.
6. _____ You <u>were</u> the only one who showed up.
7. _____ You <u>was</u> so much fun at the party.
8. _____ The pens and pencils <u>are</u> in the supply cabinet.

9. _____ Those clothes <u>was</u> for charity.

10. _____ He <u>were</u> asleep when you called.

◄ **P r a c t i c e 2 3** **Correcting** Correct the verb errors in Practice 22 by rewriting each incorrect sentence.

1. _____

2. _____

3. _____

4. _____

5. _____

6. _____

7. _____

8. _____

9. _____

10. _____

◄ **P r a c t i c e 2 4** **Completing** Fill in each blank in the following sentences with the correct form of *be* in the tense indicated.

1. I _____ a runner in school. (past)

2. You _____ the most generous person I know. (present)

3. Yesterday, the sheep _____ on that hill. (past)

4. At this moment, I _____ very happy. (present)

5. It _____ dark outside, so you had better stay home. (present)

6. He _____ my brother. (present)

7. The humidity and the flies _____ torturous in Africa. (present)

8. You _____ my favorite aunt. (present)

9. The dog in that picture _____ named Old Man Ruff. (past)

10. It _____ never polite to point at people. (present)

♦ *P r a c t i c e   2 5*   **Writing Your Own**

A. Write a sentence of your own for each of the following forms of *be*.

1. am _____

2. were _____

3. is _____

4. are _____

5. was _____

B. Write five sentences of your own using forms of *be*, and underline the verbs in each sentence.

1. _____

2. _____

3. _____

4. _____

5. _____

PROBLEMS WITH *do*

Another verb that causes sentence problems in the present and past tenses is *do*. The following chart shows these problems. Learn the correct forms, and proofread to avoid errors.

The Verb *do*

Present Tense

Singular		Plural	
INCORRECT	CORRECT	INCORRECT	CORRECT
NOT *I does*	*I* **do**	**NOT** *we does*	*we* **do**
NOT *you does*	*you* **do**	**NOT** *you does*	*you* **do**
NOT *he, she, it do*	*he, she, it* **does**	**NOT** *they does*	*they* **do**

Past Tense

Singular		Plural	
INCORRECT	CORRECT	INCORRECT	CORRECT
NOT *I done*	*I **did***	**NOT** *we done*	*we **did***
NOT *you done*	*you **did***	**NOT** *you done*	*you **did***
NOT *he, she, it done*	*he, she, it **did***	**NOT** *they done*	*they **did***

REVIEWING PROBLEMS WITH *do*

What are two common errors made with do?

_____

_____

How can you prevent these errors?

_____

◆ **P r a c t i c e   2 6**   **Identifying** Underline the correct forms of *do* in each of the following sentences.

1. I (done, did) my homework on time.
2. Scott (do, does) well at his summer job.
3. They (do, does) their exercise every night.
4. Jessica (do, did) her speech on violence.
5. She always (done, does) a good job.
6. You (do, does) eat a lot of food.
7. The doctor (do, does) rounds at the hospital every day.
8. My outdoor grill (does, done) steaks really well.
9. My sister (do, did) the best she could.
10. We (done, did) the assignment correctly.

◀ *P r a c t i c e 2 7*   **Identifying** Put an X next to the sentence if the underlined form of *do* is incorrect.

1. _____ He <u>do</u> his laundry at three in the morning.
2. _____ I <u>done</u> a quick patch on the tire.
3. _____ My uncle and aunt <u>do</u> the cooking all the time.
4. _____ Some people <u>does</u> their hair funny.
5. _____ The young worker <u>does</u> the dishes.
6. _____ We <u>done</u> everything we could think of.
7. _____ The camera <u>done</u> the work.
8. _____ He <u>do</u> his work on time.
9. _____ He <u>does</u> a hilarious comedy act.
10. _____ You <u>did</u> all the chores.

◀ *P r a c t i c e 2 8*   **Correcting** Correct the verb errors in Practice 27 by rewriting each incorrect sentence.

1. _____
2. _____
3. _____
4. _____
5. _____
6. _____
7. _____
8. _____
9. _____
10. _____

◀ *P r a c t i c e 2 9*   **Completing** Fill in each blank in the following sentences with the correct forms of *do* in the tense indicated.

1. I _____ the jig last night. (past)

2. She _____ her papers quickly. (present)

3. They _____ the job easily. (past)

4. They _____ the weather at 6:00 and 10:00. (present)

5. Last quarter, we _____ basic training together. (past)

6. You _____ math every night to keep up. (present)

7. She _____ wash her hair every day. (present)

8. The man _____ the books for my uncle's business. (present)

9. Tomas _____ the training for Carlos. (past)

10. I _____ the lettering on the poster. (past)

◆ P r a c t i c e   **3 0**   **Writing Your Own**

A. Write a sentence of your own for each of the following forms of *do*.

1. do _____

2. did _____

3. does _____

4. does _____

5. did _____

B. Write five sentences of your own using forms of *do*, and underline the verbs in each sentence.

1. _____

2. _____

3. _____

4. _____

5. _____

PROBLEMS WITH *have*

Along with *be* and *do*, the verb *have* causes sentence problems in the present and past tenses. The following chart demonstrates these problems. Learn the correct forms, and proofread to avoid errors with *have*.

The Verb *have*

Present Tense

Singular		Plural	
INCORRECT	CORRECT	INCORRECT	CORRECT
NOT *I has*	*I* **have**	**NOT** *we has*	*we* **have**
NOT *you has*	*you* **have**	**NOT** *you has*	*you* **have**
NOT *he, she, it have*	*he, she, it* **has**	**NOT** *they has*	*they* **have**

Past Tense

Singular		Plural	
INCORRECT	CORRECT	INCORRECT	CORRECT
NOT *I has*	*I* **had**	**NOT** *we has*	*we* **had**
NOT *you have*	*you* **had**	**NOT** *you has*	*you* **had**
NOT *he, she, it have*	*he, she, it* **had**	**NOT** *they has*	*they* **had**

REVIEWING PROBLEMS WITH *have*

What are two common errors made with **have**?

_____

_____

How can you prevent these errors?

_____

◆ **P r a c t i c e   3 1**   **Identifying** Underline the correct forms of *have* in each of the following sentences.

1. I (has, have) your telephone number.
2. It (have, has) too many holes in it to work properly.
3. Charles (have, has) plenty of time.
4. The ceiling fans (has, had) broken.
5. We (have, has) the deadline in mind.
6. The clowns (has, have) a long day ahead of them.
7. You (had, has) the last laugh.
8. Madam Zoya's predictions (has, have) all come true.
9. Your paragraphs (has, have) great organization.
10. We (has, had) little to say to them.

◆ **P r a c t i c e   3 2**   **Identifying** Put an X next to the sentence if the underlined form of *have* is incorrect.

1. _____ We <u>had</u> a wonderful time last night.
2. _____ Samantha <u>has</u> some good news for you.
3. _____ I <u>has</u> the worst sinus headache.
4. _____ The nurses <u>has</u> time off.
5. _____ Yesterday, Aziz <u>has</u> on the most expensive suit.
6. _____ I <u>have</u> everything I need for the trip.
7. _____ Brian <u>has</u> the story wrong.
8. _____ The scarf <u>have</u> a small flaw.
9. _____ The trees in the front yard <u>has</u> no leaves.
10. _____ It <u>have</u> many inches of snow on top.

◆ **P r a c t i c e   3 3**   **Correcting** Correct the verb errors in Practice 32 by rewriting each incorrect sentence.

1. _____

2. _____

3. _____

4. _____

5. _____

6. _____

7. _____

8. _____

9. _____

10. _____

◆ **P r a c t i c e   3 4   Completing** Fill in each blank in the following sentences with the correct form of *have* in the tense indicated.

1. The boys and girls _____ an early bedtime. (present)

2. I _____ a strange dream last night. (past)

3. We _____ fun at the beach. (past)

4. This _____ the directions for the party. (present)

5. We _____ an obligation to the court. (present)

6. Islands _____ many weather changes throughout the day. (present)

7. She _____ the answer all along. (past)

8. Cleo, my cat, _____ a small white star on her head. (past)

9. You _____ the bride's ring just a few minutes ago. (past)

10. Now you _____ the broken one. (present)

◆ **P r a c t i c e   3 5   Writing Your Own**

A. Write a sentence of your own for each of the following forms of *have*.

1. have _____

2. has _____

3. had _____

4. had _____

5. have _____

B. Write five sentences of your own using forms of *have*, and underline the verbs in each sentence.

1. _____

2. _____

3. _____

4. _____

5. _____

CHAPTER REVIEW

You might want to reread your answers to the questions in the review boxes before you do the following exercises.

Review P r a c t i c e 1   Reading List five verbs from the paragraph by Lansey Namioka on page 178, and complete the following tasks.

_____

_____

_____

_____

_____

1. Write the present tense of each verb.

_____

_____

_____

_____

_____

2. Write the past tense of each verb.

_____

_____

_____

_____

_____

3. Write the past participle of each verb with a helping verb.

_____

_____

_____

_____

_____

4. Write the *-ing* form of each verb with a helping verb.

_____

_____

_____

_____

_____

◆ *Review P r a c t i c e 2* **Identifying** Underline the incorrect verb forms in each of the following sentences.

1. The children laughs at the clown's funny faces.
2. Veronica and Mike done the dance moves perfectly.
3. Maisy has forget her pager again.
4. Yesterday, you ask me the funniest thing.

5. We been the best of friends.

6. Oh no! You has a bug in your hair.

7. The monkeys plucks fleas off of each other.

8. I were filthy from the dust storm.

9. We eating everything in sight.

10. He have the worst cold ever.

Review Practice 3 **Correcting** Correct the errors in Review Practice 2 by rewriting each incorrect sentence.

EDITING A STUDENT PARAGRAPH

Following is a paragraph written and revised by Mabel Adams in response to the writing assignment in this chapter. Read the paragraph, and underline each of her verbs.

My unique pastime, ice-skating, is something that is not really popular in all parts of the country, but no matter where I be, I always find an ice rink. I been skating my entire life. In fact, I am skating before I will walk. It is a very freeing activity. I just get on the ice and set my spirit free. I will skate for a half-hour and feel like I have been relaxing for a week. I forget all the pressures of being a student, and I remember what it is like to be a kid again when I skated alongside my boyfriend. Sometimes, I does competitions. So far, I have beat all of my opponents. To most of my friends and family, skating is a strange way to relieve stress, especially since I has a 30-minute drive to the ice rink. But I don't mind. This December, I will have skated in my spare time for 20 years.

Collaborative Activity

Team up with a partner, and place an X above the nine verb errors in Mabel's paragraph. Then, working together, use what you have learned in this chapter to correct these errors. Rewrite the paragraph with your corrections.

EDITING YOUR OWN PARAGRAPH

Now return to the paragraph you wrote and revised at the beginning of this chapter. Underline each of your verbs.

Collaborative Activity

Exchange paragraphs with your partner, and circle any verb errors that you find in your partner's paragraph.

Individual Activity

On the Error Log in Appendix 4, record any verb errors that your partner found in your paragraph. Then, to complete the writing process, correct these errors by rewriting your paragraph.

CHAPTER 12

SUBJECT-VERB AGREEMENT

✅ CHECKLIST for Correcting Subject-Verb Agreement Problems

> ✔ Do all subjects agree with their verbs?

Almost every day, we come across situations that require us to reach an agreement with someone. For example, you and a friend might have to agree on which movie to see, or you and your manager might have to agree on how many hours you'll work in the coming week. Whatever the issue, agreement is essential in most aspects of life—including writing. In this chapter, you will learn how to resolve conflicts in your sentences by making sure your subjects and verbs agree.

Notice how subjects and verbs in the following sentences by Maxine Hong Kingston work together in agreement:

Once in a long while, four times so far for me, my mother brings out the metal tube that holds her medical diploma. On the tube are gold circles crossed with seven red lines each-"joy" ideographs in abstract. There are also little flowers that look like gears for a gold machine. According to the scraps of labels with Chinese and American addresses, stamps, and postmarks, the family airmailed the can from Hong Kong in 1950. It got crushed in the middle, and whoever tried to peel the labels off stopped because the red and gold paint came off too, leaving silver scratches that rust. Somebody tried to pry the end off before discovering that the tube pulls apart. When I open it, the smell of China flies out, a thousand-year-old bat flying heavy-headed out of the Chinese caverns where bats are as white as dust, a smell that comes from long ago, far back in the brain. Crates from Canton, Hong Kong, Singapore, and

Taiwan have that smell too, only stronger because they are more recently come from the Chinese.

In this paragraph, the author describes an old family treasure through her senses. Before continuing in this chapter, take a moment to write about an object that is important to you. Save your work because you will use it later in the chapter.

WRITING ASSIGNMENT: A TREASURED OBJECT

Think of some objects that are important to you or to people close to you. How do the objects look, sound, feel, taste, or smell? Do certain senses bring back specific memories? How do they make you feel? Write a paragraph describing your most treasured object for someone who has never seen it.

REVISING YOUR WRITING

Now revise the first draft of your paragraph before you focus on editing. Use the Revising Checklist on pages 24–25 to help you with your revision. Make sure your paragraph has a good topic sentence and is well developed. Then check your paragraph for unity, organization, and coherence.

SUBJECT-VERB AGREEMENT

Subject-verb agreement simply means that singular subjects must be paired with singular verbs and plural subjects with plural verbs. Look at this example:

Singular: **She lives** in California.

The subject *she* is singular because it refers to only one person. The verb *lives* is singular and matches the singular subject. Here is the same sentence in plural form:

Plural: **They live** in California.

The subject *they* is plural, referring to more than one person, and the verb *live* is also plural.

REVIEWING SUBJECT-VERB AGREEMENT
....

What is the difference between singular and plural?

_____

_____

What kind of verb goes with a singular subject?

_____

What kind of verb goes with a plural subject?

_____

Practice 1 Identifying Underline the verb that agrees with its subject in each of the following sentences.

1. Terri (run, runs) every morning.
2. Mike (is, are) a talented football player.
3. After school, she (drives, drive) straight home.
4. The truckers (was, were) helpful to the stranded motorist.
5. The Garcias (travels, travel) quite often.
6. My sister (creates, create) art from metal scraps.
7. The St. Louis Cardinals (has, have) many loyal fans.
8. The Army (recruits, recruit) at the local colleges.
9. Massage therapy (is, are) expensive but worth the price.
10. My dog, Rusty, (is, are) my best friend.

Practice 2 Identifying Put an X next to the sentence if its subject and verb do not agree. Underline the subject and verb.

1. _____ We envies athletic ability.
2. _____ Disgruntled employees are difficult to control.
3. _____ Ian believes in his girlfriend.
4. _____ The paintings sells for a lot of money.
5. _____ Adriana try to study hard.

6. _____ The friends fights over stupid things.

7. _____ The new TV shows has great potential.

8. _____ Most kids loves rock music.

9. _____ Stella drives very fast.

10. _____ The play are about to begin.

◆ **P r a c t i c e 3 Correcting** Correct the subject-verb agreement errors in Practice 2 by rewriting each incorrect sentence.

1. _____

2. _____

3. _____

4. _____

5. _____

6. _____

7. _____

8. _____

9. _____

10. _____

◆ **P r a c t i c e 4 Completing** Fill in each blank with a present-tense verb that agrees with its subject. Avoid *is*, *are*, *was*, and *were*.

1. The nudity in the movie _____ inappropriate.

2. They _____ the trip will be exciting.

3. The computer automatically _____ the latest version of your document every few minutes.

4. After the holidays, Cassandra _____ for two weeks.

5. Cheerleaders _____ for the school's team to win.

6. Looking out my office window, I _____ at a brick wall.

7. Jack _____ he got the lead for the play.

8. Race car drivers _____ at very high speeds.

9. Eating carrots _____ people's eyesight.

10. Fire fighters _____ several fires in a week.

◆ Practice 5   Writing Your Own

A. Write a sentence of your own using each of the following words as subjects.

1. a backpack _____

2. Mike _____

3. the cars _____

4. his dogs _____

5. the computer _____

B. Write five sentences of your own, and underline the subject and verb in each sentence.

1. _____

2. _____

3. _____

4. _____

5. _____

WORDS SEPARATING SUBJECTS AND VERBS

With sentences that are as simple and direct as *She lives in California,* checking that the subject and verb agree is easy. But problems can arise when words come between the subject and the verb. Often the words between the subject and verb are prepositional phrases. If you follow the advice given in

Chapter 7, you will be able to find the subject and verb: *Cross out all the prepositional phrases in a sentence. The subject and verb will be among the words that are left.* Here are some examples:

Prepositional Phrases: The **donation** ~~for the charity center~~ **is** ~~in my car.~~

When you cross out the prepositional phrases, you can tell that the singular subject, *donation*, and the singular verb, *is*, agree.

Prepositional Phrases: The **stars** ~~in the sky~~ **twinkle** ~~at night~~.

When you cross out the prepositional phrases, you can tell that the plural subject, *stars*, and the plural verb, *twinkle*, agree.

REVIEWING WORDS SEPARATING SUBJECTS AND VERBS

What words often come between subjects and verbs?

_____

What is an easy way to identify the subject and verb in a sentence?

_____

P r a c t i c e 6   Identifying Underline the verb that agrees with the subject in each of the following sentences. Cross out the prepositional phrases first.

1. There (is, are) so many reasons why people shouldn't smoke.
2. They usually (stays, stay) late.
3. Neither one of the students (was, were) ready for the exam.
4. Four of the jurors (was, were) caught for misconduct.
5. Bananas dipped in chocolate (is, are) great over ice cream.
6. My neighbor of 12 years (goes, go) to the hockey game every week.
7. My suitcase with all of my gifts (appears, appear) to have been stolen.
8. A few cans of soda (helps, help) me stay awake to study.

9. We sometimes (fights, fight) during vacation.

10. Ling (screams, scream) really loudly at concerts.

◆ **P r a c t i c e   7   Identifying** Place an X next to the sentence if its subject and verb do not agree. Cross out the prepositional phrases first.

1. _____ The teacher in the audience seem familiar with the speaker.

2. _____ Roman architecture still influences architecture today.

3. _____ Penn and Teller is famous magicians.

4. _____ The reports on my desk belong to the finance department.

5. _____ Ranch dressing on a salad taste the best.

6. _____ The workers in the yard wants overtime work.

7. _____ Horror films and suspense dramas at the theatre gives me nightmares.

8. _____ The keys on the sofa fits the back door.

9. _____ The motorists on that highway drive too fast.

10. _____ One of her many talents are dancing.

◆ **P r a c t i c e   8   Correcting** Correct the subjects and verbs that do not agree in Practice 7 by rewriting each incorrect sentence.

1. _____

2. _____

3. _____

4. _____

5. _____

6. _____

7. _____

8. _____

9. _____

10. _____

◆ **P r a c t i c e   9   Completing** Fill in each blank in the following sentences with a verb that agrees with its subject and makes sense. Cross out the prepositional phrases first.

1. Many travelers on this trip _____ trains to planes.

2. Our award-winning roses on the back patio _____ throughout the summer.

3. The decorative dragons on this silk _____ good fortune.

4. The beef and the noodles on the stove _____ seasoning.

5. The clothes in the dryer _____ folding.

6. A pool above the ground _____ value to a house.

7. The Alamo Dome in Texas _____ many sporting events and concerts.

8. The four of us _____ watching scary movies.

9. Tom Hanks _____ many types of characters.

10. The woman with the poodle and funny glasses always _____ me laugh.

◆ **P r a c t i c e   1 0   Writing Your Own**

A. Write a sentence of your own for each of the following prepositional phrases.

1. behind the couch _____

2. around that mountain _____

3. with the red hair _____

4. in our company _____

5. on our team _____

B. Write five sentences of your own with prepositional phrases, and underline the subject and verb in each sentence. Cross out the prepositional phrases first.

1. _____

2. _____

3. _____

4. _____

5. _____

MORE THAN ONE SUBJECT

Sometimes a subject consists of more than one person, place, thing, or idea. These subjects are called **compound** (as discussed in Chapter 7). Follow these three rules when matching a verb to a compound subject:

1. When compound subjects are joined by *and,* use a plural verb.

   Plural: **Maria** and **Tom were** my best friends.

   The singular words *Maria* and *Tom* together make a plural subject. Therefore, the plural verb *were* is needed.

2. When the subject appears to have more than one part but the parts refer to a single unit, use a singular verb.

   Singular: **Vinegar and oil** is great on a salad.

   Vinegar is one item and *oil* is one item, but one is not eaten without the other, so they form a single unit. Because they are a single unit, they require a singular verb—*is*.

3. When compound subjects are joined by *or* or *nor,* make the verb agree with the subject closest to it.

   Singular: Neither **bananas** nor **chicken was** available at the store.

   The part of the compound subject closest to the verb is *chicken,* which is singular. Therefore, the verb must be singular—*was*.

   Plural: Neither **chicken** nor **bananas were** available at the store.

   This time, the part of the compound subject closest to the verb is *bananas,* which is plural. Therefore, the verb must be plural—*were*.

REVIEWING SUBJECT-VERB AGREEMENT
WITH MORE THAN ONE SUBJECT

Do you use a singular or plural verb with compound subjects joined by
and?

_____

Why should you use a singular verb with a subject like macaroni and
cheese?

_____

If one part of a compound subject joined by or *or* nor *is singular and the*
other is plural, how do you decide whether to use a singular or plural
verb?

_____

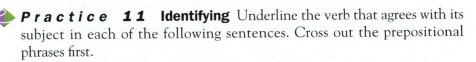 **Practice 11** **Identifying** Underline the verb that agrees with its
subject in each of the following sentences. Cross out the prepositional
phrases first.

1. Wine and cheese (is, are) a good appetizer.
2. Neither your smile nor your laughter (cheers, cheer) me today.
3. The brakes and alignment (needs, need) adjusting on the car.
4. The cupboards and refrigerator in this house (is, are) empty.
5. A hamburger and fries from Burger King (is, are) my favorites.
6. Neither man nor bullets (harms, harm) Superman.
7. Banshees and leprechauns (is, are) Irish folk characters.
8. Biscuits and gravy (is, are) a wonderful Southern breakfast.
9. Either the gophers or the dog (digs, dig) in the backyard.
10. My aunt and uncle (live, lives) in San Diego, California.

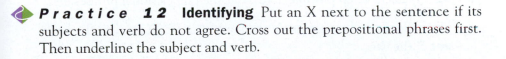 **Practice 12** **Identifying** Put an X next to the sentence if its
subjects and verb do not agree. Cross out the prepositional phrases first.
Then underline the subject and verb.

1. _____ Neither the fish nor the ham were cooked well.

2. _____ "Ball and chain" are an expression referring to one's spouse.

3. _____ Paper and an ink cartridge for the printer need to be ordered.

4. _____ Sam and Jim from my school draws very well.

5. _____ Louisiana and Georgia are humid states.

6. _____ Either the flies or the heat in the summer annoy me.

7. _____ Sour cream and onion on chips are my favorite dip.

8. _____ Either the movers or I are responsible for packing the glasses.

9. _____ Ham and cheese with mayonnaise makes a great sandwich.

10. _____ Pens and pencils belongs in the third drawer.

◆ Practice 13   Correcting Correct the subjects and verbs that do not agree in Practice 12 by rewriting each incorrect sentence.

1. _____

2. _____

3. _____

4. _____

5. _____

6. _____

7. _____

8. _____

9. _____

10. _____

◆ Practice 14   Completing Fill in each blank in the following sentences with a verb that agrees with its subject and makes sense. Avoid *is*, *are*, *was*, and *were* when possible. Cross out the prepositional phrases first.

1. The balloons and streamers for the party _____ in the back-seat of the car.

2. Neither the picture nor the wall hangings _____ good on the wall.

3. Colds and flus _____ usually caught in the winter.

4. Peanut butter and jelly _____ good for lunch.

5. Dinner and a movie with someone you like _____ a good date.

6. Sun and water _____ plants grow.

7. The managers and the staff in this office _____ a break.

8. Either this lotion or this oil _____ me to break out.

9. Neither the girls nor the boys from the third grade _____ well.

10. The CDs and the DVDs _____ in the entertainment center.

◆ **P r a c t i c e   1 5   Writing Your Own**

A. Write a sentence of your own using the following words as subjects.

1. beer and peanuts _____

2. neither my father nor mother _____

3. the actors and their bodyguards _____

4. either the sweater or the pants _____

5. the rabbits and chickens _____

B. Write five sentences of your own with compound subjects, and under-line the subject and verb in each sentence. Cross out the prepositional phrases first.

1. _____

2. _____

3. _____

4. _____

5. _____

VERBS BEFORE SUBJECTS

When the subject follows its verb, the subject may be hard to find, which makes the process of agreeing subjects and verbs difficult. Subjects come after verbs in two particular situations—when the sentence begins with *Here* or *There* and when a question begins with *Who, What, Where, When, Why,* or *How*. Here are some examples:

Verb Before Subject: Here **are** the **contestants** ~~for the game~~.

Verb Before Subject: There **is paper** ~~in the filing cabinet~~.

In sentences that begin with *Here* or *There*, the verb always comes before the subject. Don't forget to cross out prepositional phrases to help you identify the subject. One of the words that's left will be the subject, and then you can check that the verb agrees with it.

                                              v   s

Verb Before Subject: Where **are** the **keys** ~~to this lock~~?

                                              v   s   v

Verb Before Subject: When **are you graduating** ~~from college~~?

In questions that begin with *Who, What, When, Where, Why,* and *How*, the verb comes before the subject, as in the first example, or is split by the subject, as in the last example.

REVIEWING VERBS BEFORE SUBJECTS

Where will you find the verb in sentences that begin with Here *or* There?

_____

Where will you find the verb in questions that begin with Who, What, Where, When, Why, *and* How?

_____

◆ **P r a c t i c e   1 6   Identifying** Underline the verb that agrees with its subject in each of the following sentences. Cross out the prepositional phrases first.

1. Here (stands, stand) the statue of our state bird.
2. There up the tree (goes, go) our cat.
3. Who (is, are) the person responsible?
4. Where (is, are) the staples for the stapler?
5. How (is, are) dinner coming along?
6. There (grazes, graze) a wild deer in our yard.
7. Here (plays, play) the children.
8. What (is, are) Jim and Tanya doing for Halloween?
9. There (is, are) a snake in my boot.
10. Whom (is, are) you taking to the Bahamas?

◆ **Practice 17** **Identifying** Put an X next to the sentence if the subject and verb do not agree. Cross out the prepositional phrases first. Then underline the subject and verb.

1. _____ There are several reasons for this strategy.
2. _____ Who is the nurses for this procedure?
3. _____ What is you doing with all those leftovers?
4. _____ Here sit the dogs for the parade.
5. _____ There jumps the frogs from the pond.
6. _____ Whom are you taking to the baseball game?
7. _____ Why is you wearing those clothes?
8. _____ Here is the new TV.
9. _____ How are your back today?
10. _____ Here is the cleaning people for your house.

◆ **Practice 18** **Correcting** Correct the subjects and verbs that do not agree in Practice 17 by rewriting each incorrect sentence.

1. _____

2. _____

3. _____

4. _____

5. _____

6. _____

7. _____

8. _____

9. _____

10. _____

◆ **P r a c t i c e 1 9 Completing** Fill in each blank in the following sentences with a verb that agrees with its subject and makes sense. Avoid *is*, *are*, *was*, and *were* when possible. Cross out the prepositional phrases first.

1. Here _____ our horses after the ride.

2. There _____ the nervous father-to-be.

3. Who _____ that girl with the red blouse?

4. What _____ Ling thinking?

5. There _____ the coals from last night's fire.

6. How _____ the beginning of the poem?

7. Where _____ Jane and Jill last week?

8. Here _____ the water from the creek.

9. Here _____ the performers for tonight's show.

10. Where _____ those old shoes?

◆ **P r a c t i c e 2 0 Writing Your Own**

A. Write a sentence of your own beginning with each of the following words.

1. here _____

2. there _____

3. who _____

4. what _____

5. how _____

B. Write five sentences of your own with the verb before its subject, and underline the subject and verb in each sentence. Cross out the prepositional phrases.

1. _____

2. _____

3. _____

4. _____

5. _____

COLLECTIVE NOUNS

Collective nouns name a group of people or things. Examples include such nouns as *army, audience, band, class, committee, crew, crowd, family, flock, gang, jury, majority, minority, orchestra, senate, team,* and *troop.* Collective nouns can be singular or plural. They are singular when they refer to a group as a single unit. They are plural when they refer to the individual actions or feelings of the group members.

                         s   v

Singular: The **orchestra plays** every Friday.

Orchestra refers to the entire unit or group. Therefore, it requires the singular verb *plays*.

                        s   v

Plural: The **orchestra play** different instruments.

Here *orchestra* refers to the individual members, who each play an instrument, so the plural verb *play* is used.

REVIEWING COLLECTIVE NOUNS

When is a collective noun singular?

_____

When is a collective noun plural?

_____

_____

◆ **P r a c t i c e   2 1**   **Identifying** Underline the verb that agrees with its subject in each of the following sentences. Cross out the prepositional phrases first.

1. A troupe of acrobats (fly, flies) through the air one by one.
2. The senate (was, were) looking separately at their calendars.
3. The crew (is, are) all doing errands.
4. The class of 2005 (experience, experiences) many new opportunities.
5. A crowd of enthusiastic people (yell, yells) encouragement to the speaker.
6. The audience (clap, claps) wildly when he walks on stage.
7. The army (march, marches) in uniform lines.
8. The gang of children (scream, screams) together in delight.
9. The jury (was, were) deadlocked.
10. The minority (is, are) in the right.

◆ **P r a c t i c e   2 2**   **Identifying** Put an X next to the sentence if the subject and verb do not agree. Cross out the prepositional phrases first. Then underline the subjects and verbs.

1. _____ My gang of friends is going to Magic Mountain.
2. _____ The committee for finance decide money issues.
3. _____ A crew of sailors whistles every time she walks by.
4. _____ The majority of the voters plans a vote on Monday.
5. _____ The jury are passing the verdict on the accused.
6. _____ The flock of birds is flying in formation.
7. _____ The band play "Wipe Out" at every game.
8. _____ My family visits one another for every holiday.

9. _____ A troupe of entertainers performs in our town once a year.
10. _____ My brother's class of graduating students like the new caps and gowns.

◀ **P r a c t i c e 2 3 Correcting** Correct the subjects and verbs that do not agree in Practice 22 by rewriting each incorrect sentence.

1. _____

2. _____

3. _____

4. _____

5. _____

6. _____

7. _____

8. _____

9. _____

10. _____

◀ **P r a c t i c e 2 4 Completing** Fill in each blank in the following sentences with a verb that agrees with its subject and makes sense. Avoid *is*, *are*, *was*, and *were* when possible. Cross out the prepositional phrases first.

1. The team of football players _____ silently going through individual preparations for the game.

2. The majority _____ the voice of the minority.

3. The committee _____ taken a break from the long meeting.

4. Our class always _____ the most money for charity.

5. The orchestra in the pit _____ playing badly.

6. The family _____ going on vacation this summer.

7. The army _____ across the land.

8. Only a minority of the citizens _____ cheated by the new tax.

9. The crowd of onlookers _____ shocked by the scene.

10. The class with the most rowdy students _____ pleased with the teacher.

◆ **P r a c t i c e 2 5** **Writing Your Own**

A. Write a sentence of your own using each of the following collective nouns as subjects.

1. crowd _____

2. army _____

3. family _____

4. senate _____

5. audience _____

B. Write five sentences of your own with collective nouns as subjects, and underline the subject and verb in each sentence. Cross out the prepositional phrases first.

1. _____

2. _____

3. _____

4. _____

5. _____

INDEFINITE PRONOUNS

Indefinite pronouns do not refer to anyone or anything specific. Some indefinite pronouns are always singular, and some are always plural. A few can be either singular or plural, depending on the other words in the sentence. When an indefinite pronoun is the subject of a sentence, the verb must agree with the pronoun. Here is a list of indefinite pronouns.

Indefinite Pronouns

ALWAYS SINGULAR		ALWAYS PLURAL	EITHER SINGULAR OR PLURAL
another	neither	both	all
anybody	nobody	few	any
anyone	none	many	more
anything	no one	others	most
each	nothing	several	some
either	one		
everybody	other		
everyone	somebody		
everything	someone		
little	something		
much	whoever		

                         s   v

Singular: **Something changes** at home every day.

                         s   v

Everybody hates this hot weather.

                     s   v

Plural: **Several made** the long hike.

                     s   v

Many stay longer than necessary.

The pronouns that can be either singular or plural are singular when they refer to singular words and plural when they refer to plural words.

                     s   v

Singular: **Some** of Sarah's water **was** gone.

Some is singular because it refers to *water*, which is singular. The singular verb *was* agrees with the singular subject *some*.

                  s   v

Plural: **Some** of Sarah's friends **were** at her graduation.

Some is plural because it refers to *friends*, which is plural. The plural verb *were* agrees with the plural subject *some*.

REVIEWING INDEFINITE PRONOUNS
....

What is an indefinite pronoun?

_____

When are all, any, more, most, and **some** *singular or plural?*

_____

_____

◆ **P r a c t i c e   2 6   Identifying** Underline the verb that agrees with its subject in each of the following sentences. Cross out the prepositional phrases first.

1. Many (hope, hopes) she will win the contest.
2. Everyone who ate at that restaurant (is, are) expected to get sick.
3. Somebody (spike, spikes) the punch at every party.
4. Someone usually (joins, join) Victor for dinner.
5. Each of the cars (was, were) too expensive.
6. None of the vendors (has, have) change for a dollar.
7. Many kinds of people (visits, visit) Florida each year.
8. Not many of the workers (leaves, leave) the job on time.
9. Someone in the class usually (becomes, become) involved in this activity.
10. The one on top of the TV (belongs, belong) to Jason.

◆ **P r a c t i c e   2 7   Identifying** Put an X next to the sentence if its subject and verb do not agree. Cross out the prepositional phrases first. Then underline the subject and verb.

1. _____ Several of the diners eats only vegetarian meals.
2. _____ Many of the people trip on the first step.

3. _____ Nothing in this refrigerator taste good to me today.

4. _____ More of the wild animals is moving into the city.

5. _____ Both of the students in the class tries very hard.

6. _____ Everybody pretends to like her.

7. _____ All of the money are for your business trip.

8. _____ Most of the crime scene have been destroyed.

9. _____ No one paces the floor as much as you do.

10. _____ Few of the invited guests plans to arrive late.

◀ **P r a c t i c e   2 8   Correcting** Correct the subjects and verbs that do not agree in Practice 27 by rewriting each incorrect sentence.

1. _____

2. _____

3. _____

4. _____

5. _____

6. _____

7. _____

8. _____

9. _____

10. _____

◀ **P r a c t i c e   2 9   Completing** Fill in each blank in the following sentences with a verb that agrees with its subject and makes sense. Cross out the prepositional phrases first.

1. A few of the cats _____ their shots.

2. Some of the water _____ on the carpet.

3. Someone _____ eating my lunch.

4. Both of the boys _____ late for their appointments.

5. Nothing _____ more important than your health.

6. Somebody in this room _____ keeping a secret.

7. Several of the videos _____ destroyed in the heat.

8. Most of the mud _____ on me.

9. All of the barking dogs _____ to the neighbor.

10. Each person _____ a different superstition.

◆ *P r a c t i c e* *3 0*   **Writing Your Own**

A. Write a sentence of your own using the following indefinite pronouns as subjects, and combine them with one of the following verbs: *is, are, was, were*.

1. each _____

2. others _____

3. several _____

4. most _____

5. some _____

B. Write five sentences of your own using indefinite pronouns as subjects, and underline the subject and verb in each sentence. Cross out the prepositional phrases first.

1. _____

2. _____

3. _____

4. _____

5. _____

CHAPTER REVIEW

You might want to reread your answers to the questions in the review boxes before you do the following exercises.

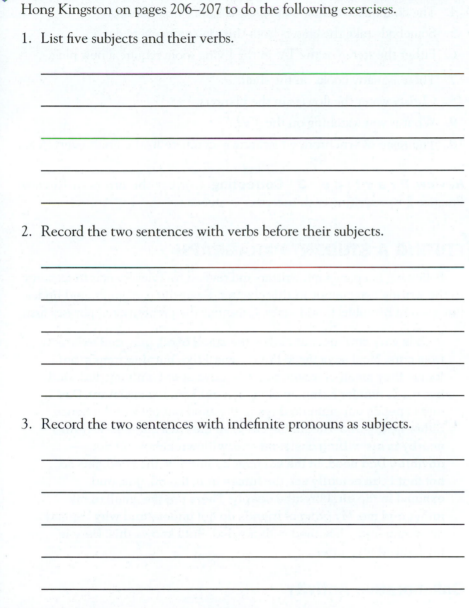

Review P r a c t i c e 1 **Reading** Refer to the paragraph by Maxine
Hong Kingston on pages 206–207 to do the following exercises.

1. List five subjects and their verbs.

   _____

   _____

   _____

   _____

   _____

2. Record the two sentences with verbs before their subjects.

   _____

   _____

   _____

   _____

   _____

3. Record the two sentences with indefinite pronouns as subjects.

   _____

   _____

   _____

   _____

   _____

Review P r a c t i c e 2 **Identifying** Underline the incorrect verbs in
each of the following sentences. Cross out the prepositional phrases first.

   1. We speaks in clear, forceful voices.
   2. The rabbits and the chickens in the back shed shares the same feed.

3. A few of the memos for today's meeting was misplaced.

4. The committee of new employees ask a lot of questions.

5. Somebody take the erasers from this classroom every day.

6. Either the stereo or the TV in the living room require a new plug.

7. There is many books on the shelf.

8. Christy water the flowers in the planters.

9. What is you watching on the TV?

10. The team of synchronized swimmers compete in the finals every year.

◆ *Review P r a c t i c e 3* **Correcting** Correct the errors in Review Practice 2 by rewriting each incorrect sentence.

EDITING A STUDENT PARAGRAPH

Following is a paragraph written and revised by Tyler Francis in response to the writing assignment in this chapter. Read the paragraph, and underline each of his subjects and verbs. Cross out the prepositional phrases first.

It is very strange, but I loves the smell of oil, gas, and exhaust from cars. Most says these things smell like burning fumes, but for me they smell of warm, carefree days spent with my dad. Dad has a passion for fixing up old cars, and I am his assistant. Dad and I spends our summer days in the shed out back of the house. Either he are underneath the car or in the car's engine. Hovering nearby is his willing assistant, me, with wrenches, oil, rags— anything Dad need. In the summer by midday, the shed gets so hot that I can actually see the fumes from the oil, gas, and exhaust in the air. I breathe deeply: There are the smell of my father and me. My gang of friends do not understand why I spend my summer in a hot shed with my dad. But I knows this: Here is my fondest memories.

Collaborative Activity

Team up with a partner, and underline the nine agreement errors in Tyler's paragraph twice. Then, working together, use what you have learned in this chapter to correct these errors. Rewrite the paragraph with your corrections.

EDITING YOUR OWN PARAGRAPH

Now return to the paragraph you wrote and revised at the beginning of this chapter. Underline each of your subjects and verbs.

Collaborative Activity

Exchange paragraphs with your partner, and circle any agreement errors that you find in your partner's paragraph.

Individual Activity

On the Error Log in Appendix 4, record the agreement errors that your partner found in your paragraph. Then, to complete the writing process, correct these errors by rewriting your paragraph.

CHAPTER 13

MORE ON VERBS

✅ CHECKLIST for Correcting Tense and Voice Problems

> ✔ Are verb tenses consistent?
> ✔ Are sentences written in the active voice?

Verbs communicate the action and time of each sentence. So it is important that you use verb tense consistently. Also, you should strive to write in the active, not the passive, voice. This chapter provides help with both of these sentence skills.

Notice how energetic and consistent the verb tenses are in the following paragraph by Robert Fulghum.

I like sorting the clothes—lights, darks, in-betweens. I like setting the dials—hot, cold, rinse, time, heat. These are choices I can understand and make with decisive skill. I still haven't figured out the new stereo, but washers and dryers I can handle. The bell dings—you pull out the warm, fluffy clothes, take them to the dining-room table, sort and fold them into neat piles. I especially like it when there's lots of static electricity, and you can hang socks all over your body and they will stick there.

In this paragraph, Robert Fulghum describes a chore he enjoys because it's not complicated. Before continuing in this chapter, take a moment to write about your favorite or most dreaded chore. Save your work because you will use it later in the chapter.

 WRITING ASSIGNMENT: MY FAVORITE OR MOST DREADED CHORE

Do you have a favorite or most dreaded chore? What is it? How do you go about doing it? Why do you like or dislike this chore? Write a paragraph explaining this chore to your peers.

> 🖊️ **REVISING YOUR WRITING**
>
> Revise the first draft of your paragraph before you focus on editing. Use the Revising Checklist on pages 24–25 to help you with your revision. Make sure your paragraph has a good topic sentence and is well developed. Then check your paragraph for unity, organization, and coherence.

CONSISTENT VERB TENSE

Verb tense refers to the time an action takes place—in the present, the past, or the future. The verb tenses in a sentence should be consistent. That is, if you start out using one tense, you should not switch tenses unless absolutely necessary. Switching tenses can be confusing. Here are some examples:

	Present
NOT	When the doorbell **rings** all through the evening and the ghosts and goblins

Present · Past
come out for candy, then it **was** Halloween.

	Present
CORRECT	When the doorbell **rings** all through the evening and the ghosts and goblins

Present · Present
come out for candy, then it **is** Halloween.

	Past · Present
NOT	They **rushed** to the hospital when they **hear** that you were having the baby.

	Past · Past
CORRECT	They **rushed** to the hospital when they **heard** that you were having the baby.

	Future · Present
NOT	We **will send** you a postcard, and we **buy** you some souvenirs from the Virgin Islands.

	Future · Future
CORRECT	We **will send** you a postcard, and we **will buy** you some souvenirs from the Virgin Islands.

REVIEWING CONSISTENT VERB TENSES

Why should verb tenses be consistent?

_____

_____

What problem do inconsistent verb tenses create?

_____

_____

◆ **P r a c t i c e 1 Identifying** Put a C next to the sentence if the tenses of the underlined verbs are consistent.

1. _____ The dog <u>keeps</u> scratching his ear and <u>will need</u> medical attention.
2. _____ She <u>is</u> my sister and <u>looks</u> like me.
3. _____ You <u>will receive</u> my message soon and <u>will need</u> to act quickly.
4. _____ The contestants <u>will be arriving</u> tomorrow morning and <u>needed</u> room assignments.
5. _____ We <u>heard</u> the good news yesterday, so we <u>leave</u> immediately to congratulate you.
6. _____ The rules of the game <u>were</u> hard to understand, and they <u>tried</u> my patience.
7. _____ I <u>like</u> the taste of cherries but <u>hate</u> cherry pie.
8. _____ The performers <u>were</u> interesting to watch and <u>play</u> well.
9. _____ Your car <u>will be</u> ready in one hour, and you <u>will need</u> to pick it up then.
10. _____ Because you <u>are</u> ill, the sheets on the bed <u>need</u> stripping.

◆ **P r a c t i c e 2 Identifying** Put an I next to the sentence if the tenses of the underlined verbs are inconsistent.

1. _____ You <u>need</u> to water the lawn so that the grass <u>did</u> not <u>die</u>.
2. _____ The baby <u>cried</u> all last night, and I <u>paced</u> the floor.
3. _____ The cows <u>escaped</u> from the pasture and <u>will roam</u> into town.
4. _____ *Scooby Doo* <u>is</u> my favorite cartoon, and I <u>watched</u> it every day.

5. _____ This dress <u>looks</u> lovely while you <u>were wearing</u> it.

6. _____ Timmy <u>poured</u> milk on the carpet and <u>cleaned</u> it up with paper towels.

7. _____ You <u>are</u> the neatest person, and you never <u>leave</u> a mess.

8. _____ The cups and saucers <u>were broken</u> during the move, but the glasses <u>are</u> not.

9. _____ Food <u>cooks</u> quickly in the microwave, but it <u>tastes</u> better from the oven.

10. _____ Barbie's laugh <u>is</u> very irritating, and she <u>laughed</u> all the time.

◆ **P r a c t i c e 3 Correcting** Correct the inconsistent verbs in Practice 2 by rewriting each incorrect sentence.

1. _____

2. _____

3. _____

4. _____

5. _____

6. _____

7. _____

8. _____

9. _____

10. _____

◆ **P r a c t i c e 4 Completing** Fill in each blank in the following sentences with a consistent verb that makes sense.

1. I _____ over the toys in the living room and _____ my ankle.

2. The students _____ to the convention in Spain, where they _____ their presentations.

3. When Jackson _____, he _____ me his new address.

4. The papers _____ behind the desk, but I _____ them anyway.

5. Some people _____ sports, and others just _____ them.

6. I _____ over the fence and _____ into the house.

7. Most people _____ because they _____ happy.

8. Vitamin B _____ you energy and _____ your body heal faster.

9. Exercise _____ stress while it _____ the body.

10. The leaves _____ from the trees in autumn and _____ back in the spring.

◆ *P r a c t i c e* **5**   **Writing Your Own**

A. Write a sentence of your own for each of the following sets of verbs, making sure your tenses are consistent.

1. love, hate _____

2. wash, clean _____

3. plant, grow _____

4. run, jump _____

5. smell, taste _____

B. Write five sentences of your own using consistent verb tenses, and underline the verbs in each sentence.

1. _____

2. _____

3. _____

4. _____

5. _____

USING THE ACTIVE VOICE

In the **active voice,** the subject performs the action. In the **passive voice,** the subject receives the action. Compare the following two examples:

Passive Voice: The clothes **were washed** yesterday **by Valerie.**

Active Voice: **Valerie washed** the clothes yesterday.

The active voice adds energy to your writing. Here is another example. Notice the difference between active and passive.

Passive Voice: The picture **was painted** for this office **by my brother.**

Active Voice: **My brother painted** the picture for this office.

REVIEWING ACTIVE AND PASSIVE VOICE
....

What is the difference between the active and passive voice?

_____

_____

Why is the active voice usually better than the passive?

_____

 P r a c t i c e   6   Identifying Underline the active-voice verbs in each of the following sentences.

1. Pamela boiled water for the spaghetti.
2. Cassey bought flowers for her father.
3. The sun baked the ground.
4. Mark took his dog to the vet.
5. My brother smoked a turkey for the Easter picnic.
6. The computer translated the French document into English.
7. The artist created a statue for the opening ceremony.
8. Dakota beat the dirt off the rug.

9. The black widow weaves a strong web.

10. Every morning, my mother made a pot of coffee.

◆ **P r a c t i c e   7   Identifying** Put a P next to each sentence that is in the passive voice.

1. _____ Jarrett played with Issa today.

2. _____ The flowers were sent to the wedding.

3. _____ A ticket was given to the driver.

4. _____ The clothes were dried by the sun.

5. _____ We mailed invitations to our family and friends.

6. _____ The bleach was spilled on my shirt by Jean.

7. _____ A message was received in secret.

8. _____ Ants invaded my kitchen.

9. _____ The man was attacked by the dog.

10. _____ The new baby was placed in its mother's arms.

◆ **P r a c t i c e   8   Correcting** Rewrite each passive-voice sentence in Practice 7 in the active voice.

1. _____

2. _____

3. _____

4. _____

5. _____

6. _____

7. _____

8. _____

9. _____

10. _____

◆ *P r a c t i c e 9*   **Completing** Fill in each blank in the following sentences with an active-voice verb that makes sense.

1. The news _____ current events around the nation.

2. I _____ calamine lotion on my mosquito bites.

3. The TV in my bedroom _____ a fuse when I turned it on.

4. Dexter _____ the presents in the car.

5. My favorite soda _____ Coca-Cola.

6. Clive _____ his appointment with time to spare.

7. The scientists _____ a new gene.

8. The winds _____ over 100 mph.

9. The computer _____ to me, "You've got mail."

10. Fifi _____ chasing the ducks in the park.

◆ *P r a c t i c e 1 0*   **Writing Your Own**

A. Write a sentence of your own putting each of the following subjects and verbs in the passive voice.

1. my mom gives _____

2. he feels _____

3. the twins bought _____

4. the team threw _____

5. prisoners made _____

B. Rewrite each of your sentences from Practice 10A in the active voice.

1. _____

2. _____

3. _____

4. _____

5. _____

CHAPTER REVIEW

You might want to reread your answers to the questions in all the review boxes before you do the following exercises.

◆ *Review P r a c t i c e 1* **Reading** Refer to the paragraph by Robert Fulghum on page 232 to do the following exercises.

1. Rewrite the paragraph in the past tense, keeping verb tenses consistent.

_____

_____

_____

_____

_____

_____

2. Rewrite the paragraph in the passive voice. Notice how the paragraph loses energy.

_____

_____

_____

_____

_____

_____

◆ *Review P r a c t i c e 2* **Identifying** Underline any inconsistent or passive verbs in each of the following sentences.

1. When the phone rings, I refused to answer it.

2. The boat was tugged to shore by the fisherman.

3. This new recipe was created by my uncle.

4. They parked in the lot and walk a mile to the park's entrance.

5. The students were taken on an off-campus field trip.

6. Tim and Bill will fish this summer, and then they camped.

7. Since I love chocolate, I ate it all the time.

8. The kitten was cleaned by its mother.

9. The solar panels heat up when the sun came out.

10. The corrections were made by Mrs. Smith.

 Review P r a c t i c e 3 Correcting Correct the verb errors in Review Practice 2 by rewriting each incorrect sentence.

EDITING A STUDENT PARAGRAPH

Following is a paragraph written and revised by Mindy Holcombe in response to the writing assignment in this chapter. Read the paragraph, and underline each of her verbs.

> I hate doing household chores, but I especially hated emptying the dishwasher. Since I'm short, emptying the dishwasher has two basic stages: the places I can reach and the places I can't reach. The silverware is emptied by me first because I can reach the drawer where it belongs. Then all the plastic containers are unloaded, which I coordinate by color. I put these away in the bottom cupboard, which, of course, I will be able to reach. Last and most hated comes the dinnerware and glasses. I take the plates and bowls out of the dishwasher and stacked them on the kitchen counter. The glasses are done in the same manner. Then I make a little room on the counter and will climb up. This is the only way I can reach the cupboards above the kitchen counter. Since the glasses are on the top shelf, I have to stand up, which usually made me dizzy. One of these days, I'm going to look down only to find the ground rushing up to meet me. Maybe then my roommate will not ask me to empty the dishwasher anymore.

Collaborative Activity

Team up with a partner, and underline the eight inconsistent and passive-voice verbs twice in Mindy's paragraph. Then, working together, use what you have learned in this chapter to correct these errors. Rewrite the paragraph with your corrections.

EDITING YOUR OWN PARAGRAPH

Now return to the paragraph you wrote and revised at the beginning of this chapter. Underline each of your verbs.

Collaborative Activity

Exchange papers with your partner, and circle any verb errors that you find in your partner's paper.

Individual Activity

On the Error Log in Appendix 4, record any verb errors that your partner found in your paragraph. To complete the writing process, correct these errors by rewriting your paragraph.

UNIT TESTS

Unit Test 1 Identifying

Underline the verb errors in each of the following sentences.

1. The boys done a great job with the backyard.
2. My brother cutted his leg.
3. George and Martha is two characters from an Edward Albee play.
4. When the full moon rises over the mountains, the wolves howled.
5. I flirted with the girl next to me and make her smile.
6. The football players has run around the field 10 times.
7. Jared has ate all the macaroon cookies again.
8. We eatted dinner before the movie.
9. Here is several good reasons for this meeting.
10. The shortest boy on the track team run the fastest.

11. She will fly into Boston on the third and gave her speech on the fourth.

12. The criminals fledded from the scene of the crime.

13. The choir have sung that song many times.

14. Jonathon bended the pipe with his car.

15. What is you doing in the garage every night?

16. Last night, all of the food will be eaten by the guests.

17. The dogs been barking at the tree all night.

18. The children hidded from their babysitter.

19. Jenny eats whatever she wants but didn't gain weight.

20. There are no reason for this chaos.

Unit Test 2 Correcting

Correct the verb errors in Unit Test 1 by rewriting each incorrect sentence.

Unit Test 3 Identifying

Underline the verb errors in the following paragraph.

My mother has the most whimsical sense of style. She loves frogs.
In the living room are a frog lamp, a frog hanging from the bathroom towel rack, and a huge concrete frog will sit in the entryway,
which everybody stumble over. And if you looks closely, you can
find little figurines all over the house. Geese of various sizes is
scattered around the entertainment center. A pack of hunting dogs
was placed on the kitchen counter by my mom. Little rabbits,
turtles, and cats snuggles in the warm earth in the household
plants. But the most whimsical and cherished decoration of all are
the hand-carved totem pole that stands in the living room. This has
come through the generations, even though nobody know who
made it. Fanciful woodland animals appear all around it. Merry
little sprites and elves dances through the woods as a maiden
rests in her bower. I have spent hours tracing the designs with
my fingers, fantasizing about the story behind the maiden's smile.
Some day this will belong to me, and I passed it down to my
children. I hope it sparks their imagination as much as it has mine.

Unit Test 4 Correcting

Correct the verb errors in Unit Test 3 by rewriting the paragraph.

UNIT WRITING ASSIGNMENTS

1. Put yourself into the scene in the photograph. What is embarrassing about it? Who is involved and what probably happened? How does the picture make you feel? Why are you reacting this way?

2. Have you ever had a misunderstanding with a friend or relative that wasn't your fault? How did the misunderstanding come about? Was anyone to blame, or was the situation simply a misunderstanding? Who was involved? What did you do? How did this event make you feel?

3. Have you ever performed an act of kindness with no thought to yourself? What did you do, and why did you do it? What kind of sacrifice, if any, did you make? How did your actions make you feel?

4. We often see things differently when we are children, like our impressions of our parents. As we grow older, we begin to see things from a more mature perspective. Is there a situation, such as getting punished, or a person that you now understand differently from how you did in your childhood? What did you think as a child, and what do you think now? What has made your perceptions change? Do you have a better understanding of the situation or person?

5. Create your own writing assignment (with the help of your instructor), and write a response to it.

PRONOUNS

Pronouns generally go almost unnoticed in writing and speaking, even though these words can do anything nouns can do. In fact, much like your inborn sense of balance, pronouns work in sentences to make your writing precise and coherent. Without pronouns, writers and speakers would find themselves repeating nouns over and over, producing sentences that are unnatural and boring. For example, notice how awkward the following paragraph would be without pronouns:

Robert wrote a rough draft of Robert's essay last night. Then Robert asked Robert's girlfriend to read over Robert's essay with Robert. After Robert's girlfriend helped Robert find errors, Robert made corrections. Then Robert set aside the essay for a day before Robert took the essay out and began revising again.

When we let pronouns take over and do their jobs, we produce a much more fluent paragraph:

Robert wrote a rough draft of his essay last night. Then he asked his girlfriend to read over his essay with him. After she helped Robert find errors, he made corrections. Then he set aside the essay for a day before he took it out and began revising again.

Problems with pronouns occur when the words pronouns refer to aren't clear or when pronouns and their antecedents—the words they refer to— are too far apart. In this unit, we will deal with the following aspects of pronouns:

Chapter 14: Pronoun Problems
Chapter 15: Pronoun Reference and Point of View
Chapter 16: Pronoun Agreement

PRONOUN PROBLEMS

☑ CHECKLIST for Using Pronouns

> ✔ Are all subject pronouns used correctly?
>
> ✔ Are all object pronouns used correctly?
>
> ✔ Are all possessive pronouns used correctly?
>
> ✔ Are pronouns used in *than* or *as* comparisons in the correct form?
>
> ✔ Are the pronouns *this*, *that*, *these*, and *those* used correctly?

Pronouns are words that take the place of nouns. They help us avoid repeating nouns. In this chapter, we'll discuss five types of pronoun problems: (1) using the wrong pronoun as a subject, (2) using the wrong pronoun as an object, (3) using an apostrophe with a possessive pronoun, (4) misusing pronouns in comparisons, and (5) misusing demonstrative pronouns.

Notice how a variety of pronouns help Lois Smith Brady create smooth paragraphs.

Eventually [love] even found me. At 28, I met my husband in a stationery store. I was buying a typewriter ribbon, and he was looking at Filofaxes. I remember that his eyes perfectly matched his faded jeans. He remembers that my sneakers were full of sand. He still talks about those sneakers and how they evoked his childhood—bonfires by the ocean, driving on the sand in an old Jeep—all those things that he cherished.

How did I know it was true love? Our first real date lasted for nine hours; we just couldn't stop talking. I had never been able to dance in my life, but I could dance with him, perfectly in step. I have learned that it's love when you finally stop tripping over your toes.

In this paragraph, Brady describes how she knew she had found true love from the moment of her first date. Before continuing in this chapter, take a moment to describe one of your first dates or your dream date. Save your work because you will use it later in this chapter.

 WRITING ASSIGNMENT: A SPECIAL DATE

Think about your first real date or your dream date. Describe the date as fully as you can in a paragraph. Consider who, what, when, where, why, and how. Was the date a success?

 REVISING YOUR WRITING

Revise the first draft of your paragraph before you focus on editing. Use the Revising Checklist on pages 24–25 to help you with your revision. Make sure your paragraph has a good topic sentence and is well developed. Then check your paragraph for unity, organization, and coherence.

PRONOUNS AS SUBJECTS

Single pronouns as subjects usually don't cause problems.

Subject Pronoun: **I** gave to charity.

Subject Pronoun: **They** flew to Dallas.

You wouldn't say "*Me* gave to charity" or "*Them* flew to Dallas." But an error often occurs when a sentence has a compound subject and one or more of the subjects is a pronoun.

NOT   The boys and **us** played ball.

CORRECT   The boys and **we** played ball.

NOT   **Him** and **me** rode together.

CORRECT   **He** and **I** rode together.

To test whether you have used the correct form of the pronoun in a compound subject, try each subject alone:

Subject Pronoun?   **The boys and us** played ball.

Test: **The boys** played ball. **YES**

Test:	**Us** played ball. **NO**
Test:	**We** played ball. **YES**
Correction:	**The boys and we** played ball.

Here is a list of subject pronouns.

Subject Pronouns

Singular	Plural
I	we
you	you
he, she, it	they

REVIEWING PRONOUNS AS SUBJECTS

Name two subject pronouns.

_____

How can you test whether you are using the correct pronoun as the subject of a sentence?

_____

 P r a c t i c e   1   Identifying Underline the correct subject pronoun in each of the following sentences.

1. The parents and (them, they) are having a conference.
2. The previous year, you and (she, her) were the best of friends.
3. (Him, He) and she have been dating for three years now.
4. The bikers and (we, us) had the best time driving through the canyon.
5. From a distance, (she, her) and Iris looked alike.
6. During the soccer game, you and (I, me) yelled until we were hoarse.
7. You and (they, them) look funny together.
8. Christine, John, and (us, we) went to Disneyland separately but at the same time.

9. Hey! You and (her, she) ate all the Oreo cookies.

10. At the swim party, the children and (they, them) dived into the pool with their clothes on.

♦ **P r a c t i c e   2   Identifying** Put an X next to the sentence if the underlined pronoun is incorrect.

1. _____ Last night, <u>him</u> and I helped with the dishes.

2. _____ The dogs and <u>us</u> ran wild across the playground.

3. _____ He and <u>me</u> are going to the Madonna concert.

4. _____ We and <u>you</u> can fit in that phone booth.

5. _____ In the spring, you and <u>I</u> are going fly-fishing.

6. _____ Last year, Jim, Tanya, and <u>we</u> car-pooled together.

7. _____ You and <u>me</u> should be lab partners.

8. _____ <u>They</u> and the receptionist have all gone to lunch.

9. _____ My mother and <u>her</u> have known each other forever.

10. _____ <u>Him</u> and I felt that you were very kind.

♦ **P r a c t i c e   3   Correcting** Correct the pronoun errors in Practice 2 by rewriting each incorrect sentence.

1. _____

2. _____

3. _____

4. _____

5. _____

6. _____

7. _____

8. _____

9. _____

10. _____

◆ **P r a c t i c e   4   Completing** Fill in each blank in the following sentences with a subject pronoun that makes sense.

1. Jamie and _____ decided to go to the same college and room together.

2. During the storm, Nicole, Brad, and _____ took shelter in the basement.

3. You and _____ need to come to an agreement.

4. After dinner, the students and _____ are going to the library to study.

5. She and _____ are getting married this June.

6. _____ and some of the parents have set up a reading area for the children.

7. The scientists and _____ are trying to discover a new planet in the solar system.

8. A famous graphic artist and _____ did the cover for this book.

9. The lifeguard and _____ both jumped in to save the swimmer.

10. Joseph, who is a great gardener, and _____, who is a wonderful decorator, designed my Asian garden.

◆ **P r a c t i c e   5   Writing Your Own**

A. Write a sentence of your own for each of the following compound subjects.

1. you and I _____

2. we and they _____

3. Sara and she _____

4. you and he _____

5. she and we _____

B. Write five sentences of your own using compound subject pronouns, and underline the subject pronouns in each sentence.

1. _____

2. _____

3. _____

4. _____

5. _____

PRONOUNS AS OBJECTS

One of the most frequent pronoun errors is using a subject pronoun when the sentence calls for an object pronoun. The sentence may require an object after a verb, showing that someone or something receives the action of the verb. Or it may be an object of a preposition that is required (see page 80 for a list of prepositions).

NOT	She gave Alisha and **I** some candy.
CORRECT	She gave Alisha and **me** some candy.

NOT	This is just between you and **I**.
CORRECT	This is just between you and **me**.

Like the subject pronoun error, the object pronoun error usually occurs with compound objects. Also like the subject pronoun error, you can test whether you are using the correct pronoun by using each object separately.

Object Pronouns?	She gave Alisha and **I** some candy.
Test:	She gave **Alisha** some candy. **YES**
Test:	She gave **I** some candy. **NO**
Test:	She gave **me** some candy. **YES**
Correction:	She gave **Alisha and me** some candy.

Here is a list of object pronouns:

Object Pronouns

Singular	Plural
me	us
you	you
him, her, it	them

Reviewing Pronouns as Objects

In what two places are pronouns used as objects?

_____

How can you test whether you have used the correct pronoun as the object in a sentence?

_____

◆ **P r a c t i c e   6   Identifying** Underline the correct object pronouns in each of the following sentences.

1. We went to the party with Maria and (he, him).
2. My grandfather will give you and (I, me) a ride to the mall.
3. They watched you and (her, she) do your dance routines.
4. The professional golf teacher instructed them and (us, we).
5. My new girlfriend is standing beside my parents and (she, her).
6. The ice-cream vendor gave Hoang and (they, them) some free ice cream.
7. Grandmother mailed invitations to you and (he, him).
8. The show scared Bubba and (he, him).
9. My parents gave my sister and (I, me) $100 for the trip.
10. The spider webs were caught on (them, they) and Diane.

◆ **P r a c t i c e   7   Identifying** Put an X next to the sentence if the underlined pronoun is incorrect.

1. _____ Kendra invited John and <u>I</u> to the movies.
2. _____ The cutest boys in the class danced with her and <u>I</u>.
3. _____ The baby ducks are waddling behind <u>they</u> and us.
4. _____ Jim and George are bouncing the ball to Sandy and <u>her</u>.
5. _____ The argument is between <u>she</u> and him.
6. _____ I found my little sister with <u>him</u> and her.

7. _____ The chaperones are walking in front of Elkie and <u>he</u>.

8. _____ Margot can go down the water slide after John and <u>he</u>.

9. _____ The competition is between <u>them</u> and us.

10. _____ The doctor gave Valerie and <u>we</u> some candy after the shot.

◆ **P r a c t i c e   8   Correcting** Correct the pronoun errors in Practice 7 by rewriting each incorrect sentence.

1. _____

2. _____

3. _____

4. _____

5. _____

6. _____

7. _____

8. _____

9. _____

10. _____

◆ **P r a c t i c e   9   Completing** Fill in each blank in the following sentences with an object pronoun that makes sense.

1. Jeremy took off running after Judy and _____.

2. Between you and _____, we can do anything.

3. The actor read his lines to them and _____.

4. We watched the children and _____.

5. Thanks to _____ and her, we have raised enough money for the trip.

6. Your mom is seated in the middle of _____ and the Turners.

7. The karate instructor made _____ and you perform in front of the class.

8. I was in awe of Cassandra and _____.

9. Charles gave the food not to Jimmy but to _____.

10. The high winds almost blew us and _____ over.

◆ **P r a c t i c e   1 0**   **Writing Your Own**

A. Write a sentence of your own for each of the following compound object pronouns.

1. you and me _____

2. him and her _____

3. us and them _____

4. Ben and him _____

5. Shawna and her _____

B. Write five sentences of your own using object pronouns, and underline the object pronouns in each sentence.

1. _____

2. _____

3. _____

4. _____

5. _____

POSSESSIVE PRONOUNS

Possessive pronouns show ownership (**my** boat, **his** bed, **our** horse). (See page 71 for a list of pronouns.) An apostrophe is used with nouns to show ownership (**Jack's** cat, the **worker's** tools, the **committee's** vote). But an apostrophe is never used with possessive pronouns.

Possessive Pronouns

Singular	Plural
my, mine	our, ours
your, yours	your, yours
his, her, hers	their, theirs

NOT   That truck is **their's.**

CORRECT   That truck is **theirs.**

NOT   The apple on the counter is **your's.**

CORRECT   The apple on the counter is **yours.**

NOT   The cat licked **its'** paws.

CORRECT   The cat licked **its** paws.

REVIEWING POSSESSIVE PRONOUNS
....

When do you use an apostrophe with a noun?

_____

Do possessive pronouns take apostrophes?

_____

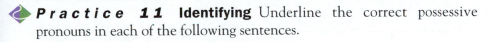 **P r a c t i c e   1 1   Identifying** Underline the correct possessive pronouns in each of the following sentences.

1. I wouldn't listen to (her, her's) excuses anymore.
2. The winning essay was (hers, his').
3. Glorianna is (his', his) girlfriend.
4. (Our, Our's) play was a success.
5. Those antique cars are (theirs, their's).
6. Are the Snoopy pajamas (yours, your's)?
7. That money was (mine's, mine).

8. The blue sweater is (his, his').

9. The dog chased (its, its') tail around and around.

10. (Their, Their's) garden is the loveliest on the block.

◆ **P r a c t i c e   1 2**   **Identifying** Put an X next to the sentence if the underlined pronoun is incorrect.

1. _____ <u>His</u> cell phone rang in class.

2. _____ <u>Her's</u> clothes are muddy.

3. _____ These assignments are <u>your's</u>.

4. _____ Those water balloons are <u>their's</u>.

5. _____ <u>Their</u> gifts were the most expensive.

6. _____ The dirty clothes on the floor are <u>our's</u>.

7. _____ <u>His</u> charm will not get him out of this situation.

8. _____ The horse swished <u>it's</u> tail in agitation.

9. _____ That plane behind the barn is <u>theirs</u>.

10. _____ <u>My's</u> hair is falling out.

◆ **P r a c t i c e   1 3**   **Correcting** Correct the pronoun errors in Practice 12 by rewriting each incorrect sentence.

1. _____

2. _____

3. _____

4. _____

5. _____

6. _____

7. _____

8. _____

9. _____

10. _____

◀ **P r a c t i c e   1 4**   **Completing** Fill in each blank in the following sentences with a possessive pronoun that makes sense.

1. This brand-new truck is _____.

2. Those punk rock clothes are definitely _____.

3. The artwork is _____.

4. _____ ghost is haunting this house.

5. _____ dog barks at everybody.

6. According to _____ notes, we should have turned left.

7. People have the right to _____ own beliefs.

8. Those are _____ goals and ambitions for the future.

9. My father rolled _____ eyes at my suggestions.

10. You spent _____ money!

◀ **P r a c t i c e   1 5**   **Writing Your Own**

A. Write a sentence of your own for each of the following possessive pronouns.

1. my _____

2. theirs _____

3. hers _____

4. yours _____

5. its _____

B. Write five sentences of your own using possessive pronouns, and underline the possessive pronouns in each sentence.

1. _____

2. _____

3. _____

4. _____

5. _____

PRONOUNS IN COMPARISONS

Sometimes pronoun problems occur in comparisons with *than* or *as*. An object pronoun may be mistakenly used instead of a subject pronoun. To find out if you are using the right pronoun, you should finish the sentence as shown here.

NOT   She can crochet better than **me.**

CORRECT She can crochet better than **I** [can crochet].

NOT   Beatrice is as good a runner as **him.**

CORRECT Beatrice is as good a runner as **he** [is].

Hint: Sometimes an object pronoun is required in a *than* or *as* comparison. But errors rarely occur in this case because the subject pronoun sounds so unnatural.

NOT   Elaine likes him more than she likes **I.**

CORRECT Elaine likes him more than she likes **me.**

REVIEWING PRONOUNS IN COMPARISONS

What causes pronoun problems in comparisons?

_____

_____

How can you test whether to use a subject pronoun or an object pronoun in a than *or* as *comparison?*

_____

_____

 **P r a c t i c e 1 6** **Identifying** Underline the correct pronoun in each of the following comparisons.

1. You have more pride than (they, them) could ever have.

2. Her dog makes more noise than (her, she)!

3. I am never as jealous as (she, her).

4. Thelma isn't as tall as (him, he).

5. He always has to work later than (me, I).

6. We have experienced as many troubles as (them, they).

7. She always drives faster than (he, him).

8. Erika isn't as good a gymnast as (she, her).

9. She thinks that she is more worthy than (them, they).

10. Most of the time, I'm better at math than (he, him).

P r a c t i c e 1 7 Identifying Put an X next to the sentence if the underlined pronoun is incorrect.

1. _____ He can read out loud better than <u>me</u>.

2. _____ Gabriel has more skill than <u>them</u>.

3. _____ Cynthia is as good a race-car driver as <u>he</u> is.

4. _____ Reyna can hold her breath longer than <u>him</u>.

5. _____ Veronica can jump higher than <u>I</u>.

6. _____ Carla is more popular than <u>her</u>.

7. _____ Manuel isn't as creative as <u>she</u>.

8. _____ He is as cold as <u>her</u>.

9. _____ We are just as friendly as <u>they</u>.

10. _____ Cordelia confides in you more than she confides in <u>I</u>.

P r a c t i c e 1 8 Correcting Correct the pronoun errors in Practice 17 by rewriting each incorrect sentence.

1. _____

2. _____

3. _____

4. _____

5. _____

6. _____

7. _____

8. _____

9. _____

10. _____

◆ *P r a c t i c e   1 9*   **Completing** Fill in each blank in the following sentences with pronouns that are correct.

1. He quits his job even more often than _____.

2. Every day, I like you more than I like _____.

3. I do believe that I am more tired than _____.

4. They are trying to recover the ball just as hard as _____.

5. Vinny and Clark are more suave than _____.

6. They push their children harder than _____ do.

7. Glenda isn't as selfish as _____.

8. Isabella likes Nolan more than she likes _____.

9. We have a better defense than _____.

10. I bet that I can play chess better than _____ can.

◆ *P r a c t i c e   2 0*   **Writing Your Own**

A. Write a sentence of your own using each of the following pronouns in comparisons.

1. I _____

2. they _____

3. she _____

4. he _____

5. we _____

B. Write five sentences of your own using pronouns in comparisons, and underline the pronouns in comparisons in each sentence.

1. _____

2. _____

3. _____

4. _____

5. _____

DEMONSTRATIVE PRONOUNS

There are four demonstrative pronouns: *this*, *that*, *these*, and *those*. **Demonstrative pronouns** point to specific people or objects. Use *this* and *these* to refer to items that are near and *that* and *those* to refer to items farther away. Look at the following examples.

Demonstrative (near):	**This** is my new computer.
Demonstrative (near):	**These** are library books.
Demonstrative (farther):	**That** is the bank.
Demonstrative (farther):	**Those** are the frames for the pictures.

Sometimes demonstrative pronouns are not used correctly.

	Incorrect	Correct
NOT	this here, that there	this, that
NOT	these here, these ones	these
NOT	them, those there, those ones	those

NOT	**Them** are the memos she typed.
CORRECT	**Those** are the memos she typed.

NOT	I'll give you **these here** clothes.
CORRECT	I'll give you **these** clothes.

NOT	**Those ones** were in the garage.
CORRECT	**Those** were in the garage.

NOT	**Those there** are the cards.
CORRECT	**Those** are the cards.

When demonstrative pronouns are used with nouns, they become adjectives.

Pronoun:	**That** is your dog.
Adjective:	**This dog** is his.

Pronoun: **Those** are memories you will always cherish.

Adjective: You will always cherish **those memories.**

The problems that occur with demonstrative pronouns can also occur when these pronouns act as adjectives.

NOT   Please hand me **that there** pen.

CORRECT   Please hand me **that** pen.

REVIEWING DEMONSTRATIVE PRONOUNS

Name the four demonstrative pronouns.

_____   _____   _____   _____

Give two examples of errors with demonstrative pronouns.

_____

_____

◆ **Practice 21** **Identifying** Underline the correct demonstrative pronoun in each of the following sentences.

1. (These, These here) are my favorite shows.
2. (Those, Them) are the people responsible.
3. Mary pushed (that there, that) all the way down the hall.
4. Janet gave (those there, those) to Manuel.
5. Are all of (these, these here) going in the truck?
6. (Those, Those ones) should be loaded first.
7. Anya is familiar with (these ones, these).
8. What will you give me for (this, this here)?
9. (That, That there) is the first house ever built in this town.
10. (Them, These) will grow into your grass and will be hard to remove.

◆ **Practice 22** **Identifying** Put an X next to the sentence if the underlined demonstrative pronoun is incorrect.

1. _____ <u>Those</u> were reserved for VIPs.
2. _____ <u>This here</u> is the best meal I've ever made.
3. _____ <u>Them</u> are the color swatches from the decorator.
4. _____ <u>These</u> are the keys you thought you'd lost.
5. _____ Will you put <u>these here</u> in the mail?
6. _____ <u>Those</u> were the best days of my life.
7. _____ <u>That</u> will never do.
8. _____ Before you go, <u>these here</u> need to be fixed.
9. _____ <u>Those ones</u> are for you, and <u>these ones</u> are for me.
10. _____ <u>Those there</u> on the sofa belong to my dad.

◢ **P r a c t i c e   2 3   Correcting** Correct the pronoun errors in Practice 22 by rewriting each incorrect sentence.

1. _____

2. _____

3. _____

4. _____

5. _____

6. _____

7. _____

8. _____

9. _____

10. _____

◢ **P r a c t i c e   2 4   Completing** Fill in each blank in the following sentences with a demonstrative pronoun that is correct.

1. _____ is the old bell from the tower.

2. _____ was the worst experience I have ever had.

3. What is _____?

4. _____ of you standing at the back of the line should be patient.

5. Please take _____ to the dry cleaner.

6. Where did you find _____?

7. _____ should make the long hike more bearable.

8. Nolan stored _____ in the basement.

9. _____ are the exercises we have to have finished by Monday.

10. _____ was the longest day I've ever lived through!

◆ **Practice 25 Writing Your Own**

A. Write a sentence of your own for each of the following demonstrative pronouns. Make sure you use them as pronouns and not as adjectives.

1. this _____

2. that _____

3. these _____

4. those _____

B. Write five sentences of your own using demonstrative pronouns, and underline the demonstrative pronouns in each sentence. Make sure you use them as pronouns and not as adjectives.

1. _____

2. _____

3. _____

4. _____

5. _____

CHAPTER REVIEW

You might want to reread your answers to the questions in all the review boxes before you do the following exercises.

Review P r a c t i c e 1 **Reading** Refer to the paragraphs by Lois Smith Brady on page 246 to do the following exercises.

1. List four different subject pronouns from the paragraphs.

_____

_____

_____

_____

2. List the two object pronouns from the paragraphs.

_____

_____

3. List four possessive pronouns from the paragraphs.

_____

_____

_____

_____

Review P r a c t i c e 2 **Identifying** Underline the pronoun errors in each of the following sentences.

1. This here is a mystery.
2. You told she and I different stories.
3. These funky glasses are his'.
4. Noemi isn't as good with punctuation as him.
5. The whale blew air out it's blowhole.

6. Them are definitely mine.

7. We have to keep the surprise between you and I.

8. Julianna can talk faster than her.

9. The students and us took a rest from the examinations.

10. Jessica, Andy, and me decided to eat out tonight.

◆ *Review P r a c t i c e 3* **Correcting** Correct the pronoun errors in Review Practice 2 by rewriting each incorrect sentence.

◢ EDITING A STUDENT PARAGRAPH

Following is a paragraph written and revised by Angelina Santos in response to the writing assignment in this chapter. Read the paragraph, and underline each of her pronouns.

My's first date almost turned me against dating forever. It was a blind date to an amusement park set up by my best friend, Claire, who was going with her boyfriend, Roger. They and us made small talk during the two-hour drive. Once there, Norman was a perfect gentleman, buying Claire and I souvenirs, holding the door open for she and me, and always saying thank you. But all of that there changed once we decided to ride the Boomerang. Norman bought a huge lemonade right before we got on the ride. I told him that I didn't think it was a good idea to take the drink on the ride since we were going to be slung up and down from one end of the ride to the other. "Don't worry," he said, "it has a lid." Sure enough, as we accelerated forward and upward, the lid popped off, and lemonade went everywhere. By the time the ride stopped, I was covered in the sweet, sticky stuff. Needless to say, I was angry with him. He didn't even apologize, just asked me what my problem was and told me that he was a better sport than me. Unfortunately, this here wasn't the worst part of the date. As we were leaving the park, I got attacked by a bee and was stung on my neck. I had to ride home covered in lemonade with a throbbing bee sting on my neck and Norman, the person responsible for my torment, at my side. There was no small talk this time.

Collaborative Activity

Team up with a partner and place an X above the seven pronoun errors in Angelina's paragraph. Then, working together, use what you have learned in this chapter to correct these errors. Rewrite the paragraph with your corrections.

EDITING YOUR OWN PARAGRAPH

Now return to the paragraph you wrote and revised at the beginning of this chapter. Underline each of your pronouns.

Collaborative Activity

Exchange paragraphs with your partner, and circle any pronoun errors that you find in your partner's paragraph.

Individual Activity

On the Error Log in Appendix 4, record the pronoun errors that your partner found in your paragraph. To complete the writing process, correct these errors by rewriting your paragraph.

PRONOUN REFERENCE AND POINT OF VIEW

CHAPTER 15

✅ CHECKLIST for Correcting Problems with Pronoun Reference and Point of View

> ✔ Does every pronoun have a clear antecedent?
> ✔ Are pronouns as close as possible to the words they refer to?
> ✔ Do you maintain a single point of view?

Anytime you use a pronoun, it must clearly refer to a specific word. The word it refers to is called its **antecedent.** Two kinds of problems occur with pronoun references: The antecedent may be unclear, or the antecedent may be missing altogether. You should also be careful to stick to the same point of view in your writing. If, for example, you start out talking about "I," you should not shift to "you" in the middle of the sentence.

Notice how the pronouns in the following paragraph by William Kowinski work with their antecedents to communicate a consistent point of view.

The mall is a common experience for the majority of American youth; they have probably been going there all their lives. Some ran within their first large open space, saw their first fountain, bought their first toy, and read their first book in a mall. They may have smoked their first cigarette or first joint or turned them down, had their first kiss or lost their virginity in the mall parking lot. Teenagers in America now spend more time in the mall than anywhere else but home and school. Mostly it is their choice, but some of that mall time is put in as a result of two-paycheck and single-parent households and the lack of other viable alternatives.

In this paragraph, the author gives examples of the things teenagers have done at a mall. Before continuing in this chapter, take a moment to write about the things people do before making a purchase. Save your work because you will use it later in this chapter.

 WRITING ASSIGNMENT: PEOPLE'S SHOPPING HABITS

Have you ever taken the time to observe people at a shopping mall? What do they do? How are they different? Do gender and age play a part in people's actions in a crowd? What can you conclude about these people from their actions?

 REVISING YOUR WRITING

Revise the first draft of your paragraph before you focus on editing. Use the Revising Checklist on pages 24–25 to help you with your revision. Make sure your paragraph has a good topic sentence and is well developed. Then check your paragraph for unity, organization, and coherence.

PRONOUN REFERENCE

Sometimes a sentence is confusing because the reader can't tell what a pronoun is referring to. The confusion may occur because the pronoun's antecedent is unclear or is completely missing.

Unclear Antecedents

In the following examples, the word each pronoun is referring to is unclear.

Unclear: A box and a key lay on the beach. As Miguel reached for **it,** the surf came in. (Was Miguel reaching for the box or the key? Only Miguel knows for sure.)

Clear: A box and a key lay on the beach. As Miguel reached for **the box,** the surf came in.

Clear: A box and a key lay on the beach. As Miguel reached for **the key,** the surf came in.

Unclear:	Sandra told Denise that **she** shouldn't wear that color. (Does *she* refer to Sandra or Denise? Only the writer knows.)
Clear:	Sandra told Denise that **Sandra** shouldn't wear that color.
Clear:	Speaking with Denise, **Sandra** told **her** not to wear that color.

How can you be sure that every pronoun you use has a clear antecedent? First, you can proofread carefully. Probably an even better test, though, is to ask a friend to read what you have written and tell you if your meaning is clear or not.

Missing Antecedents

Every pronoun should have a clear antecedent, the word it refers to. But what happens when there is no antecedent at all? The writer's message is not communicated. Two words in particular should alert you to the possibility of missing antecedents: *it* and *they*.

The following sentences have missing antecedents:

| Missing Antecedent: | In a survey, it shows that most people are happy with the president. (What does *it* refer to? It has no antecedent.) |
| Clear: | **A recent survey** shows that most people are happy with the president. |

| Missing Antecedent: | **They** say that the wise know when to speak and when not to. (Who is *they*?) |
| Clear: | **An old saying** states that the wise know when to speak and when not to. |

REVIEWING PRONOUN REFERENCE

....

What is an antecedent?

_____

How can you be sure every pronoun you use has a clear antecedent?

_____

_____

What two words warn you that an antecedent may be missing?

_____   _____

 **P r a c t i c e 1 Identifying** Underline the pronouns with missing or unclear antecedents in the following sentences.

1. It says that you need a cup of sugar.
2. Billy and Damian drove together, yet he doesn't have his license.
3. Before Saul and Andrew left the house, he closed all the windows.
4. My checkbook and lunch were sitting on the counter, but when I reached for it, I tripped and fell.
5. I love to eat strawberries and chocolate, but it gives me a rash.
6. Kenny and Ed have known each other almost all their lives, but now he is moving away.
7. She bought a Coke and an ice cream and then spilled it all over herself.
8. They say a leopard never changes its spots.
9. When Tammy and Makesha decided to take a vacation, she didn't realize she was getting sick.
10. Your shorts and shirt are on your bed, but it's still too wet to wear.

P r a c t i c e 2 Identifying Put an X next to each sentence with a missing or unclear antecedent.

1. _____ They always tell me to look both ways before crossing the street.
2. _____ Talking to Tomás, Jim asked if he was interested in a job.
3. _____ It says that we can expect a booming economy.
4. _____ My grandparents always tell me that "pretty is as pretty does."
5. _____ Jon and Carlos decided to buy the same costume for the masquerade party, but he looks dumb in it.

6. _____ Even though Cindy and Lena like each other, she picks fights all the time.

7. _____ According to the news, we can expect more rain.

8. _____ Jeff told Marc that he would be leaving his job soon.

9. _____ In last year's poll, they revealed the cause of the crises.

10. _____ When I spoke to Randy and Gage, they told me where everyone was meeting.

P r a c t i c e   3   Correcting Correct the pronoun errors in Practice 2 by rewriting each incorrect sentence.

1. _____

2. _____

3. _____

4. _____

5. _____

6. _____

7. _____

8. _____

9. _____

10. _____

P r a c t i c e   4   Completing Fill in each blank in the following sentences with either a pronoun or a noun to make the sentence clear.

1. César, James, and Juan have gone to pick out a new car for _____.

2. I tried to grab the coffeepot and cups, but _____ fell to the ground first.

3. When she spoke to Esther, _____ said that you couldn't go.

4. After you saw Harim and David, what did _____ have to say?

5. I looked for my lost shoe and sweater and found the _____ under my bed.

6. When Jack and Frank argue, _____ always wins.

7. When the proud parents and _____ saw the new baby, they expressed their joy.

8. The roses and the jasmine both require direct sunlight, but the _____ need more water.

9. Whenever I look at Misty and Kelly, _____ always smiles.

10. I went to the market for bread and eggs, but I forgot _____ when I got to the checkout line.

♦ *P r a c t i c e* **5** **Writing Your Own**

A. Write a sentence of your own using pronouns that refer to the following antecedents.

1. Mary and Jane _____

2. The cash and the grocery list _____

3. Heath, Eddie, and Emilio _____

4. the news _____

5. an old saying _____

B. Write five sentences of your own using pronouns and antecedents, and underline the pronouns and antecedents in each sentence.

1. _____

2. _____

3. _____

4. _____

5. _____

SHIFTING POINT OF VIEW

Point of view refers to whether a statement is made in the first person, the second person, or the third person. Each person—or point of view—requires different pronouns. The following chart lists the pronouns for each point of view.

Point of View

First Person:	*I, we*
Second Person:	*you, you*
Third Person:	*he, she, it, they*

If you begin writing from one point of view, you should stay in that point of view. Do not shift to another point of view. For example, if you start out writing "I," you should continue with "I" and not shift to "you." Shifting point of view is a very common error in college writing.

Shift: If **a person** doesn't save money, **you** will have nothing left for retirement.

Correct: If **a person** doesn't save money, **he or she** will have nothing left for retirement.

Shift: I moved to Los Angeles because **you** could meet movie stars there.

Correct: I moved to Los Angeles because **I** could meet movie stars there.

REVIEWING POINT OF VIEW

What is point of view?

_____

_____

What does it mean to shift point of view?

_____

_____

P r a c t i c e   6   Identifying Underline the pronouns that shift point of view in the following sentences.

1. We should really leave now since you know the traffic will be bad.

2. They can ask the administrative assistant for help if you have questions.

3. I decided to put my money in my checking account because you can draw on it easily.

4. The dog needs to be careful in this area because you could easily get hit by a car.

5. I looked up at the stars; you could see them so clearly in the country.

6. Somebody keeps leaving me love notes on my desk, and you'd better confess.

7. Since I lost all my money last year on vacation, you should always carry traveler's checks.

8. We decided to get out of the hot sun, yet still they suffered.

9. People were looking around and asking questions; you were confused.

10. I've always wanted a little black dress because you know I'll look elegant in it.

P r a c t i c e   7   Identifying Put an X next to the sentence if the underlined pronouns shift point of view.

1. _____ I am nice to all strangers because you never know whom you might meet.

2. _____ People can't be too careful with our money.

3. _____ A body needs lots of water to keep you healthy.

4. _____ The workers decided to cross the picket line because they wanted to end the strike.

5. _____ People are not an island unto themselves, even if you think you are.

6. _____ I like going to rock concerts because they find it both exciting and relaxing.

7. _____ A person can get a great deal right now at the car dealership if he or she has good credit.

8. _____ John ate so many cookies that he got sick.

9. _____ One shouldn't listen at closed doors; <u>you</u> will never hear anything nice.

10. _____ A person should ask for help when <u>you</u> are in trouble.

◆ **P r a c t i c e 8 Correcting** Correct the pronoun errors in Practice 7 by rewriting each incorrect sentence.

1. _____

2. _____

3. _____

4. _____

5. _____

6. _____

7. _____

8. _____

9. _____

10. _____

◆ **P r a c t i c e 9 Completing** Fill in each blank in the following sentences with pronouns that stay in the same point of view.

1. I should listen to these different types of music since _____ never know what _____ will like.

2. They have had a wonderful time, and _____ plan on returning soon.

3. I buy my groceries in bulk because _____ know that _____ am getting a bargain.

4. Since you are the one in love with her, _____ should call her.

5. We have always loved this spot for picnics, and _____ intend to meet here at least once a year.

6. You can find the best sales at discount centers if _____ know how to look.

7. Marion ran for two miles before _____ ran out of energy.

8. They can't leave this issue alone; _____ are determined to resolve it tonight.

9. I enjoy walking in the park because _____ feel that nature relieves stress.

10. I won't admit to seeing the alien since _____ believe no one will listen.

◀ **P r a c t i c e   1 0   Writing Your Own**

A. Write a sentence of your own for each of the following pronouns. Be sure the pronouns have clear antecedents and do not shift point of view.

1. you _____

2. they _____

3. it _____

4. I _____

5. we _____

B. Write five sentences of your own using personal pronouns that have clear antecedents and do not shift point of view. Underline the pronouns and antecedents in each sentence.

1. _____

2. _____

3. _____

4. _____

5. _____

CHAPTER REVIEW

You might want to reread your answers to the questions in all the review boxes before you do the following exercises.

◆ **Review P r a c t i c e   1 Reading** Refer to the paragraph by William Kowinski on page 268 to do the following exercises.

1. List five pronouns and their antecedents from the paragraph.

PRONOUN   ANTECEDENT

_____   _____

_____   _____

_____   _____

_____   _____

_____   _____

2. Does the paragraph shift point of view?

_____

◆ **Review P r a c t i c e   2 Identifying** Label each of the following sentences U if the antecedent is unclear, M if the antecedent is missing, or S if the sentence shifts point of view.

1. _____ Both Tina and Abigail asked Jim out on a date, but he only said yes to her.

2. _____ It says that there is a big dance tonight.

3. _____ In a current medical study, it shows that more women are suffering heart attacks than ever before.

4. _____ I love to read in the bathtub because it relaxes you.

5. _____ Everyone is so busy that they didn't send Christmas cards this year.

6. _____ I put the cell phone and the credit card right here, but now I can't find it.

7. _____ In this poll, it says that more people are for the new law than against it.

8. _____ Jesse told Kevin that he was going to cook dinner that night.

9. _____ I am going to wear my fake Rolex watch and carry my fake Gucci purse because everyone will think you're rich.

10. _____ They say love is worth the pain.

Review P r a c t i c e   3   Correcting Correct the pronoun errors in Review Practice 2 by rewriting each sentence.

EDITING A STUDENT PARAGRAPH

Following is a paragraph written and revised by Sergio Cardenas in response to the writing assignment in this chapter. Read the paragraph, and underline each of his pronouns.

> They say that women are gatherers and men are hunters. You never truly understood this statement until I watched a man for a good hour at the mall. I knew he was married, or at least attached, by the mounds of shopping bags—but no female—surrounding him. The obviously overwhelmed man was slumped on a bench with only his upper torso visible due to all the shopping clutter. Eventually, the man's significant other relieved him of the packages, dropped off their 10-year-old son, and proceeded to search the mall for an outfit to match the shoes that she bought on sale. The bewildered yet relieved man took his son's hand, looked around, stood up, sat down, checked his watch, and yawned. Then he heard a sports announcer yell, "Touchdown!" It was on. The man and his son tracked the sound to a 64-inch big-screen TV just inside a department store entrance. Slowly he circled his prey, sniffing out the accessories. Then, decisively, he moved in for the kill. "Charge it!" he said.

Collaborative Activity

Team up with a partner, and put an X above the five pronoun errors in Sergio's paragraph. Then, working together, use what you have learned in this chapter to correct these errors. Rewrite the paragraph with your corrections.

EDITING YOUR OWN PARAGRAPH

Now return to the paragraph you wrote and revised at the beginning of this chapter. Underline each of your pronouns.

Collaborative Activity

Exchange paragraphs with your partner, and circle any pronoun reference or point-of-view errors you find in your partner's paper.

Individual Activity

On the Error Log in Appendix 4, record any pronoun errors that your partner found in your paragraph. To complete the writing process, correct these errors by rewriting your paragraph.

PRONOUN AGREEMENT

CHAPTER 16

✔️ CHECKLIST for Correcting Pronoun Agreement Problems

> ✔ Do all pronouns and their antecedents agree in number (singular or plural)?
>
> ✔ Do any pronouns that refer to indefinite pronouns agree in number?
>
> ✔ Are any pronouns used in a sexist way?

As you learned in Chapter 12, subjects and verbs must agree for clear communication. If the subject is singular, the verb must be singular; if the subject is plural, the verb must be plural. The same holds true for pronouns and the words they refer to—their *antecedents*. They must agree in number—both singular or both plural.

Notice that all the pronouns and their antecedents agree with one another in the following paragraph by David Gardner, former president of the University of California.

In a world of ever-accelerating competition and change in the conditions of the workplace, of ever-greater danger, and of ever-larger opportunities for those prepared to meet them, educational reform should focus on the goal of creating a Learning Society. At the heart of such a society is the commitment to a set of values and to a system of education that affords all members the opportunity to stretch their minds to full capacity, from early childhood through adulthood, learning more as the world itself changes. Such a society has as a basic foundation the idea that education is important not only because of what it contributes to one's career goals but also because of the value it adds to the general quality of one's life. Also at the heart of the Learning Society are educational opportunities extending far beyond the traditional institutions of learning, our schools and colleges. They extend into homes and workplaces; into libraries, art galleries, museums, and science centers; indeed, into every place where the individual can develop and mature in work and life. In our view, formal schooling in youth is the essential foundation for learning throughout one's life. But without lifelong learning, one's skills will become rapidly dated.

In this paragraph, the author talks about the importance of lifelong learning. Before continuing in this chapter, take a moment to write about your experiences with test taking. Save your work because you will use it later in this chapter.

 WRITING ASSIGNMENT: THE ROLE OF TESTS IN YOUR LIFE

How do you respond to tests? Are they a good way for you to learn? Or do they produce negative results for you? Explain one of your test-taking experiences.

 REVISING YOUR WRITING

Revise the first draft of your paragraph before you focus on editing. Use the Revising Checklist on pages 24–25 to help you with your revision. Make sure your paragraph has a good topic sentence and is well developed. Then check your paragraph for unity, organization, and coherence.

Usually, pronoun agreement is not a problem, as these sentences show:

Singular: **Mr. Parker** dropped **his** pager.

Plural: **Marianne** and **Marvin** gave **their** opinions.

INDEFINITE PRONOUNS

Pronoun agreement may become a problem with indefinite pronouns. Indefinite pronouns that are always singular give writers the most trouble.

NOT **One** of the contestants did **their** dance routine.
(How many students did the dance routine? Only one, so use a singular pronoun.)

CORRECT **One** of the contestants did **her** dance routine.

CORRECT **One** of the contestants did **his** dance routine.

NOT	**Somebody** left the lights on in **their** car. (How many people left their lights on? *One person,* so use a singular pronoun.)
CORRECT	**Somebody** left the lights on in **her** car.
CORRECT	**Somebody** left the lights on in **his** car.

Here is a list of indefinite pronouns that are always singular.

Singular Indefinite Pronouns

another	everybody	neither	one
anybody	everyone	nobody	other
anyone	everything	none	somebody
anything	little	no one	someone
each	much	nothing	something
either			

Hint: A few indefinite pronouns can be either singular or plural, depending on their meaning in the sentence. These pronouns are *any, all, more, most,* and *some.*

Singular: **Most** of the senior class had **its** orientation today.

Plural: **Most** of the seniors had **their** orientation today.

In the first sentence, *class* is considered a single body, so the singular pronoun *its* is used. In the second sentence, the *seniors* are individuals, so the plural pronoun *their* is used.

REVIEWING INDEFINITE PRONOUNS

Why should a pronoun agree with the word it refers to?

_____

Name five indefinite pronouns that are always singular.

_____ _____ _____ _____ _____

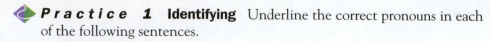

P r a c t i c e   1   Identifying Underline the correct pronouns in each of the following sentences.

1. Everybody has (his or her, their) forms completed.
2. Each of the committee members remembered (his or her, their) meeting.
3. Some of the horses shook (its, their) heads.
4. All of the men had (his, their) pictures taken with the actress.
5. No one forgot (his or her, their) books today.
6. More of the ceramic figurines had to have (its, their) surfaces reglazed.
7. Another of the Roman statues was missing (its, their) arm.
8. Everything has (its, their) proper place and time.
9. One of the doctors dropped (his or her, their) stethoscope.
10. Every one of these cats has had (its, their) tail bobbed.

P r a c t i c e   2   Identifying Put an X next to the sentence if the underlined pronoun does not agree with its antecedent.

1. _____ Paula and Rebecca got help revising <u>their</u> papers.
2. _____ Any one of the sculptors will have <u>his</u> or <u>her</u> cell phone on.
3. _____ Another of the officers turned <u>their</u> siren on.
4. _____ Everyone had <u>their</u> immunization shots.
5. _____ All of the man's hair has lost <u>their</u> color.
6. _____ At least one of the actresses will have <u>her</u> agent with her.
7. _____ Someone is remembering <u>their</u> childhood.
8. _____ Nobody knows where <u>their</u> tickets are.
9. _____ Each of the boys practiced <u>his</u> lessons.
10. _____ Anybody with <u>their</u> children should board the plane first.

P r a c t i c e   3   Correcting Correct the pronoun errors in Practice 2 by rewriting each incorrect sentence.

1. _____

2. _____

3. _____

4. _____

5. _____

6. _____

7. _____

8. _____

9. _____

10. _____

◆ *P r a c t i c e*   **4**   **Completing** Fill in each blank in the following sentences with a pronoun that agrees with its antecedent and makes sense.

1. Somebody is playing _____ stereo too loud.

2. Another of the beauty queens needs _____ dress fixed.

3. All of the cars had _____ engines overhauled.

4. Everyone should listen to _____ elders.

5. Each of my dogs had _____ hair groomed today.

6. Some of the singers lost _____ voices.

7. Something has _____ claws in me!

8. Any of the pantsuits, with _____ matching scarves, will look good on you.

9. Most of the roads have had _____ potholes fixed.

10. Everybody has _____ warmest clothes on.

◆ *P r a c t i c e*   **5**   **Writing Your Own**

A. Write a sentence of your own for each of the following sets of pronouns.

1. anybody, his or her _____

2. most, their _____

3. something, its _____

4. each, its _____

5. all, their _____

B. Write five sentences of your own using indefinite pronouns as subjects. Underline the pronouns in each sentence, and check for agreement.

1. _____

2. _____

3. _____

4. _____

5. _____

AVOIDING SEXISM

In the first section of this chapter, you learned that you should use singular pronouns to refer to singular indefinite pronouns. For example, the indefinite pronoun *someone* requires a singular pronoun, *his* or *her,* not the plural *their.* But what if you don't know whether the person referred to is male or female? Then you have a choice: (1) You can say "he or she" or "his or her"; (2) you can make the sentence plural; or (3) you can rewrite the sentence to avoid the problem altogether. What you should not do is ignore half the population by referring to all humans as males.

NOT	If **anyone** has questions, **they** should ask us.
NOT	If **anyone** has questions, **he** should ask us.
CORRECT	If **anyone** has questions, **he or she** should ask us.
CORRECT	If **people** have questions, **they** should ask us.
NOT	**Everyone** forgot to bring **their** spending money.
NOT	**Everyone** forgot to bring **his** spending money.
CORRECT	**Everyone** forgot to bring **his or her** spending money.
CORRECT	**All the travelers** forgot to bring **their** spending money.

Sexism in writing can also occur in ways other than with indefinite pronouns. We often assume that doctors, lawyers, and bank presidents are men and that nurses, teachers, and secretaries are women. But that is not accurate.

NOT   Each **policeman** is assigned **his** own locker.
               (Why automatically assume that every member of the
               police force is male?)

CORRECT   Each **police officer** is assigned **his or her** own locker.

NOT   The **chairman** should run all department meetings.
               (Because both men and women can head departments,
               boards, and committees, a more appropriate term is
               chairperson or *chair*.)

CORRECT   The **chair** should run all department meetings.

NOT   A good **receptionist** keeps **her** area clear of clutter.
               (Why leave the men who are receptionists out of the
               sentence?)

CORRECT   A good **receptionist** keeps **his or her** area clear of clutter.

CORRECT   Good **receptionists** keep **their** areas clear of clutter.

Reviewing Sexism in Writing

....

What is sexism in writing?

_____

*What are two ways to get around the problem of using male pronouns to
refer to both women and men?*

_____   _____

Give two other examples of sexism in writing.

_____   _____

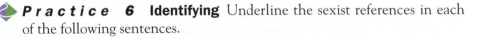 **P r a c t i c e   6   Identifying** Underline the sexist references in each
of the following sentences.

1. Each administrative assistant should leave a number where she can be
   reached.

2. A welder must always wear his face shield.

3. No one can complain about his paycheck this month.

4. Everyone has his own way of doing things.

5. Ask a salesman for his advice on this product.

6. Somebody just drove his car over the median.

7. With a little instruction, anyone can balance her checkbook.

8. Take this to your lawyer for his signature.

9. Each person is responsible for his own ride.

10. One of the receptionists didn't lock her file cabinet.

◆ **P r a c t i c e   7   Identifying** Put an X next to the sentence if it has sexist references.

1. _____ A nurse left her name tag on the counter.

2. _____ Each of my co-workers was rewarded for submitting his or her ideas.

3. _____ A firefighter learns how to fight his way through smoke and flames.

4. _____ Ask a teacher if she knows the answer.

5. _____ A whistle tells the construction worker when it is time to eat his or her lunch.

6. _____ Each of the students passed his midterm exam.

7. _____ Somebody forgot to turn off her computer in the computer lab.

8. _____ Every mailman must deliver all the mail in his bag every day.

9. _____ A good manager always listens to his employees.

10. _____ The doctors gave their patients good advice.

◆ **P r a c t i c e   8   Correcting** Correct the pronoun errors in Practice 7 by rewriting each incorrect sentence.

1. _____

2. _____

3. _____

4. _____

5. _____

6. _____

7. _____

8. _____

9. _____

10. _____

P r a c t i c e   9   Completing Fill in each blank in the following sentences with a pronoun that is correct.

1. I heard that one of the gardeners broke _____ truck.

2. An opera singer can stretch _____ vocal cords to many octaves.

3. No customer in our restaurant will have _____ MasterCard refused.

4. Each child should bring a permission slip signed by _____ parents.

5. All of the dentists have _____ teeth checked once a year.

6. Ask one of the chefs if you can taste _____ dish.

7. Scuba divers should check _____ air tanks periodically.

8. If a mechanic wants to make more money, _____ should stay open for business on the weekends.

9. Someone trimmed _____ hair in the bathroom and left a mess.

10. A race-car driver's main priority is _____ tires.

P r a c t i c e   1 0   Writing Your Own

A. Write a sentence of your own for each of the following antecedents. Include at least one pronoun in each sentence.

1. politician _____

2. flight attendant _____

3. dancer _____

4. secret agent _____

5. trucker _____

B. Write five sentences of your own using antecedents and pronouns that avoid sexist references. Underline the pronouns in each sentence.

1. _____

2. _____

3. _____

4. _____

5. _____

CHAPTER REVIEW

You might want to reread your answers to the questions in all the review boxes before you do the following exercises.

◆ *Review P r a c t i c e 1* **Reading** Refer to the paragraph by David Gardner on pages 281–282 to do the following exercises.

A. List five pronouns and their antecedents from the paragraph.

PRONOUN	ANTECEDENT
_____	_____
_____	_____
_____	_____
_____	_____
_____	_____

B. Write two sentences with sexist references based on Gardner's paragraph.

1. _____

2. _____

 **Review P r a c t i c e   2 Identifying** Underline the pronoun or sexist errors in each of the following sentences.

1. Everyone who wants his parking validated should see the receptionist.

2. If a surfer isn't careful, she could get hit by her surfboard.

3. Anyone can look like they're rich, even if they aren't.

4. Most of the birds have built its nests.

5. A good writer keeps her notebook close by.

6. It is a law that a motorcyclist must wear his helmet.

7. A policeman gave warnings to the speeding motorists.

8. Somebody left their laundry at the laundromat.

9. Each of the cherries had their pit removed.

10. Waitresses work hard for their tips.

 **Review P r a c t i c e   3 Correcting** Correct the pronoun errors, including sexist references, in Review Practice 2 by rewriting each incorrect sentence.

EDITING A STUDENT PARAGRAPH

Following is a paragraph written and revised by Jarrod Cervantes in response to the writing assignment in this chapter. Read the paragraph; then underline each of his pronouns once and their antecedents twice.

> I know how to write. I know how to structure my
>
> thoughts in an organized, cohesive manner, and I
>
> can convey those thoughts in written form. However, I
>
> cannot write on command. To say to me, "OK, you have X
>
> amount of time to answer this midterm prompt," causes
>
> instant paralysis of the brain. I brainstorm. I pray. I want
>
> to throw up. But my brain doesn't open. According to the
>
> teacher, anybody can pass a timed writing exam if he is
>
> prepared. But that is not the case when I face a written

exam. I can study for a week straight, draft outlines, and remember important facts. But all of these efforts magically disappear when I receive the test. I look around and notice everyone with their heads bent, frantically writing away. I hear somebody tapping his pencil on the desk and wonder if they are as nervous as I am. Then the fear of judgment settles in. Each teacher, in her infinite wisdom, doesn't seem to realize that she's passing judgment on *me*, not just my writing, for my writing is a reflection of myself.

Collaborative Activity

Team up with a partner, and place an X above the six pronoun errors in Jarrod's paragraph. Then, working together, use what you have learned in this chapter to correct these errors. Rewrite the paragraph with your corrections.

EDITING YOUR OWN PARAGRAPH

Now return to the paragraph you wrote and revised at the beginning of this chapter. Underline your pronouns once and antecedents twice.

Collaborative Activity

Exchange paragraphs with your partner, and circle any pronoun agreement errors or sexist references that you find in your partner's paragraph.

Individual Activity

On the Error Log in Appendix 4, record any pronoun errors that your partner found in your paragraph. To complete the writing process, correct these errors by rewriting your paragraph.

UNIT TESTS

Here are some exercises that test your understanding of all the material in this unit: Pronoun Problems, Pronoun Reference and Point of View, and Pronoun Agreement.

Unit Test 1 Identifying

Underline the pronoun errors in each of the following sentences.

1. You are just as big hearted as him.
2. I will make my's own destiny.
3. I casually surveyed the room over the rim of my dark glasses, but you couldn't see anyone.
4. Alyssa and Martha both ran as fast as they could, but she won the race.
5. A sitter should spend some time simply playing with her charges.
6. Jeremy and her are designing my furniture.
7. Anybody can become familiar with his own writing process.
8. Them in the back seat are going to storage.
9. Somebody has their hands in my cookie jar!
10. They say a bird in the hand is worth two in the bush.
11. One of the accountants left his calculator behind.
12. Diane loses her patience more with Jim than with I.
13. In last year's books, it shows a marked rise in profits.
14. You cannot eat those there; they will spoil your appetite.
15. During the outdoor symphony, him and her proposed to one another at the same time.
16. When Julia heard Cindy and he yell, she went racing toward them.
17. These lemon cakes are her's.
18. Each of the toys came with their own batteries.
19. People shouldn't fear the sun altogether since you do get several essential vitamins from its light.
20. These here were left outside and are ruined.

Unit Test 2 Correcting

Correct the pronoun errors in Unit Test 1 by rewriting each sentence.

Unit Test 3 Identifying

Underline the pronoun errors in the following paragraph.

They say that the apple doesn't fall far from the tree, and I guess that's true. My mom is a chocolate lover. Brittany and Jennifer, my twin sisters, and me are chocolate lovers, too. Perhaps the word "love" isn't the right choice because this here is not just a craving, but an obsession. We will eat any kind: dark, light, white, Swiss, German, with nuts, without nuts, and so on. I remember when Brittany and Jennifer were just five years old. Mom had given them and I these huge chocolate bunnies for Easter. Being the older sister, you know that I was entitled to a percentage of that chocolate. So I bullied the twins into giving me the ears. I fell asleep that night dreaming of all that warm, smooth, sweet stuff, until I was rudely awakened by the sound of fire engines and my screaming family. Our living room was on fire. The firemen said that the fire was started in the fireplace. Somebody had tried to burn their chocolate bunny. The bubbling chocolate spilled onto the carpet and caught fire. Imagine my surprise to learn the bunny was mine. In this case, revenge wasn't so sweet. Mom and Dad denied us our chocolate for one month. From that moment on, I respected my sisters' rights to have and to hold her own chocolate. I have to admit that the twins have a greater passion for chocolate than me because she opened up her own chocolate shop, *Sweet Chocolate*, which Mom now manages. The other twin is now the chief executive officer of a top-name chocolate factory, and she loves her job. But I too am doing my part in this legacy: I am a wife and a mother who is passing on her's chocolate genetics—in moderation, of course—to her children.

Unit Test 4 Correcting

Correct the pronoun errors in Unit Test 3 by rewriting the paragraph.

UNIT WRITING ASSIGNMENTS

1. What do you think the accompanying picture is pointing out? Are the people related? What is the adult trying to teach the child? Is the child responding? Why or why not? Are they happy, sad, frustrated? Use your imagination to explain the type of relationship between the adult and child.

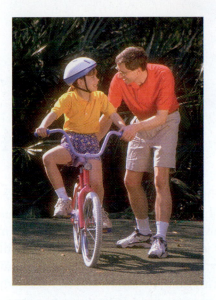

2. Your best friend has asked you to design the cover of his first rap CD, *Incognito*. What would your design be? Why this design? What colors would you use and why? How effective do you think your cover will be in marketing your friend's CD?

3. If you had to pick one word to describe your room, what would it be? Give examples of things in your room to help explain why you chose this word.

4. Most people feel there is a right way and a wrong way to do a particular chore, such as washing the car or mowing the lawn. Is there a particular chore that you insist be done a certain way? What is the chore? Explain the right way to go about doing it and the reason your way is the best.

5. Create your own assignment (with the help of your instructor), and write a response to it.

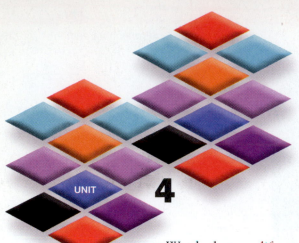

MODIFIERS

Words that modify—usually called adjectives and adverbs—add details to sentences, describing, limiting, or identifying so that sentences become more vivid and interesting. They work like accessories in our everyday lives. Without jewelry, scarves, ties, and cuff links, we are still dressed. But accessories give a little extra flair to our wardrobe. Without modifiers, our writing would be bland, boring, and lifeless. However, to use adjectives and adverbs correctly, you need to learn about their different forms and functions.

In the chapters in this unit, you will learn about adjectives, adverbs, and various problems with the placement of these words in sentences:

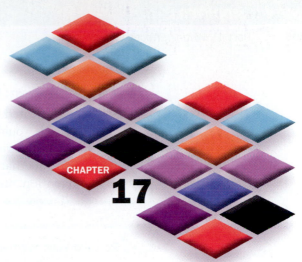

ADJECTIVES

 CHECKLIST for Using Adjectives Correctly

> ✔ Are all adjectives that show comparison used correctly?
> ✔ Are the forms of *good* and *bad* used correctly?

Adjectives are modifiers. They help us communicate more clearly (I have a *brown* jacket; I want a *black* one) and vividly (the concert was *loud* and *wild*). Without adjectives, our language would be drab and boring.

Notice how the adjectives work in the following paragraph by Rebecca Zurier.

The story of the American firehouse is part of that particular social institution, the American fire company. The building's size, shape, and character reflect the organization's development from a voluntary association—a cross between a lodge and a baseball team—into a branch of municipal government. Eighteenth-century firehouses were simply places to store a town's supply of fire engines, buckets, hooks, and ladders. Built in an easily accessible location, the firehouse could be a plain wooden shed or incorporated into a larger public structure—usually brick but sometimes stone—that served several functions. As responsibility for fire protection shifted from the community at large to private, fraternal companies, firehouses took on the character of clubhouses, with lavish second-story meeting rooms over the garage. Before long, the buildings themselves came to be seen as flamboyant architectural emblems—as distinctive a part of the company's regalia as its uniform.

In this paragraph, Rebecca Zurier talks about the evolution of the firehouse in the United States. Before continuing in this chapter, take a moment to write about something you would like to build or invent. Save your work because you will use it later in this chapter.

WRITING ASSIGNMENT: MY CREATION

Have you ever created something from scratch? Is there a building or product that you would like to design to make life easier? Maybe it's a walk-through aquarium or a pencil that won't run out of lead or computer software that keeps your computer from crashing. Think of a helpful invention, and write a paragraph describing it.

 REVISING YOUR WRITING

Revise the first draft of your paragraph before you focus on editing. Use the Revising Checklist on pages 24–25 to help you with your revision. Make sure your paragraph has a good topic sentence, is well developed, and is well organized. Then check your paragraph for unity and coherence.

USING ADJECTIVES

Adjectives are words that modify—or describe—nouns or pronouns. Adjectives often tell how something or someone looks: *dark, light, tall, short, large, small*. Most adjectives come before the words they modify, but with linking verbs (such as *is, are, look, become*, and *feel*), adjectives follow the words they modify.

Adjectives Before a Noun:	We walked down the **narrow, winding** path.
Adjectives After a Linking Verb:	The path was **narrow** and **winding**.

REVIEWING ADJECTIVES

What are adjectives?

_____

Where can you find adjectives in a sentence?

_____

P r a c t i c e   1   Identifying Underline the adjectives in each of the following sentences. Do not count possessive pronouns as adjectives. Some sentences have more than one adjective.

1. My long, white dress was caught in the car door.
2. The reunion committee is meeting at noon.
3. You are rude to say those mean things.
4. This is an important date.
5. Eugene's wedding was emotional and fun.
6. Katie got a new car for her eighteenth birthday.
7. The den carpet has brown soda stains.
8. Friskie, our tabby cat, had five kittens.
9. The weather forecast says we will have three feet of snow.
10. Harriet wrote a long list for the grocery store.

P r a c t i c e   2   Identifying Put an X next to the sentence if the underlined word is not an adjective.

1. _____ This is a boring day.
2. _____ The computer was old.
3. _____ You wrote a good essay.
4. _____ My brother is strong and brave.
5. _____ Our last vacation was in May.
6. _____ Could you hand me the yellow pencil?
7. _____ The new telephone rang loudly.
8. _____ Jimmy was nervous and worried.
9. _____ My English professor would not accept my late assignment.
10. _____ *The Rover* is a funny play.

P r a c t i c e   3   Correcting Correct the errors in Practice 2 by listing the correct adjectives here.

1. _____   4. _____

2. _____   5. _____

3. _____   6. _____

7. _____   9. _____

8. _____   10. _____

◆ *P r a c t i c e   4*   **Completing** Fill in each blank in the following paragraph with an adjective that makes sense.

Yesterday, I drove to the department store to buy a pair of (1) _____ shoes. I needed them to match my (2) _____ dress, which I bought for the (3) _____ party. The shoes looked (4) _____ and (5) _____. When I got to the store, the parking lot was (6) _____, and I had a (7) _____ time finding a place to park. Then I reached for my purse, and I was (8) _____ when I realized that I had left it in my apartment. I had to drive all the way back home to retrieve my (9) _____ purse because that's where all of my money was. When I finally got back to the store, it took me (10) _____ minutes to find another parking spot. At that point, I was determined to find that pair of shoes!

◆ *P r a c t i c e   5*   **Writing Your Own**

A. Write a sentence of your own for each of the following adjectives.

1. pretty _____

2. scared _____

3. friendly _____

4. hopeful _____

5. blue _____

B. Write five sentences of your own using adjectives. Underline the adjectives in each sentence.

1. _____

2. _____

3. _____

4. _____

5. _____

COMPARING WITH ADJECTIVES

Most adjectives have three forms: a **basic** form, a **comparative** form (used to compare two items or indicate a greater degree), and a **superlative** form (used to compare three or more items or indicate the greatest degree).

For positive comparisons, adjectives form the comparative and superlative in two different ways.

1. For one-syllable adjectives and some two-syllable adjectives, use *-er* to compare two items and *-est* to compare three or more items.

Basic	Comparative (used to compare two items)	Superlative (used to compare three or more items)
large	larger	largest
cool	cooler	coolest
rain	rainier	rainiest
happy	happier	happiest

2. For some two-syllable adjectives and all longer adjectives, use *more* to compare two items and *most* to compare three or more items.

Basic	Comparative (used to compare two items)	Superlative (used to compare three or more items)
loyal	more loyal	most loyal
hopeful	more hopeful	most hopeful
beautiful	more beautiful	most beautiful
trustworthy	more trustworthy	most trustworthy

For negative comparisons, use *less* to compare two items and *least* to compare three or more items.

	Comparative (used to compare	Superlative (used to compare
Basic	two items)	three or more items)
wild	less wild	least wild
silly	less silly	least silly
enormous	less enormous	least enormous

Hint: Some adjectives are not usually compared. For example, one person cannot be "more dead" than another. Here are some more examples.

broken	*final*	*square*
empty	*impossible*	*supreme*
equal	*singular*	*unanimous*

REVIEWING ADJECTIVE FORMS

When do you use the comparative form of an adjective?

_____

When do you use the superlative form of an adjective?

_____

How do one-syllable and some two-syllable adjectives form the comparative and superlative in positive comparisons?

_____

How do some two-syllable adjectives and all longer adjectives form the comparative and superlative in positive comparisons?

_____

How do you form negative comparisons?

_____

◆ **P r a c t i c e 6 Identifying** Identify the underlined adjectives in the following sentences as basic (B), comparative (C), or superlative (S).

1. _____ Ivan Rodriguez is the <u>most talented</u> catcher in professional baseball.
2. _____ Inez is so <u>generous</u> to let me borrow her notes.
3. _____ This year's talent show was even <u>funnier</u> than last year's.
4. _____ We ran to the <u>front</u> door and knocked loudly.
5. _____ There is a <u>black</u> mark on your chin.
6. _____ The gardens in your backyard are <u>less healthy</u> than those in your front yard.
7. _____ James is the <u>most spoiled</u> child I know.
8. _____ My friend is buying the <u>latest</u> album by Justin Timberlake.
9. _____ Yvette's New Year's resolution is to be <u>less disrespectful</u> to her parents.
10. _____ Are you taking that <u>exciting</u> chemistry class this semester?

◆ **P r a c t i c e   7   Identifying** Underline the adjectives in each of the following sentences. Do not count possessive pronouns as adjectives.

1. This month was hotter than last month.
2. Our hotel was more expensive than yours.
3. I have less valuable jewelry than my sister.
4. This was the most stressful day of the week.
5. Bong Yul gave the longest presentation of anyone in the class.
6. My dad was less worried about my grades than about my job at the department store.
7. Chris's car is more economical than mine.
8. The longest line is the one for tickets.
9. I know that you are richer than I am.
10. Tabitha was the least likely person to cut class.

◆ **P r a c t i c e   8   Correcting** Change the positive comparisons in Practice 7 to negative and the negative comparisons to positive.

1. _____

2. _____

3. _____

4. _____

5. _____

6. _____

7. _____

8. _____

9. _____

10. _____

◆ **P r a c t i c e   9   Completing** Fill in each blank in the following paragraph with the correct comparative or superlative form of the adjective in parentheses.

   I was cleaning out the refrigerator when I realized that there were three packs of sandwich meat. I threw out the (1) _____ (old) one and put the other two on a shelf where I would remember to use them. The orange juice that I made a week ago tasted (2) _____ (bitter) than I thought it should, so I threw that away also. But those were not the (3) _____ (gross) things in there. I found a piece of fruit that was (4) _____ (black) than chocolate, and I think it used to be a peach. I also found a bag of grapes that looked (5) _____ (wrinkled) than raisins, a jar of jelly with furry white spots on top, and some leftover Chinese food that smelled (6) _____ (rotten) than an old gym sock. When I opened the freezer, I found that the ice cream was (7) _____ (frozen) than the meat, which had turned a yucky gray color. There was freezer burn on everything but the frozen burritos, which were the (8) _____ (appetizing) things in there. I couldn't believe it had been two months or (9) _____ (long) since we had cleaned the refrigerator and freezer! When my roommate got home, she shook her head and thanked me for doing the (10) _____ (disgusting) job in the house.

► P r a c t i c e   1 0   Writing Your Own

A. Write a sentence of your own for each of the following comparative and superlative forms.

1. most frustrated _____

2. less hassled _____

3. more flexible _____

4. least friendly _____

5. most pleasant _____

B. Write five sentences of your own using comparative and superlative adjectives, and underline the adjectives in each sentence.

1. _____

2. _____

3. _____

4. _____

5. _____

COMMON ADJECTIVE ERRORS

Two types of problems occur with adjectives used in comparisons.

1. Instead of using one method for forming the comparative or superlative, both are used. That is, both *-er* and *more* or *less* are used to compare two items or both *-est* and *most* or *least* are used to compare three or more items.

NOT	The new glue was **more weaker** than the old glue.
CORRECT	The new glue was **weaker** than the old glue.

NOT	Derrick was the **most smartest** employee of the company.
CORRECT	Derrick was the **smartest** employee of the company.

2. The second type of error occurs when the comparative or superlative is used with the wrong number of items. The comparative form should be used for two items and the superlative for three or more items.

NOT	Post-it Notes were the **newest** of the two products.
CORRECT	Post-it Notes were the **newer** of the two products.

NOT	Superglue was the **stickier** of the many 3M products.
CORRECT	Superglue was the **stickiest** of the many 3M products.

REVIEWING COMMON ADJECTIVE ERRORS

Can you ever use -er + more or -est + most?

_____

When do you use the comparative form of an adjective?

_____

When do you use the superlative form of an adjective?

_____

◆ **P r a c t i c e   1 1   Identifying** Put a C next to underlined adjectives in the following sentences that are correct.

1. _____ Which of these three brands of batteries is the <u>best</u>?
2. _____ Mikela is the <u>shorter</u> of her five sisters.
3. _____ Tiger Woods is the <u>most popular</u> golfer at the tournament.
4. _____ Today I did the <u>most craziest</u> thing.
5. _____ We are going to New York to see my mother's <u>younger</u> brother.
6. _____ This office is <u>more busier</u> than the one next door.
7. _____ Mandy's coin collection is <u>older</u> than mine.
8. _____ Zack is <u>least honest</u> than Nathan.

9. _____ This essay assignment is <u>more harder</u> than the last one.

10. _____ The <u>quietest</u> person in the class is Tim.

◆ **P r a c t i c e   1 2** **Identifying** Underline the incorrect adjective forms in each of the following sentences.

1. *Lord of the Rings: The Return of the King* was the most longest movie I have ever seen.

2. My brother is the shortest of the two of us.

3. This class is the most boring of my five classes.

4. Seth is watching his most favoritest cartoon.

5. Yours is the prettiest house on the block.

6. Vanity is the ugliest sin.

7. The fruit at the farmer's market was less fresh than at the roadside stand.

8. Ray is the most friendliest of all of my friends.

9. My voice is the louder among all of my family members.

10. Janette likes the most confusing mystery novels.

◆ **P r a c t i c e   1 3** **Correcting** Correct the five adjective errors in Practice 11 and the five adjective errors in Practice 12 by rewriting each incorrect sentence.

1. _____

2. _____

3. _____

4. _____

5. _____

6. _____

7. _____

8. _____

9. _____

10. _____

◆ **P r a c t i c e   14   Completing** Fill in each blank in the following paragraph with the correct adjective form.

Science is the (1) _____ (more difficult/most difficult) subject for me to understand. No matter how hard I study, I never get (2) _____ (higher/more higher) grades than C's on my science exams. My sister Kimber and I usually have the same GPA, but I have always considered myself to be a little (3) _____ (smarter/more smarter) than she is. Most subjects just seem (4) _____ (easier/more easier) for me. However, when it comes to the sciences, she is definitely the (5) _____ (more talented/most talented) one. She takes good notes, so studying is usually a lot (6) _____ (least stressful/less stressful) for her. I personally hate studying, but maybe that's because my notes are (7) _____ (more unorganized/most unorganized) than Kimber's. I think that science itself is the (8) _____ (scariest/most scariest) thing I've ever had to learn. If someone could find a way to make science classes (9) _____ (more enjoyable/most enjoyable), I think I would learn to be (10) _____ (more relaxed/most relaxed) about them.

◆ **P r a c t i c e   15   Writing Your Own**

A. Write a sentence of your own for each of the following adjectives.

1. kindest _____

2. more helpful _____

3. most gorgeous _____

4. smaller _____

5. more pleasant _____

B. Write five sentences of your own using comparative and superlative adjectives, and underline the adjectives in each sentence.

1. _____

2. _____

3. _____

4. _____

5. _____

USING *GOOD* AND *BAD* CORRECTLY

The adjectives *good* and *bad* are irregular. They do not form the comparative and superlative like most other adjectives. Here are the correct forms for these two irregular adjectives:

Basic	**Comparative** (used to compare two items)	**Superlative** (used to compare three or more items)
good	better	best
bad	worse	worst

Problems occur with *good* and *bad* when writers don't know how to form their comparative and superlative forms.

NOT more better, more worse, worser, most best, most worst, bestest, worstest

CORRECT better, worse, best, worst

These errors appear in sentences in the following ways:

NOT These overexposed pictures are the **bestest** mistake that we ever made.

CORRECT These overexposed pictures are the **best** mistake that we ever made.

NOT The drought got **more worse** with each dry day.

CORRECT The drought got **worse** with each dry day.

REVIEWING *Good* AND *Bad*

What are the three forms of good?

_____   _____   _____

What are the three forms of bad?

_____   _____   _____

◆ **P r a c t i c e   1 6   Identifying** Put a C next to underlined forms of *good* and *bad* in the following sentences that are correct.

1. _____ That was the <u>bestest</u> pie you have ever made.

2. _____ I need a <u>better</u> grade on this test to pass the class.

3. _____ Professional wrestling is the <u>most worst</u> sport anyone could have invented.

4. _____ Washing the dog inside the house was a <u>bad</u> decision.

5. _____ Our trip to Tulsa was the <u>most best</u> vacation we have ever taken.

6. _____ I like the pink paint <u>more better</u> than the blue paint.

7. _____ Megan did a <u>good</u> job on her oral presentation.

8. _____ The boys' attitudes are <u>more good</u> than the girls'.

9. _____ My stomach ache is <u>worse</u> than it was 20 minutes ago.

10. _____ Our cats have taken the <u>best</u> seats in the house.

◆ **P r a c t i c e   1 7   Identifying** Underline the incorrect adjective form in each of the following sentences.

1. This was the worst day of my life.

2. That's the bestest decision I have heard so far.

3. I liked the movie, but I thought the ending could have been better.

4. After she stood out in the rain, Charity's cold got worse.

5. Carmenita likes take-and-bake pizza better than delivery.

6. I don't know anything more worse than your news.

7. I ate at the best Mediterranean restaurant in town.

8. Lee was surfing the Internet to find the most best deal on a Chevy Blazer.

9. My cats always behave more good than my dogs.

10. Of all my friends, Jameson has the worse handwriting.

P r a c t i c e   1 8   Correcting Correct the five adjective errors in Practice 16 and the five adjective errors in Practice 17 by rewriting each incorrect sentence.

1. _____

2. _____

3. _____

4. _____

5. _____

6. _____

7. _____

8. _____

9. _____

10. _____

P r a c t i c e   1 9   Completing Fill in each blank in the following paragraph with the correct form of *good* and *bad*.

Last Tuesday, I was having a really (1) _____ day. I was late to work, which made my boss think that I was the (2) _____ employee he has. While I was on my lunch break, my car broke down, and the mechanic said I had a (3) _____ transmission. To make matters (4) _____, he said it would cost $500 to replace it. I had to borrow my (5) _____ friend's bicycle to get home, and then I got a ticket for not wearing a helmet. I honestly thought that day was never going to get (6) _____. When I finally got home, I checked my mail and found some (7) _____ news. There was a

card from my grandma with a $20 bill inside, thanking me for being
the (8) _____ granddaughter she has. (I happen to be the *only*
granddaughter she has, but that's another story.) Grandma wished
me a (9) _____ day and reminded me to call her. At that point,
I realized that I am very lucky to have someone who wants to talk to
me, even when I have nothing (10) _____ to talk about.

◆ **P r a c t i c e   2 0**   **Writing Your Own**

A. Write a sentence of your own using the following forms of *good* and *bad.*

1. good _____

2. better _____

3. worse _____

4. bad _____

5. best _____

B. Write five sentences of your own using forms of *good* and *bad*, and underline these forms.

1. _____

2. _____

3. _____

4. _____

5. _____

CHAPTER REVIEW

You might want to reread your answers to the questions in the review
boxes before you do the following exercises.

◆ **Review P r a c t i c e   1**   **Reading** Refer to the paragraph by Rebecca
Zurier on page 297 to do the following exercises.

1. List five adjectives.

   _____

   _____

   _____

   _____

   _____

2. Provide the comparative and superlative forms of each of the following adjectives from Zurier's paragraph.

Basic	**Comparative**	**Superlative**
lavish	_____	_____
plain	_____	_____
accessible	_____	_____
large	_____	_____
flamboyant	_____	_____

 **Review P r a c t i c e 2 Identifying** Underline the incorrect adjectives in each of the following sentences.

1. The bestest job I ever had was at Mike's Pizza.
2. Tiffany was more lazier than Sally was today.
3. The most biggest flag flies over the gas station.
4. Of the two boys, John was the tallest.
5. When Cheyenne got engaged, she couldn't have been more happier.
6. Yesterday I felt lousy, but today I feel worser.
7. We have small mice in our attic that are the most cutest things I've ever seen.
8. There are 12 pine trees on our street, and the taller one is in our front yard.

9. Your first essay was good, but this is even more good.

10. The bananas on the counter are more riper today.

◆ **Review P r a c t i c e 3 Correcting** Correct the incorrect adjectives in Review Practice 2 by rewriting the sentences.

EDITING A STUDENT PARAGRAPH

Following is a paragraph written and revised by Brady Johnson in response to the writing assignment in this chapter. Read the paragraph, and underline each of his adjectives. Look specifically for comparative and superlative adjectives.

> One thing that I have always wanted to invent is an automatic vacuum for the house. It would be like the ones used in swimming pools, only more better. Since my parents started making me vacuum our house five years ago, it has been my least favorite chore. I hate dragging the heavy vacuum up and down the stairs, and the cord is never long enough. If I could invent an automatic vacuum, it would have a more thinner body, so it could go easily down the halls. It would also have a more longer cord and more powerful suction. A person could just turn it on and let it go. Of course, it would suck up anything in its path, so a person would have to be careful about what was left on the ground. Overall, though, I think it would make vacuuming the most easiest task.

Collaborative Activity

Team up with a partner, and mark an X above the four adjectives that are not in the correct form. Then, working together, use what you have learned in this chapter to correct these errors.

EDITING YOUR OWN PARAGRAPH

Now return to the paragraph you wrote and revised at the beginning of this chapter. Underline each of your adjectives.

Collaborative Activity

Exchange paragraphs with your partner, and circle any adjective errors that you find in your partner's paragraph. Check specifically the comparative and superlative adjectives.

Individual Activity

On the Error Log in Appendix 4, record any adjective errors that your partner found in your paragraph. To complete the writing process, correct these errors by rewriting your paragraph.

ADVERBS

☑ CHECKLIST for Using Adverbs

> ✔ Are all adverbs that show comparison used correctly?
> ✔ Are *good/well* and *bad/badly* used correctly?

Like adjectives, adverbs help us communicate more clearly (she walked *quickly*) and more vividly (he sat *comfortably*). They make sentences more interesting.

See how the adverbs work in the following paragraphs by Russell Baker.

Scientists have been struck by the fact that things that break down virtually never get lost, while things that get lost hardly ever break down.

A furnace, for example, will invariably break down at the depth of the first winter cold wave, but it will never get lost. A woman's purse, which after all does have some inherent capacity for breaking down, hardly ever does; it almost invariably chooses to get lost.

Some persons believe this constitutes evidence that inanimate objects are not entirely hostile to man and that negotiated peace is possible. After all, they point out, a furnace could infuriate a man even more thoroughly by getting lost than by breaking down, just as a glove could upset him far more by breaking down than by getting lost.

In this paragraph, Russell Baker points out that inanimate objects can let you down when you least expect it. Before continuing in this chapter, take a moment to write about an unexpected experience you have had. Save your work because you will use it later in the chapter.

WRITING ASSIGNMENT: THE UNEXPECTED

Unexpected events happen all the time in life—especially with inanimate objects. What unexpected experiences have you had? Who or what was involved? How did you handle the unexpected element? Write a paragraph explaining a particular event that comes to mind.

 REVISING YOUR WRITING

Revise the first draft of your paragraph before you focus on editing. Use the Revising Checklist on pages 24–25 to help you with your revision. Make sure your paragraph has a good topic sentence, is well developed, and is well organized. Then check your paragraph for unity and coherence.

USING ADVERBS

Adverbs modify verbs, adjectives, and other adverbs. They answer the questions *how? when? where? how often?* and *to what extent?* Look at the following examples.

How:	The air bag inflated **instantly** during the accident.
When:	My car **always** breaks down when I have an important date.
Where:	Don't park your car **there.**
How often:	Maggie drives to Los Angeles **weekly.**
To what extent:	Traffic is **extremely** heavy on the weekends.

Some words are always adverbs, including *here, there, not, never, now, again, almost, often,* and *well*.

Other adverbs are formed by adding *-ly* to an adjective:

Adjective	Adverb
light	lightly
loud	loudly
busy	busily

Hint: Not all words that end in *-ly* are adverbs. Some, such as *friendly*, *early*, *lonely*, *chilly*, and *lively*, are adjectives.

REVIEWING ADVERBS

What are adverbs?

_____

What five questions do adverbs answer?

_____ _____ _____ _____ _____

List four words that are always adverbs.

_____

How do many adverbs end?

_____

◆ **P r a c t i c e   1   Identifying** Underline the adverbs in each of the following sentences.

1. He spoke rudely to me.
2. We are meeting promptly at 5:00 p.m.
3. Do you come to this park often?
4. I think I left my wallet there.
5. Blake decided to hold fund-raisers monthly.
6. Jose is very excited about his wife's pregnancy.
7. He did not attend class today.
8. I was late to my dentist's appointment.
9. The snow is falling lightly on the ground.
10. Roosevelt proudly displayed his art in the gallery.

◆ **P r a c t i c e   2   Identifying** Put an X next to the sentence if the underlined word is not an adverb.

1. _____ I spoke quietly to my <u>best</u> friend in class.

2. _____ My girlfriend sent me <u>lovely</u> flowers on my birthday.

3. _____ <u>Rock</u> the baby gently.

4. _____ Will you be able to help me <u>now</u>?

5. _____ Grace is very <u>happy</u> about her new job.

6. _____ The CD is permanently <u>stuck</u> in the computer.

7. _____ My books got quite <u>wet</u> in the rain.

8. _____ Jason learned to type <u>quickly</u>.

9. _____ I will not make that mistake <u>again</u>.

10. _____ Luis receives a <u>salary</u> bonus annually.

P r a c t i c e   3   Correcting Correct the errors in Practice 2 by listing the actual adverbs here, including those that were identified correctly.

1. _____   6. _____

2. _____   7. _____

3. _____   8. _____

4. _____   9. _____

5. _____   10. _____

P r a c t i c e   4   Completing Fill in each blank in the following paragraph with an adverb.

One day, I (1) _____ volunteered to take my two friends home from school. The rain was falling (2) _____ on the ground, so we ran (3) _____ to my car. It was parked on the far side of the parking lot, and I could (4) _____ remember where it was. I (5) _____ pulled out my keys, and we (6) _____ jumped inside. After we had driven around the corner, my friend (7) _____ remembered that she had (8) _____ forgotten to pick up her financial aid check. She said she (9) _____ needed the money, and she (10) _____ begged me to go back to campus. I (11) _____ gave in, and we turned the car around.

◆ **P r a c t i c e 5 Writing Your Own**

A. Write a sentence of your own for each of the following adverbs.

1. wildly _____

2. honestly _____

3. almost _____

4. kindly _____

5. never _____

B. Write five sentences of your own, and underline the adverbs in each.

1. _____

2. _____

3. _____

4. _____

5. _____

COMPARING WITH ADVERBS

Like adjectives, most adverbs have three forms: a **basic** form, a **comparative** form (used to compare two items), and a **superlative** form (used to compare three or more items).

For positive comparisons, adverbs form the comparative and superlative forms in two different ways:

1. One-syllable adverbs use *-er* and *-est* to form the comparative and superlative.

Basic	Comparative (used to compare two items)	Superlative (used to compare three or more items)
soon	sooner	soonest
fast	faster	fastest

2. Adverbs of two or more syllables use *more* to compare two items and *most* to compare three or more items.

Basic	Comparative (used to compare two items)	Superlative (used to compare three or more items)
quickly	more quickly	most quickly
gently	more gently	most gently
easily	more easily	most easily

For negative comparisons, adverbs, like adjectives, use *less* to compare two items and *least* to compare three or more items.

Basic	Comparative (used to compare two items)	Superlative (used to compare three or more items)
quickly	less quickly	least quickly
gently	less gently	least gently
easily	less easily	least easily

Hint: Like adjectives, certain adverbs are not usually compared. Something cannot last "*more* eternally" or work "*more* invisibly." The following adverbs cannot logically be compared.

endlessly	*eternally*	*infinitely*
equally	*impossibly*	*invisibly*

REVIEWING ADVERB FORMS

When do you use the comparative form of an adverb?

_____

When do you use the superlative form of an adverb?

_____

How do one-syllable adverbs form the comparative and superlative in positive comparisons?

_____

How do adverbs of two or more syllables form the comparative and superlative in positive comparisons?

_____

How do adverbs form negative comparisons?

_____

◆ **Practice 6 Identifying** Identify the underlined adverbs in the following sentences as basic (B), comparative (C), or superlative (S).

1. _____ The swimmer dived <u>gracefully</u> into the water.
2. _____ That new teacher treated us <u>less fairly</u> than Mrs. Wright did.
3. _____ The boys danced <u>wildly</u> on the stage.
4. _____ The trick-or-treaters were knocking <u>loudly</u> on my door.
5. _____ She is the <u>most completely</u> prepared student in the class.
6. _____ This newsletter is published <u>weekly</u> by our fraternity.
7. _____ I have been visiting you <u>less often</u> because I have no transportation to your house.
8. _____ My essay was <u>more hastily</u> written than yours was.
9. _____ Greta <u>never</u> asked me for my opinion.
10. _____ You are <u>hardly</u> ever working.

◆ **Practice 7 Identifying** Underline the adverbs in each of the following sentences.

1. The river is flowing less swiftly than usual.
2. I use the library more frequently than my roommate.
3. I like to go shopping there.
4. I was absent less often than my friend.
5. I am taking that class again.
6. We were both upset about the service, but Cammy spoke more angrily to the server.
7. They are most likely to be at the dance.
8. Rachel walked less gracefully after her knee surgery.

9. The other actors were brave, but I said my lines more timidly.

10. Of all the children in day care, my son was screaming the loudest.

P r a c t i c e 8 Correcting Change the positive comparisons in Practice 7 to negative ones and the negative comparisons to positive ones.

1. _____

2. _____

3. _____

4. _____

5. _____

6. _____

7. _____

8. _____

9. _____

10. _____

P r a c t i c e 9 Completing Fill in each blank in the following paragraph with the correct comparative or superlative form of the adverb in parentheses.

I was 15 pounds overweight last summer because I had been eating (1) _____ (foolishly) than usual. I was also exercising (2) _____ (regularly) because I had taken on a second job. My friend introduced me to a new diet that was the (3) _____ (sensibly) organized one I had ever heard of. According to this diet, breakfast and lunch would be (4) _____ (strictly) planned than dinner. I could eat a piece of fruit or a bagel, but I couldn't snack between meals. I didn't really like the food options I had, but I was

(5) _____ (seriously) worried that a piece of fruit wouldn't be enough to satisfy my appetite. Snacking between meals was my biggest problem, and I was visiting the snack machine at work (6) _____ (often) than the water fountain. In fact, that scenario had to be completely reversed. I had to drink lots and lots of water, which meant that I made visits to the bathroom (7) _____ (frequently) than I ever had before. My co-workers cracked jokes about my trips to the bathroom, but the one who was (8) _____ (genuinely) supportive was Bill. Apparently, Bill wanted to start a diet too, and he was (9) _____ (honestly) interested in the success of my weight loss than in the side effects of drinking so much water. When I eventually lost the 15 pounds, Bill hugged and congratulated me, but even (10) _____ (importantly), he said that I looked great.

◆ P r a c t i c e 1 0   Writing Your Own

A. Write a sentence of your own for each of the following adverb forms.

1. the superlative form of *sweetly* _____

2. the positive basic form of *wisely* _____

3. the comparative form of *patiently* _____

4. the negative superlative form of *harshly* _____

5. the comparative form of *boldly* _____

B. Write five sentences of your own, and underline the adverbs in each sentence.

1. _____

2. _____

3. _____

4. _____

5. _____

ADJECTIVE OR ADVERB?

One of the most common modifier errors with modifiers is using an adjective when an adverb is called for. Keep in mind that adjectives modify nouns and pronouns, whereas adverbs modify verbs, adjectives, and other adverbs. Adverbs *do not* modify nouns or pronouns. Here are some examples.

NOT　　　She fastened the seat belt **tight.** [adjective]

CORRECT　She fastened the seat belt **tightly.** [adverb]

NOT　　　We were **real** frightened after the accident. [adjective]

CORRECT　We were **really** frightened after the accident. [adjective]

REVIEWING THE DIFFERENCE BETWEEN ADJECTIVES AND ADVERBS
....

How do you know whether to use an adjective or an adverb in a sentence?

_____

_____

Give an example of an adverb in a sentence.

_____

Give an example of an adjective in a sentence.

_____

P r a c t i c e   1 1   **Identifying** Put a C next to the sentence if the underlined word is correct.

1. _____ Handle the antiques <u>gently</u> so they don't break.
2. _____ Talk to your teacher <u>nice</u>, and he'll be more willing to work with you.

3. _____ I washed my windows, and now I can see <u>clearly</u> through them.

4. _____ Sophia was <u>real</u> worried about the midterm.

5. _____ The baby crawled <u>quickly</u> across the floor.

6. _____ We worked <u>busily</u> until midnight.

7. _____ The laptop was <u>real</u> expensive when we bought it.

8. _____ He sat <u>lazily</u> on the sofa all day.

9. _____ Shannon drove <u>slow</u> during her driving test.

10. _____ We painted the room <u>colorful</u> to create a cheery atmosphere.

P r a c t i c e   1 2   **Identifying** Underline the incorrect adverb forms in the following sentences.

1. You tied your shoelaces too loose, and your shoes are falling off your feet.

2. I set up my computer real quickly, and I think I missed something.

3. She peeked quietly into the room where the baby was sleeping.

4. We sat sleepily in our chairs.

5. When we left the party, we told Joe that we had a really good time.

6. Run quick to the phone to call the police!

7. If you want the best deal, you have to shop wise.

8. Tina wants to go very bad, but she doesn't have enough money.

9. He signed his name sloppily on the paper.

10. If you had built the cabinet properly, it wouldn't be falling apart.

P r a c t i c e   1 3   **Correcting** Correct the five adverb errors in Practice 11 and the five adverb errors in Practice 12 by rewriting each incorrect sentence.

_____

_____

_____

_____

_____

_____

_____

_____

_____

_____

♦ **P r a c t i c e   1 4   Completing** Fill in each blank in the following paragraph with the correct form of the modifier in parentheses.

I (1) _____ (recent/recently) discovered that I am not very good at interior decorating. I had been watching a special on the Home Improvement channel, and I saw this (2) _____ (real/really) neat way to paint a wall. It's called woodgraining, and it looked very easy when the experts did it on TV. They painted the wall a dark brown and then went over it (3) _____ (slow/slowly) with a special brush, which gave the wall a woodgrain effect. The brush has ridges in it that catch the paint and drag it (4) _____ (careful/carefully) into lines. I just knew my dining room would look great with this technique, so I drove (5) _____ (quick/quickly) to the hardware store and bought the necessary supplies. As I began the project, I (6) _____ (sudden/suddenly) realized that it was going to take longer than I had (7) _____ (original/originally) expected. I had no idea how to control the brush, and I (8) _____ (soon/soonly) became frustrated. I practiced and practiced, and it looked better (9) _____ (eventual/ eventually), but it was not (10) _____ (near/nearly) as beautiful as the wall the experts painted. Next time, I'm hiring a professional.

◆ P r a c t i c e 1 5 Writing Your Own

A. Write a sentence of your own using each of the following adverbs correctly.

1. really _____

2. faithfully _____

3. poorly _____

4. happily _____

5. amazingly _____

B. Write five sentences of your own, and underline the adverbs in each sentence.

1. _____

2. _____

3. _____

4. _____

5. _____

DOUBLE NEGATIVES

Another problem that involves adverbs is the **double negative**—the use of two negative words in one clause. Examples of negative words include *no, not, never, none, nothing, neither, nowhere, nobody, barely,* and *hardly.* A double negative creates the opposite meaning of what is intended.

NOT   I **never** had **no** seat belts in my car.

The actual meaning of these double negatives is "I did have seat belts in my car."

CORRECT   I **never** had seat belts in my car.

NOT   My brother does**n't** wear seat belts **nowhere.**

The actual meaning of these double negatives is "My brother wears seat belts somewhere."

CORRECT   My brother does**n't** wear seat belts **anywhere.**

Double negatives often occur with contractions.

NOT   There are**n't hardly** any cars in the parking lot.

The actual meaning of these double negatives is "There are quite a few cars in the parking lot."

CORRECT   There are **hardly** any cars in the parking lot.

Using two negatives is confusing and grammatically wrong. Be on the look-out for negative words, and use only one per clause.

REVIEWING DOUBLE NEGATIVES
....

What is a double negative?

_____

List five negative words.

_____   _____   _____   _____   _____

Why should you avoid double negatives?

_____

P r a c t i c e   1 6   Identifying Put a C next to the sentence if the underlined negative expression is correct.

1. _____ I <u>don't never</u> want to see you again.
2. _____ This is <u>not</u> a good idea.
3. _____ Aren't you <u>ever</u> going home?
4. _____ Ada <u>couldn't hardly</u> concentrate on the test.
5. _____ We <u>never</u> see Grandpa anymore.
6. _____ My mother <u>wasn't anywhere</u> to be found.
7. _____ I thought my car battery was dead, but there <u>wasn't nothing</u> wrong with it.

8. _____ We <u>didn't</u> see <u>nobody</u> at the game.

9. _____ The alarm went off, but there was <u>no</u> evidence of a burglary.

10. _____ <u>Neither</u> of us wanted to be here.

◆ *P r a c t i c e   1 7*   **Identifying** Underline the incorrect negatives in the following sentences.

1. Nobody never attended the meetings.
2. There isn't nowhere I'd rather be than here with you.
3. My best friend isn't barely one month younger than I am.
4. I didn't have no choice.
5. Lara is nice, but she isn't no saint.
6. Ramell can't get out of bed no more.
7. Nobody left me no food in the house.
8. The phone rang for ten minutes, but there wasn't no answer.
9. I didn't want a date for the Christmas party, and I didn't go with nobody.
10. That fish isn't hardly cooked.

◆ *P r a c t i c e   1 8*   **Correcting** Correct the negative errors in Practice 17 by rewriting the incorrect sentences.

1. _____

2. _____

3. _____

4. _____

5. _____

6. _____

7. _____

8. _____

9. _____

10. _____

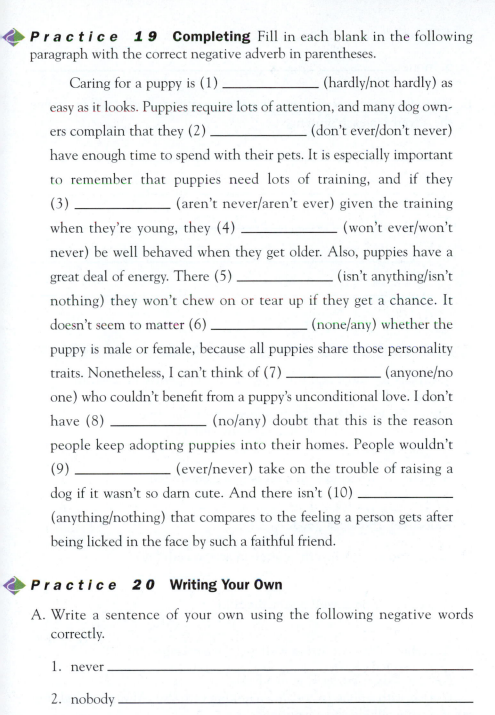

P r a c t i c e   1 9   Completing Fill in each blank in the following paragraph with the correct negative adverb in parentheses.

Caring for a puppy is (1) _____ (hardly/not hardly) as easy as it looks. Puppies require lots of attention, and many dog own-ers complain that they (2) _____ (don't ever/don't never) have enough time to spend with their pets. It is especially important to remember that puppies need lots of training, and if they (3) _____ (aren't never/aren't ever) given the training when they're young, they (4) _____ (won't ever/won't never) be well behaved when they get older. Also, puppies have a great deal of energy. There (5) _____ (isn't anything/isn't nothing) they won't chew on or tear up if they get a chance. It doesn't seem to matter (6) _____ (none/any) whether the puppy is male or female, because all puppies share those personality traits. Nonetheless, I can't think of (7) _____ (anyone/no one) who couldn't benefit from a puppy's unconditional love. I don't have (8) _____ (no/any) doubt that this is the reason people keep adopting puppies into their homes. People wouldn't (9) _____ (ever/never) take on the trouble of raising a dog if it wasn't so darn cute. And there isn't (10) _____ (anything/nothing) that compares to the feeling a person gets after being licked in the face by such a faithful friend.

P r a c t i c e   2 0   Writing Your Own

A. Write a sentence of your own using the following negative words correctly.

1. never _____

2. nobody _____

3. nowhere _____

4. barely _____

5. none _____

B. Write five sentences of your own using negative adverbs, and underline the adverbs in each sentence.

1. _____

2. _____

3. _____

4. _____

5. _____

USING *GOOD/WELL* AND *BAD/BADLY* CORRECTLY

The pairs *good/well* and *bad/badly* are so frequently misused that they deserve special attention.

Good is an adjective; *well* is an adverb or an adjective.
Use *good* with a noun (n) or after a linking verb (lv).

$$\qquad\qquad\qquad\qquad\qquad\qquad\qquad\qquad\qquad n$$

Adjective: Wearing your seat belt is a **good** idea.

$$\qquad\qquad\qquad lv$$

Adjective: He looks **good.**

Use *well* for someone's health or after an action verb (av).

$$\qquad\qquad\qquad\qquad\qquad lv$$

Adjective: She is **well** again. [health]

$$\qquad\qquad\qquad\qquad\qquad\qquad\qquad av$$

Adverb: The car drives **well** since we changed the oil.

Bad is an adjective; *badly* is an adverb.
Use *bad* with a noun (n) or after a linking verb (lv). Always use *bad* after *feel* if you are talking about emotions.

Adjective: He uses **bad** language.   ⁿ

Adjective: I feel **bad** that I got a ticket.   ^{lv}

Use *badly* with an adjective (adj) or after an action verb (av).

Adverb: The car was **badly** damaged.   ^{adj}

Adverb: He drives **badly**.   ^{av}

REVIEWING *Good/Well* AND *Bad/Badly*

When should you use the adjective good?

_____

When should you use the adjective well? *The adverb* well?

_____

When should you use the adjective bad?

_____

When should you use the adverb badly?

_____

◆ **P r a c t i c e   2 1**   **Identifying** Put a C next to the sentence if the underlined word is used correctly.

1. _____ He drives <u>bad</u> when he's upset.

2. _____ You did a <u>good</u> job on that exam.

3. _____ Kelly handled the awkward situation <u>well</u>.

4. _____ I wanted to go to the movie <u>badly</u>, but I had to study.

5. _____ Jerome felt <u>well</u> about his performance last night.

6. _____ The basketball team played <u>badly</u> in the big tournament.

7. _____ You've been sick, but now you're <u>good</u> again.

8. _____ This is a <u>bad</u> situation.

9. _____ Selena is doing <u>well</u> in rehearsals.

10. _____ If I finish this project, I will feel <u>good</u> about myself.

♦ **P r a c t i c e   2 2   Identifying** Underline the incorrect forms of *good*, *well*, *bad*, and *badly* in the following sentences.

1. If you do your job good, you'll probably get a raise.

2. Anika felt well about her decision.

3. The police are often portrayed bad in movies.

4. She spoke bad about her parents.

5. Gabrielle was in the hospital for pneumonia, but now she is good again.

6. Diane's pregnancy is going bad, and she has been very sick.

7. We feel badly that you can't come to our housewarming party.

8. Do you know that girl very good?

9. I know you like Tyrone, but I think his attitude is badly.

10. Jackie is learning what sports she can play good.

♦ **P r a c t i c e   2 3   Correcting** Correct the adjective and adverb errors in Practice 22 by rewriting each incorrect sentence.

1. _____

2. _____

3. _____

4. _____

5. _____

6. _____

7. _____

8. _____

9. _____

10. _____

P r a c t i c e   2 4 Completing Fill in each blank in the following paragraph with the correct word in parentheses.

James wanted so (1) _____ (bad/badly) to make the baseball team that he practiced long and hard all summer. When school started in the fall, he went to a really (2) _____ (good/well) baseball camp, and he spent eight weeks training with the best coaches in town. He became very (3) _____ (good/well) at pitching, and he could hit home runs (4) _____ (good/well) too. Practice finally began for baseball. James came early to every practice and tried his best, but he was so nervous that sometimes he handled the ball (5) _____ (bad/badly). He couldn't throw the ball as (6) _____ (good/well) and was having trouble pitching fastballs. He didn't look (7) _____ (good/well) swinging the bat either. It was as if something had invaded his body just to make him look (8) _____ (bad/badly) in front of everyone. He felt so (9) _____ (bad/badly) about his performance at practice that he made even more errors. Finally, his coach took him aside and told him to relax. He spent the weekend calming down and concentrating, and the following week he was a (10) _____ (good/well) baseball player again.

P r a c t i c e   2 5 Writing Your Own

A. Write a sentence of your own using the following words correctly.

1. good _____

2. badly _____

3. well _____

4. bad _____

5. good _____

B. Write five sentences of your own using adverbs, and underline the adverbs in each sentence.

1. _____

2. _____

3. _____

4. _____

5. _____

CHAPTER REVIEW

You might want to reread your answers to the questions in all the review boxes before you do the following exercises.

Review P r a c t i c e 1 **Reading** Refer to the paragraphs by Russell Baker on page 316 to do the following exercises.

1. List five adverbs in Baker's paragraphs.

_____

_____

_____

_____

_____

2. Provide the comparative and superlative forms of the following adverbs from Baker's paragraphs.

Basic	Comparative	Superlative
entirely	_____	_____
thoroughly	_____	_____

3. Provide the adverb forms of the following adjectives from the model paragraphs on page 316.

Adjective	**Adverb**
cold	_____
inherent	_____

 Review P r a c t i c e   2   Identifying Underline the incorrect adverb forms in the following sentences.

1. Hold on tight to this rope!
2. I thought you did really good in the play.
3. Becky made a real bad mistake.
4. The groom stood proud at the altar, watching his bride.
5. My father doesn't show me no respect.
6. This soup tastes badly.
7. Listen quiet to the CD because I'm trying to study.
8. The Rodriguez family never go nowhere without their dog.
9. I didn't do nothing to hurt you.
10. You drive so bad that other drivers are afraid of you.

Review P r a c t i c e   3   Correcting Correct the adverb errors in Review Practice 2 by rewriting the sentences.

 EDITING A STUDENT PARAGRAPH

Following is a paragraph written and revised by Manuel Astonomo in response to the writing assignment in this chapter. Read the paragraph, and underline each of his adverbs.

I will never forget the day I received my driver's license. I thought I was *real* important, and I honestly thought I could conquer the world. Though I didn't have no driving experience, I convinced my parents to let me take their new convertible for a joy ride. They were reluctant at first, but they most generously agreed to my foolish request. I immediately drove to my best friend's house, and we eventually found three other guys. We then drove proud to the burger place where students often gather. After visiting with some cute girls for about an hour, we decided to leave and see a movie. However, as I was backing *slow* out of my parking spot, I bumped into a post. I couldn't believe it! I hadn't never seen that post before, and I know I looked behind me when I put the car in reverse. Well, there was only minor damage to the bumper, but I knew my parents would be awful upset. With that in mind, we decided to see the movie and deal with my parents later.

Collaborative Activity

Team up with a partner and mark an X above the four adverb errors in Manuel's paragraph. Underline the two double negatives twice. Then, working together, use what you have learned in this chapter to correct these errors. Rewrite the paragraph with your corrections.

EDITING YOUR OWN PARAGRAPH

Now return to the paragraph you wrote and revised at the beginning of this chapter. Underline each of your adverbs.

Collaborative Activity

Exchange paragraphs with your partner, and circle any adverb errors that you find in your partner's paragraph. Underline any double negatives twice.

Individual Activity

On the Error Log in Appendix 4, record any adverb errors that your partner found in your paragraph. To complete the writing process, correct these errors by rewriting your paragraph.

MODIFIER ERRORS

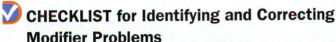

✅ CHECKLIST for Identifying and Correcting Modifier Problems

> ✔ Are modifiers as close as possible to the words they modify?
> ✔ Are any sentences confusing because the words that the modifiers refer to are missing?

As you know, a modifier describes another word or group of words. Sometimes, however, a modifier is too far from the words it refers to (*misplaced modifier*), or the word it refers to is missing altogether (*dangling modifier*). As a result, the sentence is confusing.

Notice how the modifiers work in the following paragraph by David Macaulay.

Using a keyboard to control a complex computer program is awkward and slow. The advent of the mouse and icons makes a computer much easier to use and also gives programs much greater flexibility. The mouse is a controller that is moved over a mat or desktop. As it moves, electric pulses inform the computer of its exact change in position. The computer responds by shifting a cursor over the picture in the same direction as the mouse. The computer can be given commands by moving the mouse so that the cursor points to an icon, and then "clicking" its switch. The command represented by the selected icon is then carried out.

In this paragraph, Macaulay describes how a computer mouse works. Before continuing in this chapter, take a moment to describe something that you know a great deal about. Save your work because you will use it later in the chapter.

WRITING ASSIGNMENT: HOW IT WORKS

Think of something that you use every day and are very familiar with. Choose something like a guitar, a cell phone, or a microwave. Could you describe it to someone else? How does it work? What does a person have to do to use it? Write a paragraph describing the process of operating or using this object.

REVISING YOUR WRITING

Revise the first draft of your paragraph before you focus on editing. Use the Revising Checklist on pages 24–25 to help you with your revision. Make sure your paragraph has a good topic sentence, is well developed, and is well organized. Then check your paragraph for unity and coherence.

MISPLACED MODIFIERS

A modifier should be placed as close as possible to the word or words it modifies, but this does not always happen. A **misplaced modifier** is too far from the word or words it refers to, making the meaning of the sentence unclear. Look at these examples.

> **NOT**   The gardener prunes the tree that grows in the back-yard **in May.**

(Does the tree in the backyard grow only in May? Probably not. But the gardener prunes it only in May. So the modifier *in May* needs to be moved closer to the word it actually modifies.)

> **CORRECT**   **In May,** the gardener prunes the tree that grows in the backyard.

> **NOT**   I need to upgrade the computer in that office **that doesn't have a mouse.**

(It is the computer, not the office, that doesn't have a mouse. So the modifier *that doesn't have a mouse* needs to be moved closer to the word it modifies.)

> **CORRECT**   I need to upgrade the computer **that doesn't have a mouse** in that office.

Certain modifiers that limit meaning are often misplaced, causing problems. Look at how meaning changes by moving the limiting word *only* in the following sentences:

Only Rachel plans to meet Sally for lunch at The Pepper.
(No one but Rachel will meet Sally.)

Rachel **only** plans to meet Sally for lunch at The Pepper.
(Rachel plans to meet her but might not show up.)

Rachel plans **only** to meet Sally for lunch at The Pepper.
(Rachel plans to meet Sally for lunch and do nothing else.)

Rachel plans to meet **only** Sally for lunch at The Pepper.
(Rachel plans to meet no one but Sally.)

Rachel plans to meet Sally **only** for lunch at The Pepper.
(Rachel does not plan to meet for any other reason.)

Rachel plans to meet Sally for lunch **only** at The Pepper.
(Rachel plans to have lunch there but no other meals.)

Rachel plans to meet Sally for lunch at The Pepper **only.**
(Rachel does not plan to meet at any other place.)

Here is a list of common limiting words.

almost	hardly	merely	only
even	just	nearly	scarcely

REVIEWING MISPLACED MODIFIERS

What is a misplaced modifier?

_____

How can you correct a misplaced modifier?

_____

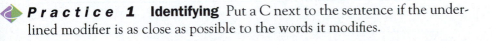 **P r a c t i c e   1   Identifying** Put a C next to the sentence if the underlined modifier is as close as possible to the words it modifies.

1. _____ The bank called me about a canceled check <u>at work</u>.
2. _____ We drove to the farmer's market <u>on the corner</u>.
3. _____ Jermaine left his jersey on the back porch <u>for the big game</u>.
4. _____ Jamal told Lisa that <u>to lose weight</u> she had no motivation.
5. _____ The book <u>by John Steinbeck</u> is on the counter.
6. _____ Shannon's son and my nephew are <u>on the same baseball team</u>.
7. _____ I heard a funny noise when I was in the garage <u>that sounded like a cat</u>.
8. _____ Isabelle told Ryan <u>in a magazine</u> about a compatibility quiz.
9. _____ We made cookies in the kitchen <u>with lots of chocolate chips</u>.
10. _____ Carrie waited <u>until the last minute</u> to start the project.

◆ **P r a c t i c e   2   Identifying** Underline the misplaced modifiers in each of the following sentences.

1. Anne lost a filling while shopping from a molar.
2. I told them that we would have lunch today in the park last weekend.
3. As a young child, my parents tried not to spoil me.
4. Paul sold his bike to me after he got a new one as a present for $150.
5. Eunice used shampoo on her hair from the beauty salon.
6. The best movie ever made was *Jaws* in 3D.
7. Thomas told Renee that to pass the exam she would be wise.
8. I need to check out the book about Edgar Allen Poe with the blue spine.
9. The basketball team held a car wash from our college.
10. My diary is in the closet under my collection of quarters.

◆ **P r a c t i c e   3   Correcting** Correct the modifier errors in Practice 2 by rewriting each incorrect sentence.

1. _____

2. _____

3. _____

4. _____

5. _____

6. _____

7. _____

8. _____

9. _____

10. _____

▶ **P r a c t i c e   4   Completing** Fill in each blank in the following paragraph with a modifier. Include at least two phrases.

When Stephanie was born, her parents owned a (1) _____ car that had many miles on it. They took many vacations in the car, even going (2) _____ one year. It was a dependable car, but it was very small and (3) _____. Needless to say, when Stephanie came along, her parents realized their need for (4) _____ transportation. They (5) _____ started shopping around for (6) _____ roomy vehicles that would fit her baby car seat and still have room for (7) _____. A salesman talked them into buying a minivan, which they had initially thought was (8) _____. Eventually, they came to (9) _____ the car and found it was perfect for them. Sixteen years later, when Stephanie got her driver's license, the (10) _____ became her car, and her parents bought a new Toyota.

▶ **P r a c t i c e   5   Writing Your Own**

A. Write a sentence of your own for each of the following modifiers.

1. after the rain _____

2. since we arrived _____

3. while making dinner _____

4. before she saw him _____

5. though we couldn't hear it _____

B. Write five sentences of your own using modifiers correctly, and underline the modifiers in each sentence.

1. _____

2. _____

3. _____

4. _____

5. _____

DANGLING MODIFIERS

Modifiers are "dangling" when they have nothing to refer to in a sentence. **Dangling modifiers** (starting with an *-ing* word or with *to*) often appear at the beginning of a sentence. Here is an example.

> **NOT**   **Surfing the Internet,** my computer mouse is very helpful.

A modifier usually modifies the words closest to it. So the phrase *Surfing the Internet* modifies *my computer mouse*. But my mouse doesn't surf the Internet. In fact, there is no logical word in the sentence that the phrase modifies. It is left dangling. You can correct a dangling modifier in one of two ways—by inserting the missing word that is being referred to or by rewriting the sentence.

> **CORRECT**   **Surfing the Internet,** I find my computer mouse very helpful.

> **CORRECT**   **When I am surfing the Internet,** my computer mouse is very helpful.

> **NOT**   **To play the lottery,** a ticket must be bought.

> **CORRECT**   **To play the lottery, you** must buy a ticket.

> **CORRECT**   You must buy a ticket if you want **to play the lottery.**

NOT	The bag for charity was full **after going through our old clothes.**
CORRECT	**After going through our old clothes, we** had a full bag for charity.
CORRECT	**After we went through our old clothes, we** had a full bag for charity.
CORRECT	The bag for charity was full **after we went through our old clothes.**

REVIEWING DANGLING MODIFIERS

What is a dangling modifier?

_____

How do you correct a dangling modifier?

_____

_____

P r a c t i c e   6   Identifying Put a C next to the sentence if the under-lined modifier is correct.

1. _____ <u>To determine the winner</u>, the contest has a panel of five judges.
2. _____ <u>Taking a shower</u>, the power went out in our house.
3. _____ <u>Waiting for the news</u>, the man started to sweat.
4. _____ <u>Holding the child</u>, the cold weather made me wish I had a blanket.
5. _____ <u>To prevent sunburn</u>, Tina applied sunscreen.
6. _____ <u>Before walking the dog</u>, the garage needed to be swept out.
7. _____ <u>To give up smoking</u>, I had to get the support of my friends.
8. _____ <u>While walking to the bus stop</u>, Jennifer told Aaron she would meet him after class.
9. _____ <u>Doing my psychology homework</u>, I fell asleep.
10. _____ <u>Watching television</u>, the popcorn was falling between the sofa cushions.

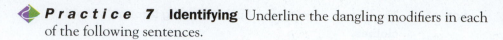 **P r a c t i c e 7 Identifying** Underline the dangling modifiers in each of the following sentences.

1. Thinking the team would never win the tournament, the calendar marked the big day.
2. To remain in this fraternity, dues must be paid.
3. While drawing in the coloring book, the crayons broke.
4. Before jumping in the pool, the diving board was very slippery.
5. To visit South America, a passport must be obtained.
6. Flying first class in the commercial jet, the seat would not recline.
7. To upgrade the computer, more memory was installed.
8. To change the oil in my car, the filter must be replaced.
9. After waiting in line for an hour, the post office worker closed her window.
10. To feed the children dinner, macaroni and cheese was prepared.

P r a c t i c e 8 Correcting Correct the modifier errors in Practice 7 by rewriting each incorrect sentence.

1. _____

_____

2. _____

3. _____

4. _____

_____

5. _____

6. _____

_____

7. _____

8. _____

9. _____

_____

10. _____

◆ **P r a c t i c e 9 Completing** Fill in each blank in the following paragraph with a modifier. Include at least two phrases.

(1) _____, everything at Macy's goes on sale. The salespeople run around frantically, preparing (2) _____ clothes and other items. Hundreds of (3) _____ people show up at the doors, often arriving before the store opens. Within a few hours, shoppers are (4) _____, and all of the beautifully arranged items become (5) _____. I personally witnessed one of these big sales when (6) _____. It was (7) _____ to see the number of people fighting over everything in sight. I wondered if they really needed the items or were just (8) _____. After I made my few purchases, I left (9) _____. I was glad to be out of the confusion and back (10) _____.

◆ **P r a c t i c e 1 0 Writing Your Own**

A. Write a sentence of your own for each of the following phrases.

1. clear and sunny _____

2. taking my coat _____

3. to communicate with my parents _____

4. getting a haircut _____

5. to visit Paris _____

B. Write five sentences of your own using phrases as modifiers, and underline the phrases.

1. _____

2. _____

3. _____

4. _____

5. _____

CHAPTER REVIEW

You might want to reread your answers to the questions in all the review boxes before you do the following exercises.

◆ *Review P r a c t i c e 1*   **Reading**   Referring to the paragraph by David Macaulay on page 339, list 10 modifiers the author used correctly.

1. _____

2. _____

3. _____

4. _____

5. _____

6. _____

7. _____

8. _____

9. _____

10. _____

◆ *Review P r a c t i c e 2*   **Identifying**   Underline any misplaced or dangling modifiers in the following sentences.

1. Joanne told Sam that she would take him to dinner tonight last Wednesday.

2. Checking the time, the clock said it was exactly 1:00 p.m.

3. Fishing in the lake, the boat sprang a leak.

4. To iron your shirts, spray starch is needed.

5. My souvenirs are on the table from Texas.

6. We made the floral arrangements from my garden with lots of daffodils.

7. To turn off the television, the remote must be used.

8. Scanning pictures from our vacation, my printer broke.

9. Moving the furniture for the carpet cleaners, the sofa landed on my toe.

10. Peter just bought a classic Mustang from a used-car dealer with white racing stripes.

Review P r a c t i c e   3   Correcting Correct the misplaced or dangling modifiers in Review Practice 2 by rewriting the sentences.

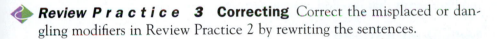

EDITING A STUDENT PARAGRAPH

Following is a paragraph written by Steven Banks in response to the writing assignment in this chapter. Read the paragraph, and underline as many modifiers as you can. Don't forget modifiers of more than one word.

> My favorite invention is the toaster oven. The toaster is in the kitchen with a glass door. To make toast and bagels, every morning it is used. Being the oldest of four children, it is usually very difficult to prepare a quick breakfast for everyone. But the toaster is very helpful and easy to use. To determine the appropriate cook time, the dial must be set on the chosen temperature. Opening the glass door, the rack inside is where the toast or bagel is placed. Then the door is shut, and the lever on the front is pressed down. After cooking for the specified time, a bell will ring to signal that the food is ready to eat. I will be moving into the dorms next quarter, and my mom promised to buy a new toaster oven for me yesterday. I just know that having a toaster oven in my dorm room will earn me a reputation as a great cook.

Collaborative Activity

Team up with a partner, and put brackets around the seven modifier errors (five dangling modifiers and two misplaced modifiers). Then, working together, use what you have learned in this chapter to correct these errors. Rewrite the paragraph with your corrections.

EDITING YOUR OWN PARAGRAPH

Now go back to the paragraph you wrote and revised at the beginning of this chapter, and underline as many modifiers as possible.

Collaborative Activity

Exchange paragraphs with your partner, and put brackets around the modifier errors that you find in your partner's paragraph.

Individual Activity

On the Error Log in Appendix 4, record any modifier errors that your partner found in your paragraph. To complete the writing process, correct these errors by rewriting your paragraph.

UNIT TESTS

Here are some exercises that test your understanding of all the material in this unit: Adjectives, Adverbs, and Modifier Errors.

Unit Test 1 Identifying

In each of the following sentences, underline the adverbs and adjectives used incorrectly. Put brackets around any misplaced or dangling modifiers.

1. That was the bestest meal I have ever eaten.
2. You did good on this report, so I think you'll get a pay raise.
3. To bake a cake, a greased pan is needed.
4. Fred started shopping here because the sales clerks are more friendlier than in any other store.
5. Devon couldn't never understand geometry, no matter how much he studied it.
6. Jogging to the dock, the boat left without us.
7. I tried real hard, but I just couldn't move that rock by myself.

8. Melanie went to the mall with Sheena, wearing her new jacket.

9. Of all the students in the class, Jade is the more intelligent.

10. I left the wallet on the cafeteria table that I got from my sister.

11. Sit quiet, so you don't disturb anyone.

12. You couldn't sing more worse than Toni.

13. Looking under the bed, my shoes were right in front of me.

14. I couldn't barely hear what you were whispering.

15. Between Konrad and Luke, Konrad is the tallest.

16. She did bad on the test, so she wants to do an assignment for extra credit.

17. Having lost his job, Mike didn't have nowhere to go.

18. I heard the song that we requested at the concert in the car.

19. There are 14 houses on this block, and mine is by far the bigger.

20. I think it would be more better if you sat with your family and I with mine.

Unit Test 2 Correcting

Correct the adjective, adverb, and modifier errors in Unit Test 1 by rewriting each incorrect sentence.

Unit Test 3 Identifying

In the following paragraph, underline the adverbs and adjectives used incorrectly. Put brackets around any misplaced or dangling modifiers.

During my first year of college, I wrote for the campus newspaper about our sports teams. I was assigned to cover the men's basketball games, the women's swim meets, and all of the tennis matches. Needless to say, I was kept quite busy going to real exciting sports events. Of the three sports, I thought the swim meets were more fun. Cheri and Julia were the two swim coaches, and they were so cooperative. The only problem I had was keeping up with the deadlines. To get an article published in a weekly paper, a draft had to be submitted by Tuesday evening. Wednesday the editors reviewed it for corrections or changes, and Thursday it was laid out for press. This tight schedule didn't leave no room for procrastination; however, it made me a better writer. Because the deadlines were so strict, I had no choice but to sit down with my pen and paper. Something even more better was that I learned how to take good notes. Listening for important details, my notes were very organized. I also learned how to manipulate the tone of my articles, making them sound positive even when the teams weren't doing so good. Writing for the paper was the most toughest experience I've had, but it was also the most rewarding.

Unit Test 4 Correcting

Correct the adjective, adverb, and modifier errors in Unit Test 3 by rewriting the paragraph.

UNIT WRITING ASSIGNMENTS

1. Where is this scene? Imagine what kinds of animals live in this area. Do people also live here? What is the weather like? Imagine that you are camping here, and write about a typical day in this area.

2. What is your personal writing process? What do you do to prepare yourself for writing? What are your favorite prewriting techniques? What do you look for in revision? Describe your writing process from beginning to end, using as many details as possible.

3. We all have our idiosyncrasies, especially when it comes to doing everyday tasks. How do you go about doing an everyday task, such as washing laundry or driving to school? Write about the process you go through to perform this activity.

4. Describe the first major holiday that you can remember. Who was there? What happened? How did you feel? Write about the holiday using as many details as you can.

5. Create your own assignment (with the assistance of your instructor) and write a response to it.

PUNCTUATION

Can you imagine streets and highways without stoplights or traffic signs? Driving would become a life-or-death adventure as motorists made risky trips with no signals to guide or protect them. Good writers, like conscientious drivers, prefer to leave little to chance. They observe the rules of punctuation to ensure that their readers arrive at their intended meaning. Without punctuation, sentences would run together, ideas would be unclear, and words would be misread. Writers need to use markers, like periods, commas, and dashes, to help them communicate as efficiently and effectively as possible.

Look at the difference punctuation makes in the meaning of the following letter.

Dear John:

I want a man who knows what love is all about. You are generous, kind, thoughtful. People who are not like you admit to being useless and inferior. You have ruined me for other men. I yearn for you. I have no feelings whatsoever when we're apart. I can be forever happy—will you let me be yours?

Susan

Dear John,

I want a man who knows what love is. All about you are generous, kind, thoughtful people, who are not like you. Admit to being useless and inferior. You have ruined me. For other men, I yearn. For you, I have no feelings whatsoever. When we're apart, I can be forever happy. Will you let me be?

Yours, Susan

This unit will help you write the love letter you actually want to write—with the punctuation that gets your message across. It will also provide you with guidelines for using the following punctuation.

END PUNCTUATION

CHAPTER 20

✔ CHECKLIST for Using End Punctuation

> ✔ Does each sentence end with a period, a question mark, or an exclamation point?
> ✔ Are question marks used when asking questions?
> ✔ Do sentences that exclaim end with exclamation points?

End punctuation signals the end of a sentence in three ways: The **period** ends a statement, the **question mark** signals a question, and the **exclamation point** marks an exclamation.

Notice how the end punctuation works in the following paragraph by Nigel Hawkes.

On another occasion, the 66-year-old Pope threatened to have the artist physically thrown down from the scaffolding if he did not work faster. "When will it be ready?" demanded Julius. "When it is ready," replied Michelangelo shortly. The Pope flushed with anger and mimicked, "When it is ready! When it is ready!" He then raised his walking stick in rage and struck Michelangelo on the shoulder.

In this paragraph, author Nigel Hawkes describes an emotional conversation that took place between Michelangelo Buonarroti and Pope Julius II. Before continuing in this chapter, take a moment to record an emotional event in your life. Save your work because you will use it later in this chapter.

WRITING ASSIGNMENT: EMOTIONS

Think of an event in your life when your emotions were raging. You might have been extremely happy, sad, excited, confused, or frustrated. What was taking place? Why was the event so emotional? Who else was involved? Write a paragraph telling about what happened and what was said. Try to remember as many details as you can.

REVISING YOUR WRITING

Revise the first draft of your paragraph before you focus on editing. Use the Revising Checklist on pages 24–25 to help you with your revision. Make sure your paragraph has a good topic sentence, is well developed, and is well organized. Then check your paragraph for unity and coherence.

PERIOD

1. A **period** is used with statements, mild commands, and indirect questions.

Statement:	Michelangelo painted the Sistine Chapel.
Command:	Paint the Sistine Chapel.
Indirect Question:	I wonder if he had any help painting the Sistine Chapel.

2. A period is also used with abbreviations and numbers.

Abbreviations:	Mrs. Baker lives at 7901 Broad St., next door to Dr. Janet Rodriguez.
Numbers:	$15.85 10.5 $659.95 .075

REVIEWING PERIODS

What are the three main uses of a period?

_____

What are two other uses of a period?

_____

P r a c t i c e   1 **Identifying** Add missing periods to each of the following sentences when necessary.

1. The geometry class is too full
2. Dr Woo is my dentist.
3. I wonder if there is another piece of cake
4. I made $25065 at my yard sale this weekend.
5. I can't remember if I mailed that check
6. Keep your hands to yourself
7. Ms Kahn bought a new BMW.
8. Sales tax is now 725% throughout most of California.
9. Geoff didn't want to go
10. My grandmother is selling her house on Maple St to move to Orange Ave.

 P r a c t i c e   2 **Identifying** Put an X next to each sentence that contains a period error.

1. _____ I am taking the day off
2. _____ I want to know what you are doing.
3. _____ I can sell the chair for $3000, or about two hours of work.
4. _____ I wonder if Mr Thompson can help me.
5. _____ Will you be at Seventh St and Pine Ave this afternoon?
6. _____ My checking account has a balance of $105,90.
7. _____ Dr. Edwards, please check my blood pressure.
8. _____ Dr Otto is my math instructor.
9. _____ We need to take the trash out tonight
10. _____ I work for the US ambassador to Ecuador.

 P r a c t i c e   3 **Correcting** Correct the punctuation errors in Practice 2 by rewriting each incorrect sentence.

1. _____

2. _____

3. _____

4. _____

5. _____

6. _____

7. _____

8. _____

9. _____

10. _____

◆ *P r a c t i c e* **4 Completing** Add periods to the following paragraph.

   The woman, Mrs. Chambers, rushed into the emergency room She was 38 weeks pregnant and going into labor Mr Chambers had been sitting at home while his wife ran errands He had no idea what was going on until he received a call from St Vincent's Hospital, telling him that his wife had been admitted Dr Bustamonte delivered their baby within the hour, and Mr Chambers arrived just in time. Unfortunately, in his hurry to get to the hospital, Mr Chambers forgot the camcorder, the camera, and even a change of clothes for his wife But aside from those minor details, the family went home with a healthy little boy and a bill for $1,56988

◆ *P r a c t i c e* **5 Writing Your Own**

   A. Write a sentence of your own for each of the following directions.

   1. a statement about Mr. Guerra

   _____

   2. an indirect question about Jefferson St.

   _____

   3. a statement about $934.59

   _____

   4. a command to do the laundry

   _____

5. an indirect question about the weather

_____

B. Write five sentences of your own—two statements, two commands, and one indirect question—using periods correctly.

1. _____

2. _____

3. _____

4. _____

5. _____

QUESTION MARK

The **question mark** is used after a direct question.

Question Mark: What do you know about Michelangelo?

Question Mark: "What do you know about Michelangelo?" the teacher asked.

REVIEWING QUESTION MARKS

What is the main role of a question mark?

_____

Give an example of a question.

_____

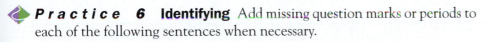 **P r a c t i c e   6   Identifying** Add missing question marks or periods to each of the following sentences when necessary.

1. You can sit here if you want to

2. "Do you think this dress is too purple " she asked.

3. I heard you remembered my birthday

4. Is there a reason for this bill

5. "Can you help me with my Spanish homework" Marshall asked

6. Mabel wondered, "What should I wear today"

7. Why won't my Gerber daisies stay alive

8. I wonder what his address is

9. Is Greg still the one in charge of this program

10. "Where will you be living" I asked

◆ **P r a c t i c e   7   Identifying** Put an X next to each sentence that contains a question mark error.

1. _____ Are you kidding.

2. _____ I wonder if Steve registered for this class?

3. _____ Janie asked, "What is taking so long?"

4. _____ This cannot happen today?

5. _____ What seems to be the problem?

6. _____ I can't remember if Kimo is allergic to dairy products?

7. _____ "Would you like something to drink?" the waitress asked?

8. _____ You are planning to be there, right?

9. _____ I can't believe you haven't cleaned this room?

10. _____ Brigitte asked the teacher what she meant?

◆ **P r a c t i c e   8   Correcting** Correct the punctuation errors in Practice 7 by rewriting each incorrect sentence.

1. _____

2. _____

3. _____

4. _____

5. _____

6. _____

7. _____

EDITING CHECKLIST ✔

SENTENCES

✔ Does each sentence have a main subject and verb?
✔ Do all subjects and verbs agree?
✔ Do all pronouns agree with their nouns?
✔ Are modifiers as close as possible to the words they modify?

PUNCTUATION AND MECHANICS

✔ Are sentences punctuated correctly?
✔ Are words capitalized properly?

WORD CHOICE AND SPELLING

✔ Are words used correctly?
✔ Are words spelled correctly?

FOLD HERE

FOLD HERE

REVISING CHECKLIST

TOPIC SENTENCE
✔ Does the topic sentence convey the paragraph's controlling idea?
✔ Does the topic sentence appear as the first or last sentence of the paragraph?

DEVELOPMENT
✔ Does the paragraph contain *specific* details that support the topic sentence?
✔ Does the paragraph include *enough* details to explain the topic sentence fully?

UNITY
✔ Do all the sentences in the paragraph support the topic sentence?

ORGANIZATION
✔ Is the paragraph organized logically?

COHERENCE
✔ Do the sentences move smoothly and logically from one to the next?

8. _____

9. _____

10. _____

◆ **P r a c t i c e   9   Completing** Add question marks to the following paragraph.

Being a professional photographer is not a glamorous job. Sometimes I ask myself, "Why are you doing this" because it definitely isn't easy. On more than one occasion, I have had to work with uncooperative people, and I wonder silently, "Why are they here if they don't want to smile for me Didn't they make this appointment Didn't they call *me* for *my* services " Nonetheless, I keep taking their pictures. At least three times I've had to ask men, "Will you please take the toothpick out of your mouth" And they look at me as if they really think the toothpick makes them look sexy. Can you imagine how uncivilized that is However, when I wake up each morning, I really do look forward to seeing who will come through my studio door. I've had the opportunity to capture a baby's first smile, the proud sparkle in a new bride's eye, and a grandmother's soft touch as she read to her grandson. Now, what other job could give me that for my résumé

◆ **P r a c t i c e   10   Writing Your Own**

A. Write a question of your own for each of the following directions.

1. a question about gardening

    _____

2. a question Fawn asked about her car tires

    _____

3. a question about breakfast

    _____

4. a question Toni asked about computer paper

    _____

5. a question Matt asked about basketball

_____

B. Write five direct questions of your own, using question marks correctly.

1. _____

2. _____

3. _____

4. _____

5. _____

EXCLAMATION POINT

The **exclamation point** indicates strong feeling.

If it is used too often, it is not as effective as it could be. You shouldn't use more than one exclamation point at a time.

Exclamation Point: Never!

Exclamation Point: I can't believe it!

Exclamation Point: That is insulting!

Exclamation Point: "That is insulting!" he said.

REVIEWING EXCLAMATION POINTS

What is the main use of an exclamation point?

_____

Give an example of an exclamation.

_____

◆ **P r a c t i c e   1 1**   **Identifying** Add missing exclamation points to each of the following sentences where necessary.

1. "Not in my house" the mother yelled.

2. Get over it

3. "You won ten dollars" I said in astonishment.

4. Shame on you

5. "Two points" he screamed.

6. Get off my foot

7. "One more chance" she begged.

8. Come back

9. We made it

10. "He finally asked me out" she exclaimed.

P r a c t i c e   1 2   **Identifying** Put an X next to each sentence that contains an exclamation point error.

1. _____ Did you tell me the truth!

2. _____ Don't you dare!

3. _____ Yeah, we won.

4. _____ "Thank God!" she said.

5. _____ What have you been doing in here!

6. _____ Can you tell me how to get to New Mexico!

7. _____ "It's going to explode," the man shouted!

8. _____ Chandra told the disc jockey, "My favorite artist is Whitney Houston!"

9. _____Get off my bike!

10. _____ "That's it," Shannon screamed!

P r a c t i c e   1 3   **Correcting** Correct the punctuation errors in Practice 12 by rewriting each incorrect sentence.

1. _____

2. _____

3. _____

4. _____

5. _____

6. _____

7. _____

8. _____

9. _____

10. _____

◆ **P r a c t i c e   1 4**   **Completing** Add exclamation points to the following paragraph.

   The last baseball game I saw was between the Texas Rangers and the Seattle Mariners during the summer of 2001. I am a big fan of the Rangers, even during their bad seasons. Posters saying "Go Rangers" hang proudly on my bedroom walls. Sometimes I even bring them to the games. During this particular game, the Rangers were up by one run at the bottom of the ninth inning. Seattle was at bat, and there were already two outs. Doug Davis was pitching for the Rangers, and Ichiro Suzuki was at bat. "Strike him out" I yelled from my seat, but the first pitch was a ball. "No way" I screamed. "That's a horrible call" Yet the next pitch was another ball. I couldn't believe it The bases were empty, and this was looking like a victory for Texas, but Davis was going to give it away. "Throw a strike" I shouted at the top of my lungs, and finally he did. "Two more, Davis" I begged. Whoosh The pitch flew by Suzuki at the speed of light, and the ump called out, "Strike" One more pitch went out—*whoosh* "Strike three" yelled the ump, and the stands erupted in applause. Victory for the Rangers That was one of the happiest days of my life.

◆ **P r a c t i c e   1 5**   **Writing Your Own**

A. Write an exclamation of your own for each of the following directions.

   1. an exclamation about cockroaches

   _____

   2. an exclamation about childbirth

   _____

3. an exclamation by Brittany about a broken ankle

_____

4. an exclamation by Steve about a touchdown

_____

5. an exclamation about bad food

_____

B. Write five sentences of your own expressing strong feelings, using exclamation points correctly.

1. _____

2. _____

3. _____

4. _____

5. _____

CHAPTER REVIEW

You might want to reread your answers to the questions in all the review boxes before you do the following exercises.

*Review P r a c t i c e **1** **Reading** Refer to the paragraph by Nigel Hawkes on page 355 to do the following exercises.

1. Rewrite the following sentence to make it an indirect question.
   "When will it be ready?" demanded Julius.

   _____

2. Rewrite the following statement to make it a direct question.
   He then raised his walking stick in rage and struck Michelangelo on the shoulder.

_____

_____

3. List the two uses of exclamation points.

_____

_____

Review P r a c t i c e 2 Identifying Underline the periods, question marks, and exclamation points that are used incorrectly in the following sentences.

1. Have you seen my little brother.
2. "Go?" Marcus yelled to Cho, who was preparing to bungee-jump at the fairgrounds.
3. "Will you come help me paint my house!" Vernon asked.
4. Get out of my way.
5. Can you open this jar of pickles for me.
6. I wonder if Tom knows his door is open?
7. "Yeah?" Isabel screamed when she learned she was pregnant.
8. My porch light is burned out?
9. "Could you repeat that!" she asked.
10. I can't remember where I left my wallet?

Review P r a c t i c e 3 Correcting Correct the punctuation errors in Review Practice 2 by rewriting the incorrect sentences.

EDITING A STUDENT PARAGRAPH

Following is a paragraph written and revised by Marina Jones in response to the writing assignment in this chapter. Read the paragraph, and underline each of her periods, question marks, and exclamation points.

> Last summer, I belonged to a book club. It was full of nice people, and I became good friends with many of the ones my age? Unfortunately, the club was growing too rapidly, and soon there were too many new members. When that happened, the structure of the club fell

apart? Instead of discussing books, the people would get together just to eat munchies and complain about things! Soon the leaders sent out a survey, asking the club members for comments and suggestions. I thought this would be my chance to explain how uncomfortable I was feeling! They asked things like "What kinds of things could we do to make it a better? club! " and I answered all of the survey questions honestly. What I didn't expect was that one of the club leaders took all of my answers personally, and she was suddenly very mad at me. I was confused by her response, and I asked myself, "What could I possibly have said wrong?" She told me that my answers were sarcastic and mean. I was shocked? "How! " I tried to ask her, but she kept avoiding me. When I finally met with her, she began to cry. "You hurt me? " she yelled, and I was still in shock. I apologized profusely and tried to understand, and eventually I think she forgave me. Still, I don't think I'll be going back to that book club again.

Collaborative Activity

Team up with a partner and put brackets around the nine end punctuation errors in Marina's paragraph. Then, working together, use what you have learned in this chapter to correct these errors. Rewrite the paragraph with your corrections.

EDITING YOUR OWN PARAGRAPH

Now return to the paragraph you wrote and revised at the beginning of this chapter, and underline your periods, question marks, and exclamation points.

Collaborative Activity

Exchange paragraphs with your partner, and circle any errors in end punctuation that you find in your partner's paragraph.

Individual Activity

On the Error Log in Appendix 4, record any end punctuation errors that your partner found in your paragraph. To complete the writing process, correct these errors by rewriting your paragraph.

CHAPTER 21

COMMAS

☑ CHECKLIST for Using Commas

✔ Are commas used to separate items in a series?

✔ Are commas used to set off introductory material?

✔ Is there a comma before *and, but, for, nor, or, so,* and *yet* when they are followed by an independent clause?

✔ Are commas used to set off interrupting material in a sentence?

✔ Are commas used to set off direct quotations?

✔ Are commas used correctly in numbers, dates, addresses, and letters?

The **comma** is the most frequently used punctuation mark, but it is also the most often misused. Commas make reading sentences easier because they separate the parts of sentences. Following the rules in this chapter will help you write clear sentences that are easy to read.

Look at some commas at work in the following paragraph by Deborah Tannen.

I broke the class into small groups to discuss the issues raised in the readings and to analyze their own conversational transcripts. I devised three ways of dividing the students into groups: one by the degree program they were in, one by gender, and one by conversational style, as closely as I could guess it. This meant that when the class was grouped according to conversational style, I put Asian students together, fast talkers together, and quiet students together. The class split into groups six times during the semester, so they met in each grouping twice. I told students to regard the groups as examples of interactional data and to note the different ways they participated in the different groups. Toward the end of the term, I gave them a questionnaire asking about their class and group participation.

In this paragraph, Deborah Tannen describes how she organizes student group activities based on the students' individual personalities. Before continuing in this chapter, take a moment to record some of your own observations. Save your work because you will use it later in this chapter.

WRITING ASSIGNMENT: CLASSROOM BEHAVIOR

What are some of your observations about classroom behavior? What behaviors characterize the students in your English class? Are the dynamics of your English class different from the dynamics of your other classes? What differences and similarities do you see? What conclusions can you draw from these observations? Write a paragraph comparing the students in two of your classes.

REVISING YOUR WRITING

Revise the first draft of your paragraph before you focus on editing. Use the Revising Checklist on pages 24–25 to help you with your revision. Make sure your paragraph has a good topic sentence, is well developed, and is well organized. Then check your paragraph for unity and coherence.

COMMAS WITH ITEMS IN A SERIES

Use commas to separate items in a series.
    This means that you should put a comma between all items in a series.

Series: The class required that we read 2 novels, 20 short stories, and 12 poems.

Series: The students exchanged their essays, read them, and gave each other suggestions.

Series: Tonight I need to finish an essay, read a short story, and answer the questions on page 15.

Sometimes this rule applies to a series of adjectives in front of a noun, but sometimes it does not. Look at these two examples.

Adjectives with Commas:	The **long, boring** lecture is finally over.
Adjectives without Commas:	The **last red** encyclopedia is checked out of the library.

Both of these examples are correct. So how do you know whether or not to use commas? You can use one of two tests. One test is to insert the word "and" between the adjectives. If the sentence makes sense, use a comma. Another test is to switch the order of the adjectives. If the sentence still reads clearly, use a comma between the two words.

Test 1: The **long and boring** lecture is finally over. **OK, so use a comma**

Test 2: The **boring, long lecture** is finally over. **OK, so use a comma**

Test 1: The **last and red** encyclopedia is checked out of the library. **NO comma**

Test 2: The **red last** encyclopedia is checked out of the library. **NO comma**

Reviewing Commas with Items in a Series

Why use commas with items in a series?

_____

Where do these commas go?

_____

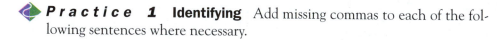 **Practice 1 Identifying** Add missing commas to each of the following sentences where necessary.

1. Emily Dickinson Robert Frost and T. S. Eliot are my favorite poets.

2. My two-year-old son loves to watch Elmo videos, read picture books and color with crayons.

3. Carlos plans on going out to dinner, ordering an expensive meal and enjoying a glass of wine on his birthday.

4. Marty discovered that he's allergic to roses daffodils and mums.

5. Crystal has two dogs, four cats and eight goldfish.

6. We studied *The Tempest, A Midsummer Night's Dream* and *Twelfth Night* in my Shakespeare class.

7. On their vacation, they visited the Grand Canyon Yellowstone National Park, and Old Faithful.

8. I stayed up too late last night studying visiting with my friends, and cleaning my dorm room.

9. My brother, my sister and my cousin started their own business.

10. Christine can play shortstop, catcher and second base.

▶ **P r a c t i c e 2   Identifying** Put an X next to the sentence if any commas in the underlined part of the sentence are missing or used incorrectly.

1. _____ If I win the lottery, I will go to Paris, buy a new house, and pay off my student loans.

2. _____ My best friend can play tennis golf and, racquetball.

3. _____ Charise's fat brown puppy is chewing on my sandals.

4. _____ The piano, the desk, and the entertainment center need to be dusted.

5. _____ I gave my old jeans, my leather jacket and the television to charity.

6. _____ When we went to the hockey game, we ate ice cream popcorn and red licorice.

7. _____ Every day, Debra goes to work, goes to night school, and works out at the gym.

8. _____ Third Watch, ER, and NYPD Blue are all very interesting TV dramas.

9. _____ The old red barn needs to be painted.

10. _____ The salmon the prime rib, and the crab legs are this restaurant's signature dishes.

▶ **P r a c t i c e 3   Correcting** Correct the comma errors in Practice 2 by rewriting each incorrect sentence.

1. _____

2. _____

3. _____

4. _____

5. _____

6. _____

7. _____

8. _____

9. _____

10. _____

◆ *P r a c t i c e 4* **Completing** Add the missing commas to the following paragraph.

When the strangers arrived in the quiet town, they saw a private village a brick silo and a white house. Next to the house was a pigpen a chicken yard and a granary. Hard mud filled the pigpen, but there were no pigs. The doors of the house were dirty the rain gutters were hanging from the rooftops and two windows were broken. Beyond the barn was a small garden of geraniums roses and azaleas. The house appeared to be occupied by a young couple two small boys and a teenage girl. The scattered toys in the front yard gave the strangers this impression. It didn't look like anyone was home, but the strangers hoped the residents wouldn't be gone long. They just wanted a warm meal a soft bed and a pleasant conversation for one night.

◆ *P r a c t i c e 5* **Writing Your Own**

A. Write a sentence of your own for each of the following series.

1. three kinds of animals

   _____

2. three places to spend money

   _____

3. three occupations

_____

4. three things to do at the beach

_____

5. three things to buy at the grocery store

_____

B. Write five sentences of your own using commas correctly to separate items in a series.

1. _____

2. _____

3. _____

4. _____

5. _____

COMMAS WITH INTRODUCTORY WORDS

Use a comma to set off an introductory word, phrase, or clause from the rest of its sentence.

If you are unsure whether to add a comma, try reading the sentence with your reader in mind. If you want your reader to pause after the introductory word or phrase, you should insert a comma.

Introductory Word:	**Yes,** I finished my essay.
Introductory Word:	**Actually,** the class was more interesting than I thought it would be.
Introductory Phrase:	**All in all,** this is a very competitive group.
Introductory Phrase:	**To save time,** I did my homework during my lunch break.
Introductory Clause:	**As the papers were being passed out,** everyone was nervous.

Introductory Clause: **When the professor wrote on the chalk-board, we began taking notes.**

REVIEWING COMMAS WITH INTRODUCTORY WORDS

Why use commas with introductory words, phrases, and clauses?

_____

How can you tell if a comma is needed?

_____

_____

P r a c t i c e   6   **Identifying**   Add missing commas to each of the following sentences where necessary.

1. If I'm lucky we will be getting married in May.
2. Just because you asked I'll tell you the whole story.
3. Well Rebecca isn't choosing sides right now.
4. When we were in class someone belched very loudly.
5. Yes your best option is perhaps to talk to him.
6. Basically there is no other way to get there.
7. As they were walking the man tripped over his shoelaces.
8. Having completed his homework Ned went to bed.
9. In what was for her a noble gesture she volunteered to help.
10. Ultimately there will be one winner.

P r a c t i c e   7   **Identifying**   Put an X next to the sentence if any commas in the underlined part of the sentence are missing or used incorrectly.

1. _____ <u>To be totally honest,</u> I've never liked math classes.
2. _____ <u>Of course</u> I'd love to help you with that project.
3. _____ <u>Hoping, to see some changes</u> we all voted in the last student body election.
4. _____ <u>When they asked, for my opinion,</u> I spoke honestly.

5. _____ Because Camille was with me, I felt brave.

6. _____ Not knowing, what we were up against, we were a little nervous.

7. _____ When she was tired Sara drank lots of coffee.

8. _____ Thank goodness, the hardest part is over.

9. _____ Fortunately Mike, is on the panel too.

10. _____ In hindsight that was a bad decision.

◆ **P r a c t i c e   8   Correcting** Correct the comma errors in Practice 7 by rewriting each incorrect sentence.

1. _____

2. _____

3. _____

4. _____

5. _____

6. _____

7. _____

8. _____

9. _____

10. _____

◆ **P r a c t i c e   9   Completing** Add the missing commas to the following paragraph.

Finally our squad is ready for the big cheerleading competition. Being one of the 10 men on the team I always feel lots of pressure and anxiety. The women count on us to lift, hold, and catch them without a flaw. Really it's not just dropping the girls that I worry about. Every minor mistake takes points away from our total score. When I was in high school cheerleading was just for girls. Now that I'm in college I have a whole different view. The cheerleading squad depends on big, strong men, and the best squads seem to have the most men. Unfortunately it is often difficult to recruit men to cheer. For some reason, many people don't think it's a "manly" thing to do. Personally I can't think of anything more manly than catching a petite cheerleader in a short skirt and swinging her up over my head. It always makes me think of Tarzan and Jane.

◆ Practice 10   Writing Your Own

A. Write a sentence of your own for each of the following introductory words, phrases, or clauses.

1. Well _____

2. When I was in junior high _____

3. After the song started _____

4. Honestly _____

5. To be more specific _____

B. Write five sentences of your own using commas correctly to set off introductory words, phrases, or clauses.

1. _____

2. _____

3. _____

4. _____

5. _____

COMMAS WITH INDEPENDENT CLAUSES

Use a comma before *and, but, for, nor, or, so,* and *yet* when they join two independent clauses. (Remember that an independent clause must have both a subject and a verb.)

Independent Clauses: The instructor put us in small groups, **and** she gave us a new assignment.

Independent Clauses: The essay was difficult to read, but I learned some new vocabulary words.

Hint: Do not use a comma when a single subject has two verbs.

no
comma

         s   v   v

The **instructor put** us in small groups and **gave** us a new assignment.

Adding a comma when none is needed is one of the most common errors in college writing assignments. Only if the second verb has its own subject should you add a comma.

comma

         s   v   s   v

The **instructor put** us in small groups, and **she gave** us a new assignment.

REVIEWING COMMAS WITH INDEPENDENT CLAUSES

Name three coordinating conjunctions.

_____ _____ _____

When should you use a comma before a coordinating conjunction?

_____

Should you use a comma before a coordinating conjunction when a single subject has two verbs?

_____

P r a c t i c e   1 1   **Identifying** Add missing commas to the following sentences where necessary.

1. We made a batch of cookies and we ate too much dough.
2. I wasn't happy about the decision nor did I appreciate their rude comments.
3. Justin waited by the phone yet it never rang.
4. We bought lots of new clothes but many things shrank in the wash.
5. This will be my last night at this job or I'm going to go crazy.

6. The coin collection is in the closet so I think it is in a safe place.

7. I looked for Christina but I didn't see her.

8. I am going to the beach for that is the only place where I can relax.

9. My computer crashed so I'm glad I have a backup.

10. Carmen used to dream of being an astronaut but she realized that she's afraid of heights.

◆ **P r a c t i c e   1 2**   **Identifying** Put an X next to the sentence if any commas in the underlined part of the sentence are missing or used incorrectly.

1. _____ Mom went to the outlet <u>mall and</u> she bought a new jacket for me.

2. _____ My car ran out of <u>gas but</u> the gas gauge said I had a full tank.

3. _____ Greg organized a local baseball <u>league and</u> did lots of fund-raising.

4. _____ I can't stay <u>long for</u> I have a paper to write.

5. _____ My brother is out with his <u>girlfriend or</u> he's working late tonight.

6. _____ Junior is usually late to <u>class, but</u> he's always prepared.

7. _____ I've been <u>dieting yet</u> I haven't lost any weight.

8. _____ I'm going to order either the chicken <u>parmesan, or</u> the fettuc-cine Alfredo.

9. _____ James is taking a trip to <u>Missouri, and</u> he's visiting his grandparents.

10. _____ I have a doctor's appointment in 20 <u>minutes so</u> I have to leave right now.

◆ **P r a c t i c e   1 3**   **Correcting** Correct the comma errors in Practice 12 by rewriting each incorrect sentence.

1. _____

2. _____

3. _____

4. _____

5. _____

6. _____

7. _____

8. _____

9. _____

10. _____

 **P r a c t i c e 1 4 Completing** Add the missing commas to the following paragraph.

The trainers at the Los Angeles Zoo watch the animals closely so they are usually prepared for anything. One of the elephants, Orion, was becoming extremely overweight and the trainers began to worry about him. Orion was very intelligent but he was also very lazy. The trainers started him on a cardiovascular exercise program and within a few months, Orion lost 600 pounds. Then the trainers worried that the exercise might be too much for Orion was 42 years old. They wondered if his heart would be able to take all of this activity, so they called in some veterinarians. The vets brought in an ultrasound machine but they could not detect Orion's heartbeat. They decided that his heart was too deep for the ultrasound to pick up or that his sternum was too thick for the ultrasound machine. Eventually, the vets found other instruments and they determined that Orion was a very healthy elephant. This was a very challenging experience yet it was also very helpful. The vets and trainers learned a great deal about the elephant's anatomy and that will help them deal with Orion in the future.

P r a c t i c e 1 5 Writing Your Own

A. Write a sentence of your own using each of the following coordinating conjunctions with two independent clauses.

1. and _____

2. so _____

3. but _____

4. or _____

5. yet _____

B. Write five sentences of your own using commas correctly with independent clauses and coordinating conjunctions.

1. _____

2. _____

3. _____

4. _____

5. _____

COMMAS WITH INTERRUPTERS

Use a comma before and after a word or phrase that interrupts the flow of a sentence.

Most words that interrupt a sentence are not necessary for understanding the main point of a sentence. Setting them off makes it easier to recognize the main point.

Word: I didn't study for the exam, **however,** because I had to work late.

Word: The exchange student, **Frida,** is from Sweden.

Phrase: The city with the most hotels, **according to this travel journal,** is Las Vegas.

Phrase: This book, ***The Long Valley,*** is a collection of Steinbeck's short stories.

Phrase: James Whitaker, **the chair of the English Department,** is retiring.

A very common type of interrupter is a clause that begins with *who, whose, which, when,* or *where* and is not necessary for understanding the main point of the sentence:

Clause: The new instructor, **who came here from UC Berkeley,** is teaching the American literature class.

Because the information "who came here from UC Berkeley" is not necessary for understanding the main idea of the sentence, it is set off with commas.

> **Clause:**   The public library, **which is downtown,** provides several books on tape.

The main point here is that the public library provides books on tape. Since the other information isn't necessary to understanding the sentence, it can be set off with commas.

Hint: Do not use commas with *who, whose, which, when,* or *where* if the information is necessary for understanding the main point of the sentence.

> My brother **who joined the Navy** came home for Christmas.

Because the information in the *who* clause is necessary to understand which brother came home for Christmas, you should not set it off with commas.

Hint: Do not use commas to set off clauses beginning with *that*.

> The movie theater **that is on Elm Street** is showing *Jurassic Park III*.

REVIEWING COMMAS WITH INTERRUPTERS

Why should you use commas to set off words and phrases in the middle of a sentence?

_____

When should you use commas with who, whose, which, when, *or* where*?*

_____

_____

When should you not use commas before these words?

_____

♦ **P r a c t i c e   1 6   Identifying** Add missing commas to each of the following sentences where necessary.

1. I'm driving my car a Nissan Sentra, on a long road trip.
2. The alligator tamer Steve, is crazy.
3. I will take a nap which I'm looking forward to before the big party.
4. Gardening, Juana's favorite pastime is very hard work.
5. Yvonne read that book *Martin Eden* in her literature class.
6. I need to get a tan obviously before I leave for Hawaii.
7. Paint the house please before our relatives get here.
8. The best restaurant in town according to this article is Fish Lips on Truxton Avenue.
9. I need the credit card that is in your wallet Honey to buy a pair of shoes.
10. Basketball is the best sport however for exercise.

♦ **P r a c t i c e   1 7   Identifying** Put an X next to the sentence if there are any comma errors in the underlined part of the sentence.

1. _____ I bought this <u>car however,</u> because of the extended warranty.
2. _____ Jimmy's favorite <u>character, Buzz Lightyear,</u> is from *Toy Story*.
3. _____ <u>Pink, a female musician</u> is in concert this weekend.
4. _____ The <u>vacuum cleaner which I hate,</u> is in the hall closet.
5. _____ My <u>aunt, who made this bread,</u> lives in New Mexico.
6. _____ The <u>remote control, that is on the coffee table,</u> works the TV, VCR, and DVD player.
7. _____ I need to go to the <u>office which is on the north side of the building</u> to get the tickets.
8. _____ My next-door <u>neighbor, whose cat always torments mine,</u> works for the school district.
9. _____ Jack has been dating <u>Lisa the girl from Texas</u> for about five months.
10. _____ You are the <u>one, of course,</u> who will win this election.

♦ **P r a c t i c e   1 8   Correcting** Correct the comma errors in Practice 17 by rewriting each incorrect sentence.

1. _____

2. _____

3. _____

4. _____

5. _____

6. _____

7. _____

8. _____

9. _____

10. _____

Practice 19   Completing Add the missing commas to the following paragraph.

Doing laundry is my favorite household chore. I have to sort the clothes of course before I throw them all into the washing machine, but I am very picky about what items can be washed together. I put the colors the dark ones in one pile, and the whites go in another. But there are in-between colors like tans and beiges that I cannot put in either stack. Those colors get their own pile. The whites and only the whites are washed in hot water, and sometimes I will put in a little bleach. The colors are always washed in warm or cold usually cold because I don't want the colors to "bleed." I love my washing machine which was quite expensive because it can handle very large loads. Four people live in this house, so believe me their laundry stacks up quickly. Most of the other chores like washing dishes and dusting I will gladly give away, but save the laundry for me.

Practice 20   Writing Your Own

A. Write a sentence of your own using each of the following phrases or clauses as interrupters.

1. who was 16 years old _____

   2. however _____

   3. of course _____

   4. which changes every year _____

   5. whose bike is in my garage _____

B. Write five sentences of your own using commas correctly with interrupting phrases or clauses.

   1. _____

   2. _____

   3. _____

   4. _____

   5. _____

COMMAS WITH DIRECT QUOTATIONS

Use commas to mark direct quotations.

   A direct quotation records a person's exact words. Commas set off the exact words from the rest of the sentence, making it easier to understand who said what.

Direct Quotation: The instructor said, **"The exam will be next Friday."**

Direct Quotation: **"The exam will be next Friday,"** the instructor said.

Direct Quotation: **"The exam,"** said the instructor, **"will be next Friday."**

Hint: If a quotation ends with a question mark or an exclamation point, do not use a comma. Only one punctuation mark is needed.

NOT   **"What was the question?,"** he asked.

CORRECT   **"What was the question?"** he asked.

REVIEWING COMMAS WITH DIRECT QUOTATIONS

Why should you use commas with a direct quotation?

_____

Should you use a comma if the quotation ends with a question mark or an exclamation point? Why or why not?

_____

P r a c t i c e   21   Identifying Add missing commas to the following sentences where necessary.

1. "Yeah Dodgers!" they screamed.
2. "We'll meet you at the park" Suki said.
3. Tina quietly whispered "Don't eat the rice."
4. "I can't see where I'm going" said Wanda.
5. "When you get to Real Road," he said "turn right."
6. "I can't find my lucky pencil" she said sadly.
7. "If you've finished your homework" said the teacher "pass it forward."
8. Rachel screamed "A spider is on my head!"
9. "We need more envelopes for this office" said the receptionist.
10. "Take me to your leader" commanded the alien.

P r a c t i c e   22   Identifying Put an X next to the sentence if there are any comma errors in the underlined part of the sentence.

1. _____ Shawn <u>said, "I</u> think this is a good day for tennis."
2. _____ "Take me <u>dancing" said</u> Helen Hunt's character in *As Good As It Gets*.
3. _____ "I can't <u>believe" she said</u>, <u>"that</u> you are going to miss the big event."
4. _____ "We got the <u>loan!" Simone</u> shouted in glee.
5. _____ Julian <u>asked "Where</u> are we supposed to meet?"
6. _____ "Do these pants make me look <u>fat?," she</u> asked.

7. _____ "Go to <u>work</u>," he said, "<u>and</u> I'll take you to dinner when you get home."

8. _____ "If you <u>insist</u>," she said, "<u>then</u> that's the way it will be."

9. _____ Tara <u>snapped</u> "Get back in line!"

10. _____ "Is this fish <u>fresh</u>?" I asked the waitress.

◆ **P r a c t i c e   2 3   Correcting** Correct the comma errors in Practice 22 by rewriting each incorrect sentence.

1. _____

2. _____

3. _____

4. _____

5. _____

6. _____

7. _____

8. _____

9. _____

10. _____

◆ **P r a c t i c e   2 4   Completing** Add the missing commas to the following paragraph.

"I'm looking for some plants for my garden" Annabel told the man at the nursery. "What kinds of plants did you have in mind?" he asked her. "Well, something that can tolerate heat" she said "because my garden gets lots of sun." "If you want flowers" he said "roses are always nice, and these petunias would do well." Annabel thought about them and said "I need something that spreads out, too like a ground cover." "Oh" he said "I have just the thing for you! Try this verbena." "Will it spread out pretty far?" she asked. "Absolutely" he assured her "and it will be full of little flowers." "I'll take it" she said, pulling out her wallet.

 **P r a c t i c e 2 5** **Writing Your Own**

A. Write a sentence of your own for each of the following quotations.

1. a direct quotation about the weather

_____

2. a direct quotation about your job

_____

3. a direct quotation about television

_____

4. a direct quotation about dinner

_____

5. a direct quotation about attending class regularly

_____

B. Write five sentences of your own using commas correctly with direct quotations.

1. _____

2. _____

3. _____

4. _____

5. _____

OTHER USES OF COMMAS

Other commas clarify information in everyday writing.

Numbers: What is **2,667,999** divided by **10,300?**

Dates: Mike and Melissa were married on **August 1, 2000,** in Cincinnati.

Notice that there is a comma both before and after the year.

Addresses: Nicole moved from **Lamont, California,** to **8900 New Fork Lane, Aspen, CO 81612.**

Notice that there is no comma between the state and the zip code.

States: They moved from San Antonio, Texas, to Phoenix, Arizona.

Notice that there is a comma both before and after a state.

Letters: **Dear Alyson,**

Yours truly,

REVIEWING OTHER USES OF COMMAS

Give one example of commas in each of the following situations:

Numbers _____

Dates _____

Addresses _____

Letters _____

Why are these commas important?

_____

♦ **P r a c t i c e   2 6**   **Identifying** Add missing commas to the following where necessary.

1. The murder took place near 4000 Chester Avenue.
2. More than 55600 excited fans rushed onto the field.
3. February 14 2004 was the worst Valentine's Day I have ever had.
4. My car needs a new transmission, but it will cost over $1200.
5. We had $3565 in tax deductions last year.
6. Quincy is looking into buying a house at 355 Park Way.
7. Dear Mark
8. The next assessment exam is on March 4 2005.

9. Our new address is 4800 Jackson Place, Richmond VA 23221.

10. Sincerely yours

P r a c t i c e   2 7   Identifying Put an X next to the sentence if there are any comma errors in the underlined part of the sentence.

1. _____ My grandmother lives at 3,230 Eureka Street.

2. _____ On June 10, 2006 I will graduate from this university.

3. _____ The boys are camping in Denver, Colorado.

4. _____ This stadium holds 300,00 people.

5. _____ We moved from Jackson, Mississippi, to Oakland, California.

6. _____ We were married on December 3 2003.

7. _____ I only paid $1566 for my new bedroom furniture.

8. _____ There are approximately 450000 people living in this city.

9. _____ William built a house at 2244 Knoxbury Street, Miami, FL, 33012.

10. _____ The winner of the contest will receive $5000,00 in prize money.

P r a c t i c e   2 8   Correcting Correct the comma errors in Practice 27 by rewriting each incorrect sentence.

1. _____

2. _____

3. _____

4. _____

5. _____

6. _____

7. _____

8. _____

9. _____

10. _____

 **P r a c t i c e   2 9   Completing** Add the missing commas to the following paragraph.

My cousin joined the Marines on June 20 1996 and after boot camp, he was sent to Okinawa Japan. At this base, he worked in communications. Since he was such a quick learner, he advanced in rank very quickly. Soon he was responsible for more than 1500 other Marines. His paychecks were not very much—approximately $2000 each month—however, he was single and didn't have any big bills. After three years and many other tours, the Marines asked him if he was planning to stay in the service. He had a great reputation, and they wanted him to keep advancing in rank. My cousin thought about it for a long time, but he decided that he would be happier back in the civilian world. After his discharge, he bought a house in Topeka Kansas and fell in love with a wonderful girl. Several of my cousin's Marine friends were at their wedding on November 16 2001 to share in their happiness.

P r a c t i c e   3 0   Writing Your Own

A. Write a sentence of your own for each of the following items.

1. your current address

_____

2. the date you were born

_____

3. the number of students at your school

_____

4. the amount of money you would like to make in one year

_____

5. the address of your campus library

_____

B. Write five sentences of your own using commas correctly with numbers, dates, and addresses.

1. _____

2. _____

3. _____

4. _____

5. _____

CHAPTER REVIEW

You might want to reread your answers to the questions in all the review boxes before you do the following exercises.

*Review **P r a c t i c e**   **1** Reading* Refer to the paragraph by Deborah Tannen on pages 368–369 to do the following exercises.

1. List the two sentences that use commas to separate items in a series.

_____

_____

_____

_____

2. List one introductory phrase that is set off with a comma.

_____

_____

3. List the sentence that uses a comma with two independent clauses.

_____

_____

4. Rewrite the following sentence from the paragraph with an interrupter and commas.

I broke the class into small groups to discuss the issues raised in the readings.

_____

5. Rewrite the following sentence from the paragraph to make it a direct quotation, using commas correctly.

I told students to regard the groups as examples of interactional data and to note the different ways they participated in the different groups.

_____

_____

6. Add another sentence to the following sentence, using commas correctly with numbers or dates.

Toward the end of the term, I gave them a questionnaire asking about their class and group participation.

_____

 **Review P r a c t i c e   2 Identifying** Underline the incorrect and missing commas in each of the following sentences.

1. When we went to the store we forgot to buy milk.
2. Cesar tried to move the refrigerator, but it was too heavy.
3. Fortunately this is the last chemistry class that I have to take.
4. "Really " she said, "I never meant to hurt, your feelings."
5. I sat next to Carter, my best friend at the concert.
6. We started this class on September 7 2004.
7. Chaney brought chips salsa, and soft drinks to the party.
8. The empty deserted farmhouse, caught fire yesterday.
9. We need to raise $100 500 in donations.
10. I found the special paper pen and ink, that I need at a stationery store.

Review Practice 3 Correcting Correct the comma errors in Review Practice 2 by rewriting each incorrect sentence.

EDITING A STUDENT PARAGRAPH

Following is a paragraph written and revised by Marla Anderson in response to the writing assignment in this chapter. Read the paragraph, and think about where commas should be.

> The students in my English class and the students in my theater class are very different. In theater the students just won't be quiet and settle down. This is probably because the theater students are talkative outgoing people. Usually the class gets out of hand which I don't like. When it gets really bad it sounds like there are 1 000 people in one small classroom. Sometimes I just want to yell "Shut up!" The students in my English class however are very quiet and serious. They usually listen well pay close attention to the teacher and maintain order in the class. I think I probably learn more in this class but it can get boring at times. I'll just be glad when June 10 2005 comes because then I'll be a certified social worker and I'll be finished with my degree.

Collaborative Activity

Team up with a partner, and find the 15 missing commas in Marla's paragraph. Then, working together, use what you have learned in this chapter to label each error from the following list.

1   Commas with items in a series
2   Commas with introductory words
3   Commas with independent clauses
4   Commas with interrupters
5   Commas with direct quotations
6   Commas with numbers, dates, addresses, and letters

Finally, rewrite the paragraph with your corrections.

EDITING YOUR OWN PARAGRAPH

Now return to the paragraph you wrote and revised at the beginning of this chapter. Underline each of your commas.

Collaborative Activity

Exchange paragraphs with your partner, and circle any comma errors that you find in your partner's paragraph.

Individual Activity

Using the six rules governing comma usage, identify the rule for each of the comma errors your partner found in your paragraph. On the Error Log in Appendix 4, record your comma errors. Finally, to complete the writing process, correct these errors by rewriting your paragraph.

APOSTROPHES

CHAPTER 22

 CHECKLIST for Using Apostrophes

✔ Are apostrophes used correctly in contractions?

✔ Are apostrophes used correctly to show possession?

The **apostrophe** looks like a single quotation mark. Its two main purposes are to indicate where letters have been left out and to show ownership.

Let's watch some apostrophes at work in the following paragraph by Alan Monroe.

Someone has said, "Let me hear a voice, and I'll tell you what sort of person he or she is." This statement is, of course, exaggerated; nonetheless, its essential truth is borne out both by common experience and by scientifically conducted experiments. The tone of people's voices varies from normal when they're angry, excited, sleepy, or terrified. Habits of temperament such as nervousness, irritability, or aggressiveness likewise seem to be reflected in one's habitual speaking voice; people are inclined, therefore, to judge one's personality largely on the sound of the voice. A person whose tones are too sharp and nasal is often thought of as being a nagging person. A person whose voice is harsh and guttural is judged to be crude and rough. Weak, thin voices suggest weakness in character. These judgments may, at times, be absolutely contrary to fact; more often they're close to the truth. But whether true or false, such judgments are important in that they color the listener's attitude toward all that the speaker does or says. They're often a major factor in determining the first impression speakers make on their audience.

In this paragraph, Alan Monroe discusses the importance of a speaker's voice. Before continuing in this chapter, take a moment to discuss your feelings about talking in public. Save your work because you will use it later in this chapter.

 WRITING ASSIGNMENT: TALKING IN PUBLIC

Do you feel comfortable talking in front of other people? Are there certain situations that make you uneasy? What about classroom situations? Do you like to answer questions and participate in class discussions? Are you the kind of person who tends to dominate discussions, or are you the one who will sit on the sidelines and listen? Write a paragraph describing your reactions when you have to talk in public.

 REVISING YOUR WRITING

Revise the first draft of your paragraph before you focus on editing. Use the Revising Checklist on pages 24–25 to help you with your revision. Make sure your paragraph has a good topic sentence, is well developed, and is well organized. Then check your paragraph for unity and coherence.

MARKING CONTRACTIONS

Use an apostrophe to show that letters have been omitted to form a contraction.

A **contraction** is the shortening of one or more words. Our everyday speech is filled with contractions.

I will	=	I'll (*w* and *i* have been omitted)
do not	=	don't (*o* has been omitted)
let us	=	let's (*u* has been omitted)

Here is a list of commonly used contractions.

Some Common Contractions

I am	=	*I'm*	*you will*	=	*you'll*
I would	=	*I'd*	*he is*	=	*he's*
I will	=	*I'll*	*she will*	=	*she'll*
you have	=	*you've*	*it is*	=	*it's*

we have	=	*we've*	*do not*	=	*don't*
we will	=	*we'll*	*did not*	=	*didn't*
they are	=	*they're*	*have not*	=	*haven't*
they have	=	*they've*	*could not*	=	*couldn't*

Hint: Two words that are frequently misused are *it's* and *its*.

it's = contraction: it is (or it has)   **It's** too late to go to the movie.

its = pronoun: belonging to it   **Its** eyes are really large.

To see if you are using the correct word, say the sentence with the words *it is*. If that is what you want to say, add an apostrophe to the word.

?   I wonder if **its** on the dresser.

Test: I wonder if **it is** on the dresser.   **YES, add an apostrophe**

This sentence makes sense with *it is*, so you should write *it's*.

Correct: I wonder if **it's** on the dresser.

?   The horse stomped **its** foot.

Test: The horse stomped **it is** foot.   **NO, so no apostrophe**

This sentence does not make sense with *it is*, so you should not use the apostrophe in *its*.

Correct: The horse stomped **its** foot.

REVIEWING CONTRACTIONS

What is the purpose of an apostrophe in a contraction?

_____

Write five contractions and tell which letters have been omitted.

_____   _____

_____   _____

_____   _____

_____   _____

_____   _____

What is the difference between it's and its?

_____

◆ **P r a c t i c e 1** **Identifying** Add missing apostrophes to the following sentences where necessary.

1. My husband wonders why babies dont come with instruction manuals.
2. Sylvia wont be attending the class reunion.
3. Theyre going to Mustang Island for the weekend.
4. You shouldnt have said that.
5. Gretchen said shes feeling much better now.
6. Isnt it funny that we were in the same class all semester and never knew it?
7. If you could help me with this, Id really appreciate it.
8. Weve been so busy lately that we forgot to RSVP for the party.
9. Elise cant make it tonight, but shell be there tomorrow.
10. Its a funny thing that our chicken always lays its eggs in my dads boot.

◆ **P r a c t i c e 2** **Identifying** Put an X next to the sentence if an apostrophe is missing or used incorrectly.

1. _____ Youve got to leave before my parents get home.
2. _____ My sister said that she's applying to UCLA.
3. _____ I think wel'l be able to make it.
4. _____ Amber did'nt have a ride to class.
5. _____ We're going to the mountains on Friday.
6. _____ Its a nice day today.
7. _____ He said they've been here before.
8. _____ Can you write the report while Im making the display?
9. _____ The cat knocked it's bowl over last night.
10. _____ Hows this plan going to work?

◆ **P r a c t i c e 3** **Correcting** Correct the apostrophe errors in Practice 2 by rewriting each incorrect sentence.

1. _____

2. _____

3. _____

4. _____

5. _____

6. _____

7. _____

8. _____

9. _____

10. _____

P r a c t i c e   4   Completing Add apostrophes to the contractions in the following paragraph.

Gordon Foster couldnt drive fast enough to pick up his wife, Betsy, from the airport. Shed been at a conference in Tennessee for five days, and he couldnt wait to see her again. Shes one of the nutritionists for the city's hospital, and they re always being sent to meetings and lectures out of state. When shes gone, Gordon cant stand it. They ve only got two children, and the kids are now in high school, so its not that hes stuck changing diapers or preparing bottles. He just doesnt like being without Betsy. Sometimes shell shake her head and laugh at how dependent Gordon is. But its pretty obvious that she enjoys being missed so much.

P r a c t i c e   5   Writing Your Own

A. Write a sentence of your own for each of the following contractions.

1. he's _____

2. they'll _____

3. couldn't _____

4. doesn't _____

5. we'd _____

B. Write five sentences of your own using apostrophes correctly in contractions.

1. _____

2. _____

3. _____

4. _____

5. _____

SHOWING POSSESSION

Use an apostrophe to show **possession.**

1. For a singular word, use *'s* to indicate possession or ownership. You can always replace a possessive with *of* plus the noun or pronoun.

   the team**'s** leader   =   the leader **of the team**
                                    (the team possesses the leader)

   Edward**'s** car   =   the car **of Edward**
                                    (Edward possesses the car)

   the teacher**'s** rules   =   the rules **of the teacher**
                                    (the teacher possesses the rules)

   tomorrow**'s** weather   =   the weather **of tomorrow**
                                    (tomorrow "owns" or "possesses" the weather)

2. For plural nouns ending in *-s*, use only an apostrophe.

   the students**'** books   =   the books **of the students**

   the sisters**'** bedroom   =   the bedroom **of the sisters**

   the writers**'** convention =   the convention **of the writers**

   the tourists**'** hotel   =   the hotel **of the tourists**

3. For plural nouns that do not end in *-s*, add *'s*.

   the men**'s** bathroom   =   the bathroom **of the men**

   the children**'s** toys   =   the toys **of the children**

   the women**'s** tea party =   the tea party **of the women**

REVIEWING POSSESSIVES

How do you mark possession or ownership for a singular word?

_____

How do you mark possession or ownership for a plural word that ends in -s?

_____

How do you mark possession or ownership for a plural word that doesn't end in -s?

_____

 **P r a c t i c e   6   Identifying** Add missing apostrophes to each of the following sentences where necessary.

1. Janets last day at work will be Wednesday.
2. From here on, this receptionists job includes filing documents.
3. All of the neighborhood boys bicycles need to stay out of the street.
4. My cousins car is in the shop.
5. Thomass pencil is on my desk.
6. Robin made cookies for Secretaries Day.
7. This teams 12 wins put it in second place.
8. The lawyers briefcase hit me in the leg as I walked by.
9. I never could understand Mr. Davidsons sense of humor.
10. The dentists drill needs to be sterilized after each patient.

P r a c t i c e   7   Identifying Put an X next to the sentence if an apostrophe is missing or used incorrectly.

1. _____ Jennifer's dad is on his way to Boston.
2. _____ Dustin wrecked his moms car last night.
3. _____ The two dog's food dish is full of bugs.
4. _____ Damians walls are covered with Post-it Notes.

5. _____ My one brothers' dream is to climb Mount Everest.

6. _____ Uncle Bobs' boat sank in Lake Erie.

7. _____ They broke into their friend's room and left a present.

8. _____ Can you see the childrens' department from here?

9. _____ The many customers complaints have been reviewed.

10. _____ Are you going to Eddies' birthday party?

◆ **P r a c t i c e   8   Correcting** Correct the apostrophe errors in Practice 7 by rewriting each incorrect sentence.

1. _____

2. _____

3. _____

4. _____

5. _____

6. _____

7. _____

8. _____

9. _____

10. _____

◆ **P r a c t i c e   9   Completing** Add apostrophes to the possessive nouns in the following paragraph.

Last year we spent Mothers Day at the Rollerama with my little sister. We decided that our familys time together was important, so we promised each other we would stay together all day. Beths passion is to roller-skate. Dads passion is not to roller-skate. I was somewhere in the middle, and Mom was just enjoying the days activities. The roller rinks entrance fee was waived that day, and all the other prices were discounted. My sisters friends were there, and I was embarrassed to be there. But I have to admit that I had fun.

P r a c t i c e   1 0   Writing Your Own

A. Create possessive nouns from the following phrases, and write a sentence
   of your own for each one.

1. the program of the children

   _____

2. the dress code of the school

   _____

3. the lunch break of the workers

   _____

4. the cookies of the grandmother

   _____

5. the problems of Susanna

   _____

B. Write five sentences of your own using apostrophes correctly in possessive nouns.

1. _____

2. _____

3. _____

4. _____

5. _____

COMMON APOSTROPHE ERRORS

Two common errors occur with apostrophes. The following guidelines
will help you avoid these errors.

No Apostrophe with Possessive Pronouns

Do not use an apostrophe with a possessive pronoun.

Possessive pronouns already show ownership, so they do not need an apostrophe.

Incorrect	Correct
his'	his
her's or hers'	hers
it's or its'	its
your's or yours'	yours
our's or ours'	ours
their's or theirs'	theirs

No Apostrophe to Form the Plural

Do not use an apostrophe to form a plural word.

This error occurs most often with plural words ending in *-s*. An apostrophe indicates possession or contraction; it does *not* indicate the plural. Therefore, a plural word never takes an apostrophe unless it is possessive.

NOT	The **bike's** are in the garage.
CORRECT	The **bikes** are in the garage.

NOT	He bought a new pair of **shoe's** yesterday.
CORRECT	He bought a new pair of **shoes** yesterday.

NOT	I saw eight hockey **game's** this season.
CORRECT	I saw eight hockey **games** this season.

REVIEWING APOSTROPHE ERRORS

List three possessive pronouns.

_____   _____   _____

Why don't possessive pronouns take apostrophes?

_____

What is wrong with the apostrophe in each of the following sentences?
The last float in the parade is ours'.

_____

There must be 100 floats' in the parade.

_____

 **P r a c t i c e   1 1   Identifying** Add missing apostrophes in the following sentences where necessary.

1. We help with Dads projects whenever he's around.
2. My supervisors files are a mess!
3. I thought your presentation was great, but I really enjoyed Mistys and hers.
4. Kyles going to his grandfathers house.
5. Dust Susans lamps while Im cleaning out her refrigerator.
6. That parrot used to be theirs, but now its Sydneys.
7. Winston received five awards at yesterdays ceremony.
8. I thought I had good penmanship until I saw Terrences.
9. If the neighbors dog barks at you, give him a treat.
10. One of those chairs legs is broken.

P r a c t i c e   1 2   Identifying Put an X next to the sentence if an apostrophe is missing or used incorrectly.

1. _____ That new car is her's.
2. _____ I lost my handouts, so I had to borrow theirs.
3. _____ There were four nails' in my front tire.
4. _____ This is my paper, but can I see your's?
5. _____ Jackson ordered pizza's for our meeting.
6. _____ Office Depot has computer's on sale.
7. _____ Do you have his telephone number?
8. _____ These book's are going to the basement.
9. _____ You can sit at any of the tables in this room.
10. _____ When they ran out of their soft drinks, I offered to share our's.

◆ **P r a c t i c e   1 3**   **Correcting** Correct the apostrophe errors in Practice 12 by rewriting each incorrect sentence.

1. _____

2. _____

3. _____

4. _____

5. _____

6. _____

7. _____

8. _____

9. _____

10. _____

◆ **P r a c t i c e   1 4**   **Completing** Correct the apostrophe errors in the following paragraph.

After breakfast, Sam walked around the cabin. Bug's had come in through the hole in the screen door, and Sam squashed some of them with his' bare hand's. The cabin was especially quiet, so he began looking through the cabinet's in the kitchen. He was hungry, but he didn't want to bother any of the other campers'. He found a jar of grape jelly that was labeled "Homemade by Marci," and he tasted it. He also found some homemade biscuit's that he knew were her's too, but he didn't think she'd mind if he ate them. When he'd just about filled his' stomach, Marci walked into the room. She smiled at him and gave him two napkin's to wipe the jelly off of his face.

◆ **P r a c t i c e   1 5**   **Writing Your Own**

A. Write a sentence of your own for each of the following possessive pronouns.

1. hers _____

2. its _____

3. his _____

4. yours _____

5. theirs _____

B. Write five sentences of your own using apostrophes correctly.

1. _____

2. _____

3. _____

4. _____

5. _____

CHAPTER REVIEW

You might want to reread your answers to the questions in the review boxes before you do the following exercises.

Review P r a c t i c e 1 Reading Refer to the paragraph by Alan Monroe on page 395 to do the following exercises.

1. List four contractions from the paragraph.

_____   _____

_____   _____

2. List four possessive nouns with apostrophes.

_____   _____

_____   _____

3. List two possessive pronouns.

_____   _____

4. List four plural nouns that end in *-s*.

_____   _____

_____   _____

◆ **Review Practice 2 Identifying** Underline the words missing apostrophes or the words in which apostrophes are used incorrectly in each of the following sentences.

1. Terrys piano needs to be tuned.
2. The library's hour's change every six month's.
3. Some of the actor's werent familiar with their lines.
4. Im going to the mall to buy pant's like your's.
5. My geranium's havent bloomed yet.
6. Its impossible to see those planet's without a telescope.
7. Shes going to Magic Mountain for the day.
8. The waters too cold for swimming right now.
9. My principals wife is one of my aunts friend's.
10. I shouldnt have told you about that new house of their's.

◆ **Review Practice 3 Correcting** Correct the apostrophe errors in Review Practice 2 by rewriting the sentences.

1. _____

2. _____

3. _____

4. _____

5. _____

6. _____

7. _____

8. _____

9. _____

10. _____

EDITING A STUDENT PARAGRAPH

Following is a paragraph written and revised by Willie Perkins in response to the writing assignment in this chapter. Read the paragraph, and underline each of his words with apostrophes.

I like to talk, especially when I have an audience. I'm usually the one coming up with conversation topic's, trying to make people laugh, and "breaking the ice." Sometimes in a classroom situation, though, its different. I dont mind answering question's that the instructor poses, but sometimes Im afraid that Ill say the wrong thing and make a fool of myself. The difference is that in social situations, I'm not being judged. Everyone's trying to be friend's and have fun. In a classroom, the instructor is waiting to see if I know what Im talking about. The instructor's always judging me, but that's the instructors job. Though I'm not always the one to dominate class discussion's, I do like to participate in them. I'd much rather we talk in groups than listen to lectures. I like to hear other students opinions, because sometimes they'll bring up very interesting points. Although talking in front of people can sometimes be intimidating, its a very good way to learn about yourself.

Collaborative Activity

Team up with a partner, and mark an X above the eight words that are missing apostrophes in Willie's paragraph. Place a second underline under the four plural nouns that use apostrophes incorrectly. Then, working together, use what you have learned in this chapter to correct these errors. Rewrite the paragraph with your corrections.

EDITING YOUR OWN PARAGRAPH

Now return to the paragraph you wrote and revised at the beginning of this chapter. Underline each word that contains an apostrophe.

Collaborative Activity

Exchange paragraphs with your partner, and circle any missing or misplaced apostrophes or words missing apostrophes that you find in your partner's paragraph.

Individual Activity

On the Error Log in Appendix 4, record the apostrophe errors that your partner found in your paragraph. To complete the writing process, correct these errors by rewriting your paragraph.

QUOTATION MARKS

 CHECKLIST for Using Quotation Marks

> ✔ Are quotation marks used to indicate someone's exact words?
> ✔ Are all periods and commas inside quotation marks?
> ✔ Are words capitalized correctly in quotations?
> ✔ Are quotation marks used to indicate the title of a short work, such as a short story or a poem?

Quotation marks are punctuation marks that work together in pairs. Their most common use is to indicate someone's exact words. They are also used to mark the title of a short piece of writing, such as a short story or a poem.

Note how quotation marks are used in the following paragraph by Anna Quindlen.

My husband, a bred-in-the-bone Boyfriend, was terrified of this aspect of having children, convinced that on the morning after our first son was born he would awaken with a drawerful of pajamas and cardigan sweaters and the urge to say things like, "Now, son, I think we should have a little talk about that." Not a chance. His most recent foray into fatherhood was to teach both his children the words to "You Give Love a Bad Name." The eldest can also play air guitar along with the song. On the one hand, I hate "You Give Love a Bad Name," although my children sing it rather well. On the other hand, my husband would not think twice about scandalizing a Confederate ball by bidding $150 in gold to dance with me. And, like Scarlett, when someone said, "She will not consider it, sir," I know what I would say without a moment's hesitation: "Oh, yes, I will."

In this paragraph, Anna Quindlen writes about music's role in her marriage. Before continuing in this chapter, take a moment to record your ideas about music. Save your work because you will use it later in this chapter.

 WRITING ASSIGNMENT: MUSIC

Are you interested in music? Do you play music or enjoy listening to it? How has music affected you personally? Has it helped you make friends, or has it helped you learn more about yourself? Write a paragraph explaining your thoughts about music and the role it plays in your life.

 REVISING YOUR WRITING

Revise the first draft of your paragraph before you focus on editing. Use the Revising Checklist on pages 24–25 to help you with your revision. Make sure your paragraph has a good topic sentence, is well developed, and is well organized. Then check your paragraph for unity and coherence.

DIRECT QUOTATIONS

Use quotation marks to indicate a **direct quotation**—someone's exact words.

Here are some examples that show the three basic forms of a direct quotation.

Direct Quotation: "This is a great song," said the teenager.

In this example, the quoted words come first.

Direct Quotation: The teenager said, "This is a great song."

In the example above, the quoted words come after the speaker is named.

Direct Quotation: "This," the teenager said, "is a great song."

In this example, the quoted words are interrupted, and the speaker is named in the middle. This form emphasizes the first few words.

INDIRECT QUOTATIONS

If you just talk about someone's words, you do not need quotation marks. Indirect quotations usually include the word *that*, as in *said that*. In questions, the wording is often *asked if*. Look at these examples of **indirect quotations.**

Direct Quotation: "I'm joining a rock band," said Rick.

These are Rick's exact words, so you must use quotation marks.

Indirect Quotation: Rick **said that** he is going to join a rock band.

This sentence explains what Rick said but does not use Rick's exact words. So quotation marks should not be used.

Direct Quotation: "There will be a jazz concert next weekend," said Donna.

Indirect Quotation: Donna **said that** there will be a jazz concert next weekend.

Direct Quotation: "Could you sing at my wedding?" Jordan asked.

Indirect Quotation: Jordan **asked if** I could sing at her wedding.

REVIEWING QUOTATION MARKS WITH QUOTATIONS

How do you show that you are repeating someone's exact words?

_____

What is an indirect quotation?

_____

◆ **P r a c t i c e   1   Identifying** Add missing quotation marks to the following sentences where necessary.

1. Nadia said, I really liked visiting with you yesterday.
2. Murphy asked, Can we start this project tonight?

3. I called the phone company and said, My phone has been disconnected."

4. "Take me to the game with you, Stefan begged.

5. "This is the only afternoon, I said, when we can get these things finished."

6. "Are you ready? they asked us.

7. The firefighters yelled to the woman, Jump out the window!

8. Charles told me, He didn't do well on the last test.

9. "Stand up and cheer! yelled the cheerleaders.

10. This dip is outstanding, I told her.

♦ **P r a c t i c e   2   Identifying** Put an X next to the sentence if quotation marks are missing or used incorrectly.

1. _____ "Run! yelled the first base coach.

2. _____ Ricardo said, The apple pie "tastes delicious."

3. _____ "Going to the movies," she said, "is my favorite pastime."

4. _____ Angela asked if "we could help her with her car."

5. _____ Jackie replied, "Of course, you are invited.

6. _____ "Is this the best you could do?" I asked.

7. _____ "Give me one reason," he said, why I should believe you."

8. _____ Nicole said "that she wanted to see Big Ben."

9. _____ "Can I get you something to drink? the hostess asked.

10. _____ "Don't forget," she said, "that we have a test tomorrow."

♦ **P r a c t i c e   3   Correcting** Correct the quotation mark errors in Practice 2 by rewriting each incorrect sentence.

1. _____

2. _____

3. _____

4. _____

5. _____

6. _____

7. _____

8. _____

9. _____

10. _____

◆ *P r a c t i c e* **4** **Completing** Add quotation marks to the following paragraph.

Kevin had the day off, so he called Marty and asked, Do you want to play golf today? Well, I don't know, said Marty. What do you mean? asked Kevin. Marty explained, I promised my girlfriend we'd go to the beach. The beach? Kevin said. Well, it's our six-month anniversary, Marty said. You don't count months for anniversaries, Kevin responded, because anniversaries mark only years. Marty didn't follow his logic. The word is related to the word *annual,* which means yearly, Kevin continued, so you don't owe her anything until you have dated for one year. Marty thought for a minute and then replied, I think you should be the one to explain that to my girlfriend. No thanks, Kevin replied. I'd have better luck finding someone else to golf with!

◆ *P r a c t i c e* **5** **Writing Your Own**

A. Write a sentence of your own for each of the following items.

1. a question Rochelle asked

   _____

2. a statement spoken by a police officer

   _____

3. an exclamation spoken by Randy

   _____

4. an indirect question that Tabitha asked

   _____

5. a statement spoken by the plumber

_____

B. Write five sentences of your own using quotation marks correctly.

1. _____

2. _____

3. _____

4. _____

5. _____

CAPITALIZING AND USING OTHER PUNCTUATION MARKS WITH QUOTATION MARKS

When you are quoting someone's complete sentences, begin with a capital letter and use appropriate end punctuation—a period, a question mark, or an exclamation point. You do not need to capitalize the first word of a quotation if it is only part of a sentence. Here are some examples.

Capitalize the first letter of the first word being quoted, and put a period at the end of the sentence if it is a statement. Separate the spoken words from the rest of the sentence with a comma.

"This is a very good band," he said.
She said, "Turn up the stereo."

If the quotation ends with a question mark or an exclamation point, use that punctuation instead of a comma or a period.

He yelled, "Stop that car!"
"Why are you leaving?" she asked.

In a quotation that is interrupted, capitalize the first word being quoted, but do not capitalize words in the middle of the sentence. Use a comma both before and after the interruption. End with a period if it is a statement.

"Yes," said the guitar player, "we will give you a concert."

You do not need to capitalize the first word of a quotation that is only part of a sentence.

My mom told me to relax and "have faith."

Hint: Look at the examples again. Notice that periods and commas always go inside the quotation marks.

NOT	"No", he said, "this isn't the way to Woodstock".
CORRECT	"No," he said, "this isn't the way to Woodstock."

REVIEWING CAPITALIZATION AND PUNCTUATION WITH QUOTATION MARKS

When you quote someone's exact words, why should you begin with a capital letter?

_____

Where do commas go in relation to quotation marks? Where do periods go?

_____

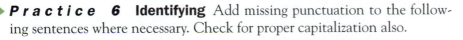 **P r a c t i c e   6   Identifying** Add missing punctuation to the following sentences where necessary. Check for proper capitalization also.

1. "These are the best cookies I have ever eaten, she remarked.
2. What happened to Jeremy? Terry asked.
3. Fatima smiled and said, thanks so much for coming by to see me."
4. "Take this class with me, said my friend.
5. Rachel exclaimed, "I passed the test!"
6. "Could you drop these off for me? Greta asked.
7. The nurse instructed, Lie down on your side."
8. Ouch! My ankle's broken! screamed Tim.
9. "I think I'm feeling sick, said Aiko.
10. "We're meeting at lunch in the cafeteria, he said.

◆ *P r a c t i c e   7* **Identifying** Put an X next to the sentence if it contains capitalization or punctuation errors.

1. _____ "Give up", he said as he tackled his opponent.

2. _____ Rudolfo complained, "There's no more turkey in the refrigerator."

3. _____ "Walk me to my car, she said, "so I can talk to you."

4. _____ The tree trimmer asked, "How long has that tree been infected?"

5. _____ "Have you seen," I asked, "That new horror movie?"

6. _____ "If you leave," she told him, don't come back."

7. _____ My neighbor asked, "can we borrow your wheelbarrow?"

8. _____ Landon said, "My fraternity is having a big fund-raiser."

9. _____ Michael greeted his guests and said, "welcome to my home."

10. _____ "This," she said, "is my favorite part of the game."

◆ *P r a c t i c e   8* **Correcting** Correct the errors in Practice 7 by rewriting each incorrect sentence.

1. _____

2. _____

3. _____

4. _____

5. _____

6. _____

7. _____

8. _____

9. _____

10. _____

◆ *P r a c t i c e   9* **Completing** Add quotation marks and other necessary punctuation to the following paragraph.

I took my tomcat to a local pet groomer and asked her, How much would it cost to get this cat bathed? Well, does he have fleas? she asked. Not that I know of, I replied. Then that will make it cheaper she said because he won't need to be dipped. Dipped? I asked. Yes, she explained we have a flea dip that is really effective on cats, but it's more expensive. Well, I think he only needs a normal bath I said. Actually, she said, he's pretty clean already. I think he just needs a good brushing. OK I said, how much would that cost? She stroked my cat's back and answered, I'll do it for $20.

◀ P r a c t i c e   **1 0**   **Writing Your Own**

A. Write a sentence of your own for each of the following direct quotations.

1. "Get off the bus!"

   _____

2. "Maureen is coming over for dinner."

   _____

3. "Are you sure we have ice cream?"

   _____

4. "Hand me that book."

   _____

5. "You need a new tennis racket."

   _____

B. Write five sentences of your own using quotation marks correctly.

1. _____

2. _____

3. _____

4. _____

5. _____

QUOTATION MARKS AROUND TITLES

Put quotation marks around the titles of short works that are parts of larger works. The titles of longer works are put in italics (or underlined).

Quotation Marks	Italics/Underlining
"The Wild Swans" (short story)	*Hans Andersen's Fairy Tales* (book)
"Mud Master" (poem)	*The Collected Poems of Wallace Stevens* (book)
"There's Your Trouble" (song)	*Home* (CD)
"Losing Weight the Easy Way" (magazine article)	*Parenting* (magazine)
"Power Bills on the Rise" (newspaper article)	*Orange County Register* (newspaper)
"The Inferno" (episode of a TV show)	*Third Watch* (TV series)

REVIEWING QUOTATION MARKS WITH TITLES

When do you put quotation marks around a title?

_____

When do you italicize (or underline) a title?

_____

◆ **P r a c t i c e   1 1**   **Identifying** Add missing quotation marks in the following sentences where necessary.

1. Last night's episode of *Law & Order* was called The Verdict.
2. *People* magazine ran an article called Hollywood Threatens Strike!
3. The Joyce Carol Oates story A Good Man Is Hard to Find was made into a movie last summer.

4. We always sing Hit Me with Your Best Shot when we go to the karaoke bar.

5. Wedding Bells Are Ringing was a great article in February's *Bride's Magazine*.

6. Mark Twain wrote the essay How to Tell a Story after he wrote the book *The Adventures of Huckleberry Finn*.

7. The *Boston Globe* conducted a survey asking people about the president's new bill.

8. Aretha Franklin's best song ever was Respect.

9. Birches by Robert Frost was published in 1916.

10. Every time I hear I Will Remember You on the radio, I cry.

◆ **P r a c t i c e   1 2   Identifying** Put an X next to the sentences in which the titles are punctuated incorrectly.

1. _____ "Beloved" is my favorite novel by Toni Morrison.

2. _____ When I hear the Beach Boys sing "Surfin' USA," it makes me want to go to the beach.

3. _____ I read some good gardening advice in Making Roses Your Friends in *American Gardener Magazine*.

4. _____ The "Denver Herald" ran an article on the recent snowstorm.

5. _____ I can't wait to watch "American Idol" tonight.

6. _____ *Success Is Counted Sweetest* is a popular poem by Emily Dickinson.

7. _____ "The Weakest Link" is having the "Celebrity Episode" next Thursday night.

8. _____ "Brown-Eyed Girl" is the theme song for our charity event.

9. _____ Xavier read a great article in "Newsweek" about the recent election.

10. _____ My literature class studied Hawthorne's short story "Young Goodman Brown" this quarter.

◆ **P r a c t i c e   1 3   Correcting** Correct the quotation mark errors in Practice 12 by rewriting each incorrect sentence.

1. _____

2. _____

3. _____

4. _____

5. _____

6. _____

7. _____

8. _____

9. _____

10. _____

◆ *P r a c t i c e   1 4*   **Completing** Place quotation marks around the titles of short works, and underline the titles of long works in the following paragraph.

Marjorie Clemens is a popular celebrity agent in Hollywood. She spotted the band Four Up when it was playing in a small hometown talent show. The group sang Hangin' with My Girl, and Marjorie knew it would be a hit. She put Four Up in contact with Arista Records, who released the album Just Four Fun only a few months later. Soon all of the teen magazines, such as Bop and Teen Dream, were printing articles about Four Up. The guys were stunned by their overnight success as they read articles titled Four Up Not Coming Down and Americans Want These Guys Four Keeps. Three years later, a journalist named Walt Gentry worked with them on a book he titled One, Two, Three, Four Up: Counting on Our Fans. But just when the group had become a household name, the lead singer, Eric Bassy, left for a solo career. Music fans all over America were in tears as they read Four Up Is One Down across the front page of the newspapers.

◆ *P r a c t i c e   1 5*   **Writing Your Own**

A. Write a sentence of your own for each of the following titles. Make up a title if you can't think of one.

1. a short story _____

2. a song title _____

3. a newspaper article _____

4. a poem _____

5. a magazine article _____

B. Write five sentences of your own using quotation marks correctly.

1. _____

2. _____

3. _____

4. _____

5. _____

CHAPTER REVIEW

You might want to reread your answers to the questions in all the review boxes before you do the following exercises.

◆ *Review* **P r a c t i c e** *1* **Reading** Refer to the paragraph by Anna Quindlen on page 411 to do the following exercises.

1. List the three direct quotations in the paragraph.

_____

_____

_____

_____

_____

2. List the one song title in the paragraph.

_____

◆ ***Review P r a c t i c e 2***   **Identifying** Mark an X above each place where punctuation is used incorrectly or missing.

1. Seth is watching his favorite video, I said.

2. Austin asked Can I use your shower?

3. Arlene titled her essay The Truth About Being Twenty.

4. When we arrived at the hotel, the valet asked if "we wanted him to park the car."

5. Zane memorized Roethke's poem My Papa's Waltz for his English class.

6. When Mother Teresa died, the *New York Times* ran an article with the headline Saint Taken Home.

7. When you get back she said let's go out to dinner.

8. Edgar said that "we could meet at his house."

9. We sang Happy Birthday to Fran in class today.

10. I read an article in *Tennis Weekly* titled How Venus Williams Stays in the Game.

◆ ***Review P r a c t i c e 3***   **Correcting** Correct the quotation marks and other punctuation errors in Review Practice 2 by rewriting each of the sentences.

✎ EDITING A STUDENT PARAGRAPH

Following is a paragraph written and revised by Scott Flores in response to the writing assignment in this chapter. Read the paragraph, and underline each of his quotation marks.

> Listening to music is my favorite way to relax. The only instrument that I can play is my stereo, but I like to play it nice and loud. I really enjoy alternative rock

bands, such as Blink 182. I listen to the band's CD "Cheshire Cat" almost every single day. Touchdown Boy is my favorite song, even though my mother hates the lyrics. She always screams, Turn that music down!" But all of my friends like the music too. In fact, I didn't realize that Blink 182 had so many fans. I went to a concert last month and saw about 20 people from my school standing in the audience. I've heard people say, Classical music is the best," but I believe that all music is an expression. It's both an expression of the artist and an expression of the person or people listening to it. With that in mind, I'd say that alternative rock expresses my personality best.

Collaborative Activity

Team up with a partner, and underline twice the six quotation mark errors (including the missing quotation marks) in Scott's paragraph. Then, working together, use what you have learned in this chapter to correct these errors. Rewrite the paragraph with your corrections.

EDITING YOUR OWN PARAGRAPH

Now return to the paragraph you wrote and revised at the beginning of this chapter. Underline each of your quotation marks.

Collaborative Activity

Exchange paragraphs with your partner, and circle any quotation mark errors that you find in your partner's paragraph.

Individual Activity

On the Error Log in Appendix 4, record any quotation mark errors that your partner found in your paragraph. To complete the writing process, correct these errors by rewriting your paragraph.

OTHER PUNCTUATION MARKS

CHAPTER **24**

✓ CHECKLIST for Using Semicolons, Colons, Dashes, and Parentheses

> ✔ Are semicolons used to join two closely related complete sentences?
> ✔ Are long items in a series that already contain commas separated by semicolons?
> ✔ Are colons used correctly to introduce a list?
> ✔ Are dashes used to emphasize or further explain a point?
> ✔ Are parentheses used to include additional, but not necessary, information?

This chapter explains the uses of the **semicolon**, **colon**, **dash**, and **parentheses**. We'll look at these punctuation marks one by one.

Note how the following paragraph by Joan Didion uses those punctuation marks correctly.

But Las Vegas seems to offer something other than "convenience"; it is merchandising "niceness," the facsimile of proper ritual, to children who do not know how else to find it, how to make the arrangements, how to do it "right." All day and evening long on the Strip, one sees actual wedding parties, waiting under the harsh lights at a crosswalk, standing uneasily in the parking lot of the Frontier while the photographer hired by The Little Church of the West ("Wedding Place of the Stars") certifies the occasion, takes the picture: the bride in a veil and white satin pumps, the bridegroom usually in a white dinner jacket, and even an attendant or two, a sister or a best friend in hot-pink *peau de soie*, a flirtation veil, a carnation nosegay. "When I Fall in Love It Will Be Forever," the organist plays, and then a few bars of Lohengrin. The mother cries; the stepfather, awkward in his role, invites the chapel hostess to join them for a drink at the Sands. The hostess declines with a professional smile; she has already transferred her interest to the group waiting outside. One bride out, another in, and again the sign goes up on the chapel door: "One moment please—Wedding."

In this paragraph, Joan Didion describes a Las Vegas wedding. Before continuing in this chapter, take a moment to record your thoughts about some rituals in your life. Save your work because you will use it later in this chapter.

WRITING ASSIGNMENT: RITUALS IN YOUR LIFE

What rituals have you participated in or observed? How did you feel about these rituals? Why do we have rituals? What one ritual holds special memories for you? Write a paragraph explaining this ritual to your class.

REVISING YOUR WRITING

Revise the first draft of your paragraph before you focus on editing. Use the Revising Checklist on pages 24–25 to help you with your revision. Make sure your paragraph has a good topic sentence, is well developed, and is well organized. Then check your paragraph for unity and coherence.

SEMICOLONS

Semicolons are used to separate equal parts of a sentence. They are also used to avoid confusion when listing items in a series.

1. Use a semicolon to separate two closely related independent clauses.

    An independent clause is a group of words with a subject and a verb that can stand alone as a sentence. You might use a semicolon instead of a coordinating conjunction (*and, but, for, nor, or, so, yet*) or a period. Any one of the three options would be correct.

	Independent	Independent
Semicolon:	Carter wants to buy a new truck**;** **he** took one for a test drive yesterday.	
Conjunction:	Carter wants to buy a new truck**,** **so** he took one for a test drive yesterday.	

| Period: | Carter wants to buy a new truck. **He** took one for a test drive yesterday. |

2. Use a semicolon to join two independent clauses that are connected by such words as *however, therefore, furthermore, moreover, for example,* or *consequently.* Put a comma after the connecting word.

Independent   Independent

Semicolon:	Studying for exams is hard work**; however,** getting good grades is important.
Semicolon:	You promised to help me paint the house**; therefore,** I expect you to be here.
Semicolon:	She had a weakness for sweets**; for example,** she couldn't resist chocolate candy.

3. Use a semicolon to separate items in a series when any of the items contain commas.

| **NOT** | To avoid leaving anyone out, we invited all of our friends from high school, college, and work, my mother's bridge club, and my father's tennis buddies. |
| **CORRECT** | To avoid leaving anyone out, we invited all of our friends from high school, college, and work; my mother's bridge club; and my father's tennis buddies. |

REVIEWING SEMICOLONS

How are semicolons used between two independent clauses?

_____

_____

How are semicolons used with items in a series?

_____

 P r a c t i c e   1   Identifying Add missing semicolons or other punctuation to the following sentences where necessary.

1. We went to the drive-in we ordered the cheeseburger special.
2. Monica borrowed $10 from me she needed lunch and bus fare.

3. This weekend, we need to spray the trees, bushes, and flowers for bugs paint the fence and wash the car.

4. This book has been on the best-seller list for a month, but I didn't think it was very good.

5. The curtains need to be cleaned however, I think I can put them in the washing machine.

6. Bathe the baby put him in a new diaper, socks, and pajamas and fix him a bottle.

7. Catherine took that picture when she was in Italy it became her favorite.

8. We threw Pilar a big baby shower consequently she had lots of thank-you notes to write.

9. Please bring me an aspirin I have a horrible headache.

10. I don't agree with his teaching methods furthermore I won't be taking any more classes from him.

◆ *P r a c t i c e   2*   **Identifying** Put an X next to the sentence if it contains errors with semicolons.

1. _____ My house caught fire; I lost all of my pictures from elementary school.

2. _____ We have saved more than $3,000, therefore; it is time that we took a nice vacation.

3. _____ We need to leave right now the movie; starts in five minutes.

4. _____ Jonathan is our strongest runner; he should be the first man in our relay team.

5. _____ Mr. Cheng raises corn; wheat; and oranges on his farm.

6. _____ Deena works at Stairway to Beauty; she cuts hair and does nails.

7. _____ Our toilet overflowed and flooded our carpet, consequently, our insurance premium was raised.

8. _____ The sale items include the furniture, appliances, and bedding; some of the ceiling fans, and the patio furniture.

9. _____ I vacuumed the carpets, but; I didn't polish the hardwood floors.

10. _____ We have two orange cats in our neighborhood, however, I think one of them belongs to Mrs. Ayala.

◆ **Practice 3 Correcting** Correct the punctuation errors in Practice 2 by rewriting each incorrect sentence.

1. _____

2. _____

3. _____

4. _____

5. _____

6. _____

7. _____

8. _____

9. _____

10. _____

◆ **Practice 4 Completing** Add semicolons to the following paragraph.

This summer, my friend Laura had to have knee surgery. She's a very active person she dances and plays volleyball constantly. She has had to sit still for two weeks now, which is almost impossible for her. She is one of those people who can't quit moving she's always in constant motion. If she's not dancing around while she's talking to you, she's sitting in an odd position she's extremely limber. I don't know how much longer she has to stay off her knee I hope it's not long. I think she'll go crazy soon I can already see her dancing in her mind.

◆ **Practice 5 Writing Your Own**

A. Write a sentence of your own of each of the following types.

1. two closely related independent clauses joined with a semicolon

_____

2. two independent clauses joined by the word "nonetheless"

    _____

3. a list that has items that include commas

    _____

4. two independent clauses joined by the word "however"

    _____

5. two independent clauses joined by the words "for example"

    _____

B. Write five sentences of your own using semicolons correctly.

1. _____

2. _____

3. _____

4. _____

5. _____

COLONS

Colons introduce a list or idea that follows them.

1. The main use of the colon is to introduce a list or thought. Here are some examples:

    Colon: Bring the following items with you to the beach: a swim-suit, a towel, sun block, and sunglasses.

    Colon: The mall opened several new stores: Gap, Bath and Beauty, Victoria's Secret, and Old Navy.

    Colon: The answer is clear: take the trip.

    The most common error with colons is using one where it isn't needed.

2. Do not use a colon after the words *such as* or *including*. A complete sentence must come before a colon.

NOT   Use only primary colors, **such as:** blue, yellow, and red.

CORRECT Use only primary colors, **such as** blue, yellow, and red.

NOT   They traveled to many places this summer, **including:** New Mexico and Arizona.

CORRECT They traveled to many places this summer, **including** New Mexico and Arizona.

3. In addition, you should not use a colon after a verb or after a preposition. Remember that a complete sentence must come before a colon.

NOT   The best forms of cardiovascular exercise **are:** tennis and aerobics.

CORRECT The best forms of cardiovascular exercise **are** tennis and aerobics.

NOT   Put the clothes **in:** the closet, the dresser, or the armoire.

CORRECT Put the clothes **in** the closet, the dresser, or the armoire.

REVIEWING COLONS

What is the main use of a colon?

_____

Why should you not use a colon after such words as is *or* of?

_____

◆ **P r a c t i c e   6   Identifying** Add missing colons to the following sentences where necessary.

1. Grandpa served in three wars World War II, Korea, and Vietnam.

2. My favorite slush flavors are bubble gum, grape, and cherry.

3. We bought three new pieces of furniture a dresser, an armoire, and a desk.

4. The ending of this book was awful disappointing, predictable, and pathetic.

5. Could you hand me a pencil, a pen, and some paper?

6. We have three choices for the movie tonight *Harry Potter and the Prisoner Azkaban, Cold Mountain,* or *The Lord of the Rings: The Fellowship of the Ring.*

7. I'll take some food a hot dog, a jumbo pretzel, and an ice-cream cone.

8. My favorite NHL teams are the Dallas Stars, the San Jose Sharks, and the Chicago Blackhawks.

9. Yolanda only has three classes left to take chemistry, astronomy, and statistics.

10. I want to have a career in law enforcement, teaching, or accounting.

◆ **P r a c t i c e   7   Identifying** Put an X next to the sentence if it contains colon errors.

1. _____ We need to bring these things with us, as well as: the sodas, the chips, and the hot dogs.

2. _____ Nathan has: three goals, graduate from college, get accepted by Harvard Law School, and meet Judge Ito.

3. _____ My father always told me to: take pride in myself, believe in my abilities, and trust my instincts.

4. _____ Computers are good for many things: they speed communication, they organize finances, and they format important documents.

5. _____ I learned a great deal in this class: how to proofread, how to check spelling, and how to use colons.

6. _____ My best friends are: Shawna, Kayla, and Margie.

7. _____ I knew she was lying when she: started playing with her hair, wouldn't look me in the eyes, and tried to change the subject.

8. _____ If you forget everything else, remember the following things: be patient, try your best, and forgive yourself.

9. _____ Darren left four things: on the nightstand—his wallet, his glasses, his passport, and his keys.

10. _____ On our vacation, we are going to: Disneyland, Lake Tahoe, and Mount Rushmore.

◆ **P r a c t i c e   8   Correcting** Correct the colon errors in Practice 7 by rewriting each incorrect sentence.

1. _____

2. _____

3. _____

4. _____

5. _____

6. _____

7. _____

8. _____

9. _____

10. _____

◆ *P r a c t i c e* **9** **Completing** Add colons to the following letter.

Dear Howard,

Here are our choices for dinner tonight barbecue the steak in the freezer, heat the leftover lasagna in the fridge, or order a pizza. If you decide on barbecue, I'll need you to do a few things sweep off the back porch, refill the propane tank at the hardware store, and go to the market for barbecue sauce. There are only three brands of barbecue sauce I like. They are Hunts, El Paso, and O'Malley's. Thank you so much for this help. If you decide on pizza, make sure you tell them to add my favorite veggies mushrooms, bell peppers, and olives. If you have any questions, please call me at work. I should be home for dinner.

Thanks again,
Vera

◆ *P r a c t i c e* **10** **Writing Your Own**

A. Write a sentence of your own for each of the following directions, using colons correctly. Remember that a complete sentence must come before a colon.

1. three reasons to eat fast food

   _____

2. three colors in your bedroom

   _____

3. three things on a to-do list

   _____

4. three sports cars you would like to drive

   _____

5. three reasons to own a computer

   _____

B. Write five sentences of your own using colons correctly.

   1. _____

   2. _____

   3. _____

   4. _____

   5. _____

DASHES AND PARENTHESES

Dashes and parentheses set ideas off from the rest of their sentence.

Dashes

Dashes emphasize ideas.

1. Use dashes to emphasize or draw attention to a point.

   Dash: Nancy pinpointed her biggest source of stress—her husband.

In this example, the beginning of the sentence introduces an idea, and the dash then sets off the answer.

> **Dash:** Faithfulness and honesty—these are the keys to a lasting relationship.

In this example, the key words are set off at the beginning and the explanation follows. Beginning this way adds some suspense to the sentence.

> **Dashes:** Patrick gave me a very nice birthday gift—a crystal vase—and I was quite impressed.

The dashes divide this sentence into three distinct parts, which makes the reader pause and think about each part.

Parentheses

Whereas dashes set off material that the writer wants to emphasize, **parentheses** do just the opposite. They are always used in pairs.

2. Use parentheses to set off information that is interesting or helpful but not necessary for understanding the sentence.

> **Parentheses:** My second cousin (**who owns an auto parts store**) is coming to visit.

> **Parentheses:** The best coffee in town (**if you don't mind waiting in line**) is at a coffeehouse called Common Grounds.

3. Parentheses are also used to mark a person's life span and to number items in a sentence. They are always used in pairs. Here are some examples:

> **Parentheses:** Charles Dickens (**1812–1870**) wrote the long novel *Bleak House*.

> **Parentheses:** I have three important errands today: (**1**) pick up the dry cleaning, (**2**) mail the bills, and (**3**) order the flowers.

REVIEWING DASHES AND PARENTHESES

What is the difference between dashes and parentheses?

_____

_____

When do you use dashes?

_____

When do you use parentheses?

_____

_____

 P r a c t i c e   1 1   **Identifying** Figure out whether the underlined words require dashes or parentheses, and add them to the following sentences where necessary.

1. My brother has one love in his life   <u>tennis shoes.</u>
2. We made a foolish purchase   <u>an old Model-T</u>   and ended up spending too much money restoring it.
3. This restaurant   <u>owned by a Vietnamese family</u>   serves great French food.
4. <u>Photography</u>   that is the one thing I can do well.
5. Tillie   <u>who lives next door to my mother</u>   fell yesterday and broke her hip.
6. Lisa opened her mailbox to find the surprise of her life   <u>a check for $500,000.</u>
7. Richard opened his new office in the Haberfeld Center   <u>the tall brick building</u>   to attract more customers.
8. Juanita is staying at my house so she can   <u>1</u>   feed my dogs,   <u>2</u>   water my houseplants, and   <u>3</u>   pick up my mail.
9. Bernadette Bradley   <u>1816–1880</u>   was one of the founders of this city.
10. My computer   <u>a Compaq Presario</u>   cost $1,200 when I bought it.

 P r a c t i c e   1 2   **Identifying** Put an X next to the sentence if it contains errors with dashes or parentheses.

1. _____ I wanted to buy this jacket but (I didn't have enough money).

2. _____ Mandy who plays tennis with my brother is going to Yale next year.

3. _____ There is only one solution—take more time off work.

4. _____ Greta made a good point—and I agree—Bill should not be in charge of that department.

5. _____ Charles Divine lived (from 1919 to 1988).

6. _____ (Courage and respect) these are two things I look for in a man.

7. _____ We gave Janner a television—a big-screen TV—so that he could enjoy the Super Bowl.

8. _____ The highest priorities are 1 the customer complaints, 2 the late bills, and 3 this month's invoices.

9. _____ I could sum up all of my problems with two words (money management).

10. _____ Movies and music—two things every American teen is interested in.

◆ **P r a c t i c e   1 3   Correcting** Correct the punctuation errors in Practice 12 by rewriting each incorrect sentence.

1. _____

2. _____

3. _____

4. _____

5. _____

6. _____

7. _____

8. _____

9. _____

10. _____

◆ **P r a c t i c e   1 4   Completing** Add dashes or parentheses around the underlined words in the following paragraph.

When Dad found Skipper — or rather, Skipper found Dad — it was a hot summer day in my southern Kentucky hometown. For most of his life, Dad had never cared for pets, but the sight of that skinny, flea-infested puppy seemed to open his heart. Filthy and smelly — that's how I described Skipper when I first saw him. Skipper was curled up in the corner of an abandoned warehouse — the old Carter's Machinery building — that Dad's company was preparing to tear down. Dad carried Skipper to his truck and drove him to the neighborhood vet — who usually treated large farm animals. The vet gave Dad something for the fleas — Bug-Out Flea Dip — and some vitamins to add to his food. He told Dad that Skipper was lucky to be found. If he'd been on the streets much longer, he would have surely picked up some kind of an infection — and most likely would have died. After a couple of weeks in our home, Skipper began to look healthy again. It took several flea baths — at least four — to get rid of the fleas, but Skipper didn't mind. As soon as Skipper was back on his feet, Dad began taking him to work with him. In no time, there was only one word to describe them — inseparable.

◆ **P r a c t i c e   1 5   Writing Your Own**

A. Write a sentence of your own of each of the following types.

1. a sentence that uses dashes to set off key words at the end

   _____

2. a sentence that uses dashes to set off key words at the beginning

   _____

3. a sentence that uses dashes to divide the sentence into three parts

   _____

4. a list of three things using parentheses around the numbers

   _____

5. a sentence that places the years of someone's life in parentheses

   _____

B. Write five sentences of your own using dashes and parentheses correctly.

1. _____

2. _____

3. _____

4. _____

5. _____

CHAPTER REVIEW

You might want to reread your answers to the questions in all the review boxes before you do the following exercises.

Review Practice 1 Reading Refer to the paragraph by Joan Didion on pages 426–427 to do the following exercises.

1. List the two sentences with semicolons, and explain the rule that applies to each.

_____

Rule: _____

_____

Rule: _____

2. List the two sentences with colons, and explain the rule that applies to each.

_____

Rule: _____

_____

Rule: _____

3. List the sentence with a dash, and explain the rule that applies to it.

_____

Rule: _____

4. List the sentence with parentheses and explain the rule that applies to it.

_____

Rule: _____

 **Review Practice 2** **Identifying** Underline the semicolons, colons, dashes, and parentheses used incorrectly in the following sentences.

1. Sinclair—Lewis 1885–1951—was an American author who won the Nobel Prize in 1930.

2. There are only three things I will do when I'm on vacation; check my e-mail, buy groceries, and read the paper.

3. She was crying for an hour today: however, she wouldn't tell us why.

4. Devon was wearing pants in my favorite color today (teal blue).

5. Pablo: who never forgets anything: locked his keys in the car.

6. Cookies and cupcakes: are my biggest weakness.

7. (This chair comes in four colors) navy, black, brown, or beige.

8. My two-year-old is a very good climber (today I found him on the refrigerator)!

9. We have to meet Mark, Julie, and Craig: walk to the park: and set up the volleyball net.

10. This class requires that we—1, read two novels, 2, write five essays, and 3, do eight hours of community service.

 **Review Practice 3** **Correcting** Correct the errors in Review Practice 2 by rewriting the sentences.

EDITING A STUDENT PARAGRAPH

Following is a paragraph written and revised by Angela Houston in response to the writing assignment in this chapter. Read the paragraph, and underline each of her semicolons, colons, dashes, and parentheses.

My family used to have the same routine from Christmas Eve to Christmas Day. This ritual started sometime when I was young (maybe around the time I was 10 or 11). On Christmas Eve: my sister, my brother, and I would get to open one present from under the tree. We were allowed to choose it; we had to get approval before we could actually open it; just in case it was an expensive gift. We loved getting a taste of Christmas before the day arrived. That night, we would set out a plate of cookies for Santa and some carrots for Rudolph—which we later learned was for Dad and Sparky the dog. We were supposed to go to bed early— after all, Santa doesn't come when children are awake. But I usually decided to do my spring cleaning early and cleaned my room until I was too tired to keep my eyes open. Then (like clockwork) my little brother would wake us up at 3:30 a.m., excited to begin the day. This was the best part of the day: waking up our parents, opening our gifts, and enjoying the morning with the family. My mom would make homemade doughnuts; the best around; before we would all go back to bed for a nap. Later that evening, we would eat a wonderful dinner and just celebrate the holiday and our family; I miss those days.

Collaborative Activity

Team up with a partner, and place a second underline beneath the 10 punctuation errors in Angela's paragraph. Then, working together, use what you have learned in this chapter to correct these errors. Rewrite the paragraph with your corrections.

EDITING YOUR OWN PARAGRAPH

Now return to the paragraph you wrote and revised at the beginning of this chapter. Underline each of your semicolons, colons, dashes, and parentheses.

Collaborative Activity

Exchange paragraphs with your partner, and circle any punctuation errors that you find in your partner's paragraph.

Individual Activity

On the Error Log in Appendix 6, record any punctuation errors that your partner found in your paragraph. To complete the writing process, correct these errors by rewriting your paragraph.

UNIT TESTS

Here are some exercises that test your understanding of all the material in this unit: End Punctuation, Commas, Apostrophes, Quotation Marks, Semicolons, Colons, Dashes, and Parentheses.

Unit Test 1 Identifying

Underline the punctuation errors in the following sentences.

1. I wonder if I left the lights on?
2. "Where's my credit card" yelled the woman in the store!
3. The gardener mowed the grass; raked the leaves; and pruned the hedges this afternoon.
4. We studied all night long; but we still missed several questions on the exam.
5. There are five yellow house's on my block.
6. Are you ready yet.
7. The magnets on my refrigerator door are from: London, Paris, and Venice.
8. I can't believe they wo'nt take personal checks here.
9. When he was a little boy; he ran around in his front yard naked.
10. My great-grandfather, Sylvester Martin—1870–1950—founded this hardware store.
11. Are you going to be here for a few more minutes!
12. Please turn off (the television) before you leave the room.
13. "If you can't find me, Paul said, I'm probably in the library."
14. I went to the post office; which is near my office; and mailed those letters.
15. At 5:00 p.m., we need to pick up Sharon, Camilla, and Tony, drive to the restaurant, and reserve a table for six.

16. The best desserts to bring are: lemon cream pie, chocolate brownies, or peach cobbler.

17. Shell be here in about 10 minutes.

18. Gary is riding his bike today because (his car ran out of gas).

19. This weekend I plan to—1—visit my sister, —2—make cookies for Eddie, and —3—finish this needlepoint.

20. "Did you drive or fly to Boston" asked Sheryl?

Unit Test 2 Correcting

Correct the punctuation errors in Unit Test 1 by rewriting each sentence.

Unit Test 3 Identifying

Underline the punctuation errors in the following paragraph.

In July, we bought our very first house? There was only one word to describe it (finally). My wife and I have three small children so it was about time for this move. We had a house-warming party on August 1, and we asked all of our friends to come see the new place. About 30 people said they would stop by, so we bought lots of: hamburgers, hot dogs, and sodas. When people started to arrive; they immediately told us how beautiful the house was. "You guys have really done a great job, they said." One of our friends—who works with my wife—was especially impressed that we did all of the landscaping ourselves. We really enjoyed visiting and showing off our new house, the party was over before we knew it. It was'nt until everyone had left that I saw what a mess they had made. There were spills on the carpet and glasses of punch left in every room. Napkins and trash had been dropped in the strangest places. "Wow" I exclaimed! "I think our house has been officially warmed!"

Unit Test 4 Correcting

Correct the punctuation errors in Unit Test 3 by rewriting the paragraph.

UNIT WRITING ASSIGNMENTS

1. Who are the people in the picture on the next page? What sport do they play? Where is this scene? Imagine that you just watched one of

their games and write about what happened. Did they win or lose? What was the score? Did anything unusual or unexpected happen during the game?

2. How do you unwind? When you have a particularly stressful day, what do you do to relax? Do you read a book, listen to music, watch television, or do something else? Write about the steps you take to get rid of stress.

3. There are some natural differences between men and women, but most often we hear about the stereotypes. The reality is that women are *not* born to be better cooks or housekeepers than men, and men are *not* the only ones capable of repairing cars. What are some of the gender stereotypes that you have personally proved wrong? For example, are you a female who has a talent for math but an aversion to needlepoint? Are you a male who doesn't mind ironing his own shirts but who cannot change the oil in his car? Describe one of your talents, interests, or dislikes that contradicts the stereotypes for your gender.

4. If you won an all-expenses-paid vacation anywhere in the world, where would you go? If you knew that whatever you wanted to do at your vacation spot would be absolutely free, what would you do? What would you like to see if you only had the chance? Write about this vacation place and the activities you would find there. Use as many details as possible.

5. Create your own assignment (with the help of your instructor), and write a response to it.

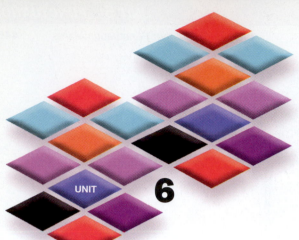

MECHANICS

The mechanical aspects of a sentence are much like the mechanical features of a car, an appliance, or a clock. They are some of the smallest—yet most important—details in a sentence. In writing, the term "mechanics" refers to capitalization, abbreviations, and numbers. We usually take these items for granted, but when they are used incorrectly, a sentence, just like a mechanical appliance with a weak spring, starts to break down.

Following a few simple guidelines will help you keep your sentences running smoothly and efficiently. They are explained in two chapters:

CAPITALIZATION

 CHECKLIST for Editing Capitalization

> ✔ Are all proper nouns capitalized?
> ✔ Are all words in titles capitalized correctly?
> ✔ Have you followed the other rules for capitalizing correctly?

Because every sentence begins with a capital letter, **capitalization** is the best place to start discussing the mechanics of good writing. Capital letters signal where sentences begin. They also call attention to certain kinds of words, making sentences easier to read and understand.

Notice how capitalization shows where a sentence begins and calls attention to specific words in the following paragraph by Judith Ortiz Cofer.

On a bus trip to London from Oxford University where I was earning some graduate credits one summer, a young man, obviously fresh from a pub, spotted me and as if struck by inspiration went down on his knees in the aisle. With both hands over his heart he broke into an Irish tenor's rendition of "Maria" from *West Side Story*. My politely amused fellow passengers gave his lovely voice the round of gentle applause it deserved. Though I was not quite as amused, I managed my version of an English smile: no show of teeth, no extreme contortions of the facial muscles—I was at this time of my life practicing reserve and cool. Oh, that British control, how I coveted it. But "Maria" had followed me to London, reminding me of a prime fact of my life: You can leave the island, master the English language, and travel as far as you can, but if you are Latina, especially one like me who obviously belongs to Rita Moreno's gene pool, the island travels with you.

In this paragraph, the young man makes an assumption about author Judith Ortiz Cofer based on her appearance. Before continuing in this chapter, take a moment to write about your experiences with snap judgments. Save your work because you will use it later this chapter.

 WRITING ASSIGNMENT: SNAP JUDGMENTS

Have you ever made a snap judgment about another person, or has someone ever assumed something false about you based on appearance? What was the judgment? What were the physical clues that led to the conclusion made? How did this make you or the other person feel? What did you learn from the experience? Write a paragraph focusing your thoughts on these questions.

 REVISING YOUR WRITING

Revise the first draft of your paragraph before you focus on editing. Use the Revising Checklist on pages 24–25 to help you with your revision. Make sure your paragraph has a good topic sentence, is well developed, and is well organized. Then check your paragraph for unity and coherence.

Correct capitalization coupled with correct punctuation adds up to good, clear writing. Here are some guidelines to help you capitalize correctly.

1. Capitalize the first word of every sentence, including the first word of a quotation that forms a sentence.

> **W**e are vacationing in Hawaii.
>
> "**W**e are vacationing in Hawaii," he said.
>
> **H**e said, "**W**e are vacationing in Hawaii."

Do not capitalize the second part of a quotation that is split.

> "**W**e are vacationing," he said, "in Hawaii."

2. Capitalize all proper nouns. Do not capitalize common nouns.

Common Nouns	Proper Nouns
person	George Washington
state	Texas
building	Eiffel Tower
river	Columbia River
airplane	*Spruce Goose*

Here are some examples of proper nouns.

People:	Cindy, Marilyn Monroe, Jack Nicholson
Groups:	Russians, New Yorkers, Cherokees, Canadians, Vietnamese
Languages:	Latin, Gaelic, German
Religions, Religious Books, Holy Days:	Taoism, Baptist, Upanishads, Bible, Lent, Good Friday, Chanukah
Organizations:	American Kennel Club, Independent Party, American Association of University Women, National Council of Teachers of English
Places:	Yosemite National Park, New Orleans, Orange County, Bunker Hill, Sunset Boulevard, Highway 99, London Bridge, Tampa International Airport
Institutions, Agencies, Businesses:	North High School, Harvard University, UCLA Harbor Hospital, Pacific Bell
Brand Names, Ships, Aircraft:	Adidas, Dr Pepper, *Spirit of St. Louis*

3. Capitalize titles used with people's names or in place of their names.

Mr. Judson L. Montgomery, Ms. Christy Waldo, Dr. Crystal Reeves
Aunt Janet, Grandpa Bill, Cousin Margaret, Sis, Nana

Do not capitalize words that identify family relationships.

NOT	I talked with **my** Grandfather last month.
CORRECT	I talked with **my** grandfather last month.
CORRECT	I talked with Grandfather last month.

4. Capitalize the titles of creative works.

Books:	*The Stand*
Short Stories:	"Barn Burning"
Plays:	*Tea Party*
Poems:	"Icarus"

Articles:	"Ah, Happiness"
Magazines:	*Life*
Songs:	"Come Together"
Albums or CDs:	*Abbey Road*
Films:	*Gladiator*
TV Series:	*King of the Hill*
Works of Art:	*The Woman in the Red Hat*
Computer Programs:	Endnotes

Do not capitalize *a, an, the,* or short prepositions unless they are the first or last word in a title.

5. Capitalize days of the week, months, holidays, and special events.

   Monday, September, Mother's Day, the Fourth of July, Ramadan, Halloween

   Do not capitalize the names of seasons: *summer, fall, winter, spring.*

6. Capitalize the names of historical events, periods, and documents.

   D-Day, the Battle of Wounded Knee, the Age of Enlightenment, the War of the Roses, the Seventies, the Bill of Rights

7. Capitalize specific course titles and the names of language courses.

   Sociology 401, Physics 300, French 202, Economic History

   Do not capitalize a course or subject you are referring to in a general way unless the course is a language.

   my math course, my English course, my German course, my economics course

8. Capitalize references to regions of the country but not words that merely indicate direction.

   If you travel west from the Midwest, you will end up in the West.

9. Capitalize the opening of a letter and the first word of the closing.

   Dear Dr. Rogers, Dear Sir, Fondest regards, Sincerely

   Notice that a comma comes after the opening and closing.

REVIEWING CAPITALIZATION

Why is capitalization important in your writing?

_____

_____

_____

What is the difference between a proper noun and a common noun?

_____

_____

 P r a c t i c e   1   Identifying Underline the correctly capitalized word or phrase in each of the following sentences.

1. According to (Mom, mom), butter is better than margarine.

2. The letter ended with (Love, Thelma; love, Thelma).

3. Sue's (Grandmother, grandmother) was a full-blooded (Crow, crow) (Indian, indian).

4. Your (Nike, nike) shoes are under the couch.

5. My (Husband, husband) is a member of the (Democratic Party, democratic party), and I am a member of the (Republican Party, republican party).

6. In our (Physics, physics) class, we are learning (Newtonian, newtonian) math.

7. You must travel (North, north) from here to get to the (East Coast, east coast).

8. Last (Summer, summer), we ran a (Marathon, marathon) for the (American Cancer Society, american cancer society).

9. Even though (*Friends, friends*) has ended, I can still watch the (Reruns, reruns) on the (Fox, fox) network.

10. My favorite computer game is (Diablo II, diablo II), but for some reason it will only run on my (Gateway, gateway) computer.

◆ **P r a c t i c e   2   Identifying** Put an X next to the sentence if any of the underlined words are capitalized incorrectly.

1. _____ Uncle John used to live in <u>Cairo</u>, Egypt, before he moved to Flower <u>street</u> in Willis, Texas.

2. _____ After graduating from <u>Permian High School</u>, I attended college at <u>South Coast University</u>.

3. _____ <u>when</u> I was 13 years old, my dog ran away.

4. _____ The letter from <u>father</u> began, "<u>dear</u> son."

5. _____ "We should leave," she said, "<u>Before</u> the rain starts."

6. _____ Sandra shopped at <u>Kmart</u> for some <u>Martha Stewart</u> bathroom accessories, some <u>Coca-Cola</u>, and a Dixie Chicks CD.

7. _____ For <u>christmas</u>, I got season tickets to the <u>red</u> <u>sox</u> games.

8. _____ I bought <u>aunt</u> Eustice a Liz Claiborne outfit.

9. _____ In <u>anthropology</u> 400, we are studying the <u>paleolithic</u> <u>age</u>.

10. _____ "Go <u>west</u>, young man," is a famous saying.

◆ **P r a c t i c e   3   Correcting** Correct the capitalization errors in Practice 2 by rewriting each incorrect sentence.

1. _____

2. _____

3. _____

4. _____

5. _____

6. _____

7. _____

8. _____

9. _____

10. _____

◆ **P r a c t i c e   4   Completing** Fill in each blank in the following sentences with a word that makes sense, and capitalize when necessary.

1. Before _____ left the country, he made sure he had his _____ watch and hearing aid.

2. When we lived in _____, we saw the _____.

3. Jane's _____, George, used to work for the _____.

4. In _____ 405, we are studying the _____ Period.

5. According to my _____ instructor, _____ was famous for his efforts.

6. People from _____ think their state is the best.

7. Travel _____ on _____ to reach _____.

8. This _____, we will celebrate _____.

9. "Everybody needs a few basic necessities," he said, "_____."

10. I belong to the _____, which helps needy families every _____.

◆ **P r a c t i c e   5   Writing Your Own** Write 10 sentences of your own that cover all nine of the capitalization rules.

1. _____

2. _____

3. _____

4. _____

5. _____

6. _____

7. _____

8. _____

9. _____

10. _____

CHAPTER REVIEW

You might want to reread your answers to the questions in the review box before you do the following exercises.

◆ *Review P r a c t i c e 1* **Reading** Refer to the paragraph by Judith Ortiz Cofer on page 447 to do the following exercises.

1. List the capitalization rule that applies to each of the following words from the paragraph.

Capitalized Words	Rule Number
On	_____
London	_____
Oxford University	_____
Irish	_____
"Maria"	_____
West Side Story	_____
English	_____
British	_____
Latina	_____
Rita Moreno's	_____

◆ *Review P r a c t i c e 2* **Identifying** Underline the capitalization errors in the following sentences.

1. I would love a dress like the one marilyn monroe wore when she sang "diamonds are a girl's best friend."

2. The letter began, "dear Mary," and then said, "You must turn North on bombay street."

3. Kim took pictures of the empire state building.

4. My Mother always makes me chocolate chip cookies when I'm feeling blue.

5. We have been learning about taoism in chinese politics 403.

6. latin may be considered a Dead Language, but it is still beneficial to english majors.

7. Aunt betty is a member of MADD, mothers against drunk driving.

8. We had dinner with senator Williams to celebrate mardi gras.

9. When *the x-files* came out, more people were convinced that the Government was covering up the existence of alien beings.

10. The death of thousands of native americans along the trail of tears was a terrible waste of human life.

◆ *Review P r a c t i c e 3* **Correcting** Correct the capitalization errors from Review Practice 2 by rewriting each incorrect sentence.

1. _____

2. _____

3. _____

4. _____

5. _____

6. _____

7. _____

8. _____

9. _____

10. _____

EDITING A STUDENT PARAGRAPH

Following is a paragraph written and revised by Susan Miller in response to the writing assignment in this chapter. Read the paragraph, and underline each capital letter.

> I have always been small—not just short, but small.
> When we lived in new jersey, mom used to have to pick
> me up and put me on the school bus. I was too small
> to manage what appeared to be a mountain of a step.
> Because I was so small, others naturally made false

judgments about my age and my intellect. On my first day at Willis High School, I knew no one. I had just finished my english literature class and was fumbling with *the complete works of william shakespeare* at my locker trying to remember the combination when a very polite young man came up to me. His name was richard marquez, and he asked me if I was lost. "No," I said, "But thank you." Obviously he didn't believe me because he then told me that the junior high school was just South of the high school—and he was serious! This was my d-day, the day I recognized just how others saw me, and it was devastating. I guess somewhere in the back of my mind I always assumed people took me seriously, even though they often thought I was five years younger than I looked. I learned a valuable lesson on that day. But I have since learned another valuable lesson about my size—people often underestimate me, and that gives me an advantage.

Collaborative Activity

Team up with a partner, and underline twice the 14 words in Susan's paragraph that are capitalized incorrectly. Then, working together, use what you have learned in this chapter to correct the errors. Rewrite the paragraph with your corrections.

EDITING YOUR OWN PARAGRAPH

Now return to the paragraph you wrote and revised at the beginning of this chapter. Underline the capitalized words in your own writing.

Collaborative Activity

Exchange paragraphs with your partner, and circle any capitalization errors that you find in your partner's paragraph.

Individual Activity

On the Error Log in Appendix 4, record any capitalization errors that your partner found in your paragraph. To complete the writing process, correct these errors by rewriting your paragraph.

CHAPTER 26

ABBREVIATIONS AND NUMBERS

☑ CHECKLIST for Using Abbreviations and Numbers

> ✔ Are titles before and after proper names abbreviated correctly?
>
> ✔ Are government agencies and other organizations abbreviated correctly?
>
> ✔ Are numbers *zero* through *nine* spelled out?
>
> ✔ Are numbers 10 and over written as figures (10, 25, 1–20, 324)?

Like capitalization, abbreviations and numbers are also mechanical features of writing that help us communicate what we want to say. Following the rules that govern their use will make your writing as precise as possible.

Notice how the consistent use of abbreviations and numbers moves the following paragraph by David Gardner along.

The educational dimensions of the risk before us have been amply documented in testimony received by the commission. For example,

- International comparisons of student achievement, completed a decade ago, reveal that on 19 academic tests American students were never first or second and, in comparison with other industrialized nations, were last seven times.

- Some 23 million American adults are functionally illiterate by the simplest tests of everyday reading, writing, and comprehension.

- About 13 percent of all 17-year-olds in the United States can be considered functionally illiterate. Functional illiteracy among minority youth may run as high as 40 percent.

- Average achievement of high school students on most standardized tests is now lower than it was when *Sputnik* was launched [1957].

- Over half the population of gifted students do not match their tested ability with comparable achievement in school.

- The College Board's Scholastic Aptitude Tests (SATs) demonstrate a virtually unbroken decline from 1963 to 1980. Average verbal scores fell over 50 points, and average mathematics scores dropped nearly 40 points.

- College Board achievement tests also reveal consistent declines in recent years in such subjects as physics and English.

- Both the number and proportion of students demonstrating superior achievement on the SATs (i.e., those with scores of 650 or higher) have also dramatically declined.

- There was a steady decline in science achievement scores of U.S. 17-year-olds as measured by national assessments of science in 1969, 1973, and 1977.

In this paragraph, David Gardner explains that the U.S. system of public education is not doing its job well. Before continuing in this chapter, take a moment to write about how well prepared you are for college. Save your work because you will use it later in this chapter.

WRITING ASSIGNMENT: HOW READY ARE YOU?

How ready are you for college work? Did your high school prepare you adequately for the classes you are now taking? Do you feel confident in your basic skills (reading, writing, and math)? What would you like to change about your academic background? What would you keep the same? Write a paragraph discussing these issues in reference to your high school.

REVISING YOUR WRITING

Revise the first draft of your paragraph before you focus on editing. Use the Revising Checklist on pages 24–25 to help you with your revision. Make sure your paragraph has a good topic sentence, is well developed, and is well organized. Then check your paragraph for unity and coherence.

ABBREVIATIONS

Abbreviations help us move communication along. They follow a set of rules when used in writing.

1. Abbreviate titles before proper names.

   > **Mr.** Jason Best, **Mrs.** Baker, **Ms.** Susan Elias, **Dr.** George Carlton, **Rev.** Sid Peterson, **Gov.** Arnold Schwarzenegger, **Sgt.** Milton Santos

   Abbreviate religious, governmental, and military titles when used with an entire name. Do not abbreviate them when used only with a last name.

NOT	We support **Gov.** Wilson.
CORRECT	We support **Governor** Wilson.
CORRECT	We thought that **Gov.** Lionel Wilson would be supported.

   Professor is not usually abbreviated: **Professor** Angela Perez will be teaching again this year.

2. Abbreviate academic degrees.

   > **B.S.** (Bachelor of Science)
   > **A.A.** (Associate of Arts)
   > **E.M.T.** (Emergency Medical Technician)

3. Use the following abbreviations with numbers.

   > **A.M.** *or* **a.m.** (ante meridiem)
   > **P.M.** *or* **p.m.** (post meridiem)
   > **B.C.** *and* **A.D.**

4. Abbreviate *United States* only when it is used as an adjective.

NOT	The **U.S.** is a capitalist society.
CORRECT	The **United States** is a capitalist society.
CORRECT	The **U.S.** president will address the people today.

5. Abbreviate only the names of well-known government agencies, businesses, and educational institutions by using their initials without periods.

   > **CIA** (Central Intelligence Agency)
   > **DMV** (Department of Motor Vehicles)
   > **AMA** (American Medical Association)
   > **USC** (University of Southern California)
   > **KCEOC** (Kern County Economic Opportunity Corporation)

6. Abbreviate state names when addressing mail or writing out the postal address. Otherwise, spell out the names of states.

> Christy moved to 504 Frontier Street, New York, **NY** 10011.
> Christy moved to New York, **New York.**

REVIEWING ABBREVIATIONS
....

When you write, are you free to abbreviate any words you want?

_____

 **P r a c t i c e 1 Identifying** Underline the correct choice in each of the following sentences.

1. (Prof., Professor) Stockton teaches English 305.
2. (Sgt., Sergeant) Williams was the toughest instructor I've ever had.
3. If the president needed to find someone's telephone number, he or she could ask the (CIA, Central Intelligence Agency) for help.
4. They visited (TX, Texas) last summer.
5. This is the year 2005 (A.D., a.d.).
6. Ginny's brother is going to be an (E.M.T., emer. med. tech.).
7. When Sally was little, she lived at 511 Arbor Drive, Lafayette, (LA, Louisiana).
8. The (U.S., United States) has one of the highest standards of living in the world.
9. The driver was passing the (YMCA, Young Men's Christian Association) when he slammed on his brakes.
10. The (AMA, A.M.A.) does not support tobacco smoking.

P r a c t i c e 2 Identifying Put an X next to the sentence if the underlined word is incorrect.

1. _____ <u>Mr.</u> Hewett helped settle the crowd down.
2. _____ My family migrated to the <u>U.S.</u> in the early 1800s.
3. _____ <u>Rev.</u> Thomas performed the marriage ceremony.
4. _____ <u>Washington</u> is a wonderful state for a vacation.

5. _____ Your new address is 121 Bennington Avenue, Iowa City, <u>Iowa</u> 52241.

6. _____ When I woke up, the alarm clock read 3:30 <u>ante</u> <u>meridiem</u>.

7. _____ <u>Prof.</u> Angus will be the guest speaker at the ceremony.

8. _____ This company reports all earnings to avoid an audit by the <u>I.R.S.</u>

9. _____ I plan to get my <u>Associate of Arts</u> degree at a community college before attending a four-year university.

10. _____ The <u>United States</u> Supreme Court will rule today.

◆ *P r a c t i c e* **3 Correcting** Correct the errors you identified in Practice 2 by rewriting each incorrect sentence.

1. _____

2. _____

3. _____

4. _____

5. _____

6. _____

7. _____

8. _____

9. _____

10. _____

◆ *P r a c t i c e* **4 Completing** Fill in each blank in the following sentences with either an abbreviation or a word that makes sense.

1. _____ Lang will be taking over this class for the rest of the quarter.

2. Karl decided to attend college at _____.

3. In four years, you could have your _____ in English, history, or philosophy.

4. _____ Williams is head of the mission from our church.

5. It is a myth that everything is bigger in the state of _____ than anywhere else.

6. The _____ is a somewhat controversial organization.

7. The U.S. _____ is strong this year.

8. The letter was addressed to 1011 Sunny Boulevard, Los Angeles, _____.

9. We moved from Spain to the _____ more than five years ago.

10. Jason was going over 75 _____ when the police officer pulled him over.

◆ *P r a c t i c e   5*   **Writing Your Own**

A. Write a sentence of your own for each of the following abbreviations.

1. Gov. _____

2. a.m. _____

3. CBS _____

4. CA _____

5. U.S. _____

B. Write five sentences of your own covering at least five of the six abbreviation rules.

1. _____

2. _____

3. _____

4. _____

5. _____

NUMBERS

Most writers ask the same question about using **numbers:** When should a number be spelled out, and when is it all right to use numerals? The following simple rules will help you make this decision.

1. Spell out numbers from *zero* to *nine*. Use figures for numbers 10 and higher.

> I own **two** houses.
> My sister has **11** dogs and **15** cats living on her ranch.

Do not mix spelled-out numbers and figures in a sentence if they refer to the same types of items. Use numerals for all numbers in that case.

> **NOT**   I have **three** reports, **11** files, and **two** memoran-
> dums to finish today.
>
> **CORRECT**   I have **3** reports, **11** files, and **2** memorandums to
> finish today.

2. For very large numbers, use a combination of figures and words.

> The company's profits this fiscal year were **$21 million.**
> His cabin in the mountains cost **$1.1 million.**

3. Always spell out a number that begins a sentence. If this becomes awkward, reword the sentence.

> **Twenty-five** apples fell from the tree.
> A total of **25** apples fell from the tree.

4. Use figures for dates, addresses, zip codes, telephone numbers, identification numbers, and time.

> On July **22, 1998,** we relocated to **2504** Box Drive, Bryan,
> TX **77805.**
> Scott's old telephone number was **(661) 555-3405.**
> My Social Security number is **101-112-1314.**
> The alarm went off at **4:30** a.m.

5. Use figures for fractions, decimals, and percentages.

> Mix **1/2** cup of butter and **2** tablespoons of vanilla in a
> saucepan.
> His GPA is **3.8.**
> Only **10** percent of the people polled were in favor of the
> measure.

Notice that *percent* is written out and is all one word.

6. Use figures for exact measurements, including amounts of money. Use a dollar sign for amounts over $1.

> The backyard is **20** feet by **22** feet.
> She paid **$10.99** for her shorts—**99 cents** more than I paid.

7. Use figures for the parts of a book.

> Chapter **9**   page **119**   Exercise **7**   questions **2** and **8**

Notice that *Chapter* and *Exercise* are capitalized.

REVIEWING NUMBERS

What is the general rule for spelling out numbers as opposed to using numerals?

_____

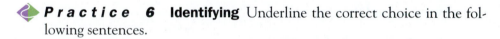 **P r a c t i c e   6   Identifying** Underline the correct choice in the following sentences.

1. I cannot make this recipe because I do not have (1/2, a half) cup of milk.
2. They found (4, four) silver coins, 15 gold coins, and (3, three) pieces of jewelry in the old chest.
3. Walk about (3, three) miles up the road, and you should see the sign.
4. This warehouse, which measures approximately (5,000, five thousand) square feet, is up for sale.
5. My brother has (2, two) motorcycles and a car, whereas I have neither.
6. The instructor assigned Chapters (10 and 11, ten and eleven) for reading.
7. Our phone rang at (2:30, two thirty) in the morning.
8. The year-long charity drive earned a little over ($1.5 million, one and a half million dollars).
9. In (2004, two thousand and four), we renewed our marriage vows.
10. (10,000, Ten thousand) people attended the rally.

P r a c t i c e   7   Identifying Put an X next to the sentence if the underlined number is in the incorrect form.

1. _____ We caught <u>3</u> fish for supper.
2. _____ Clear off an area measuring <u>twenty</u> feet by <u>thirty</u> feet.
3. _____ Approximately <u>2.9</u> percent of his sentences were compound-complex.
4. _____ <u>9</u> people perished in the flood.
5. _____ Please read Chapter <u>Two</u> for the discussion next week.
6. _____ I was born on December <u>22, 1978</u>.
7. _____ <u>Thirty</u> people showed up for the surprise party.
8. _____ The address is <u>two, three, nine</u> Woodrow Avenue.
9. _____ Only <u>five</u> percent of the people exposed actually got sick.
10. _____ They paid over <u>two thousand dollars</u> for their new carpet.

♦ **P r a c t i c e 8 Correcting** Correct the errors in Practice 7 by rewriting each incorrect sentence.

1. _____

2. _____

3. _____

4. _____

5. _____

6. _____

7. _____

8. _____

9. _____

10. _____

♦ **P r a c t i c e 9 Completing** Fill in each blank in the following sentences with a number or figure that makes sense.

1. _____ new recruits joined the army today.
2. My telephone number is _____.

3. I have _____ brothers and sisters and _____ cousins.

4. The construction on this building to bring it up to code will cost _____ million.

5. In the future, my GPA will be _____.

6. Over _____ percent of the incoming freshmen are from out of state.

7. I woke up at _____ today.

8. The dorm room measures _____ feet by _____ feet.

9. Did you complete Exercises _____ and _____?

10. This new CD cost _____.

◆ **P r a c t i c e   1 0   Writing Your Own** Write 10 sentences of your own that cover all seven of the number rules.

1. _____

2. _____

3. _____

4. _____

5. _____

6. _____

7. _____

8. _____

9. _____

10. _____

CHAPTER REVIEW

You might want to reread your answers to the questions in all the review boxes before you do the following exercises.

 **Review P r a c t i c e   1 Reading** Refer to the paragraph by David Gardner on pages 457–458 to do the following exercises.

1. List an abbreviation from the paragraph that follows each of the following abbreviation rules.

    Rule 4: _____

    Rule 5: _____

2. List all the numbers from the paragraph that follow each of the following number rules.

    Rule 1: _____

    Rule 2: _____

    Rule 4: _____

    Rule 5: _____

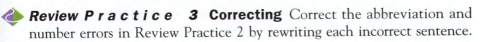 **Review P r a c t i c e   2 Identifying** Underline the abbreviation and number errors in each of the following sentences. Some sentences contain more than one error.

1. There are only 5 new houses being built with a ten-by-twelve entryway.

2. I couldn't imagine living anywhere but the U.S.

3. Over three hundred thousand claims were handled this month.

4. Sen. Wood earned his Bachelor of Science degree at the same university that my dad attended.

5. 4 contestants claimed to have the winning number.

6. The new telephone number is three, nine, eight, four, four, five, four.

7. Benjamin fled the country to avoid the Internal Revenue Service.

8. The recipe on page one hundred twenty calls for one-eighth cup of chili powder.

9. Ramon rides his motorbike forty miles to work each day.

10. The best Cajun food comes from LA.

Review P r a c t i c e   3 Correcting Correct the abbreviation and number errors in Review Practice 2 by rewriting each incorrect sentence.

EDITING A STUDENT PARAGRAPH

Following is a paragraph written and revised by Ashley Knight in response to the writing assignment in this chapter. Read the paragraph, and underline all the capitalized words, abbreviations, and numbers.

> When I graduated from High School, I thought I was prepared for college. What I discovered was that this was not so. But I think this is as much my fault as it was my school's. I knew 3 years ago I wanted to work for the Central Intelligence Agency or the FBI. And even though I did what was required of me in High School, I never learned how to study because my grades were decent enough without having to worry about it. Now I'm at a University, and I wish I had better study skills to help me manage my time better here. I'll never get my Master of Arts Degree at the rate I'm going. People in my high school were aware that many students were barely trying but making decent grades, yet they never really taught us to be prepared for crash-course study skills lessons. Of course, it's difficult for Teachers to keep an eye on four thousand students. To have learned these skills would have made my life one hundred % easier.

Collaborative Activity

Team up with a partner, and put a second underline below the 9 capitalization, abbreviation, and number errors in Ashley's paragraph. Then, working together, use what you have learned in this chapter to correct these errors. Rewrite the paragraph with your corrections.

EDITING YOUR OWN PARAGRAPH

Now return to the paragraph you wrote and revised at the beginning of this chapter. Underline all of your capitalized words, abbreviations, and numbers.

Collaborative Activity

Exchange paragraphs with your partner, and circle any capitalization, abbreviation, number, and figure errors that you find in your partner's paragraph.

Individual Activity

On the Error Log in Appendix 4, record any mechanics errors that your partner found in your paragraph. To complete the writing process, correct these errors by rewriting your paragraph.

UNIT TESTS

Here are some exercises that test your understanding of all the material in this unit: Capitalization, Abbreviations, and Numbers.

Unit Test 1 Identifying

Underline the capitalization, abbreviation, and number errors in each of the following sentences. Some sentences contain more than one error.

1. "hey, you," the boy shouted, "Throw me the ball."
2. When Kimmie was eight, she moved from the midwest to the south.
3. Rev. Dunn wrote many satirical sermons.
4. You can purchase a duplicate title for your car at the Department of Motor Vehicles.
5. While visiting Alaska, we sampled 9 different types of fish.
6. Since I gave up television for Lent, I decided to occupy myself with J.R.R. tolkien's *lord of the rings* trilogy.
7. I have always wanted to work for the Central Intelligence Agency.
8. Last spring, Barney bought his Mother a family bible for mother's day.
9. The politician spent over two million dollars on her campaign.
10. Around three thirty this afternoon, you will need to add two and a half cups of stewed tomatoes to the soup simmering on the stove.
11. This picture of my Dog ralph is hilarious.
12. Last night, I got ahead in my Sociology class by reading Chapters Twenty through Twenty-Five.
13. The new playground will measure one hundred feet by one hundred and fifty feet.
14. After the dallas cowboys game, grandpa Roland asked for his slippers and his english tea.
15. I am currently pursuing my Master of Arts degree in psychology.

16. He signed the letter, "your secret admirer."
17. 250 people were hired for the job.
18. The U.S. offers many trade opportunities to other nations.

19. In history 401, we are studying the war of 1812.
20. The state of NV was the first to legalize gambling.

Unit Test 2 Correcting

Correct the errors in Unit Test 1 by rewriting each incorrect sentence.

1. _____

2. _____

3. _____

4. _____

5. _____

6. _____

7. _____

8. _____

9. _____

10. _____

11. _____

12. _____

13. _____

14. _____

15. _____

16. _____

17. _____

18. _____

19. _____

20. _____

Unit Test 3 Identifying

Underline the capitalization, abbreviation, and number errors in the following paragraph.

In the Spring of 2003, I was out of the U.S. trying to get some much needed relaxation away from phones, work, and television. I was staying in the french countryside at uncle Mike's small villa. Unfortunately, I was unavoidably detained and could not mail my taxes in on time. Once I realized the problem, I drove North to the nearest town to call the Internal Revenue Service. But it was a holiday, and the post office was closed. I had to make the same trip the following day at 4:00 post meridiem. My french 307 class was apparently a waste of time because the lady on the other side of the counter, Missus Ideaux, who was wearing clothes from the nineteen-fifties, and I could not communicate. I followed the advice in Chapter one of my psychology text (*getting along in life*) when I counted to 3, took a deep breath, and tried once again to explain that I needed a phone. I finally reached someone at the IRS who told me that I owed over one million dollars. "1 million dollars!" I screamed. "Are you sure you have the right Social Security number?" I asked. "It's four, five, eight, two, one, seven, nine, three, eight." "Ah, yes," returned the voice on the other end. "Here is your record. You're a student getting an Associate of Arts degree. I'll make a note in your file, but you'll have to pay a three percent penalty fee and fill out some paperwork when you return to the United States." I said that was fine and hung up the phone. But before I could leave, Missus Ideaux asked for ten dollars for the phone call, which I gladly paid. Boy, was I glad to get back to my home in OR, where there is a phone in every room.

Unit Test 4 Correcting

Correct the errors in Unit Test 3 by rewriting the paragraph.

UNIT WRITING ASSIGNMENTS

1. Who do you think the people are in this picture? What is the mood of the picture? Where do you think these people are going? Are they on an adventure or just walking for pleasure? Do they have a long way to walk? Use your imagination to create the details.

2. Most of us know people who go about life in dramatically different ways, such as parents disciplining their children or friends handling relationships. Compare two people you know who have different approaches to the same task. Explain how each goes about the task and why.

3. You have been asked to write a short article for your local newspaper about the best fast-food restaurants in town. Which restaurants are they, and why are they the best? You might want to consider the atmosphere, the service, the price, and the food.

4. When we are children, play is an important part of our day. But as we get older, responsibilities soon take up most of our spare time, and our "play" changes. Now that you are an adult, what do you do for playtime? How has this changed from childhood, if at all? Why? What were the benefits of play as a child? As an adult?

5. Create your own assignment (with the help of your instructor), and write a response to it.

EFFECTIVE SENTENCES

UNIT 7

At one time or another, you have probably been a member of a team. You may have actively participated in sports somewhere or been a part of a close-knit employee group. Or maybe you have taken part in classroom discussion groups or special projects that required your cooperation with your peers. Whatever the situation, teamwork is important in many everyday situations. To be a good team member, you must perform your individual duties with others in mind as you also work.

Sentences, too, require good teamwork to be successful. Each individual word, phrase, or clause has to express its own meaning but must also work together with other words, phrases, and clauses toward the common goal of communicating a clear message. In this unit, three chapters will help you write successful sentences that work in harmony with each other to say exactly what you want to say in the best way possible:

Chapter 27: Varying Sentence Structure
Chapter 28: Parallelism
Chapter 29: Combining Sentences

VARYING SENTENCE STRUCTURE

☑ CHECKLIST for Varying Sentence Patterns

- ✔ Do you add introductory material to vary your sentence patterns?
- ✔ Do you occasionally reverse the order of some subjects and verbs?
- ✔ Do you move sentence parts to add variety to your sentences?
- ✔ Do you sometimes use questions and exclamations to vary your sentence structure?

Reading the same sentence pattern sentence after sentence can become very monotonous for your readers. This chapter will help you solve this problem in your writing. Look at the following example.

I have longed to be independent. I have a part-time job and a full-time college career. I will be moving into my new apartment soon. I have already begun to shop for secondhand furniture. I am very excited about this change in my life.

This paragraph has some terrific ideas, but they are expressed in such a monotonous way that the readers might doze off. What this paragraph needs is variety in its sentence structure.

Notice how varying sentence structures can liven up writing:

This is truly the land of opportunity, and I would have enjoyed its bounty even if I hadn't walked into Miss Hurd's classroom in 1953. But she was the one who directed my grief and pain into writing, and if it weren't for her I wouldn't have become an investigative reporter and foreign correspondent, recorded the story of my mother's life and death in *Eleni* and now my father's story in *A Place for Us*, which is also a testament to the country that took us in. She was the catalyst that sent me into journalism and indirectly caused all the good things that came after. But Miss Hurd would probably deny this emphatically.

In this paragraph, Nicholas Gage is explaining how a teacher changed his life by helping him discover his true potential. Before continuing in this chapter, take a moment to write about a time when you discovered something new about yourself. Save your work because you will use it later in this chapter.

WRITING ASSIGNMENT: SELF-DISCOVERY

Have you ever had one of those moments when you realize something about yourself that you had not previously known? What was the situation? Were you tempted into doing something you never thought you would do, or did you discover a hidden personality trait? How did you react to the situation? Have your feelings changed since your discovery? Write a paragraph explaining this discovery.

REVISING YOUR WRITING

Revise the first draft of your paragraph before you focus on editing. Use the Revising Checklist on pages 24–25 to help you with your revision. Make sure your paragraph has a good topic sentence and is well developed. Then check your paragraph for unity, organization, and coherence.

In this chapter, we will be working on sentence variety. Here are some ideas for keeping your readers awake and ready to hear your good thoughts.

ADD INTRODUCTORY WORDS

Add some introductory words to your sentences so that they don't all start the same way.

Ever since I turned 17, I have longed to be independent. **Now** I have a part-time job and a full-time college career. **In addition,** I will be moving into my new apartment soon. I have already begun to shop for secondhand furniture. I am very excited about this change in my life.

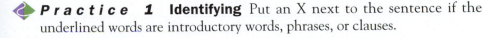

P r a c t i c e   1   Identifying Put an X next to the sentence if the underlined words are introductory words, phrases, or clauses.

1. _____ <u>When I was little</u>, I liked pickles and peanut butter.
2. _____ <u>Tigger</u>, the kitten, destroyed the couch.
3. _____ <u>Your car</u> is located down aisle 5A.
4. _____ <u>However</u>, I think I can manage to raise the money.
5. _____ <u>Even though Marciella didn't want to go</u>, she went to provide moral support.
6. _____ <u>Shonell's</u> gum pops every time that she chews it.
7. _____ <u>Initially</u>, no one grasped the strategy.
8. _____ <u>Although some of the results remain mysterious</u>, the process is now well understood.
9. _____ <u>Therefore</u>, denying her feelings led to complete chaos.
10. _____ <u>In the beginning</u>, everyone loved the old house.

◆ **P r a c t i c e 2**   **Identifying** Underline the sentence in each pair that can be turned into an introductory word, phrase, or clause.

1. It was late that night. The car started making bizarre noises.
2. Rolando was almost hit by a car. He was walking in the middle of the street.
3. Benjamin tried to sneak out of the dorm. It was 2:00 a.m.
4. Fermin complained too much. The instructor gave him extra work.
5. I was nervous to start college. It was the beginning of the semester.
6. There was a tornado yesterday. The tornado destroyed several homes.
7. It was spring. They fell in love.
8. Bring me the telephone. I will make the phone call for you.
9. Judith won't do it. I will.
10. Mario thought he smelled a cow. It was actually a pig.

◆ **P r a c t i c e 3**   **Correcting** Combine the sentences in Practice 2 by turning the sentence you underlined into an introductory word, phrase, or clause.

1. _____

2. _____

3. _____

4. _____

5. _____

6. _____

7. _____

8. _____

9. _____

10. _____

♦ *P r a c t i c e*   **4**   **Completing** Fill in each blank in the following sentences with introductory words, phrases, or clauses that make sense.

1. _____, the strawberries are not ripe enough to eat.

2. _____, I just got out of my seat and walked out of the room.

3. _____, let's make a pie instead.

4. _____, her hair turned a pale shade of green.

5. _____, the shoes were too small for her very large feet.

6. _____, you must close all the shutters and lock the windows.

7. _____, someone will have to compromise.

8. _____, you will find an old chest with clothes from the 1800s.

9. _____, everyone toured Europe except me.

10. _____, she does enjoy taking long walks at twilight.

♦ *P r a c t i c e*   **5**   **Writing Your Own**

A. Write a sentence of your own using each of the following as introductory words, phrases, or clauses.

1. yesterday _____

2. after the day ended _____

3. during the night _____

4. since my brother left _____

5. at the store _____

B. Write five sentences of your own containing an introductory word, phrase, or clause. Underline the introductory words.

1. _____

2. _____

3. _____

4. _____

5. _____

REVERSE WORDS

Reverse the order of some subjects and verbs. For example, instead of *I am so excited,* try *Am I ever excited.* You can also add or drop words and change punctuation to make the sentence read smoothly.

Ever since I turned 17, I have longed to be independent. Now I have a part-time job and a full-time college career. In addition, I will be moving into my new apartment soon. I have already begun to shop for secondhand furniture. **Am I ever** excited about this change in my life!

P r a c t i c e   6   Identifying Put an X next to the sentence if the subject and verb have been reversed.

1. _____ Out from behind the door popped a strange man.

2. _____ In the back of the trunk is a surprise for you.

3. _____ Jeremy taught the dog to play dead.

4. _____ Am I happy to see you!

5. _____ Lovely is the well-mannered person.

6. _____ "This is really confusing," thought Jerome.

7. _____ Out of the fog arose a ghostly figure.

8. _____ Completely satisfied was I.

9. _____ The pennies fell from the purse.

10. _____ Before the test is the time to ask questions.

P r a c t i c e   7   Identifying Underline the subjects and verbs that can be reversed in the following sentences.

1. I am so relieved.

2. Those men were very hungry.

3. A twig is caught in the spokes of the tire.

4. Most infants can smile by three months of age.

5. Her steps were determined and purposeful.

6. I couldn't remember my telephone number.

7. The gifts are hidden in the closet.

8. He was bored.

9. The apples and milk are in the refrigerator.

10. Rebecca almost forgot her ten-year anniversary.

◆ **P r a c t i c e   8   Correcting** Reverse the subjects and verbs in Practice 7 when possible by rewriting each sentence.

1. _____

2. _____

3. _____

4. _____

5. _____

6. _____

7. _____

8. _____

9. _____

10. _____

◆ **P r a c t i c e   9   Completing** Fill in each blank in the following sentences with a subject or verb that makes sense.

1. Forceful and clear was _____.

2. Through the small lane _____ a herd of sheep.

3. Out of the smoke _____ the _____.

4. In the garage _____ your new car.

5. _____ I ever so grateful.

6. From the tree _____ the _____.

7. Calm and collected was the _____.

8. To the ground burned the old _____.

9. On my father's land are many _____.

10. Happy _____ the person who can forgive.

◆ **P r a c t i c e   1 0   Writing Your Own**

A. Write a sentence of your own using the following reversed subjects and verbs.

1. am I _____

2. was the cow _____

3. jumped the children _____

4. asked Jay _____

5. is the person _____

B. Write five sentences of your own with subjects and verbs reversed. Underline the subjects and verbs in each sentence.

1. _____

2. _____

3. _____

4. _____

5. _____

MOVE SENTENCE PARTS

Move some parts of the sentence around. Experiment to see which order works best.

Ever since I turned 17, I have longed to be independent. Now I have a part-time job and a full-time college career. In addition, **soon**

I will be moving into my new apartment. I have already begun to shop for secondhand furniture. Am I ever excited about this change in my life!

Practice 11 Identifying Put an X next to the sentence if the underlined words can be moved.

1. _____ <u>To get Seth to agree</u>, Becca bribed him with sweets.
2. _____ <u>Fear</u> can make people do strange things.
3. _____ Samantha got very little sleep last night <u>because of all the traffic on the streets</u>.
4. _____ Cats are much cleaner <u>than dogs</u>.
5. _____ <u>Despite your great attitude</u>, some people still complained.
6. _____ I got a haircut <u>before the big date</u>.
7. _____ <u>To pass the driving test</u>, you should first practice driving.
8. _____ <u>However</u>, he said that he would certainly make an effort.
9. _____ The computer's low hum <u>almost put me to sleep</u>.
10. _____ <u>My friends</u> are always giving me advice.

Practice 12 Identifying Underline the parts of the following sentences that can be moved.

1. My favorite recipe, though, calls for 3 cups of sugar.
2. Initially, the phone wouldn't stop ringing.
3. Consequently, I do feel fine today.
4. We looked marvelous, except for the rain and mud trailing down our bodies.
5. Even if you beg and plead, I am still going to say no.
6. To help with the chores, I mowed the backyard.
7. Our house guest finally decided to go home.
8. After that first kiss, we knew we were meant to be together.
9. Before doing the errands, will you please balance the checkbook?
10. He stood there as if he was waiting for something to happen.

Practice 13 Correcting Rewrite the sentences in Practice 12 by moving the words you underlined.

1. _____

2. _____

3. _____

4. _____

5. _____

6. _____

7. _____

8. _____

9. _____

10. _____

◆ **Practice 14** **Completing** Rewrite the following paragraph by moving words and phrases around.

> At night, I always read. I love to find new places when I read that I will travel to someday. Once I discovered a boiling lake in the jungles of Dominica. By accident, I learned about a Mayan cave in Belize that was discovered by a young man's dog while it was chasing a large rat. Just yesterday, I read about 250-pound codfish in the Great Barrier Reef in Australia. I love to read to take my mind to these places before I can afford to see them in person. Forever, I will love traveling through books.

◆ **Practice 15** **Writing Your Own**

A. Write a sentence of your own for each of the words, phrases, and clauses here.

    1. however _____

    2. in the summer _____

    3. before you speak _____

4. when the sun comes up _____

5. after I study _____

B. Vary the structure of the sentences you wrote in Practice 15A by moving portions of each sentence around and rewriting it. Underline the words you moved.

1. _____

2. _____

3. _____

4. _____

5. _____

VARY SENTENCE TYPE

Use a question, a command, or an exclamation occasionally.

> Ever since I turned 17, I have longed to be independent. **Have you ever longed to be independent?** Now I have a part-time job and a full-time college career. In addition, soon I will be moving into my new apartment. I have already begun to shop for secondhand furniture. Am I ever excited about this change in my life!

◆ *Practice 16* **Identifying** Identify each of the following sentences as a statement (S), a question (Q), a command (C), or an exclamation (E). Add the appropriate end punctuation.

1. _____ Margery has a strange phobia

2. _____ Finish these reports before the end of the week

3. _____ Hey, you just took my seat

4. _____ Why are you sitting in the dark

5. _____ Which way did the horse run

6. _____ Yes, I would like some more iced tea

7. _____ Jim will be in San Francisco on Tuesday

8. _____ Walk the dog

9. _____ You are awesome

10. _____ How do I start this machine

◆ *P r a c t i c e   1 7*   **Identifying** Label the sentences in the following paragraph as statements (S), questions (Q), commands (C), or exclamations (E) in the following paragraph.

There are so many different genres of music. _____ Just pick one. _____ Progressive, alternative, rap, and country are just a few. _____ And there are even divisions of music within genres. _____ Have you ever heard of new country? _____ It's a blend of rock and country. _____ Or have you ever heard of classic rock? _____ Out of the 1960s and 1970s came that type. _____ Or have you ever heard of retroactive, big band, gansta rap, light jazz, metal, acid rock, and so on? _____ There are just too many of them to count! _____ You choose. _____

◆ *P r a c t i c e   1 8*   **Correcting** Change each of the sentences in Practice 16 from a statement, question, command, or exclamation into another type of sentence.

1. _____

2. _____

3. _____

4. _____

5. _____

6. _____

7. _____

8. _____

9. _____

10. _____

◆ *P r a c t i c e   1 9*   **Completing** Fill in each blank in the following sentences to make each into a statement, question, command, or an exclamation, and add the correct punctuation.

1. Wow! That was _____

2. Explain _____

3. What was _____

4. Take this _____

5. Hey, _____

6. I like _____

7. You just _____

8. How did he _____

9. Which of these _____

10. She felt _____

♦ **P r a c t i c e   2 0**   **Writing Your Own**

A. Rewrite each of the following sentences, making them into the sentence type indicated in parentheses.

1. How many questions are there? (statement)

   _____

2. What did you do? (exclamation)

   _____

3. Take me to your superior. (question)

   _____

4. Do I like candy? (statement)

   _____

5. Will you deliver this to the Smiths? (command)

   _____

B. Write five sentences of your own, making at least one a statement, one a question, one a command, and one an exclamation.

1. _____

2. _____

3. _____

4. _____

5. _____

REVIEWING WAYS TO VARY SENTENCE PATTERNS

Why is varying sentence patterns important in your writing?

_____

Name four ways to vary your sentence patterns.

_____

_____

_____

_____

What other kinds of sentences besides statements can you use for variety?

_____   _____   _____

CHAPTER REVIEW

You might want to reread your answers to the questions in the review box before you do the following exercises.

◆ **Review P r a c t i c e 1**   **Reading** Refer to the paragraph by Nicholas Gage on pages 474–475 to do the following exercises.

1.   List two introductory words from the paragraph.

_____

_____

2a. Record a sentence from the paragraph whose subject and verb can be reversed.

_____

2b. Write this sentence with its subject and verb reversed.

_____

3a. List two sentences that have words that can be moved.

_____

3b. Write these two sentences in another way, moving at least one word in each one.

_____

4.   Add one question, one command, and one exclamation to the paragraph.

_____

◆ **Review P r a c t i c e 2 Identifying** Underline the words or groups of words that have been added or moved in each revised sentence. Then use the list that follows to record which rule you applied to the sentence.

Rule

1. Add introductory words.
2. Reverse the order of subject and verb.
3. Move parts of the sentence around.
4. Use a question, command, or exclamation occasionally.

   1. We laughed in the rain.
        _____ Last night, we laughed in the rain.
   2. You fit all those clothes in that tiny suitcase.
        _____ How did you fit all those clothes in that tiny suitcase?

3. They decided to fly instead of drive due to the terrible conditions of the road.

_____ Due to the terrible conditions of the roads, they decided to fly instead of drive.

4. It was spring. We were competing in the biggest game of our lives.

_____ During the spring, we competed in the biggest game of our lives.

5. The bird flew out of the house.

_____ Out of the house flew the bird.

6. Indeed, she felt happy to have survived the weekend.

_____ She felt happy indeed to have survived the weekend.

7. You should listen more carefully.

_____ Listen more carefully.

8. The man came lumbering down the lane.

_____ Lumbering down the lane came the man.

9. I found my keys.

_____ Yippee, I found my keys!

10. Since then, everyone has gotten along fantastically.

_____ Everyone has gotten along fantastically since then.

Review P r a c t i c e 3 Correcting Vary the structure of the following sentences with at least three of the four ideas you learned in this chapter. Rewrite the paragraph with your changes.

Good hairdressers are hard to find. They should be good listeners. That's the first step to pleasing customers. They should also be able to visualize what their customers want. The best hairdressers always make suggestions about what will or will not look good on a person. They should do what the customer wants, though, since the customer is always right. They also need to be interested in their customers' lives.

EDITING A STUDENT PARAGRAPH

Following is a paragraph written and revised by Gabriel Alvarez in response to the writing assignment in this chapter. Read the paragraph, and check it for sentence variety.

While practicing with my band, I found out that the other band members thought I was a bit too serious, even mean at times. They said that I was "cool" and everything, but when it came to practicing music, my personality changed. They were even afraid to voice their opinions to me for fear of my reaction. I thought this was odd because I'm usually considered an easygoing person. I have often heard people say that I don't play around when it comes to my tunes. They are right. I take music very seriously. But I had no idea how seriously. I guess it took someone else to make me realize this. I will try to be more polite. I don't regret this part of my personality. If I didn't take our practices seriously, there would be no practice. The band needs someone to be in charge, and that's me. And besides, my personality changes back once practice is over.

Collaborative Activity

Team up with a partner, and put brackets around any sentence in Gabriel's paragraph that could use some variety in its structure. Then add at least one introductory element; reverse the order of one subject and verb; move some parts of a sentence around; and create at least one question, command, or exclamation. Rewrite the paragraph with your changes.

EDITING YOUR OWN PARAGRAPH

Now return to the paragraph you wrote and revised at the beginning of this chapter. Check it for sentence variety.

Collaborative Activity

Exchange paragraphs with your partner, and put brackets around any sentence that could use some variety in your partner's paragraph.

Individual Activity

Apply at least two of the guidelines you learned in this chapter to your own writing. To complete the writing process, revise any sentences that your partner marked in your paragraph by rewriting your paragraph.

CHAPTER **28**

PARALLELISM

✅ CHECKLIST for Using Parallelism

> ✔ Can you use parallelism to add coherence to your sentences and paragraphs?
> ✔ Are all items in a series grammatically balanced?

When sentences are **parallel,** they are balanced. That is, words, phrases, or clauses in a series start with the same grammatical form. Parallel structures make your sentences interesting and clear.

Notice how parallel structures create smooth and interesting writing:

To be fair, it's simplistic to dump all the woes of education on mothers and fathers. Some apathetic teachers, autocratic principals, narrow-minded school boards, lifeless textbooks, suffocating policies, and ridiculous rules must share the blame. Besides, our children are growing up in a society that's only willing to pay lip service to the need for first-class schools.

Yet none of these problems compares with the disappearance and disarray of parents. During more than a decade of reporting and writing about Florida schools, I have met hundreds of dedicated teachers with the same horror stories: parents who never set foot on school grounds, who don't show up for conferences, who insult and sometimes threaten teachers, who show little interest in what's happening to their children, and who sometimes don't seem to care if their kids are actually going to school. Over and over, teachers tell me, parents say: "Hey, you're the expert. You deal with it."

In this paragraph, Thomas French discusses who's to blame for the problems in public schools. Before continuing in this chapter, take a moment to write about a time you blamed someone or something for your own actions. Save your work because you will use it later in this chapter.

WRITING ASSIGNMENT: THE BLAME GAME

Have you ever blamed something or someone other than yourself for a problem when in fact you were to blame? What was the situation? Who was involved? What did you do and why? How did your actions make you feel? Write a paragraph describing the situation and the outcome.

 REVISING YOUR WRITING

Revise the first draft of your paragraph before you focus on editing. Use the Revising Checklist on pages 24–25 to help you with your revision. Make sure your paragraph has a good topic sentence and is well developed. Then check your paragraph for unity, organization, and coherence.

Parallel structure gives your sentences order and continuity. It helps your readers navigate through your ideas and understand what you are saying. Notice how difficult the following paragraph is to understand because the items in a series are not grammatically parallel.

> Susan had her summer all planned out. She was going to read as many romance novels as possible, will work in her garden, and will be taking piano lessons. Then her brother called her and asked if she could stay at his house for a month while he and his wife vacationed in Florida. Now she is taking care of the children, feeding the dog, and the elderly neighbor.

Words and phrases in a series should be parallel, which means they should start with the same type of word. Parallelism makes your sentence structure smoother and more interesting. Look at this sentence, for example.

NOT She was going to **read** as many romance novels as possible,

will work in her garden, and

will be taking piano lessons.

CORRECT She **will read** as many romance novels as possible,

will work in her garden, and

will be taking piano lessons.

CORRECT She was going to **read** as many romance novels as possible,

work in her garden, and

take piano lessons.

Here is another sentence that would read better if the parts were parallel:

NOT   Now she is **taking** care of the children,
                        feeding the dog, and
                        the elderly neighbor.

CORRECT Now she is **taking** care of the children,
                        feeding the dog, and
                        looking after the elderly neighbor.

CORRECT Now she is taking care of **the children,**
                        the dog, and
                        the elderly neighbor.

Now read the paragraph with these two sentences made parallel or balanced.

Susan had her summer all planned out. She was going to read as many romance novels as possible, work in her garden, and take piano lessons. Then her brother called her and asked if she could stay at his house for a month while he and his wife vacationed in Florida. Now she is taking care of the children, the dog, and the elderly neighbor.

REVIEWING PARALLELISM

What is parallelism?

_____

_____

Why should you use parallelism in your writing?

_____

◆ **P r a c t i c e 1 Identifying** Underline the parallel structures in each of the following sentences.

1. They baked me a cake, sang me a song, and bought me presents for my birthday.

2. Kiara, Jayda, Robin, and Laura were voted most likely to succeed.

3. I'm feeling even more confused, frustrated, and lost than before.

4. When you get dressed up in those clothes, fix your hair like that, and wear your sunglasses, you look like a movie star.

5. Edgar plans to rehearse with his band, watch James Bond movies, and surf the waves this summer.

6. Walk across the street, turn left, and proceed straight ahead to your destination.

7. The secretary phoned to ask if we could prepare the minutes and if we could give a short speech for the meeting.

8. In the cupboard, behind the boxes, and to the right are the blank Christmas cards from last year.

9. Lori believed that she would win the contest and that she would go to the finals.

10. Since you are so patient, kind, and generous, you should be in charge of the children.

◀ P r a c t i c e   2   Identifying Put an X next to the sentence if the underlined structures are not parallel.

1. _____ On vacation, we plan to <u>hike in the mountains</u>, <u>swim in the ocean</u>, and <u>dance under the stars</u>.

2. _____ She always turns red whenever someone <u>smiles at her</u> or <u>paying her a compliment</u>.

3. _____ He ordered <u>*Time*</u>, the <u>*New York Times*</u>, and the <u>*Los Angeles Times*</u> for his manager.

4. _____ The frog jumped <u>on the dresser</u>, <u>across the table</u>, and <u>out the window</u>.

5. _____ <u>Biking</u>, <u>talk to friends</u>, and <u>to eat pizza</u> are some of my favorite things to do.

6. _____ <u>After the television has been turned off</u>, <u>after the children have been tucked into bed</u>, and <u>we let the dog out for the night</u>, I can finally go to bed.

7. _____ I believe in you because you are <u>loyal</u>, <u>dedicated</u>, and <u>kept my secrets</u>.

8. _____ <u>Because the car was not running</u> and <u>because the rain hadn't stopped</u>, we decided to stay home.

9. _____ To start your research, you should <u>surf the Net</u>, <u>search the library</u>, and <u>you will need to interview people</u>.

10. _____ Kendra was so stressed out today that she <u>put the Windex in the refrigerator</u>, <u>put the milk in the cupboard</u>, and <u>the remote in the medicine cabinet</u>.

◆ **P r a c t i c e   3   Correcting** Correct the parallelism errors in Practice 2 by rewriting each incorrect sentence.

1. _____

2. _____

3. _____

4. _____

5. _____

6. _____

7. _____

8. _____

9. _____

10. _____

◆ **P r a c t i c e   4   Completing** Fill in the blanks in each of the following sentences with parallel structures.

1. The pictures on the wall are by _____, _____, and _____.

2. We thought that you _____ and that you _____.

3. In spite of the _____, _____, and _____, Diego managed to finish his final on time.

4. He _____, _____, and _____.

5. Because Shane _____ and _____, Marianne agreed to marry him.

6. The penny rolled _____, bounced _____, and landed.

7. The most _____, _____, and _____ person in the world just asked me out on a date.

8. This _____, _____, and _____ essay should be published.

9. It tasted like _____, _____, and _____.

10. You will find your grandmother's handmade quilts in the garage, _____, and _____.

◆ *P r a c t i c e* 5 **Writing Your Own**

A. Write a sentence of your own for each of the following parallel structures.

1. that you should have apologized and that you should try to make it up

   _____

2. through the hedges, across the stream, and over the hill

   _____

3. every time he sees her, talks to her, or mentions her name

   _____

4. blue, red-gold, and off-white

   _____

5. read, sun-bathe, and garden

   _____

B. Write five sentences of your own using parallel structures, and underline the parallel structures.

1. _____

2. _____

3. _____

4. _____

5. _____

CHAPTER REVIEW

You might want to reread your answers to the questions in the review box before you do the following exercises.

◆ *Review* **P r a c t i c e 1**   **Reading** List the two parallel structures from the paragraph by Thomas French on page 490.

1. _____

_____

2. _____

_____

_____

_____

◆ *Review* **P r a c t i c e 2**   **Identifying** Underline the faulty parallel structures in the following sentences.

1. Jake enjoys golf, soccer, and playing tennis.
2. We always take the path through the woods, around the old haunted house, and run across the meadow.
3. Minnie taught Adrian how to bait a hook, cast a lure, and avoiding falling into the river.
4. She will eat only organic foods, wear only all-natural clothes, and uses only natural beauty products.
5. Zach said that the banquet was at 6:00 p.m. and that served at 6:30 was dinner.
6. If you lay your clothes out the night before, gather your materials and set them on the table, and if you will wake up a bit earlier, you should be able to make it to work on time.
7. Please fill the car with gas, get a receipt, and I would love some donuts.

8. Take the rugs outside, hang them on the clothesline, and the dust needs to be beaten out of them.

9. Tonight Rosa plans to surprise her husband by making a romantic dinner, putting on some soft jazz, and get her parents to watch the kids.

10. On the drums, you first begin with the stride, then the main beat, and the counterbeat comes next.

Review P r a c t i c e 3 Correcting Correct the faulty parallel structures in Review Practice 2 by rewriting each sentence.

EDITING A STUDENT PARAGRAPH

Following is a paragraph written and revised by Jessie Santillion in response to the writing assignment in this chapter. Read the paragraph, and underline her words, phrases, and clauses in a series.

When I was 8 years old, I set the carpet on fire. It all started when Dad asked me to do some chores: pulling the weeds in the flowerbeds, make up the beds, and iron some clothes. After I finished pulling the weeds and making the beds, I went into the laundry room to do some ironing. When I got there, I found that LaVonne, my eldest sister, had left the iron on. I proceeded to do my ironing until the phone rang. I raced out of the room, down the hall I flew, and skidded to a halt in front of the phone. (It was always a race to see who could get to the phone first.) By the time I made it back to the ironing, the carpet was smoldering, hissing, and smoked. In my haste, I must have knocked the iron over. I stamped the fire out, grab the white oval rug from my room, and covered up my crime. That night at dinner, Mom casually asked about the carpet in the laundry room. LaVonne dropped her fork, gasped for breath, and her stricken eyes turned toward her mother. Obviously, LaVonne thought she had done the deed. I chose to remain silent. LaVonne got grounded for two months. But before the weekend came, my conscience began to devour my innocence, and so I confessed. But Mom didn't believe me! And even after crying, pleading, and I begged. Mom still didn't believe me—or so she said. In hindsight, I think that she knew that I was the criminal all along and that my conscience was punishment enough. Since that day, I have always thought twice about blaming others for my actions.

Collaborative Activity

Team up with a partner, and put an X above the six items in Jessie's paragraph that are not parallel to the other items in their series. Then, working together, use what you have learned in this chapter to correct these errors. Rewrite the paragraph with your corrections.

EDITING YOUR OWN PARAGRAPH

Now return to the paragraph you wrote and revised at the beginning of this chapter. Underline any words, phrases, and clauses in a series.

Collaborative Activity

Exchange paragraphs with your partner, and put an X above any structures in your partner's paragraph that are not parallel with others in their series.

Individual Activity

On the Error Log in Appendix 4, record any parallelism errors that your partner found in your paragraph. To complete the writing process, correct these errors by rewriting your paragraph.

COMBINING SENTENCES

CHAPTER **29**

 CHECKLIST for Combining Sentences

✔ Do you combine sentences to avoid too many short, choppy sentences in a row?

✔ Do you use different types of sentences?

Still another way to add variety to your writing is to combine short, choppy sentences into longer sentences. **Combining sentences** changes the rhythm of a paragraph and stimulates your readers' interest.

Notice how different types of sentences add variety and interest to the following paragraph.

I liked Grandma the best, though, when she told me about my mama, because it was a part of Mama that I had never seen or been close to. I didn't know that when Mama was a little girl a photographer came one day to take a picture of her and her sister in a pony cart. I couldn't imagine that they had to bribe them into good behavior by giving them each a coin. In the picture Mama is crying and biting her coin in half. It was a dime, and she wanted the bigger coin—the nickel—given to her sister. Somehow, I thought that Mama was born knowing the difference between a nickel and a dime.

In this paragraph, Erma Bombeck explores her changing perceptions of her mother. Before continuing in this chapter, take a moment to write about how your own perception of someone has changed. Save your work because you will use it later in this chapter.

WRITING ASSIGNMENT: PERCEPTIONS

We've all had moments when we discover something new about ourselves, but what about others? Have you ever been shocked to learn something about someone you thought you knew well? For example, when did you discover that one of your parents or guardians was actually human—that he or she could cry, feel pain, be silly, act immature, or make a mistake? What happened to change your view of this person? What did you discover about this person? How did this discovery make you feel? Write a paragraph explaining your changing perceptions.

REVISING YOUR WRITING

Revise the first draft of your paragraph before you focus on editing. Use the Revising Checklist on pages 24–25 to help you with your revision. Make sure your paragraph has a good topic sentence and is well developed. Then check your paragraph for unity, organization, and coherence.

Simple sentences can be combined to make three other types of sentences: compound, complex, and compound-complex.

SIMPLE SENTENCES

A **simple sentence** consists of one independent clause. Remember that a clause has a subject and a main verb.

In the following examples, notice that a simple sentence can have more than one subject and more than one verb. (For more on compound subjects and compound verbs, see Chapter 7.)

 s   v
I have many opportunities for the future.

 s   v   v
I have plans for the future and want to realize them all.

 s   s   v
Ed and Jim took the dogs for a walk.

      s   s   v   v

Margarita and I shop and gossip at the mall.

REVIEWING SIMPLE SENTENCES

What does a simple sentence consist of?

_____

Write a simple sentence.

_____

 P r a c t i c e   1   Identifying Underline the subjects once and the verbs twice in the following simple sentences.

1. The phone and the doorbell rang at the same time.
2. The carpenter measured and then cut the wood.
3. You can choose from many career opportunities.
4. The doe and her fawn were startled and ran away.
5. The math problem frustrated and confused me.
6. We wasted much time.
7. The skaters and the bikers joined forces and cleaned up the park.
8. The Kilpatricks and the McLoughlins sponsored the event.
9. The sun's light felt warm and comforting.
10. Juan and Tim smiled at the girls.

 P r a c t i c e   2   Identifying Put an S next to the sentence if it is a simple sentence. Remember to look for subjects and verbs first.

1. _____ Marvin reconfigured the computer's memory.
2. _____ My sister and my mother will be spending the weekend at an exclusive spa.
3. _____ Michael and Kim volunteer at the local shelter, and their friends provide homes for foster children.
4. _____ He calculated the distance between home and school on his bike.
5. _____ The neighbor's dogs barked all night long and annoyed me greatly.

6. _____ The child hugged his stuffed bear tightly and cried for a long time after his mother left.

7. _____ Our house and landscape were designed and built by a close friend.

8. _____ Many people are turning to solar energy; others insist on gas and electricity.

9. _____ They played Monopoly and visited all day.

10. _____ When I'm ready to leave, the suitcase and carry-on will be sitting by the door, and the taxi will be here.

◆ **P r a c t i c e   3   Correcting** Make 10 simple sentences out of the sentences in Practice 2 that are not simple.

1. _____

2. _____

3. _____

4. _____

5. _____

6. _____

7. _____

8. _____

9. _____

10. _____

◆ **P r a c t i c e   4   Completing** Fill in the blanks in each of the following sentences with subjects and verbs that complete the simple sentences.

1. _____ and _____ chased the ice-cream truck around the corner.

2. Yolanda's _____ and _____ _____ with her over the weekend and _____ the following Monday.

3. The _____ and _____ have fallen behind the bookshelf.

4. Most people _____ mild peppers to the hotter ones.

5. A _____ just bit me.

6. The fans _____ and _____ for the football team.

7. The stereo's _____ went dead.

8. Mom and Dad _____ everything and _____ to the door.

9. Your _____ is about to run outside.

10. Your _____ and _____ in your bedroom are _____ and _____ to be let out.

◆ **P r a c t i c e   5   Writing Your Own**

A. Write a simple sentence of your own for each of the following subjects and verbs.

1. laughing and singing _____

2. the dog and cat _____

3. the red sports car _____

4. are skipping and whistling _____

5. gasped _____

B. Write five simple sentences of your own, and underline the subjects and verbs.

1. _____

2. _____

3. _____

4. _____

5. _____

COMPOUND SENTENCES

A **compound sentence** consists of two or more independent clauses joined by a coordinating conjunction (*and, but, for, nor, or, so,* or *yet*). In other words, you can create a compound sentence from two (or more) simple sentences.

Simple:	Amy enjoys reading.
Simple:	Amy can read very quickly.

                        S   V   S   V

Compound: Amy enjoys reading, **and** she can read very quickly.

Simple:	Charles loves to cook for people.
Simple:	He owns his own restaurant.

                        S   V   S   V

Compound: Charles loves to cook for people, **so** he owns his own restaurant.

Simple:	Natasha and Christy wanted to stay in a fancy hotel.
Simple:	They didn't have enough money.

                        S   S   V

Compound: Natasha and Christy wanted to stay in a fancy hotel,

                S   V

but they didn't have enough money.

Hint: As the examples show, a comma comes before the coordinating conjunction in a compound sentence.

REVIEWING COMPOUND SENTENCES

What does a compound sentence consist of?

_____

Write a compound sentence.

_____

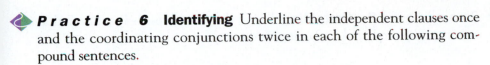 **P r a c t i c e 6** **Identifying** Underline the independent clauses once and the coordinating conjunctions twice in each of the following compound sentences.

1. The dinner looked great, and it tasted even better.
2. The marble sculpture fell during the earthquake, and it broke into many pieces.
3. It is 110 degrees outside, and our air conditioning is not working.
4. The tennis player served the ball, but it hit the net.
5. He cannot give you a ride to the store, nor can he pick up the dry cleaning.
6. You can work late today, or you can come in on Saturday.
7. Frank pushed the car with all his strength, yet he could not get it out of the mud.
8. We ran out of bait, so we used fake worms instead.
9. One of the engines failed on the airplane, but the other engines made up for the loss of power.
10. The dog chased the cat, but the cat quickly ran up a tree.

P r a c t i c e 7 **Identifying** Underline the independent clauses in the following sentences once, and underline any coordinating conjunctions twice. Then label the sentence either simple (S) or compound (C).

1. _____ Dean went to the Bahamas, and he snorkeled there for the first time.
2. _____ Jeremy was worried about his weight.
3. _____ John liked the shirt, but his girlfriend didn't.
4. _____ The computer cannot think for itself, nor can it solve every problem.
5. _____ The lock on the door was bolted.
6. _____ The sail was raised, and soon the boat was out at sea.
7. _____ My dictionary does not provide definitions of slang words.
8. _____ The cat kept sharpening its claws on my new couch, so I bought a scratching post.
9. _____ Cruise lines tend to overfeed passengers.
10. _____ Aunt Rosa's roses usually take first place at the fair.

◆ **P r a c t i c e 8 Correcting** Using the sentences in Practice 7 that are not compound, make 10 compound sentences.

1. _____
2. _____
3. _____
4. _____
5. _____
6. _____
7. _____
8. _____
9. _____
10. _____

◆ **P r a c t i c e 9 Completing** Combine each pair of simple sentences into a compound sentence.

1. Michelle loves to shop. She doesn't have any money.
2. The mascot broke his leg. He couldn't perform at tonight's game.
3. The storm blew down the power lines. We missed our favorite television show.
4. I am very hungry. There is no food in the refrigerator.
5. He didn't have much experience. He got the job anyway.
6. Cheryl cannot eat strawberries. She cannot drink milk.
7. Ants have a complex social structure. Each type of ant has a specific task within the structure.
8. Sparky, my dog, has been hit by lightning three times. He survived each episode.
9. Mr. Dupré is an excellent teacher. He enjoys working with students.
10. Chris spoke harshly to his girlfriend. Now he regrets it.

P r a c t i c e   **1 0**   **Writing Your Own**

A. Write a compound sentence of your own by adding a coordinating con-junction and an independent clause to each of the following sentences.

1. The gophers are digging holes in the yard.

_____

2. We got a new DVD player.

_____

3. Sequoia National Forest is a protected area.

_____

4. Sydney is really good at American Sign Language.

_____

5. Scientists are working on a cure for cancer.

_____

B. Write five compound sentences of your own, and underline the subjects and verbs.

1. _____

2. _____

3. _____

4. _____

5. _____

COMPLEX SENTENCES

A **complex sentence** is composed of one independent clause and at least one dependent clause. A **dependent clause** begins with either a subordinat-ing conjunction or a relative pronoun.

Subordinating Conjunctions

after	because	since	until
although	before	so	when
as	even if	so that	whenever
as if	even though	than	where
as long as	how	that	wherever
as soon as	if	though	whether
as though	in order that	unless	while

Relative Pronouns

who	whom	whose	which	that

You can use subordinating conjunctions and relative pronouns to make a simple sentence (an independent clause) into a dependent clause. Then you can add the new dependent clause to an independent clause to produce a complex sentence that adds interest and variety to your writing.

How do you know which simple sentence should be independent and which should be dependent? The idea that you think is more important should be the independent clause. The less important idea will then be the dependent clause.

Following are some examples of how to combine simple sentences to make a complex sentence.

Simple:　　Devin has a demanding job.

Simple:　　Devin really enjoys his job.

　　　　　　　　　　　　　　　　　Dep　　　　　　　　　　　　　Ind
Complex:　　**Though** Devin has a demanding job, he really enjoys it.

This complex sentence stresses that Devin enjoys his job. That the job is demanding is of secondary importance.

　　　　　　　　　　　　Ind　　　　　　　　　　　　　　　　　Dep
Complex:　　Devin has a demanding job, **though** he really enjoys it.

In the previous complex sentence, the fact that Devin's job is demanding is the important point, so it is stated in the independent clause.

Simple: Jack loves to go deep-sea fishing.

Simple: Jack is my brother.

                         Ind   Dep

Complex: Jack, **who** is my brother, loves to go deep-sea fishing.

This complex sentence answers the question "Who loves to go deep-sea fishing?" The information about Jack being the speaker's brother is of secondary importance.

                         Ind   Dep

Complex: My brother is Jack, **who** loves to go deep-sea fishing.

This complex sentence answers the question "Who is your brother?" The information that he loves to go deep-sea fishing is secondary.

REVIEWING COMPLEX SENTENCES

What does a complex sentence consist of?

_____

Write a complex sentence.

_____

◆ **P r a c t i c e   1 1   Identifying** Identify the underlined part of each sentence as either an independent (Ind) or a dependent (Dep) clause.

1. _____ Even though he enjoys working with small children, <u>they try his patience sometimes</u>.

2. _____ Thomas, <u>who won the election</u>, is now the dorm monitor.

3. _____ <u>Before you leave for work</u>, make sure the iron is turned off.

4. _____ <u>She always sneezes</u> whenever she is around daffodils.

5. _____ There is the mouse <u>that you have been trying to catch</u>!

6. _____ Of course, you can attend the wedding, <u>provided that you are invited</u>.

7. _____ <u>I wonder</u> how I can improve my grades.

8. _____ Cassandra is the employee <u>whose attendance is perfect</u>.

9. _____ <u>The winner of the talent contest is Misha Grimes</u>, who is also my sister.

10. _____ <u>We are celebrating</u> because we passed our final exams.

◆ **P r a c t i c e   1 2**   **Identifying** Underline the independent clauses once and the dependent clauses twice in each of the following sentences.

1. Your proposal, which is beautifully written, was accepted.
2. My favorite singer is Sting, who also has a B.A. in English literature.
3. Have the carpets cleaned before the new furniture arrives.
4. Aiden appreciated Joan's efforts to cheer him up, though he still felt sad.
5. Although I do want to go, I have a deadline to meet.
6. In life, you never know whom you might meet.
7. Anna believes that she is the best candidate for the position.
8. Even if the sun comes out from behind the clouds, it's still going to be cold.
9. If they try to jump over that stream, they are probably going to fall in.
10. The air conditioning is set to 72 degrees so that the computers will run properly.

◆ **P r a c t i c e   1 3**   **Correcting** Write the sentences in Practice 12 as either simple or compound sentences. You can change words when necessary.

1. _____

2. _____

3. _____

4. _____

5. _____

6. _____

7. _____

8. _____

9. _____

10. _____

◆ **P r a c t i c e   1 4   Completing** Finish each of the following sentences, and label the new clause either dependent (Dep) or independent (Ind).

1. _____ My cousin, _____, won the lottery.

2. _____ Here are the rods and reels _____.

3. _____ Thomas left the lights on _____.

4. _____ Even if the show ends by 9:00, _____.

5. _____ Whenever it snows, _____.

6. _____ _____, although he really doesn't like it.

7. _____ The presents _____ are already in the mail.

8. _____ I invested money in a CD _____.

9. _____ Before _____, make sure that the car is filled with gas.

10. _____ _____ how you finished your work so quickly.

◆ **P r a c t i c e   1 5   Writing Your Own**

A. Write a dependent clause using each of the following subordinating conjunctions and relative pronouns.

1. that _____

2. whose _____

3. after _____

4. whereas _____

5. unless _____

B. Write five independent clauses to combine with the dependent clauses you wrote in Practice 15A to make five complex sentences.

1. _____

2. _____

3. _____

4. _____

5. _____

COMPOUND-COMPLEX SENTENCES

If you combine a compound sentence with a complex sentence, you produce a **compound-complex sentence.** That means your sentence has at least two independent clauses (to make it compound) and at least one dependent clause (to make it complex). Here are some examples.

Simple:	Jarvis likes to sail.
Simple:	He is going to Cancun this summer.
Simple:	He is looking forward to sailing in Cancun.

	Ind Ind
Compound-Complex:	Jarvis likes to sail, **and** he is going to
	Dep
	Cancun this summer, **which** he is looking forward to.

Simple:	She is selling her old house.
Simple:	Her house has only one bedroom.
Simple:	She plans to buy a bigger house.

	Ind Dep
Compound-Complex:	She is selling her old house, **which** has
	Ind
	only one bedroom, **and** she plans to buy a bigger house.

Simple:	These cookies look delicious.
Simple:	The cookies are very hot.
Simple:	The cookies just came out of the oven.

Ind   Ind

Compound-Complex: These cookies look delicious, **but** they are

Dep

very hot **since** they just came out of the oven.

Hint: Notice in these examples that we occasionally had to change words in the combined sentences so they make sense.

REVIEWING COMPOUND-COMPLEX SENTENCES

What does a compound-complex sentence consist of?

_____

Write a compound-complex sentence.

_____

◆ **P r a c t i c e   1 6   Identifying** Identify the underlined part of each sentence as either an independent (Ind) or a dependent (Dep) clause.

1. _____ Alyssa, <u>who is a practical joker</u>, left a can of paint over the door, and she also put a fake mouse in the sheets.

2. _____ Even though I like to be alone sometimes, <u>I do enjoy others' company</u>, and I can make small talk.

3. _____ Golf is a difficult game, but it can be mastered <u>if a person has patience</u>.

4. _____ The man looked <u>as if he was going to burst out laughing</u>, yet he just gasped and wheezed into his napkin.

5. _____ <u>They have been married for five years</u>, and they are very happy together even though both have very different personalities.

6. _____ <u>While the boss was out of the office</u>, the employees did a little redecorating, yet they resisted the urge to play hooky.

7. _____ Whether you believe it or not, Harvey really did send you an invitation, and <u>he really does like you</u>.

8. _____ The antique-white dress, <u>which belonged to my grandmother</u>, is lovely, and I plan to have it altered for my wedding.

9. _____ We caught several bass and catfish, but they were too small for supper, so <u>we threw them back in the lake</u>.

10. _____ When the tire blew, <u>he quickly pulled the car over to the side of the road</u>, and then he called AAA.

◆ **P r a c t i c e   1 7   Identifying** Underline the independent clauses once and the dependent clauses twice in each of the following sentences.

1. Manny, who is a wonderful father, spends much time with his children, and he even takes them to work with him on occasion.

2. The books that you ordered over the Internet are in the mail, and they should reach you within three days.

3. These CDs, which I borrowed from a friend, are the best, and I am going to buy them for myself.

4. She whipped up a quick meal, and then she jumped in the bathtub when the phone rang.

5. After you accept your diploma, you should turn and smile for the camera, but you shouldn't make any silly faces.

6. We are planning the roast for our retiring chair, and we are going to prepare a slide show because we have some hilarious pictures of everyone.

7. Even though the weather is horrible outside, Luke insists on going on the trip, and he will not back down.

8. She asked him how he managed to escape without a lecture, and then she filed the information away for future use.

9. Once the liquid comes to a rolling boil, remove the mixture from the stove, but don't allow it to cool too quickly.

10. The person who gets the job must have experience with communication systems, and he or she must also have great customer service skills.

◆ **P r a c t i c e   1 8   Correcting** Write the sentences in Practice 17 as either simple, compound, or complex sentences. You can change words when necessary.

1. _____

2. _____

3. _____

4. _____

5. _____

6. _____

7. _____

8. _____

9. _____

10. _____

◀ **P r a c t i c e   1 9   Completing** Write two compound-complex sentences for each set of sentences. You may have to change some of the words to make the new sentences clear.

1. I need a new computer.
   I damaged my last computer.
   I plan to order a computer from Gateway.

   _____

   _____

2. The tea was lukewarm.
   I was thirsty.
   I drank the tea.

   _____

   _____

3. Bob owns a vintage Harley Davidson.
   Bob has been a biker for 10 years.

Bob likes to ride in the mountains.

_____

_____

4. Joshua loves to eat Reese's Peanut Butter Cups.
   He has a process for eating Reese's Peanut Butter Cups.
   Joshua will not share his Reese's Peanut Butter Cups.

_____

_____

5. Min Ling has an infectious sense of humor.
   Min Ling laughs all the time.
   Min Ling makes others laugh too.

_____

_____

◆ P r a c t i c e   2 0   Writing Your Own

A. Expand the following clauses into compound-complex sentences.

1. I know the man who was the last person to arrive

_____

2. I was reading a really good book

_____

3. They bought the house that you decorated

_____

4. I am a free spirit, and I love to travel

_____

5. so that the rain wouldn't come through the roof

   _____

B. Write five compound-complex sentences of your own and underline the
    independent clauses once and the dependent clauses twice in each
    sentence.

   1. _____

   2. _____

   3. _____

   4. _____

   5. _____

CHAPTER REVIEW

You might want to reread your answers to the questions in all the review
boxes before you do the following exercises.

Review **P r a c t i c e   *1*   Reading** Refer to the paragraph by Erma
Bombeck on page 499 to do the following exercises.

1. List the simple sentence from the paragraph.

   _____

2. List the one compound sentence from the paragraph.

   _____

   _____

3. List the four complex sentences from the paragraph.

   _____

   _____

   _____

_____

_____

_____

_____

4. Combine some of the sentences in the paragraph to create a compound-complex sentence.

_____

_____

◆ **Review P r a c t i c e   2   Identifying** Underline the independent clauses once and the dependent clauses twice in each of the following sentences. Then label each sentence simple (S), compound (C), complex (CX), or compound-complex (CCX). The following definitions will help you.

Simple	=	one independent clause
Compound	=	two or more independent clauses joined by *and, but, for, no, nor, or, so,* or *yet*
Complex	=	one independent clause and at least one dependent clause
Compound-complex	=	at least two independent clauses and one or more dependent clauses

1. _____ They often attend auctions, but they rarely bid on the antiques.

2. _____ Erin is always joking with people.

3. _____ He cooked dinner, washed the dishes, and mowed the lawn while she watched television.

4. _____ He said that you were a trustworthy employee, and he recommended that we hire you.

5. _____ Most people who are allergic to bees developed the allergy after their second sting.

6. _____ The car sputtered and died.

7. _____ This printer can print in many different colors, and it can act as a fax too.

8. _____ We brought extra water, freeze-dried food, and heavy-duty sleeping bags, and we made sure that the first-aid kit was stocked.

9. _____ A. C. Bradley was a well-known Shakespearean critic, and he is often cited in research papers.

10. _____ Whenever Sarah gets that silly smile on her face, she is thinking about her fiancé.

Review P r a c t i c e 3 Writing Your Own Combine each set of sentences to make the sentence pattern indicated in parentheses. You may need to change some wording in the sentences so they make sense. The list of sentence types in Review Practice 2 may help you with this exercise.

1. The plane may not arrive on time. We will miss our next connection. (complex)

2. Joey left for Spain. Joey got a new passport. Joey brushed up on his Spanish. (compound-complex)

3. Whole-wheat muffins or bagels are tasty. Whole-wheat muffins or bagels are healthy. (simple)

4. You had to suffer through the lecture. The lecture was extremely boring. You had to catch a plane back home. (compound-complex)

5. The phone lines were down. Cathy used her cell phone. Cathy cut the conversation short to save money. (compound-complex)

6. Simone discussed the upcoming election. Craig discussed the upcoming election. (simple)

7. Nurses have difficult jobs. Most nurses find their work worthwhile. (compound)

8. Many people entered the drawing. Only one person won. (complex)

9. You always laugh. People laugh with you. (complex)

10. Myra and Jennifer will build a fire in the fireplace. Dave and Voni will begin supper. (compound)

EDITING A STUDENT PARAGRAPH

Following is a paragraph written and revised by Tim Robertson in response to the writing assignment in this chapter. Read the paragraph, and underline the independent clauses once and the dependent clauses twice.

I found out that my older brother Mike was actually a member of the human race. It was the day when he fixed my bike. I was 6 years old. Mike was 13. I thought that he knew everything. Mike was a distant god in my eyes. It was a Saturday morning. The chain had come loose on my bike. I was crying in the garage. Mike came out. He saw me crying and said that he would fix my bike. I watched for a while. Then I got bored. Most 6-year-olds get bored easily. I went inside to find other entertainment. Soon I was in the garage again. "Are you finished yet?" I asked him. "No," he said. I repeated this routine four times within 30 minutes. On the fourth time, Mike yelled, "No, I am not finished yet. If you don't stop bugging me, I'm going to throw the chain in the garbage!" I ran screaming to my room. I slammed the door. Not five minutes later, Mike came into my room. He sat on my bed. It was lumpy from years of jumping. He pulled me onto his lap and gave me a big hug. "You know that I really do love you," he said, "even when you bug me." Mike and I had seven years separating us. Mike never seemed to have time for me. I thought that I was simply someone whom he tolerated. On that day, however, my perspective of Mike changed. He was no longer just a distant god. He was my big brother too.

Collaborative Activity

Team up with a partner, and label each of Tim's sentences S (simple), C (compound), CX (complex), or CCX (compound-complex). Then, working together, use what you have learned in this chapter to add variety to the paragraph by combining some of the sentences. Make at least two compound, two complex, and two compound-complex sentences. Rewrite the paragraph with your revisions.

EDITING YOUR OWN PARAGRAPH

Now return to the paragraph you wrote and revised at the beginning of this chapter. Underline the independent clauses once and the dependent clauses twice.

Collaborative Activity

Exchange paragraphs with your partner, and label each of your partner's sentences S (simple), C (compound), CX (complex), or CCX (compound-complex).

Individual Activity

To complete the writing process, add variety in your sentence patterns by combining some of the sentences in your paragraph.

UNIT TESTS

Here are some exercises that test your understanding of all the material in this unit: Varying Sentence Structure, Parallelism, and Combining Sentences.

Unit Test 1 Identifying

Label each of the following sentences simple (S), compound (C), complex (CX), or compound-complex (CCX).

1. _____ My boyfriend likes to go to the movies a lot, but I would rather watch TV.

    _____ He always wants to see blood-and-guts movies.

    _____ Someday I'll sneak in a romance, a drama, or seeing a comedy.

2. _____ I am ready for summer break.

    _____ I took too many units this quarter, unfortunately.

    _____ I hope that I can keep up my hectic pace through finals.

3. _____ I love to shop for groceries, cook meals, and baking.

    _____ Thank goodness my roommate loves to clean.

    _____ We decided to keep peace by doing these chores for each other.

4. _____ Monday is my favorite day of the week.

    _____ Most people think that this is very strange.

    _____ I love starting a new week, making new decisions, and my troubles are left behind me.

5. _____ My favorite brother is moving to my town.

    _____ I love being with my brother.

    _____ Being together will be like old times.

Unit Test 2 Varying

Rewrite each of the sentences in Unit Test 1 using one of the following techniques to add variety to them.

1. Add some introductory words to your sentences so that they don't all start the same way.
2. Reverse the order of some subjects and verbs.
3. Move some parts of the sentences around.
4. Use a question, command, or exclamation occasionally.

1. _____

_____

_____

2. _____

_____

_____

3. _____

_____

_____

4. _____

_____

_____

5. _____

_____

_____

Unit Test 3 Making Parallel

In the sentences you wrote in Unit Test 2, correct any items in a series that are not parallel by rewriting each series in parallel form.

1. _____

2. _____

3. _____

4. _____

_____

5. _____

Unit Test 4 Combining

Combine the sentences from Unit Test 1 using as many of the changes you made in Unit Tests 2 and 3 as possible.

1. _____

_____

2. _____

_____

3. _____

_____

4. _____

_____

5. _____

_____

UNIT WRITING ASSIGNMENTS

1. What is the ad on the next page about? What is the unspoken message in this picture? Are you persuaded by this ad? Why or why not?

2. You have been asked to prepare a speech for your English class about writing. Use your experience as a writer to persuade your audience that writing is beneficial for many different reasons. Be sure to

explain what the benefits are and why they are benefits. You may even want to narrow your topic to one type of writing.

3. You have decided to use your yard skills and mow the lawns in your neighborhood to make money during the summer. This job fits with your summer classes, and you can work as much or as little as you want. How do you plan to approach your customers? What will you do to demonstrate your talents? What will you say? Explain your approach and the reasons for your choices.

4. Create your own assignment (with the help of your instructor), and write a response to it.

CHOOSING THE RIGHT WORD

UNIT
8

Choosing the right word is like choosing the right snack to satisfy your appetite. If you don't select the food you are craving, your hunger does not go away. In like manner, if you do not choose the right words to say what is on your mind, your readers will not be satisfied and will not understand your message.

Choosing the right word depends on your message, your purpose, and your audience. It also involves recognizing misused, nonstandard, and misspelled words. We deal with the following topics in Unit 8:

Chapter 30: Standard and Nonstandard English
Chapter 31: Easily Confused Words
Chapter 32: Spelling

STANDARD AND NONSTANDARD ENGLISH

✅ CHECKLIST for Choosing the Right Word

> ✔ Do you consistently use standard English in your paper?
>
> ✔ Is your paper free of nonstandard, ungrammatical words?
>
> ✔ Have you changed any slang to standard English?

Choosing the right words for what you want to say is an important part of effective communication. This chapter will help you find the right words and phrases for the audience you are trying to reach.

Look, for example, at the following sentences. They all have generally the same message, expressed in different words.

I'm studying to become a nurse, the reason being that I want to help people.

I be studying to be a nurse so I can help people.

I'm pounding the books so I can be a nurse and help other folks.

I am pursuing a degree in nursing so that I can help others in need.

Which of these sentences would you probably say to a friend or to someone in your family? Which would you most likely say during a job interview? Which would be good for a college paper?

The first three sentences are nonstandard English. They might be said or written to a friend or family member, but they would not be appropriate in an academic setting or in a job situation. Only the fourth sentence would be appropriate in an academic paper or during a job interview.

Notice in the following paragraph how the consistent use of standard English makes a message smooth and coherent.

Just last week, I was walking down the street with my mother, and I again found myself conscious of the English I was using, the English I do use with her. We were talking about the price of new and used furniture, and I heard myself saying this: "Not waste money that way." My husband was with us as well, and he didn't notice any switch in my English. And then I realized why. It's because over the twenty years we've been together I've often used that same kind of English with him, and sometimes he even uses it with me. It has become our language of intimacy, a different sort of English that relates to family talk, the language I grew up with.

In this paragraph, Amy Tan discusses the different types of English she uses depending on the situation. Before continuing in this chapter, take a moment to record your thoughts on your language use in a typical day. Save your work because you will use it later in this chapter.

WRITING ASSIGNMENT: LANGUAGES

How many languages do you speak and write? What is your native language? How do you adjust your English to different people and different situations? Why do you adjust your language in these ways? Write a paragraph describing your language use in a typical day. Do your adjustments in language suit the different purposes and people in your life?

REVISING YOUR WRITING

Revise the first draft of your paragraph before you focus on editing. Use the Revising Checklist on pages 24–25 to help you with your revision. Make sure your paragraph has a good topic sentence and is well developed. Then check your paragraph for unity, organization, and coherence.

STANDARD AND NONSTANDARD ENGLISH

Most of the English language falls into one of two categories—either *standard* or *nonstandard*. **Standard English** is the language of college, business, and the media. It is used by reporters on television, by newspapers, in most magazines, and on Web sites created by schools, government agencies, businesses, and organizations. Standard English is always grammatically correct and free of slang.

Nonstandard English does not follow all the rules of grammar and often includes slang. Nonstandard English is not necessarily wrong, but it is more appropriate in some settings (with friends and family) than others. It is not appropriate in college or business writing. To understand the difference between standard and nonstandard English, compare the following paragraphs.

Nonstandard English

I just got a new pad and went to the grocery store to stock the fridge with some grub. Since I only had 40 bucks, I knew I oughta play it cool and just stick to the list: milk, eggs, cereal, soda, bread, peanut butter, and jelly. Irregardless of my good intentions, I sorta lost it in the frozen food section. By the time I got outta there, I must of picked up one of each kind of food— pizza, corn dogs, burritos, pies, and apple turnovers. And somewheres underneath all that stuff were the bread and the eggs. I was real embarrassed when I go to check out cuz I didn't have enough money and I had to put some of the stuff back. At that moment, I realized I was a long ways from home.

Standard English

I just got a new apartment and went to the grocery store to stock the refrigerator with some food. Since I had only $40, I knew I had to stick to my list: milk, eggs, cereal, soda, bread, peanut butter, and jelly. Regardless of my good intentions, I made too many choices in the frozen food section. By the time I got out of that aisle, I must have picked up one of each kind of food—pizza, corn dogs, burritos, pies, and apple turnovers. Somewhere underneath all that food were the bread and the eggs. I was really embarrassed when I went to check out because I didn't have enough money and I had to put some of the items back. At that moment, I realized I was a long way from home.

In the rest of this chapter, you will learn how to recognize and correct ungrammatical English and how to avoid slang in your writing.

REVIEWING STANDARD AND NONSTANDARD ENGLISH

Where do you hear standard English in your daily life?

_____

What is nonstandard English?

_____

Give two examples of nonstandard English.

_____   _____

NONSTANDARD ENGLISH

Nonstandard English is ungrammatical. It does not follow the rules of standard English that are required in college writing. The academic and business worlds expect you to be able to recognize and avoid nonstandard English. This is not always easy because some nonstandard terms are used so often in speech that many people think they are acceptable in writing. The following list might help you choose the correct words in your own writing.

ain't

NOT	He **ain't** leaving until tomorrow.
CORRECT	He **isn't** leaving until tomorrow.

anywheres

NOT	Susie can't find her glasses **anywheres.**
CORRECT	Susie can't find her glasses **anywhere.**

be

NOT	I **be** really good at art.
CORRECT	I **am** really good at art.

(For additional help with *be*, see Chapter 11, "Verb Tense.")

being as, being that

NOT	Jamal will not be joining the study group tonight, **being as** his car broke down.
CORRECT	Jamal will not be joining the study group tonight, **because** his car broke down.

coulda/could of, shoulda/should of

NOT   She **could of** made the sauce with cream instead of milk.

CORRECT   She **could have** made the sauce with cream instead of milk.

different than

NOT   This sandwich is no **different than** that sandwich.

CORRECT   This sandwich is no **different from** that sandwich.

drug

NOT   I **drug** the rug across the floor.

CORRECT   I **dragged** the rug across the floor.

enthused

NOT   Jim was **enthused** about his GPA.

CORRECT   Jim was **enthusiastic** about his GPA.

everywheres

NOT   My little sister follows me **everywheres.**

CORRECT   My little sister follows me **everywhere.**

goes

NOT   Then Nancy **goes,** I'm taking the bus.

CORRECT   Then Nancy **says,** "I'm taking the bus."

CORRECT   Then Nancy **said** that she was taking the bus.

hisself

NOT   Evan made **hisself** sick on peanut butter.

CORRECT   Evan made **himself** sick on peanut butter.

in regards to

NOT   I got your memo **in regards to** the changes.

CORRECT   I got your memo **in regard to** the changes.

irregardless

NOT   **Irregardless** of your healthy lifestyle, you still need to lower your cholesterol.

CORRECT   **Regardless** of your healthy lifestyle, you still need to lower your cholesterol.

kinda/kind of, sorta/sort of

NOT	This tastes **kinda** sweet, **sorta** like cherries.
CORRECT	This tastes **rather** sweet, **much** like cherries.

most

NOT	**Most** everyone is going.
CORRECT	**Almost** everyone is going.

must of

NOT	I **must of** left my backpack in the park.
CORRECT	I **must have** left my backpack in the park.

off of

NOT	Michael skated **off of** the ramp.
CORRECT	Michael skated **off** the ramp.

oughta

NOT	Sometimes you **oughta** say please and thank you.
CORRECT	Sometimes you **ought to** say please and thank you.

real

NOT	She was **real** glad to see us.
CORRECT	She was **really** glad to see us.

somewheres

NOT	His books are **somewheres** in that dirty room.
CORRECT	His books are **somewhere** in that dirty room.

suppose to

NOT	They were **suppose to** meet us here.
CORRECT	They were **supposed to** meet us here.

theirselves

NOT	The children hid **theirselves** throughout the house.
CORRECT	The children hid **themselves** throughout the house.

use to

NOT	I **use to** work while listening to music.
CORRECT	I **used to** work while listening to music.

ways

NOT	We are lost and a long **ways** from home.
CORRECT	We are lost and a long **way** from home.

where . . . at

NOT	**Where** is the remote control **at?**
CORRECT	**Where** is the remote control?

REVIEWING NONSTANDARD ENGLISH

What is one reason using nonstandard English in written work is easy to do?

_____

Give four examples of nonstandard English; then correct them.

_____   _____

_____   _____

_____   _____

_____   _____

◆ **P r a c t i c e   1   Identifying** Put an X next to the sentence if the underlined words are ungrammatical.

1. _____ <u>Being that</u> it is such a beautiful day, we should take our lunch on the patio.
2. _____ Alyssa <u>don't</u> like to be tickled.
3. _____ She <u>used</u> to drink coffee every morning.
4. _____ We <u>ain't</u> going to fail this test.
5. _____ Jake bought <u>himself</u> a dirt bike.
6. _____ The crowd was <u>enthused</u> about his speech.
7. _____ Those dogs <u>oughta</u> be on a leash.
8. _____ My cell phone goes <u>everywheres</u> I go.
9. _____ The computer was <u>suppose</u> to come with a color printer.
10. _____ <u>Most everyone</u> likes your idea.

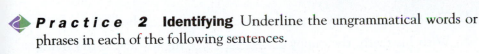

◆ **P r a c t i c e   2   Identifying** Underline the ungrammatical words or phrases in each of the following sentences.

1. Mom was real mad when I left the milk out.

2. They made theirselves a promise to spend more time together.

3. We have wandered a long ways from the path.

4. Your wallet could be anywheres in the backyard.

5. The plant have only two blooms.

6. Irregardless of how much time you spent on your paper, it still needs revision.

7. Somewheres out there is the perfect car for me.

8. Where is the phone at?

9. You could of taken the freeway instead of the back roads.

10. The receptionist must of written down the wrong phone number.

◆ **P r a c t i c e   3   Correcting** Correct the standard English errors in Practice 2 by rewriting each incorrect sentence.

1. _____

2. _____

3. _____

4. _____

5. _____

6. _____

7. _____

8. _____

9. _____

10. _____

◆ **P r a c t i c e   4   Completing** Fill in each blank in the following sentences with standard English using the list at the beginning of this chapter.

1. The girl's behavior is very different _____ the boy's.

2. With his teeth, the puppy _____ his toy across the living room.

3. Then William _____ that he would do the job.

4. They received the letter in _____ to the board meeting.

5. He fell _____ the sidewalk and sprained his ankle.

6. My little sister didn't realize that she wasn't _____ to eat the mud pies.

7. The cake _____ ready yet.

8. I _____ very fond of seafood.

9. That smells _____ bad, _____ like garbage.

10. The dog has buried my keys _____ in the backyard.

◆ P r a c t i c e 5 Writing Your Own

A. Write a sentence of your own for each of the following words and phrases.

1. should have _____

2. in regard to _____

3. ought to _____

4. must have _____

5. dragged _____

B. Write five sentences of your own using at least five of the standard English examples at the beginning of this chapter. Underline the standard English examples.

1. _____

2. _____

3. _____

4. _____

5. _____

SLANG

Another example of nonstandard English is **slang,** popular words and expressions that come and go, much like the latest fashions. For example, in the 1950s, someone might call his or her special someone *my steady.* In the 1970s, you might hear a boyfriend or girlfriend described as *foxy,* and in the 1980s, *stud* was a popular slang term for males. Today your significant other might be your *man* or *homegirl.*

These expressions are slang because they are part of the spoken language that changes from generation to generation and from place to place. As you might suspect, slang communicates to a limited audience who share common interests and experiences. Some slang words, such as *cool* and *neat,* have become part of our language, but most slang is temporary. What's in today may be out tomorrow, so the best advice is to avoid slang in your writing.

REVIEWING SLANG

What is slang?

_____

Give two examples of slang terms that were popular but aren't any longer.

_____   _____

Give two examples of slang terms that you and your friends use today.

_____   _____

P r a c t i c e   6   Identifying Put an X next to the sentence if the underlined word is slang.

1. _____ Your leather jacket is <u>slammin'</u>.
2. _____ This is good <u>grub</u>.
3. _____ Cordelia's talking <u>smack</u> again.
4. _____ I'm making <u>big bucks</u> now.
5. _____ Sam will leave when he is <u>ready</u>.
6. _____ Let's <u>chill</u> at the library for a while.

7. _____ <u>Talk to me</u> about your decision.

8. _____ We don't allow <u>scrubs</u> in our dorm.

9. _____ You deserve <u>praise</u> for your efforts.

10. _____ The hostess was <u>way</u> nice.

♦ **P r a c t i c e 7 Identifying** Underline the slang words or phrases in the following sentences.

1. These CDs are da bomb.

2. Everyone knows Jason is a player.

3. She's down with the plan.

4. You have to get your groove on at the party.

5. Me and my dawgs are going to the show.

6. Keep it real.

7. I got your back.

8. I dig your new ride.

9. Give it to me straight.

10. What's crackin'?

♦ **P r a c t i c e 8 Correcting** Correct the slang errors in Practice 7 by rewriting each sentence.

1. _____

2. _____

3. _____

4. _____

5. _____

6. _____

7. _____

8. _____

9. _____

10. _____

P r a c t i c e   9   Completing Translate each of the following slang expressions into standard English.

1. go with the flow _____

2. as if _____

3. get outta here _____

4. pump it up _____

5. fries your brain _____

6. homies _____

7. five-finger discount _____

8. keep it on the DL _____

9. give him props _____

10. give big ups _____

P r a c t i c e   1 0   Writing Your Own

A. List five slang words or expressions, and use them in sentences of your own.

  1. _____

  2. _____

  3. _____

  4. _____

  5. _____

B. Rewrite each sentence from Practice 10A using standard English to replace the slang expressions.

  1. _____

  2. _____

3. _____

4. _____

5. _____

CHAPTER REVIEW

You might want to reread your answers to the questions in all the review boxes before you do the following exercises.

◆ ***Review Practice 1*** **Reading** Rewrite the paragraph by Amy Tan on page 527 in nonstandard English.

_____

_____

_____

_____

_____

_____

◆ ***Review Practice 2*** **Identifying** Underline any nonstandard English and slang in the following sentences.

1. We're really rolling now.
2. She must of forgotten that we were going to have lunch today.
3. The monkeys at the zoo acted real hyper when they saw us.
4. That's jacked.
5. You don't understand, man.
6. Somewheres out there is the girl for you.
7. These are my peeps.
8. Where's the sugar at?
9. Say what?
10. This ain't the best idea.

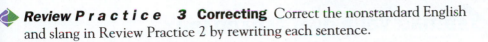

Review **P r a c t i c e** **3** **Correcting** Correct the nonstandard English and slang in Review Practice 2 by rewriting each sentence.

EDITING A STUDENT PARAGRAPH

Following is a paragraph written and revised by Jamie Franks in response to the writing assignment in this chapter. Read the paragraph, and look for any nonstandard English or slang.

> Unfortunately, I now only speak one language. I say "now" because I use to speak Spanish until I was 3, but I have lost all memory of the language. In a way, however, the statement that I only speak one language is false, because I kinda speak two languages—a form of English I use with adults and a form of English I use with my friends. And believe me, one is definitely different than the other. When I speak to my friends, I go, "Dude, I went to a phat party last night. Carly was chillin' with a hottie named Dan. Man, she was a dog." Of course, I ain't gonna say this to my grandma. I would say, "I went to a great party last night. A girl named Carly spent time with a good-looking guy named Dan, but she wasn't very attractive." Irregardless of the situation, it be real disrespectful, in some ways, to talk to adults in slang being that they don't understand, but it's also not proper. But I wouldn't talk in proper English all the time to my friends because we'd eventually never communicate. I'd be left behind somewheres in the conversation. So I do believe that language is important, and I do believe I speak two languages. They just both happen to be English.

Collaborative Activity

Team up with a partner, and underline the 17 nonstandard and slang expressions in Jamie's paragraph. Then, working together, use what you have learned in this chapter to correct these errors. Rewrite the paragraph with your corrections. Don't change any words in quotations.

EDITING YOUR OWN PARAGRAPH

Now return to the paragraph you wrote and revised at the beginning of this chapter. Look for any nonstandard English or slang.

Collaborative Activity

Exchange paragraphs with your partner, and underline any nonstandard or slang expressions that you find in your partner's paragraph.

Individual Activity

On the Error Log in Appendix 4, record any nonstandard English errors your partner found in your paragraph. To complete the writing process, correct these errors by rewriting your paragraph.

EASILY CONFUSED WORDS

CHAPTER 31

 CHECKLIST for Easily Confused Words

> ✔ Is the correct word chosen from the easily confused words?
> ✔ Are the following words used correctly: *its/it's, their/there/they're, to/too/two, who's/whose, your/you're?*

Some words are easily confused. They may look alike, sound alike, or have similar meanings, but they all play different roles in the English language.

Notice how the careful selection of words helps convey meaning in the following paragraph.

Do you consistently write more than necessary in e-mail messages? Are you swamping your readers with too many details? Do you give so much information—important, unimportant, and in no particular order— that your reader cannot easily conclude what matters and what does not? A poll published in *Oregon Business* found that 26 percent of respondents spend an hour each day reading and replying to their e-mail; 14 percent spend more than an hour. So, do everything possible to compose messages that will help your reader save time. Some guidelines include the following: (1) Limit messages to one screen so the reader will not have to scroll down, and (2) use numbers, bullets, and so on to highlight key points.

In this excerpt, Mark Hansen gives some practical advice about communicating through e-mail. Before continuing in this chapter, take a moment to respond to his suggestions. Save your work because you will use it later in this chapter.

WRITING ASSIGNMENT: THE JOYS OF TECHNOLOGY

Letter writing is a ritual from the past. Very few people take the time to write and mail letters when they have access to faster or more convenient means of communication. What is your experience with modern communication technology? How does e-mail fit into your life? Are you keeping up with the latest changes? How does technology affect your studies? Your job? Where do you think technology will be in a few years? Write a paragraph explaining your thoughts on these questions.

REVISING YOUR WRITING

Revise the first draft of your paragraph before you focus on editing. Use the Revising Checklist on pages 24–25 to help you with your revision. Make sure your paragraph has a good topic sentence and is well developed. Then check your paragraph for unity, organization, and coherence.

This chapter will help you choose the right words for your sentences.

EASILY CONFUSED WORDS, PART I

a/an: Use *a* before words that begin with a consonant. Use *an* before words that begin with a vowel (*a, e, i, o, u*).

> **a** letter, **a** cookie, **a** fax
> **an** answer, **an** eon, **an** animal

accept/except: *Accept* means "receive." *Except* means "other than."

> I **accept** your apology.
> I found all the marbles **except** the black one.

advice/advise: *Advice* means "helpful information." *Advise* means "give advice or help."

> His **advice** is sound.
> He **advises** me on financial matters.

affect/effect: *Affect* (verb) means "influence." *Effect* means "bring about" (verb) or "a result" (noun).

This decision will **affect** the final outcome.
The new law will **effect** important reforms.
The **effect** was caused by changes in weather patterns.

already/all ready: *Already* means "in the past." *All ready* means "completely prepared."

Sarah has **already** received her shots.
They were **all ready** to leave when the car broke down.

among/between: Use *among* when referring to three or more people or things. Use *between* when referring to only two people or things.

The doctors discussed the diagnoses **among** themselves.
She lives **between** those two houses.

bad/badly: *Bad* means "not good." *Badly* means "not well."

That rash on your arm looks **bad.**
He performed **badly** on his driving test.
He felt **bad** about the ruined sweater.

beside/besides: *Beside* means "next to." *Besides* means "in addition (to)."

I sat **beside** a large oak tree.
Besides smelling bad, the sneakers were covered with mud.

brake/break: *Brake* means "stop" or "the parts that stop a moving vehicle." *Break* means "shatter, come apart" or "a rest between work periods."

She put her foot on the **brake** as soon as she saw the dog.
I saw the vase **break** when it hit the floor.
I like my job, but I look forward to my lunch **break.**

breath/breathe: *Breath* means "air." *Breathe* means "taking in air."

Take a deep **breath** and count to 10.
If you **breathe** too quickly, you could hyperventilate.

choose/chose: *Choose* means "select." *Chose* is the past tense of *choose*.

You **choose** the restaurant.

He **chose** to go with his friends.

REVIEWING WORDS THAT ARE EASILY CONFUSED, PART I

Do you understand the differences in the sets of words in Part I of the list?

_____

Have you ever confused any of these words? If so, which ones?

_____

P r a c t i c e   1   Identifying Underline the correct word in each of the following sentences.

1. Can you offer any (advice, advise) on this problem?
2. Your actions will (affect, effect) the outcome.
3. The class talked quietly (among, between) themselves.
4. If you keep bending that twig, you are going to (brake, break) it.
5. The puppy (choose, chose) a spot in front of the oven to sleep.
6. That looks like (a, an) weather balloon, not a spaceship.
7. She is not a (bad, badly) child, just mischievous.
8. Please (advice, advise) me on upcoming courses.
9. The horses are (already, all ready) to be ridden.
10. The (affects, effects) of your actions were impossible to foresee.

P r a c t i c e   2   Identifying Put an X next to the sentence if the underlined word is incorrect.

1. _____ <u>Among</u> the two of us, we can cook a great meal.
2. _____ I <u>already</u> gave to that charity.
3. _____ The <u>affect</u> was subtle.

4. _____ Sometimes the air we <u>breath</u> is not healthy.

5. _____ The dog food is <u>beside</u> the dog's bowl.

6. _____ She was so nervous that she sang <u>bad</u>.

7. _____ You should listen to your <u>mother's advice</u>.

8. _____ Please don't <u>brake</u> my heart.

9. _____ <u>A</u> ant just crawled up my pant leg.

10. _____ Yesterday you <u>choose</u> the red one, but now you want the blue one.

P r a c t i c e   3   Correcting Correct the word errors in Practice 2 by rewriting each incorrect sentence.

1. _____

2. _____

3. _____

4. _____

5. _____

6. _____

7. _____

8. _____

9. _____

10. _____

P r a c t i c e   4   Completing Fill in each blank in the following sentences with a correct word that makes sense from Part I of the list of easily confused words.

1. Anna did _____ your invitation to lunch.

2. _____ dictionary is a good reference tool.

3. The loan officer has _____ left for the day.

4. _____ those two students sits my mother.

5. Why did Martin _____ to move to Ohio?

6. My accountant gives me good _____ regarding stocks.

7. That dog has turned _____, so don't pet him.

8. His yawning _____ the rest of us.

9. Mints will sweeten your _____.

10. _____ for balancing the checkbook and going to the grocery store, I don't have any plans for today.

◆ **Practice 5   Writing Your Own** Use each of the following pairs of words correctly in a sentence of your own.

1. choose/chose

_____

_____

2. breath/breathe

_____

_____

3. bad/badly

_____

_____

4. beside/besides

_____

_____

5. advice/advise

_____

_____

EASILY CONFUSED WORDS, PART II

coarse/course: *Coarse* refers to something that is rough. *Course* refers to a class, a process, or a part of a meal.

This cornmeal is **coarse.**
My future **course** is clear.
The meals in this restaurant have many **courses.**

desert/dessert: *Desert* refers to dry, sandy land or means "abandon." *Dessert* refers to the last course of a meal.

The **desert** has many strange animals.
He **deserted** the army.
The strawberry shortcake **dessert** was the best I ever had.

Hint: You can remember that *dessert* has two s's if you think of *strawberry shortcake*.

does/dose: *Does* means "performs." *Dose* refers to a specific portion of medicine.

He **does** the yard work, and I do the housework.
A large **dose** of cranberry juice will clear up that infection.

fewer/less: *Fewer* refers to things that can be counted. *Less* refers to things that cannot be counted.

Now that I am older, I have **fewer** really good friends.
I have **less** time for play now that I am in college.

good/well: *Good* modifies nouns. *Well* modifies verbs, adjectives, and adverbs. *Well* also refers to a state of health.

Jane is a **good** instructor.
She did **well** on the state exam.
My goldfish is swimming sideways; he must not feel **well.**

hear/here: *Hear* refers to the act of listening. *Here* means "in this place."

The child didn't speak until he was 4 because he couldn't **hear** well.
Here are the Easter eggs from last year—yuck!

it's/its: *It's* is the contraction for *it is* or *it has*. *Its* is a possessive pronoun.

> **It's** the best solution.
> The water buffalo flicked **its** tail at the flies.

knew/new: *Knew* is the past tense of *know*. *New* means "recent."

> He **knew** about the **new** television set.

know/no: *Know* means "understand." *No* means "not any" or is the opposite of *yes*.

> **No,** I didn't **know** that you had lived overseas.

lay/lie: *Lay* means "set down." (Its principal parts are *lay, laid, laid*.) *Lie* means "recline." (Its principal parts are *lie, lay, lain*.)

> She **lays** material out before cutting it.
> He **laid** down the heavy firewood.
> My mom **lies** on the couch to watch her soaps.
> They **lay** under the stars.

(For additional help with *lie* and *lay*, see Chapter 10, "Regular and Irregular Verbs.")

loose/lose: *Loose* means "free" or "unattached." *Lose* means "misplace" or "not win."

> Ben knocked his tooth **loose.**
> I'm fighting hard not to **lose** this game.

passed/past: *Passed* is the past tense of *pass*. *Past* refers to an earlier time or means "beyond."

> Brittany **passed** us in her car, but she didn't see us.
> We can learn about ourselves from the **past.**
> Suddenly, a bird swooped **past** me.

REVIEWING WORDS THAT ARE EASILY CONFUSED, PART II

Do you understand the differences in the sets of words in Part II of the list?

_____

Have you ever confused any of these words? If so, which ones?

_____

P r a c t i c e   6   Identifying Underline the correct word in each of the following sentences.

1. We are studying Egypt's (passed, past).
2. Put the gifts (hear, here).
3. Everybody (knew, new) about the surprise but you.
4. Jimmie flew (passed, past) me on his bike.
5. Dillon always (does, dose) well in art.
6. You must not (loose, lose) your pass, or you will not be allowed back in.
7. The bird lifted (it's, its) wings in the wind.
8. Martin's suggestions are (good, well) ideas.
9. Now that summer is almost over, there are (fewer, less) blooms on the rose bushes.
10. The ship sailed on a northern (coarse, course).

P r a c t i c e   7   Identifying Put an X next to the sentence if the underlined word is incorrect.

1. _____ Be careful because your pants are really <u>lose</u> and might fall off.
2. _____ <u>Its</u> time for you to make your entrance.
3. _____ The <u>dessert</u> can be a beautiful place if you know where to look.
4. _____ The <u>knew</u> uniforms are still in their boxes.
5. _____ The <u>does</u> she took was too strong.
6. _____ Her language was <u>coarse</u> and uncalled for.
7. _____ Speak louder since I can't <u>hear</u> you.
8. _____ There is <u>fewer</u> water in your cup than in mine.
9. _____ Ben's presentation in class went <u>good</u>.
10. _____ Since Tabitha just moved here, she doesn't <u>know</u> anybody.

P r a c t i c e   8   Correcting Correct the word errors in Practice 7 by rewriting each incorrect sentence.

1. _____

2. _____

3. _____

4. _____

5. _____

6. _____

7. _____

8. _____

9. _____

10. _____

◆ **P r a c t i c e   9   Completing** Fill in each blank in the following sentences with a correct word that makes sense from Part II of the list of easily confused words.

1. The maximum _____ is 2 tablespoons.

2. They are taking a _____ together.

3. We could _____ the class laughing all the way down the hall.

4. _____ wines go well with fruit and cheeses.

5. The _____ time you spend editing, the more mistakes you're likely to make.

6. Candice doesn't want to go to the party because she doesn't _____ how to dance.

7. Leroy always _____ a blanket down for the baby.

8. _____ perhaps the funniest thing I've seen all day.

9. This cap is too _____ for this jar.

10. I love to _____ in the sun and read a good novel.

◆ **P r a c t i c e   1 0   Writing Your Own** Use each of the following pairs of words in a sentence of your own.

1. know/no

   _____

   _____

2. passed/past

   _____

   _____

3. fewer/less

   _____

   _____

4. good/well

   _____

   _____

5. it's/its

   _____

   _____

EASILY CONFUSED WORDS, PART III

principal/principle: *Principal* means "main, most important," "a school official," or "a sum of money." A *principle* is a rule. (Think of *principle* and *rule*—both end in *-le*.)

> My **principal** reason for attending college is to get a good job.
> Our **principal** was strict but kind.
> Sometimes it's hard to live by one's **principles.**

quiet/quite: *Quiet* means "without noise." *Quite* means "very."

> We have to be **quiet** so we don't disturb the others.
> I found the book **quite** fascinating.

raise/rise: *Raise* means "increase" or "lift up." *Rise* means "get up from a sitting or reclining position."

Do not **raise** the lid on the stew; it's simmering.
As the temperature **rises,** so does everyone's temper.

set/sit: *Set* means "put down." *Sit* means "take a seated position."

You can **set** those anywhere you like.
Bailey can **sit** and watch TV for hours.

(For additional help with *sit* and *set*, see Chapter 10, "Regular and Irregular Verbs.")

than/then: *Than* is used in making comparisons. *Then* means "next."

I am older **than** my aunt.
Allen smelled the daisies, and **then** he sneezed.

their/there/they're: *Their* is possessive. *There* indicates location. *They're* is the contraction of *they are*.

Their coats are in the entryway.
We went **there** first.
They're all happy for you.

threw/through: *Threw*, the past tense of *throw*, means "tossed." *Through* means "finished" or "passing from one point to another."

The quarterback **threw** the ball.
Are you **through** with studying?
The mouse ate **through** the cupboard wall.

to/too/two: *To* means "toward" or is used with a verb. *Too* means "also" or "very." *Two* is a number.

Diane always goes **to** the reunion **to** catch up on the gossip.
The coffee was **too** strong.
We have **two** children.

wear/were/where: *Wear* means "have on one's body." *Were* is the past tense of *be*. *Where* refers to a place.

You can **wear** casual clothes but not shorts or jeans.

Where were those candles?

weather/whether: *Weather* refers to outdoor conditions. *Whether* expresses possibility.

> **Whether** you believe it or not, you can trust the **weather** to stay sunny.

who's/whose: *Who's* is a contraction of *who is* or *who has*. *Whose* is a possessive pronoun.

> **Who's** going to determine **whose** display is the best?

your/you're: *Your* means "belonging to you." *You're* is the contraction of *you are*.

> **Your** actions will tell others if **you're** a loyal friend or not.

Reviewing Words That Are Easily Confused, Part III

Do you understand the differences in the sets of words in Part III of this list?

_____

Have you ever confused any of these words? If so, which ones?

_____

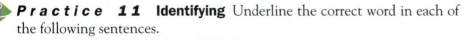 **P r a c t i c e   1 1**   **Identifying** Underline the correct word in each of the following sentences.

1. The (principal, principle) of our old high school has accepted another position.
2. (Set, Sit) in this chair until the doctor can see you.
3. She'd rather eat worms (than, then) have to watch this movie.
4. Are you (quiet, quite) sure that's what you want to do?
5. (Their, There, They're) are many decisions to be made.

6. They went (to, too, two) the wrecking yard to hunt for spare parts.

7. Kendra and Parker (were, wear, where) thrilled about the pregnancy.

8. Walk (threw, through) those doors, and turn left.

9. The (weather, whether) has turned unexpectedly cold.

10. When you (raise, rise) in the morning, don't forget to do your exercises.

♦ **P r a c t i c e   1 2   Identifying** Put an X next to the sentence if the underlined word is incorrect.

1. _____ I was <u>quiet</u> upset when I got to the station and couldn't find my train.

2. _____ Few of us are able to live strictly by our <u>principals</u>.

3. _____ That was <u>to</u> much information to digest at once.

4. _____ Allow the dough to <u>raise</u> for one hour.

5. _____ <u>Their</u> asking a lot of questions that I cannot answer.

6. _____ <u>Whose</u> giving Sheila a ride to the airport?

7. _____ Make sure the children <u>wear</u> their coats.

8. _____ The snake slithered underneath the bed, and <u>than</u> I ran screaming out the door.

9. _____ <u>Your</u> hair is snagged on a tree branch.

10. _____ I'm never going to make it <u>threw</u> this traffic on time.

♦ **P r a c t i c e   1 3   Correcting** Correct the word errors in Practice 12 by rewriting each incorrect sentence.

1. _____

2. _____

3. _____

4. _____

5. _____

6. _____

7. _____

8. _____

9. _____

10. _____

◆ **P r a c t i c e 1 4 Completing** Fill in each blank in the following sentences with a correct word that makes sense from Part III of the list of easily confused words.

1. _____ shoes are untied.

2. You must be _____ in this hospital ward.

3. If you _____ those books on that table, they are going to fall.

4. The students have prepared _____ orals in advance.

5. _____ watch is this?

6. _____ the hood of the car very carefully.

7. Benjamin always eats what she cooks for him, _____ he likes it or not.

8. There are _____ letters in the mailbox for Palmer.

9. The reporter listened intently, and _____ she took out her pen and notebook.

10. What was Gregory thinking when he _____ that rock at the beehive?

◆ **P r a c t i c e 1 5 Writing Your Own** Use each of the following sets of words in a sentence of your own.

1. quiet/quite

   _____

   _____

2. their/there/they're

   _____

   _____

3. threw/through

_____

_____

4. than/then

_____

_____

5. raise/rise

_____

_____

CHAPTER REVIEW

You might want to reread your answers to the questions in all the review boxes before you do the following exercises.

◆ *Review Practice 1* **Reading** List the nine words that could be confused from the paragraph by Mark Hansen on page 541.

_____   _____   _____

_____   _____   _____

_____   _____   _____

◆ *Review Practice 2* **Identifying** Underline the words used incorrectly in each of the following sentences.

1. It is to hot in here to pay attention.
2. Jacinta choose to tour Europe for a year before attending college.
3. My mom cannot except the fact that I am an adult.
4. It looks like its going to be another long day.
5. Peter will be getting a rise next month.
6. The kids new they could talk us into agreeing.

7. What will be the affect if we mix these two chemicals?

8. You must be absolutely quite, or else we are going to get caught.

9. Whose going to call the fire department?

10. Owen dropped his desert down the front of his shirt.

 **Review P r a c t i c e 3 Correcting** Correct the words used incorrectly in Review Practice 2 by rewriting each incorrect sentence.

EDITING A STUDENT PARAGRAPH

Following is a paragraph written and revised by Maki Okuta in response to the writing assignment in this chapter. Read the paragraph, and underline the words that may be confused.

> The technological age has arrived, and people who don't learn what technology has too offer will soon be left behind. The biggest way technology has effected everyone's lives is threw the Internet. The Internet has brought the world to every person's doorstep. If a person in Hong Kong wants to find out the whether at Catalina Island, he or she could go find the information on the Web. If a person wants to buy a house, chose a college, or even find a husband or wife, than a click of the mouse is all it takes. Pretty soon, all people will know were their kids are, can check on the house from work, or can turn on there heat in the car from inside the house. Its really quiet amazing. People who are frightened bad by technology need to learn to understand it because it's hear too stay. And soon it will be a part of every aspect of our lives.

Collaborative Activity

Team up with a partner, and add a second underline below the 13 confused words used incorrectly in Maki's paragraph. Then, working together, use what you have learned in this chapter to correct these errors. Rewrite the paragraph with your corrections.

EDITING YOUR OWN PARAGRAPH

Now return to the paragraph you wrote and revised at the beginning of this chapter. Underline the words that may be confused.

Collaborative Activity

Exchange paragraphs with your partner, and put an X above any words used incorrectly that you find in your partner's paragraph.

Individual Activity

On the Spelling Log in Appendix 5, record any word errors that your partner found in your paragraph. To complete the writing process, correct these errors by rewriting your paragraph.

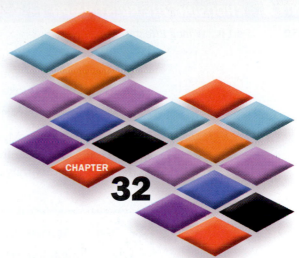

SPELLING

 CHECKLIST for Identifying Misspelled Words

> ✔ Do you follow the basic spelling rules?
> ✔ Are all words spelled correctly?

If you think back over your education, you will realize that teachers believe spelling is important. There is a good reason they feel this way: Spelling errors send negative messages. Misspellings seem to leap out at readers, creating serious doubts about the writer's abilities in general. Because you will not always have access to spell-checkers—and because spell-checkers do not catch all spelling errors—improving your spelling skills is important.

Notice how good spelling makes an author seem trustworthy.

I remember the spelling books that we used—the color, size, and shape of the books; how the words to be learned were grouped on the page. And I can remember how hard I tried to learn these words, doing just what my teacher said—printing the words over and over again, spelling a word to myself with my eyes closed and then opening my eyes to check if I was right, spelling the words for my parents before bed, going over them again and again right before the test. I can also remember what it was like to take the spelling tests—a piece of wide-margined paper and a pencil, the teacher saying the words aloud, fear and anxiety. I struggled to remember how to spell each word. Erase. No matter how I spelled a word, it looked wrong. Fear. I crossed out, printed over, went back, tried again. "One minute left." Anxiety. When my spelling papers came back they were covered with red marks, blue marks, check marks, correction marks, and poor grades. It was so humiliating, and it was always the same. No matter how much I prepared or how hard I tried, I couldn't spell most of the words. And no matter how many spelling tests I took and failed, there were always more spelling tests to take and fail. We got a new book of spelling words at the beginning of each term.

In this paragraph, Mark Levensky describes his anxiety over spelling tests. Before continuing in this chapter, take a moment to write about your own spelling ability. Save your work because you will use it later in this chapter.

WRITING ASSIGNMENT: WHAT SPELLING REVEALS

Our spelling tells a lot about us. Spelling mistakes on personal notes say we're sloppy and we don't even take time to proofread. What are your experiences with spelling? Are you a good or bad speller? What experiences have you had with your strengths or weaknesses in spelling? Write a paragraph describing your experiences and feelings.

REVISING YOUR WRITING

Revise the first draft of your paragraph before you focus on editing. Use the Revising Checklist on pages 24–25 to help you with your revision. Make sure your paragraph has a good topic sentence and is well developed. Then check your paragraph for unity, organization, and coherence.

SPELLING HINTS

The spelling rules in this chapter will help you become a better speller. But first, here are some practical hints that will also help you improve your spelling.

1. Start a personal spelling list of your own. Use the list of commonly misspelled words on pages 568–573 as your starting point.

2. Study the lists of easily confused words in Chapter 31.

3. Avoid all nonstandard expressions (see Chapter 30).

4. Use a dictionary when you run across words you don't know.

5. Run the spell-check program if you are writing on a computer. Keep in mind, however, that spell-check cannot tell if you have incorrectly used one word in place of another (such as *to, too,* or *two*).

REVIEWING HINTS FOR BECOMING A BETTER SPELLER

Name two things you can do immediately to become a better speller.

_____

Why can't you depend on a spell-check program to find every misspelled word?

_____

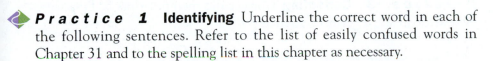 **P r a c t i c e   1   Identifying** Underline the correct word in each of the following sentences. Refer to the list of easily confused words in Chapter 31 and to the spelling list in this chapter as necessary.

1. The flames will (fascinate, fascinat) you if you stare at them long enough.
2. They received a (bicycle, bycicle) for two as a wedding present.
3. (Seperate, Separate) the egg yolks from the whites carefully.
4. The union has agreed to (cooperate, coopperate).
5. I learned (grammar, grammer) in junior high school, but I forgot most of it by the time I got to college.
6. You can (succed, succeed) at anything as long as you put your mind to it.
7. My father is a (genuse, genius) and a member of Mensa.
8. Public spelling bees used to (embarass, embarrass) me.
9. Dora's cat is a bit (weird, wierd)—he likes to take baths.
10. In the movie, the (villain, villian) gets away.

P r a c t i c e   2   Identifying Underline the misspelled words in each of the following sentences. Refer to the spelling list in this chapter as necessary.

1. There are undoutedly more people living in the United States now than ever before.
2. Ouch! I bit my tonge.
3. The cotton candy made my tooth ach.

4. Because Alyssa is allergic to wasps, we called the ambulence immediately.

5. Many soldeirs who fought in the war died from disease.

6. The original masterpiece was lost.

7. Beverly was jealus of Evan's new Mustang convertible.

8. If you drink and drive, you will lose your lisence.

9. The Louisiana bayous are a dangerous place for the inexperienced.

10. Even though Febrary is a cold month, it is filled with warmth on Valentine's Day.

◆ **P r a c t i c e 3 Correcting** Correct the spelling errors in Practice 2 by rewriting each incorrect sentence.

1. _____

2. _____

3. _____

4. _____

5. _____

6. _____

7. _____

8. _____

9. _____

10. _____

◆ **P r a c t i c e 4 Completing** Fill in each blank in the following spelling hints with accurate information.

1. Use a _____ to look up words you don't know.

2. You can always use the _____ on your computer, but you should remember that it cannot correct confused words, only misspelled words.

3. Start a _____ to help you remember words you commonly misspell.

4. Study the lists of _____ in Chapter _____.

5. Try to avoid all _____ English.

▶ P r a c t i c e   **5**   **Writing Your Own**

A. Choose the correctly spelled word in each pair, and write a sentence of your own for it. Refer to the spelling list in this chapter as necessary.

1. banana/bannana

   _____

2. volunter/volunteer

   _____

3. desision/decision

   _____

4. oposit/opposite

   _____

5. recommend/recomend

   _____

B. Write five words that you often misspell, and use each in a sentence of your own. Underline these words.

1. _____

2. _____

3. _____

4. _____

5. _____

SPELLING RULES

Four basic spelling rules can help you avoid many misspellings. It pays to spend a little time learning them now.

1. **Words that end in *-e*:** When adding a suffix beginning with a vowel (*a, e, i, o, u*), drop the final *-e*.

ache + -ing	=	aching
challenge + -ed	=	challenged
value + -able	=	valuable

   When adding a suffix beginning with a consonant, keep the final *-e*.

aware + -ness	=	awareness
improve + -ment	=	improvement
leisure + -ly	=	leisurely

2. **Words with *ie* and *ei*:** Put *i* before *e* except after *c* or when sounded like *ay* as in *neighbor* and *weigh*.

c + *ei*	(no *c*) + *ie*	Exceptions
receive	anxiety	science
receipt	niece	foreign
deceive	convenience	leisure
neighbor	fiery	height

3. **Words that end in *-y*:** When adding a suffix to a word that ends in a consonant plus *-y*, change the *y* to *i*.

silly + er	=	sillier
cry + ed	=	cried
dry + er	=	drier

4. **Words that double the final consonant:** When adding a suffix starting with a vowel to a one-syllable word, double the final consonant.

big + -est	=	biggest
quit + -er	=	quitter
bet + -ing	=	betting

With words of more than one syllable, double the final consonant if (1) the final syllable is stressed and (2) the word ends in a single vowel plus a single consonant.

beget + ing	=	begetting
permit + ing	=	permitting
uncap + ed	=	uncapped

The word *travel* has more than one syllable. Should you double the final consonant? No, you should not, because the stress is on the *first* syllable (**tra´ vel**). The word ends in a vowel and a consonant, but that is not enough. Both parts of the rule must be met.

REVIEWING FOUR BASIC SPELLING RULES

What is the rule for adding a suffix to words ending in -e (such as date + -ing)?

_____

_____

What is the rule for spelling ie and ei words (such as receive, neighbor, and friend)?

_____

_____

When do you change y to i before a suffix (such as sunny + -est)?

_____

When do you double the final consonant of a word before adding a suffix (such as cut, begin, or travel + -ing)?

_____

_____

◆ **P r a c t i c e   6   Identifying** Underline the correct word in each of the following sentences.

1. Art Fry (conceived, concieved) the idea for Post-it Notes while working at MIT.
2. In the (begining, beginning), Sandra found the class difficult.
3. Nancy has a strange hobby; she visits (cemeteries, cemeterys) and makes rubbings of the headstones.
4. He (seized, seizd) the opportunity when it came.
5. Not studying will give you (grief, greif) on the day of the exam.
6. The (groceryes, groceries) are still in the car.
7. There were (approximately, approximatly) 70 applicants for the position.
8. Charles is (getting, geting) his hair cut.
9. Darn, I didn't have the (wining, winning) ticket.
10. We are (temporarily, temporaraly) staying with my aunt.

◆ **P r a c t i c e   7   Identifying** Underline the misspelled words in each of the following sentences.

1. When I reached the door, I hesitated because I heard a strange noise.
2. My father accompanyed me on my first date.
3. The lieutenant ordered us to peel potatoes.
4. Before they agreed to buy the house, they asked that the cieling be repaired.
5. The mountain climbers faced many difficulties.
6. The oceanographer is mapping out the ocean floor.
7. The elaboratness of the room was overwhelming.
8. Now that Veronica has been accepted at Yale, she is happyer.
9. Let the dog smell your hand before you begin peting him.
10. I had problems unwraping the plastic from the CD.

◆ **P r a c t i c e   8   Correcting** Correct the spelling errors in Practice 7 by rewriting each incorrect sentence.

1. _____

2. _____

3. _____

4. _____

5. _____

6. _____

7. _____

8. _____

9. _____

10. _____

P r a c t i c e   9   Completing Complete each of the following spelling rules.

1. When adding a suffix beginning with a vowel to a word that ends in -*e*,

   _____.

2. Put *i* before *e* except after _____ or when sounded like

   _____ as in _____.

3. When adding a suffix starting with a _____ to a one-syllable

   word, _____ the final consonant.

4. When adding a suffix to a word the ends in a consonant plus -*y*, change

   the _____ to _____.

5. With words of more than one syllable, _____ the final conso-

   nant if (1) the final syllable is _____ and (2) the word ends in

   a single _____ plus a single _____.

P r a c t i c e   1 0   Writing Your Own

A. Choose the correctly spelled word in each pair, and write a sentence of
   your own for it. Refer to the spelling list in this chapter as necessary.

   1. believing/believeing

   _____

2. audience/audeince

_____

3. tried/treid

_____

4. seting/setting

_____

5. weigh/wiegh

_____

B. Write five words that you often misspell, and use them each in a sentence of your own.

1. _____

2. _____

3. _____

4. _____

5. _____

MOST COMMONLY MISSPELLED WORDS

Use the following list of commonly misspelled words to check your spelling when you write.

abbreviate	accomplish	actual
absence	accumulate	address
accelerate	accurate	adequate
accessible	ache	advertisement
accidentally	achievement	afraid
accommodate	acknowledgment	aggravate
accompany	acre	aisle

although
aluminum
amateur
ambulance
ancient
anonymous
anxiety
anxious
appreciate
appropriate
approximate
architect
arithmetic
artificial
assassin
athletic
attach
audience
authority
autumn
auxiliary
avenue
awkward
baggage
balloon
banana
bankrupt
banquet
beautiful
beggar
beginning
behavior
benefited
bicycle

biscuit
bought
boundary
brilliant
brought
buoyant
bureau
burglar
business
cabbage
cafeteria
calendar
campaign
canoe
canyon
captain
career
carriage
cashier
catastrophe
caterpillar
ceiling
cemetery
census
certain
certificate
challenge
champion
character
chief
children
chimney
coffee
collar

college
column
commit
committee
communicate
community
comparison
competent
competition
complexion
conceive
concession
concrete
condemn
conference
congratulate
conscience
consensus
continuous
convenience
cooperate
corporation
correspond
cough
counterfeit
courageous
courteous
cozy
criticize
curiosity
curious
curriculum
cylinder
dairy

dangerous

dealt

deceive

decision

definition

delicious

descend

describe

description

deteriorate

determine

development

dictionary

difficulty

diploma

disappear

disastrous

discipline

disease

dissatisfied

divisional

dormitory

economy

efficiency

eighth

elaborate

electricity

eligible

embarrass

emphasize

employee

encourage

enormous

enough

enthusiastic

envelope

environment

equipment

equivalent

especially

essential

establish

exaggerate

excellent

exceptionally

excessive

exhaust

exhilarating

existence

explanation

extinct

extraordinary

familiar

famous

fascinate

fashion

fatigue

faucet

February

fiery

financial

foreign

forfeit

fortunate

forty

freight

friend

fundamental

gauge

genius

genuine

geography

gnaw

government

graduation

grammar

grief

grocery

gruesome

guarantee

guess

guidance

handkerchief

handsome

haphazard

happiness

harass

height

hesitate

hoping

humorous

hygiene

hymn

icicle

illustrate

imaginary

immediately

immortal

impossible

incidentally

incredible

independence

indispensable
individual
inferior
infinite
influential
initial
initiation
innocence
installation
intelligence
interfere
interrupt
invitation
irrelevant
irrigate
issue
jealous
jewelry
journalism
judgment
kindergarten
knife
knowledge
knuckles
laboratory
laborious
language
laugh
laundry
league
legible
legislature
leisure
length

library
license
lieutenant
lightning
likable
liquid
listen
literature
machinery
magazine
magnificent
majority
manufacture
marriage
material
mathematics
maximum
mayor
meant
medicine
message
mileage
miniature
minimum
minute
mirror
miscellaneous
mischievous
miserable
misspell
monotonous
mortgage
mysterious
necessary

neighborhood
niece
nineteen
ninety
noticeable
nuisance
obedience
obstacle
occasion
occurred
official
omission
omitted
opponent
opportunity
opposite
original
outrageous
pamphlet
paragraph
parallel
parentheses
partial
particular
pastime
patience
peculiar
permanent
persistent
personnel
persuade
physician
pitcher
pneumonia

politician	science	tournament
possess	scissors	tragedy
prairie	secretary	truly
precede	seize	unanimous
precious	separate	undoubtedly
preferred	significant	unique
prejudice	similar	university
previous	skiing	usable
privilege	soldier	usually
procedure	souvenir	vacuum
proceed	sovereign	valuable
pronounce	spaghetti	various
psychology	squirrel	vegetable
publicly	statue	vehicle
questionnaire	stomach	vicinity
quotient	strength	villain
realize	subtle	visible
receipt	succeed	volunteer
recipe	success	weather
recommend	sufficient	Wednesday
reign	surprise	weigh
religious	syllable	weird
representative	symptom	whose
reservoir	technique	width
responsibility	temperature	worst
restaurant	temporary	wreckage
rhyme	terrible	writing
rhythm	theater	yacht
salary	thief	yearn
satisfactory	thorough	yield
scarcity	tobacco	zealous
scenery	tomorrow	zoology
schedule	tongue	

REVIEWING COMMONLY MISSPELLED WORDS

Why is spelling important in your writing?

_____

Start a personal spelling log of your most commonly misspelled words.

_____ _____ _____

_____ _____ _____

_____ _____ _____

Practice 11 Identifying Underline the correct word in each of the following sentences.

1. The gas (gauge, guage) was almost on empty.
2. Sean's uncle is a (tobacco, tabaco) farmer.
3. The (labortory, laboratory) was destroyed in the fire.
4. The choir sang a gospel (hymn, hym) to open the graduation ceremony.
5. You should see a doctor about that (coff, cough).
6. Up to three (absences, absenses) will be excused.
7. (Icicycles, Icicles) make beautiful prisms that reflect light.
8. The sea is (visible, visable) from atop that cliff.
9. (Yeild, Yield) the right-of-way to oncoming traffic.
10. Her nephew can speak five (languages, langages).

Practice 12 Identifying Underline the misspelled words in each of the following sentences.

1. Driving is a privelege, not a right.
2. Special scisors are made for left-handed people.
3. Though the twins are not identical, they are similar-looking.
4. My knowlege is lacking in this area.
5. Dean recommends the Chinese restaurant on Blossom Avenue.

6. The doctor had to reschedle my appointment.

7. Real sucess isn't gained through money.

8. I accidentally ran over my bicycle with my car.

9. Yes, Martha is familar with linear math.

10. Alisha's stomache hurts.

◆ **P r a c t i c e   1 3   Correcting** Correct the spelling errors in Practice 12 by rewriting each incorrect sentence.

1. _____

2. _____

3. _____

4. _____

5. _____

6. _____

7. _____

8. _____

9. _____

10. _____

◆ **P r a c t i c e   1 4   Completing** Fill in each blank in the following sentences with a word that makes sense from the spelling list in this chapter.

1. The _____ was caught at the airport.

2. The _____ stars look like diamonds.

3. My _____ is bothering me.

4. His new house is rather _____.

5. The show *Whose Line Is It, Anyway?* always makes people _____.

6. I filled out the _____ even though it was very long.

7. Take a picture of that _____.

8. Cassidy met her future husband in _____.

9. Don't worry; your mismatched socks aren't _____.

10. For a doctor, your writing is quite _____.

◆ **P r a c t i c e   1 5   Writing Your Own**

A. Choose the correctly spelled word in each pair, and write a sentence for
each one. Refer to the spelling list in this chapter as necessary.

1. appreciate/apprecate

    _____

2. laundry/landry

    _____

3. mariage/marriage

    _____

4. excellent/excelent

    _____

5. oposite/opposite

    _____

B. Choose five words that you often misspell from the spelling list in this
chapter, and use each in a sentence of your own. Underline these words.

1. _____

2. _____

3. _____

4. _____

5. _____

CHAPTER REVIEW

You might want to reread your answers to the questions in all the review boxes before you do the following exercises.

Review P r a c t i c e   1   Reading   Refer to the paragraph by Mark Levensky on pages 559–560 to do the following exercises.

1. List two words from the paragraph that have nonstandard versions.

From Paragraph   **Nonstandard**

_____   _____

_____   _____

2. List two words from the paragraph that are easily confused with other words.

From Paragraph   **Easily Confused Word**

_____   _____

_____   _____

3. List two words from the paragraph that might be easily misspelled.

From Paragraph   **Misspelling**

_____   _____

_____   _____

Review P r a c t i c e   2   Identifying   Underline the misspelled words in each of the following sentences. Refer to the spelling list in this chapter as necessary.

1. There is a terrable flu going around.
2. My kitten's curosity landed him in the toilet.
3. Who says chocolate isn't an essintial food group?
4. That smells delicous.
5. The show will air tommorow.

6. Catapillars may be cute, but they wreak havoc in my garden.

7. I may be an amature baseball player today, but I plan to play professional ball in a few years.

8. The bread nife is in the third drawer.

9. She has all the symtoms of someone in love.

10. That perfume is just sutle enough.

◆ **Review P r a c t i c e 3 Correcting** Correct the spelling errors in Review Practice 2 by rewriting each sentence.

EDITING A STUDENT PARAGRAPH

Following is a paragraph written and revised by Sabrina Patrova in response to the writing assignment in this chapter. Read the paragraph, and look for any misspelled words. Do not count words that are misspelled intentionally.

I'm an average speller. Just like everybody else, I usualy confuse "effect" with "affect" or "accept" with "except," have difficulty remembering if an ending should be "-ant" or "-ent," or have difficulty remembering those weird words (like "weird") that don't follow the "i before e except after c" rule. But for the most part, I tend to get by with my spelling—until I'm asked to spell in public. When someone asks me to spell a word, even the simplest word like "of," my brain freezes. (I once said "of" was spelled o-v-e) But this problem becomes most embarassing when I'm called to the chalkboard to write. My heart starts to pound. My palms get sweaty. I try counting to 10. I try taking deep breathes. I have even tryed to quickly go over the spelling rules in my mind as I approach the board. But it doesn't matter weather I no the spelling rules or not. My spelling knowledge vanishes somewhere between my desk and the board. Now, I consider myself a fairly intelligent person. My achievments are many. Yet I always look foolish in these moments, no matter how brilliant my ideas. But happyly—or perhaps sadly—I have learned that I'm not alone. Many others suffer from the same phobia. My nieghbor calls it "fear of public spelling." Perhaps we should join forces and start a support group, because until someone figures out a way to rewire or recondition the brain, I don't know how to overcome this problem. I know what spelling errors say about me: "You're lazy," "You can't write," "Your anxeity got the better of you." Even though these statements aren't true, I still hate the messages. But I'm no quiter. I'll continue that long walk to the front of the class whenever I hear, "Sabrina, could you come to the board and. . . ."

Collaborative Activity

Team up with a partner and underline the 11 misspelled words in Sabrina's paragraph. Then, working together, use what you have learned in this chapter to correct these errors. Rewrite the paragraph with your corrections.

EDITING YOUR OWN PARAGRAPH

Now go back to the paragraph you wrote and revised at the beginning of this chapter. Look for misspelled words.

Collaborative Activity

Exchange paragraphs with your partner and underline any misspelled words that you find in your partner's paragraph.

Individual Activity

On the Spelling Log in Appendix 7, record any spelling errors that your partner found in your paragraph. To complete the writing process, correct these errors by rewriting your paragraph.

UNIT TESTS

Here are some exercises that test your understanding of all the material in this unit: Standard and Nonstandard English, Easily Confused Words, and Spelling.

Unit Test 1 Identifying

Underline the words used incorrectly in each of the following sentences.

1. Everywheres I look, I see smiling, happy faces.
2. Today, Carol will chose a major.
3. These physics problems are frying my brain.
4. Surely Tom exaggerrated the story.
5. He ain't going to like your plan.
6. Its been a very long and exhausting day.
7. It's been a eon since I've seen you.
8. Being that it is so hot outside, let's go ice-skating.
9. Carlie has a vast awarness of herself.
10. The package was unwraped when Scott bought it.
11. We're going to rock the house tonight.
12. The fake blood and gore looked grusome in the moonlight.
13. That is to much information for me to process at the moment.
14. Mac was very enthused about winning the door prize.
15. Jan's new boyfriend is a hottie.
16. The little girl cryed for her lost kitten.
17. In the dessert, the temperature drops dramatically at night.
18. With her fair skin, she oughta wear sunscreen.
19. Don't touch that pan—it's firy hot.
20. Everyone can fit in the truck accept the dog.

Unit Test 2 Correcting

Correct the errors in Unit Test 1 by rewriting each incorrect sentence.

1. _____

2. _____

3. _____

4. _____

5. _____

6. _____

7. _____

8. _____

9. _____

10. _____

11. _____

12. _____

13. _____

14. _____

15. _____

16. _____

17. _____

18. _____

19. _____

20. _____

Unit Test 3 Identifying

Underline the words used incorrectly in the following paragraph.

Being that my brother got a chemistry set for his
birthday one summer, I figureed it was time to take up
science. Scott, my brother, played with the set a couple
of times, and than he forgot about it, so I five-fingered it.
I remember waiting for the weekend to come, for the
nights when everyone was asleep and no one could
censure me and the experiments could begin. The
secrecy of those nighttime rituals made me feel sorta
like an ancient goddess performing sacred rites while
the world slept and the moon shone threw my window. I
was quiet lax when it came to the rules—who needed

instructions? Needless to say, there were a few accidents in my labortory. But the joy of discovery and the thrill of creating were addictive. I never set out to actually create anything specific. The lure was the adventure itself. Now I get the same thrill from journal writing. I can mix new ingredients, feelings, and ideas and see were they take me. I can explore any crazy notion that comes into my head because they're is no censorship: I am the audeince. Occasionally, my writing becomes flammable, and if I survive the flame, I'm left with illumination. Sometimes I wait for the night to come, and when everybody is asleep and the moonlight from the window casts a glow on my computer, I write. Again I am a goddess, only this time the chemical reaction happens within my heart, my mind, my psyche, my soul. My new discovery is myself. I be the creator and the created.

Unit Test 4 Correcting

Correct the errors in Unit Test 3 by rewriting the paragraph.

UNIT WRITING ASSIGNMENTS

1. What is the child tying to persuade her parent to do in the accompanying picture? What do you think the child's strategy is? Is the child effective in persuading the parent? Why or why not?

2. Are you aware of listening to the languages that are spoken around you? Are the languages different? What can you tell from people's tone of voice even when you don't speak the language? Think of a time you went to an amusement park or a public place where you heard many different languages. What were your observations? What were the differences among the speakers? What were the similarities?

3. You have just taken the Pepsi challenge. What brand of soda—Pepsi or Coca-Cola—did you choose? Prepare an article for your college newspaper comparing the two sodas and arguing why one soda is better than the other.

4. At one time or another, we have all been let down by our computer's spell-check, and yet many of us continue to use only the computer's tools to find words used incorrectly in our papers. Why is relying only on spell-check not a good editing habit? Can spell-check catch every word used incorrectly? Why or why not? Should an author use other methods along with the computer? If so, what methods?

5. Create your own assignment (with the help of your instructor), and write a response to it.

III

PARAGRAPHS: SENTENCES IN CONTEXT

Studying their own writing puts students in a position to see themselves as language users, rather than as victims of a language that uses them.

—DAVID BARTHOLOMAE

Part III focuses on the paragraph. Even though you have been working with sentences and paragraphs throughout this text, this section makes sure you know how to write a successful paragraph, step by step. It provides both a professional and a student model for you to work with. Then it helps you apply specific revising and editing guidelines to a student paragraph and to your own writing.

CHAPTER **33**

RECOGNIZING A PARAGRAPH

As you have learned, a **paragraph** is a series of sentences that develop, illustrate, or explain a single topic. Paragraphs differ in organization and content, but they share several features that set them apart from other forms of writing. The first and perhaps easiest way to recognize a paragraph is to look at its form. You will see (as with this paragraph) that the first line of a new paragraph is indented, signaling to the reader that a new topic is being introduced.

Second, paragraphs have a controlling idea that is expressed in a **topic sentence,** which is usually the first sentence of the paragraph. The rest of the paragraph includes **details** that explain the topic sentence. Finally, a paragraph has a **concluding sentence** that sums up the information in the paragraph.

The following paragraph, by K. C. Cole, is from an essay titled "Calculated Risks." It explains how we can learn from taking some well-chosen risks.

> Of course, risk isn't all bad. Without knowingly taking risks, no one would ever walk out the door, much less go to school, drive a car, have a baby, submit a proposal for a research grant, fall in love, or swim in the ocean. It's hard to have any fun, accomplish anything productive, or experience life without taking risks—sometimes substantial ones. Life, after all, is a fatal disease, and the mortality rate for humans, at the end of the day, is 100 percent.

Before continuing, take a moment to record some of your own thoughts and observations on taking risks. Save your work because you will use it later in Part III.

WRITING YOUR OWN PARAGRAPH

Think of a risk you took that taught you a valuable lesson. What was the situation? In what way was it a risk? What did you gain from it? In what ways did it help you? Write a paragraph explaining how this risk turned out to be a valuable experience in your life.

 COLLABORATING

Swap paragraphs with a class member, and double underline and label the writer's topic sentence. Then circle three details that support that topic sentence. Finally, put a single line under the concluding sentence.

How to Read
a Paragraph

CHAPTER 34

To learn how paragraphs actually function, you should look at them from two different perspectives—from both reading and writing. In each case, you are studying paragraphs from a different angle so you can clearly understand how they work. As you progress through these next two chapters, you will see that reading and writing are companion activities that help people create meaning. When you read a paragraph, you work with the writer to understand his or her message; in other words, you convert words and sentences into ideas and thoughts. When you write a paragraph, your job is to put your own thoughts into language that communicates your message to your reader(s). In either case, you are in a partnership with the text to create meaning from the words on the page.

Every time you read an essay in this book, you will also be preparing to write your own thoughts on a similar topic—in the form of paragraphs and, in some cases, full essays. For this reason, you should pay careful attention to both the content (subject matter) and the form (language, sentence structure, organization, and development of ideas) of each essay you read. In fact, the more aware you are of each author's techniques and strategies, the more rapidly your own writing process will mature and improve.

The questions after each essay in Part IV teach you a specific way of approaching your reading that can help you understand what you read and discover the relationship of the writer's ideas to one another and to your own thoughts. These questions can also help clarify for you the connection between the writer's topic, his or her means of expression, and your own composing process. In other words, the questions are designed to help you understand and generate ideas, then discover various choices the writers make in composing their essays, and finally realize the freedom you have to make related choices in your own writing. Such an approach to the process of reading takes some of the mystery out of reading and writing and makes them manageable tasks at which anyone can succeed.

To practice recognizing the working features of a paragraph, read the following three paragraphs taken from essays in Part IV of this text. Then answer the questions after each paragraph.

FROM "A GIANT STEP" BY HENRY LOUIS GATES Jr. (p. 622)

In this paragraph, Gates writes about some ugly, heavy orthopedic shoes that he is finally able to put aside. Notice the various writing strategies that make this paragraph work so well.

We had been together since 1975, those shoes and I. They were orthopedic shoes built around molds of my feet, and they had a 2¼-inch lift. I had mixed feelings about them. On the one hand, they had given me a more or less even gait for the first time in 10 years. On the other hand, they had marked me as a "handicapped person," complete with cane and special license plates. I went through a pair a year, but it was always the same shoe, black, wide, weighing about four pounds.

1. What is the subject of this paragraph?

   _____

2. What is its topic sentence?

   _____

   Does the topic sentence state the author's position on the subject?

   _____

   _____

3. Does the author include enough details and examples to support the topic sentence?

   _____

   List at least three supporting details:

   _____

   _____

   _____

4. Are the supporting details organized as effectively as possible? Label their method of organization.

_____

_____

5. How does the author conclude the paragraph?

_____

Does the final sentence actually bring the paragraph to a close?

_____

FROM "A QUESTION OF TRUST" BY SHERRY HEMMAN HOGAN (p. 631)

In this paragraph, Hogan writes about the role of her dad's handkerchief in her discussions about her new single life. Notice the various writing techniques that make this paragraph work so well.

Some 12 years later, and newly divorced, quite a few handkerchief sessions with Dad were in order as my daughter and I faced a whole new life together. After heart-wrenching discussions at Mom and Dad's, my search for a tissue invariably ended with my father's familiar offer. Then, concerned about my going home to a dark house, my parents established a routine for their peace of mind as well as mine. Within minutes of my arrival, I would always call to say, "Hi, Dad. It's me. I'm home."

1. What is the subject of this paragraph?

_____

_____

2. What is its topic sentence?

_____

_____

_____

Does the topic sentence state the author's position on the subject?

_____

3. Does the author include enough details and examples to support the topic sentence?

_____

List at least three supporting details:

_____

_____

_____

4. Are the supporting details organized as effectively as possible? Label their method of organization.

_____

5. How does the author conclude the paragraph?

_____

Does the final sentence actually bring the paragraph to a close?

_____

_____

FROM "FERRYING DREAMERS TO THE OTHER SIDE" BY TOMÁS ROBLES (p. 640)

In this paragraph, Robles discusses some of the difficult details of bringing illegal immigrants into the United States. Notice the different strategies that make this paragraph work so well.

Before we get to the immigration checkpoint, we get out of the car and let the driver continue north. The drivers have their papers, so they can pass through the checkpoint. Then we walk into the countryside. It's dark, but we know where we're going. There are power lines that we use to guide us. We go on together, walking and walking, for five or six hours. There are lots of rattlesnakes, and you can die if they bite you. We walk on through the brush until we get to a place to rest. Then one person—only one—goes out to the road to see if the drivers are there yet. When they arrive, we get back in the cars, and off we go to Houston.

1. What is the subject of this paragraph?

    _____

2. What is its topic sentence?

    _____

    _____

    Does the topic sentence state the author's position on the subject?

    _____

3. Does the author include enough details and examples to support the topic sentence?

    _____

    List at least three supporting details:

    _____

    _____

    _____

4. Are the supporting details organized as effectively as possible? Label their method of organization.

    _____

5. How does the author conclude the paragraph?

    _____

    Does the final sentence actually bring the paragraph to a close?

    _____

◆ P r a c t i c e   1   What type of reading (novels, magazine, short stories, essays, comic books, etc.) do you like most?

_____

◆ P r a c t i c e   2   What do you like most about reading?

_____

_____

◆ P r a c t i c e   3   What do you like least about reading?

_____

_____

◆ P r a c t i c e   4   What did you learn about reading in this chapter that can help you with your writing?

_____

_____

CHAPTER 35

HOW TO WRITE A SUCCESSFUL PARAGRAPH

The key to a successful paragraph is well-built sentences—sentences that are clear and complete. In this book, you have learned how to write good sentences. Even when you wrote paragraphs in previous chapters, we focused on the sentences within those paragraphs. Now you will learn how to build an effective paragraph around a single topic. The following guidelines can serve as a blueprint for writing a paragraph on any subject.

1. ***Choose a subject that can be covered in a single paragraph.***
   Sometimes you will be given a subject to write on, and other times you will be asked to choose your own topic. If you can select your own topic, write on something you know about. If you aren't a baseball fan, you probably shouldn't write about baseball. Instead, make a list of what's on your mind and what interests you. Here, for instance, is one student's list:

   > All types of music
   > Movies
   > Psychology
   > Summer jobs
   > Basketball
   > Skateboarding
   > Space program

   Next, be sure your subject can be covered in only one paragraph. That is, your topic should not be too general. Suppose the student who made the list here decided to write on movies. That topic is far too general for a paragraph. In fact, whole books are written on movies. So she narrows her topic to science-fiction movies. But that's still too general. So she narrows her subject further to Steven Spielberg's science-fiction movies and eventually to his movie *A.I.* She finally decides to write a paragraph on why *A.I.* was Steven Spielberg's greatest science-fiction movie.

K. C. Cole, the author of the model paragraph in Chapter 33, is a science writer. She brings both math and science to life in her articles. So she might have started with a general topic like "mathematics" and then narrowed it to "statistics about people." Since this topic is still too broad for a paragraph, she probably narrowed her scope again to "risks" and finally to "calculated risks that let us have some fun in life." Now she has a topic that can be covered in a single paragraph.

2. **Write a topic sentence for your paragraph.** Your topic sentence should express the controlling idea—or the main point—of your paragraph. Although the topic sentence can be either the first or last sentence of its paragraph, making it the first is preferable because it tells the reader what your paragraph will be about.

   A topic sentence has two parts: a limited topic and a statement about that topic. The statement gives your opinion on the topic. Here are some examples.

Topic	Limited Topic	Statement
Friendship	What makes a good friend	A good friend is a good listener.
Athletics	Basketball is fun to watch.	Basketball is fun to watch because it is fast.

   K. C. Cole's topic sentence is the first sentence in her paragraph: "Of course, risk isn't all bad." Like all good topic sentences, it has two parts—a limited topic ("risk") and a statement about that topic ("isn't all bad"). She makes this statement so she can talk about the value of some risks.

3. **Develop your paragraph with details and examples that support your topic sentence.** At this point in writing your paragraph, think of yourself as a lawyer. You have stated your position in the topic sentence, and you now need details and examples to prove your point. If you aren't sure what supporting details will work best, try turning your topic sentence into a question. The way you answer this question will give you the details and examples you need.

   If Cole turned her topic sentence into a question, it might be, "Are risks all bad?" She then answers this question in her paragraph with clear details and examples. She explains that everyday activities such as walking out the door, going to school, driving a car, having a baby, submitting a proposal, falling in love, and swimming in the ocean involve taking risks. By furnishing specific, concrete examples of risks we all take every day, Cole leads the reader to her main point—that risks have value.

4. ***Organize your supporting details and examples.*** Once you know which details and examples best support your topic sentence, you need to think about how you will organize them. What should come first? Second? Last? How you organize your ideas depends on your purpose. Here are some examples:

- *Chronological (time) order:* If you are retelling an important story, you should start at the beginning and tell the story as it happened, in chronological or time order.

- *Chronological (step-by-step) order:* If you are telling how to do something or how something happened, you should explain it step by step, in a logical time sequence.

- *Spatial order:* If you are describing something physical, you will probably move from one area or location to another, such as from top to bottom, left to right, inside to outside—or the reverse.

- *From one extreme to another (least to most or most to least):* If you are using details and examples to support a specific point, they need to be organized in some meaningful way. You should suit your order to your purpose—for example, from least to most important, from most to least funny, from least to most frustrating, or from most to least exciting.

In the model paragraph, K. C. Cole arranges her examples from least to most dangerous. Walking out the door every day involves the least amount of risk compared to her other examples; swimming in the ocean is the most dangerous of her examples.

5. ***Write a concluding sentence.*** The last step in drafting your paragraph is to write a concluding sentence, a sentence that sums up what you have said in your paragraph. Summing up does not mean repeating. You should never write a concluding sentence that repeats what you have just said. Instead, aim to give the reader a feeling that the paragraph comes to a natural close. Since paragraphs are usually part of longer pieces of writing, a concluding sentence often sums up one paragraph and hints at what will come next.

K. C. Cole concludes her paragraph with two sentences. The first sums up what she said in the paragraph by explaining how the examples she lists contribute to the quality of our lives: "It's hard to have any fun, accomplish anything productive, or experience life without taking risks—sometimes substantial ones." The final sentence then brings the paragraph to a close and puts the idea of risks into a larger perspective: "Life, after all, is a fatal disease, and the mortality rate for humans, at the end of the day, is 100 percent."

6. ***Revise and edit your paragraph.*** Writing is a process, and you will realize as you write that your ideas grow, develop, and change as you express yourself. In your effort to communicate your thoughts to others, you may find a better way of saying something or come up with a more appropriate example. Therefore, after you draft your paragraph, read it over again, asking yourself the following questions:

✔ Does the topic sentence convey the paragraph's controlling idea?

✔ Does the topic sentence appear as the first or last sentence of the paragraph?

✔ Does the paragraph contain *specific* details that support the topic sentence?

✔ Does the paragraph include *enough* details to explain the topic sentence fully?

✔ Do all the sentences in the paragraph support the topic sentence?

✔ Is the paragraph organized logically?

✔ Do the sentences move smoothly and logically from one to the next?

After you have revised your paragraph for content, you can begin editing your paragraph—checking grammar, punctuation, mechanics (capitalization, abbreviations, and numbers), and spelling. You should ask questions like the following:

✔ Does each sentence have a main subject and verb?

✔ Do all subjects and verbs agree?

✔ Do all pronouns agree with their nouns?

✔ Are modifiers as close as possible to the words they modify?

✔ Are sentences punctuated correctly?

✔ Are words capitalized properly?

✔ Are words used correctly?

✔ Are words spelled correctly?

We will deal with all these questions in the next two chapters.

As a successful writer, Cole no doubt revised and edited her paragraph—probably more than once.

36

REVISING AND EDITING A STUDENT PARAGRAPH

Here is a paragraph written by Josh Ellis, a college student. As you read it, figure out what Josh's main idea is, and think of ways he might convey this idea more fully.

¹We all deal with boredom in different ways. ²Unfortunately, most of us has to deal with it far to often. ³Most people deal with boredom. ⁴By trying to distract themselves from boring circumstances. ⁵Myself, I'm a reader. ⁶So at the breakfast table over a bowl of cereal, I read the cereal box, the milk carton, the wrapper on the bread. ⁷Also, waiting in a doctor's office, I will gladly read weekly newsmagazines of three years ago, a book for 5-year-olds, advertizements for drugs, and even the physician's diplomas on the walls. ⁸That's my recipe for beating boredom, what's yours?

This paragraph is Josh's first draft, which now needs to be revised and edited. First, apply the Revising Checklist that follows to the content of Josh's draft. When you are satisfied that his ideas are fully developed and well organized, use the Editing Checklist on page 599 to correct his grammar and mechanics errors. Answer the questions after each checklist. Then write your suggested changes directly on Josh's draft.

REVISING CHECKLIST ✔

TOPIC SENTENCE

✔ Does the topic sentence convey the paragraph's controlling idea?

✔ Does the topic sentence appear as the first or last sentence of the paragraph?

DEVELOPMENT

✔ Does the paragraph contain *specific* details that support the topic sentence?

✔ Does the paragraph include *enough* details to explain the topic sentence fully?

UNITY
✔ Do all the sentences in the paragraph support the topic sentence?

ORGANIZATION
✔ Is the paragraph organized logically?

COHERENCE
✔ Do the sentences move smoothly and logically from one to the next?

Let's look at these revision strategies one by one.

Topic Sentence

✔ Does the topic sentence convey the paragraph's controlling idea?
✔ Does the topic sentence appear as the first or last sentence of the paragraph?

1. What main idea does Josh communicate in his paragraph?

   _____

2. Put brackets around Josh's topic sentence.
3. Does the topic sentence introduce his main idea?

   _____

4. Does the topic sentence appear as the first or last sentence of the paragraph?

   _____

5. Rewrite it, if necessary, to introduce all the ideas in Josh's paragraph.

   _____

Development

✔ Does the paragraph contain *specific* details that support the topic sentence?
✔ Does the paragraph include *enough* details to explain the topic sentence fully?

1. Does Josh's paragraph contain specific details that support his topic sentence?

   _____

2. List two of his details.

   _____

   _____

3. Make one detail more specific than it already is.
4. Does Josh's paragraph have enough details to make his point?

   _____

5. Add another detail to Josh's paragraph.

Unity

> ✔ Do all the sentences in the paragraph support the topic sentence?

1. Read each of Josh's sentences with his topic sentence (revised, if necessary) in mind.
2. Drop or rewrite any of his sentences that are not directly related to his topic sentence.

Organization

> ✔ Is the paragraph organized logically?

1. List Josh's details to see if his paragraph is arranged logically.

   _____

   _____

   _____

2. Move any details that are out of order.

Coherence

> ✔ Do the sentences move smoothly and logically from one to the next?

1. Circle two transitions Josh uses.
2. Explain how one of these makes Josh's paragraph easier to read.

For a list of transitions, see pages 36–37.

_____

Now rewrite Josh's paragraph with your revisions.

EDITING CHECKLIST ✔

SENTENCES
- ✔ Does each sentence have a main subject and verb?
- ✔ Do all subjects and verbs agree?
- ✔ Do all pronouns agree with their nouns?
- ✔ Are modifiers as close as possible to the words they modify?

PUNCTUATION AND MECHANICS
- ✔ Are sentences punctuated correctly?
- ✔ Are words capitalized properly?

WORD CHOICE AND SPELLING
- ✔ Are words used correctly?
- ✔ Are words spelled correctly?

Sentences

> ✔ Does each sentence have a main subject and verb?

1. Underline the subjects once and the verbs twice in your revision of Josh's paragraph. Remember that sentences can have more than one subject-verb set.

For help with subjects and verbs, see Chapter 7.

2. Does each of Josh's sentences have at least one subject and verb that can stand alone?

For help with fragments, see Chapter 8.

3. Did you find and correct Josh's fragment? If not, find and correct it now.

For help with run-togethers, see Chapter 9.

4. Did you find and correct Josh's run-together sentence? If not, find and correct it now.

> ✔ Do all subjects and verbs agree?

For help with subject-verb agreement, see Chapter 12.

1. Read aloud the subjects and verbs you underlined in your revision of Josh's paragraph.
2. Correct any subjects and verbs that do not agree.

> ✔ Do all pronouns agree with their nouns?

For help with pronoun agreement, see Chapter 16.

1. Find any pronouns in your revision of Josh's essay that do not agree with their nouns.
2. Correct any pronouns that do not agree with their nouns.

> ✔ Are modifiers as close as possible to the words they modify?

For help with modifier errors, see Chapter 19.

1. Find any modifiers in your revision of Josh's essay that are not as close as possible to the words they modify.
2. Rewrite sentences if necessary so that modifiers are as close as possible to the words they modify.

Punctuation and Mechanics

> ✔ Are sentences punctuated correctly?

For help with punctuation, see Chapters 20–24.

1. Read your revision of Josh's paragraph for any errors in punctuation.
2. Make sure the fragment and run-together sentence you revised are punctuated correctly.

> ✔ Are words capitalized properly?

---

1. Read your revision of Josh's paragraph for any errors in capitalization.

2. Be sure to check his capitalization in the fragment and run-together sentence you revised.

For help with capitalization, see Chapter 25.

Word Choice and Spelling

> ✔ Are words used correctly?

---

1. Find any words used incorrectly in your revision of Josh's paragraph.

2. Correct any errors you find.

For help with confused words, see Chapter 31.

> ✔ Are all words spelled correctly?

---

1. Use spell-check and a dictionary to check the spelling in your revision of Josh's paragraph.

2. Correct any misspelled words.

Now rewrite Josh's paragraph again with your editing corrections.

For help with spelling, see Chapter 32.

CHAPTER 37

REVISING AND EDITING YOUR OWN PARAGRAPH

Now you are ready to revise and edit the paragraph that you wrote in Chapter 33. The checklists here will help you apply what you have learned to your own writing.

REVISING CHECKLIST ✔

TOPIC SENTENCE
☐ Does the topic sentence convey the paragraph's controlling idea?
☐ Does the topic sentence appear as the first or last sentence of the paragraph?

DEVELOPMENT
☐ Does the paragraph contain *specific* details that support the topic sentence?
☐ Does the paragraph include *enough* details to explain the topic sentence fully?

UNITY
☐ Do all the sentences in the paragraph support the topic sentence?

ORGANIZATION
☐ Is the paragraph organized logically?

COHERENCE
☐ Do the sentences move smoothly and logically from one to the next?

Let's look at these revision strategies one by one.

Topic Sentence

☐ Does the topic sentence convey the paragraph's controlling idea?

☐ Does the topic sentence appear as the first or last sentence of the paragraph?

1. What is the main idea that you are trying to convey in your paragraph?
2. Put brackets around your topic sentence.
3. Does the topic sentence communicate your main idea?
4. Does the topic sentence appear as the first or last sentence of the paragraph?
5. Rewrite it, if necessary, to introduce all the ideas in your paragraph.

Development

☐ Does the paragraph contain *specific* details that support the topic sentence?

☐ Does the paragraph include *enough* details to explain the topic sentence fully?

1. Does your paragraph contain specific details that support your topic sentence? List three of your details.

   _____

   _____

   _____

2. Make one detail more specific than it already is.
3. Does your paragraph have enough details to make your point?

   _____

4. Add another detail to your paragraph.

Unity

> ☐ Do all the sentences in the paragraph support the topic sentence?

1. Read each of your sentences with your topic sentence (revised, if necessary) in mind.
2. Drop or rewrite any of your sentences that are not directly related to your topic sentence.

Organization

> ☐ Is the paragraph organized logically?

1. List your details to see if your paragraph is arranged logically.

_____

_____

_____

2. Move any details that are out of order.

Coherence

> ☐ Do the sentences move smoothly and logically from one to the next?

For a list of transitions, see pages 36–37.

1. Circle two transitions you use.
2. Explain how one of these makes your paragraph easier to read.

_____

Now rewrite your paragraph with your revisions.

EDITING CHECKLIST ✔

SENTENCES

☐ Does each sentence have a main subject and verb?

☐ Do all subjects and verbs agree?

☐ Do all pronouns agree with their nouns?

☐ Are modifiers as close as possible to the words they modify?

PUNCTUATION AND MECHANICS

☐ Are sentences punctuated correctly?

☐ Are words capitalized properly?

WORD CHOICE AND SPELLING

☐ Are words used correctly?

☐ Are words spelled correctly?

Sentences

☐ Does each sentence have a main subject and verb?

1. Underline the subjects once and the verbs twice in your revised paragraph. Remember that sentences can have more than one subject-verb set.

   For help with subjects and verbs, see Chapter 7.

2. Does each of your sentences have at least one subject and verb that can stand alone?

3. Correct any fragments you find.

   For help with fragments, see Chapter 8.

4. Correct any run-together sentences you find.

   For help with run-togethers, see Chapter 9.

☐ Do all subjects and verbs agree?

1. Read aloud the subjects and verbs you have underlined in your revised paragraph.

   For help with subject-verb agreement, see Chapter 12.

2. Correct any subjects and verbs that do not agree.

> ☐ Do all pronouns agree with their nouns?

For help with pronoun agreement, see Chapter 16.

1. Find any pronouns in your revised paragraph that do not agree with their nouns.

2. Correct any pronouns that do not agree with their nouns.

> ☐ Are modifiers as close as possible to the words they modify?

For help with modifier errors, see Chapter 19.

1. Find any modifiers in your revised paragraph that are not as close as possible to the words they modify.

2. Rewrite sentences if necessary so that your modifiers are as close as possible to the words they modify.

Punctuation and Mechanics

> ☐ Are sentences punctuated correctly?

For help with punctuation, see Chapters 20–24.

1. Read your revised paragraph for any errors in punctuation.

2. Make sure any fragments and run-together sentences you revised are punctuated correctly.

> ☐ Are words capitalized properly?

For help with capitalization, see Chapter 25.

1. Read your revised paragraph for any errors in capitalization.

2. Be sure to check your capitalization if you revised any fragments or run-together sentences.

Word Choice and Spelling

> ☐ Are words used correctly?

1. Find any words used incorrectly in your revised paragraph.
2. Correct any errors you find.

For help with confused words, see Chapter 31.

☐ Are words spelled correctly?

---

1. Use spell-check and a dictionary to check the spelling in your revision.
2. Correct any misspelled words.

For help with spelling, see Chapter 32.

Now rewrite your paragraph again with your editing corrections.

CHAPTER 38

WRITING WORKSHOP

Guidelines for Writing a Paragraph

1. Choose a subject that can be covered in a single paragraph.
2. Write a topic sentence for your paragraph.
3. Develop your paragraph with details and examples that support your topic sentence.
4. Organize your supporting details and examples.
5. Write a concluding sentence.
6. Revise and edit your paragraph.

1. Imagine that you are in this setting waiting for someone. Whom are you waiting for? Why are you in this particular place? What is the reason for your meeting? Put yourself in this scene, and talk about your reasons for being there.

2. Write a paragraph describing your ideal work environment. What factors make it ideal? Why is it a good environment for you to work in?

3. Discuss a time you were blamed for a mistake you did not make. What were the circumstances? Why were you blamed? Did you ever clear your name?

4. Create your own assignment (with the help of your instructor), and write a response to it.

Revising Workshop

Small Group Activity (5–10 minutes per writer)   In groups of three or four, each person should read his or her paragraph to the other members of the group. Those listening should record their reactions on a copy of the Peer Evaluation Form in Appendix 2A. After your group goes through this process, give your evaluation forms to the appropriate writers so that each writer has two or three peer comment sheets for revising.

Paired Activity (5 minutes per writer)   Using the completed Peer Evaluation Forms, work in pairs to decide what you should revise in your paragraphs. If time allows, rewrite some of your sentences, and have your partner check them.

Individual Activity   Rewrite your paragraph, using the revising feedback you received from other students.

Editing Workshop

Paired Activity (5–10 minutes per writer)   Swap papers with a classmate, and use the editing portion of your Peer Evaluation Form (Appendix 2B) to identify as many grammar, punctuation, mechanics, and spelling errors as you can. Mark the errors on the student paragraph using the editing symbols on the inside back cover of this book. If time allows, correct some of your errors, and have your partner check them.

Individual Activity   Rewrite your paragraph again, using the editing feedback you received from other students. Record your grammar, punctuation, and mechanics errors in the Error Log (Appendix 4) and your spelling errors in the Spelling Log (Appendix 5).

Reflecting on Your Writing

When you have completed your own paragraph, answer these five questions:

1. What was most difficult about this assignment?

2. What was easiest?

3. What did you learn about writing by completing this assignment?

4. What do you think are the strengths of your paragraph? What are its weaknesses?

5. What did you learn from this assignment about your own writing process—about preparing to write, about writing the first draft, about revising, and about editing?

IV

FROM READING TO WRITING

The best writing is rewriting.

—E. B. WHITE

Part IV is a collection of essays that demonstrate the rhetorical modes you are studying in this book. Each chapter focuses on a different rhetorical strategy and includes two essays showing the strategy at work with other rhetorical modes. Following each essay are questions to check your understanding of the selection. By charting your correct and incorrect responses to these questions in Appendix 1, you can track your general level of reading comprehension.

39

DESCRIBING

When you **describe,** you create a picture in words to show your reader something you have seen, heard, or done. The following essays describe events, actions, and thoughts so clearly that we can experience them for ourselves through words. "A Day in the Homeless Life," written by Colette Russell, describes her daily activities, joys, frustrations, and humiliations as a homeless person. In "Casa: A Partial Remembrance of a Puerto Rican Childhood" by Judith Ortiz Cofer, the author discusses the daily ritual of the women in her family.

Colette Russell

A DAY IN THE HOMELESS LIFE

Focusing Your Attention

1. We all own things that we would never part with. What are your prized possessions? If you had to live in a shelter or on the streets, what would you take with you?

2. In the essay you are about to read, the writer describes in vivid detail her daily routine as a homeless person. If you suddenly became homeless, where would you go? What would you do to get food, shelter, and comfort?

Expanding Your Vocabulary

The following word is important to your understanding of this essay.

invariably: without ever changing (paragraph 2)

1   "Good morning, ladies. It's 5 a.m. Time to get up." Ceiling lights were suddenly ablaze. This message boomed repeatedly until nearly everyone was out of bed.

Two toilets and three sinks for 50 women; no toilet paper in the morning, invariably. Three tables with benches bordered by beds on two sides were our day room, dining room, and lounge. 2

Breakfast usually arrived at 5:45 a.m., too late for those who were in the day-labor van pools. They went to work on empty stomachs, and they were the ones needing food the most. 3

Breakfast generally consisted of rolls and sausage and juice until it ran out. The coffee was unique: It didn't taste like coffee, but that's what we had to drink. 4

At 6:30 a.m. we were ordered to go down to the lobby, where we joined 50 other women either standing or sitting on wooden benches awaiting the light of day. Some talked to themselves. Some shouted angrily. Some sat motionless. Some slept sitting up. Some jumped up and down, walking away and then returning. Some chain-smoked. 5

All of us had our belongings with us. Carrying everything every step of the way every day was hard on the arms, and I felt it was a dead giveaway that I was homeless. 6

At 7:30 a.m. the clothing room opened. It was shocking to be told, "Throw away what you're wearing after you get a new outfit." No laundry, just toss out yesterday's garments. We were allotted five minutes to paw through racks looking for articles that fit. 7

I was always happy to see 8:30 a.m. roll around. Grabbing my bags, I headed down Berkeley Street away from the jam-packed, smoke-filled "holding cell." Always I felt guilty at not going to work like everyone else who hurried by as I approached the business district. 8

The main library was my daily stop. I positioned myself at a table where I could watch the clock: We had to return to the shelter before 4 p.m. to get in line for a bed. Otherwise we might miss out. 9

Reading was the high point of the day. Escape into a book. There was relative privacy at a library table. It was heavenly. I hated to leave. 10

The clock signaled the task of trudging back, at 3:45 p.m., with even heavier bags. The bags, of course, were no heavier; they just seemed heavier. 11

Back in the "yard" I joined the group already assembled. Some women never left the grounds, staying all day in the small yard by the building. God forbid. With the appearance of a staff member, we would form a line as the staffer prepared a list of our names and bed requests. 12

I was always glad when the lights went out at 9 p.m. and I could climb into bed (a bottom sheet and a blanket—no top sheet) and close my eyes and pretend I wasn't there but back in my apartment on the West Coast. 13

Twice I was robbed. Once a bag was taken. Another time my new blue underpants disappeared out of one of my bags. Who knew they were there? 14

15   Even if I were to do day labor at $4 per hour and clear $28 or so a day, how many weeks would it take to save enough for first and last month's rent on an apartment plus deposit and enough to pay for initial utilities? I was too depressed to even try to work and took frequent breaks to sit down while doing kitchen volunteer work. I was tired all the time.

16   The true stories I heard were heartbreaking. Which was the sadder?

17   One young woman with no skills and no job training had been OK financially until her CETA job ended—the program was abolished—and the YWCA raised its weekly room rate. She couldn't afford a room and couldn't find a job. She'd been in shelters for three or four years. I marveled that she was still sane. She did crossword puzzles while waiting everywhere.

18   Another older lady had held the same job for 10 years and would still have been working had not the corporation, without notice, closed up shop. She was 59 years old and out of a job, with a little severance pay and no help to find new work. She tried but was unsuccessful in finding a new job. She exhausted her savings after her unemployment ran out. One June day in 1987, she found herself homeless—no money for rent.

19   Both of these women are intelligent, honest, pleasant, clean, and neatly dressed. And both are penniless and homeless. How will they escape the shelters? Will they?

20   I got by, all right, by keeping my mouth shut around the staff and talking only with two or three women whom I knew to be sane and sociable. I was lucky. Two and a half months after I'd first gone into a shelter, my son rescued me. I was on the verge of madness, so hungry for a little privacy and peace that I was afraid I'd start screaming in my sleep and be shunted off to a mental ward.

21   Now I've got a job paying more than I've ever earned. But I remember those days and nights.

22   No one should have to live like that. Too many do—and will, I fear, unless and until we who do have homes and jobs help them end their eternal, living nightmare.

Thinking Critically About Content

1. List one detail from this essay for each of the five senses: seeing, hearing, touching, tasting, and smelling. How do these details *show* rather than *tell* the readers what a homeless life is like?

2. Why do you think the writer describes the lives of other homeless women in addition to her own?

3. Why was Russell "always glad when the lights went out at 9 p.m." (paragraph 13)?

Thinking Critically About Purpose and Audience

4. What do you think is Russell's dominant impression in this essay? Which details in paragraph 2 help create this dominant impression?

5. Who do you think is Russell's audience? Do you think people who have never been homeless can appreciate her descriptions?

6. What attitude do you think Russell wants her readers to have toward homeless people as a result of reading her essay? On what details do you base your answer?

Thinking Critically About Sentences

7. Find two sentences that are questions in Russell's essay. How do these questions help you understand the writer's attitude about the shelter?

8. What is the topic sentence of paragraph 9? Is it a good topic sentence for the details in that paragraph?

9. Write one or more complete sentences describing Russell's inner feelings about homelessness.

Judith Ortiz Cofer

CASA: A PARTIAL REMEMBRANCE OF A PUERTO RICAN CHILDHOOD

Focusing Your Attention

1. Think of a ritual that you are very familiar with, such as putting up holiday decorations, hanging the hammock for summer, or sitting on the porch in the evening. What do you like best about these rituals? Why are they important to you?

2. In the essay you are about to read, a young girl tells us about the ritual the women in her family have of sitting around and talking in the late afternoon. Think of a ritual that is important in your life and list the sights, sounds, smells, textures, and tastes that you associate with this ritual.

Expanding Your Vocabulary

The following words are important to your understanding of this essay.

café con leche: coffee with milk (paragraph 1)

embellishing: enhancing (paragraph 2)

histrionic: dramatic (paragraph 3)

conclave: private gathering (paragraph 3)

impassively: unemotionally, casually (paragraph 3)

ironic: unexpectedly amused (paragraph 3)

ministrations: aid (paragraph 3)

matriarchal: motherly (paragraph 3)

hombres: men (paragraph 4)

pueblo: village (paragraph 4)

haciendas: country homes (paragraph 4)

plait: braid (paragraph 5)

La Escuela San José: the San Jose School (paragraph 5)

La Loca: the crazy lady (paragraph 6)

bodega: grocery store (paragraph 6)

pasteles: meat pies (paragraph 6)

Gringa: white female (paragraph 7)

chameleons: people with changeable moods or habits (paragraph 7)

realm: domain (paragraph 7)

epithet: name, title (paragraph 8)

conspiratorially: mischievously (paragraph 9)

finca: property, estate (paragraph 9)

collaborators: people who band together (paragraph 10)

mesmerizing: hypnotic (paragraph 10)

denouement: conclusion (paragraph 11)

promesa: promise (paragraph 11)

lamented: agonized (paragraph 11)

infectious: spreading from one person to another (paragraph 13)

1   At three or four o'clock in the afternoon, the hour of *café con leche*, the women of my family gathered in Mamá's living room to speak of important things and retell familiar stories meant to be overheard by us young girls, their daughters. In Mamá's house (everyone called my grandmother Mamá) was a large parlor built by my grandfather to his wife's exact specifications so that it was always cool, facing away from the sun. The doorway was on the side of the house so no one could walk directly into her living room. First they had to take a little stroll through and around her beautiful garden where prize-winning orchids grew in the trunk of an

ancient tree she had hollowed out for that purpose. This room was furnished with several mahogany rocking chairs, acquired at the births of her children, and one intricately carved rocker that had passed down to Mamá at the death of her own mother.

It was on these rockers that my mother, her sisters, and my grandmother   2
sat on these afternoons of my childhood to tell their stories, teaching each other, and my cousin and me, what it was like to be a woman, more specifically, a Puerto Rican woman. They talked about life on the island, and life in *Los Nueva Yores*, their way of referring to the United States from New York City to California: the other place, not home, all the same. They told real-life stories though, as I later learned, always embellishing them with a little or a lot of dramatic detail. And they told *cuentos*, the morality and cautionary tales told by the women in our family for generations: stories that became a part of my subconscious as I grew up in two worlds, the tropical island and the cold city, and that would later surface in my dreams and in my poetry.

One of these tales was about the woman who was left at the altar. Mamá   3
liked to tell that one with histrionic intensity. I remember the rise and fall of her voice, the sighs, and her constantly gesturing hands, like two birds swooping through her words. This particular story usually would come up in a conversation as a result of someone mentioning a forthcoming engagement or wedding. The first time I remember hearing it, I was sitting on the floor at Mamá's feet, pretending to read a comic book. I may have been eleven or twelve years old, at that difficult age when a girl was no longer a child who could be ordered to leave the room if the women wanted freedom to take their talk into forbidden zones nor really old enough to be considered a part of their conclave. I could only sit quietly, pretending to be in another world, while absorbing it all in a sort of unspoken agreement of my status as silent auditor. On this day, Mamá had taken my long, tangled mane of hair into her ever-busy hands. Without looking down at me and with no interruption of her flow of words, she began braiding my hair, working at it with the quickness and determination that characterized all her actions. My mother was watching us impassively from her rocker across the room. On her lips played a little ironic smile. I would never sit still for *her* ministrations, but even then, I instinctively knew that she did not possess Mamá's matriarchal power to command and keep everyone's attention. This was never more evident than in the spell she cast when telling a story.

"It is not like it used to be when I was a girl," Mamá announced. "Then,   4
a man could leave a girl standing at the church altar with a bouquet of fresh flowers in her hands and disappear off the face of the earth. No way to track him down if he was from another town. He could be a married man, with maybe even two or three families all over the island. There was no

way to know. And there were men who did this. Hombres with the devil in their flesh who would come to a pueblo, like this one, take a job at one of the haciendas, never meaning to stay, only to have a good time and to seduce the women."

5   The whole time she was speaking, Mamá would be weaving my hair into a flat plait that required pulling apart the two sections of hair with little jerks that made my eyes water; but knowing how grandmother detested whining and *boba* (sissy) tears, as she called them, I just sat up as straight and stiff as I did at La Escuela San José, where the nuns enforced good posture with a flexible plastic ruler they bounced off of slumped shoulders and heads. As Mamá's story progressed, I noticed how my young Aunt Laura lowered her eyes, refusing to meet Mamá's meaningful gaze. Laura was seventeen, in her last year of high school, and already engaged to a boy from another town who had staked his claim with a tiny diamond ring, then left for Los Nueva Yores to make his fortune. They were planning to get married in a year. Mamá had expressed serious doubts that the wedding would ever take place. In Mamá's eyes, a man set free without a legal contract was a man lost. She believed that marriage was not something men desired, but simply the price they had to pay for the privilege of children and, of course, for what no decent (synonymous with "smart") woman would give away for free.

6   "María La Loca was only seventeen when *it* happened to her." I listened closely at the mention of this name. María was a town character, a fat middle-aged woman who lived with her old mother on the outskirts of town. She was to be seen around the pueblo delivering the meat pies the two women made for a living. The most peculiar thing about María, in my eyes, was that she walked and moved like a little girl though she had the thick body and wrinkled face of an old woman. She would swing her hips in an exaggerated, clownish way, and sometimes even hop and skip up to someone's house. She spoke to no one. Even if you asked her a question, she would just look at you and smile, showing her yellow teeth. But I had heard that if you got close enough, you could hear her humming a tune without words. The kids yelled out nasty things at her, calling her *La Loca*, and the men who hung out at the bodega playing dominoes sometimes whistled mockingly as she passed by with her funny, outlandish walk. But María seemed impervious to it all, carrying her basket of *pasteles* like a grotesque Little Red Riding Hood through the forest.

7   María La Loca interested me, as did all the eccentrics and crazies of our pueblo. Their weirdness was a measuring stick I used in my serious quest for a definition of normal. As a Navy brat shuttling between New Jersey and the pueblo, I was constantly made to feel like an oddball by my peers, who made fun of my two-way accent: a Spanish accent when I spoke English,

and when I spoke Spanish I was told that I sounded like a *Gringa*. Being the outsider had already turned my brother and me into cultural chameleons. We developed early on the ability to blend into a crowd, to sit and read quietly in a fifth story apartment building for days and days when it was too bitterly cold to play outside, or, set free, to run wild in Mamá's realm, where she took charge of our lives, releasing Mother for a while from the intense fear for our safety that our father's absences instilled in her. In order to keep us from harm when Father was away, Mother kept us under strict surveillance. She even walked us to and from Public School No. 11, which we attended during the months we lived in Paterson, New Jersey, our home base in the states. Mamá freed all three of us like pigeons from a cage. I saw her as my liberator and my model. Her stories were parables from which to glean the *Truth*.

"María La Loca was once a beautiful girl. Everyone thought she would   8 marry the Méndez boy." As everyone knew, Rogelio Méndez was the richest man in town. "But," Mamá continued, knitting my hair with the same intensity she was putting into her story, "this *macho* made a fool out of her and ruined her life." She paused for the effect of her use of the word "macho," which at that time had not yet become a popular epithet for an unliberated man. This word had for us the crude and comical connotation of "male of the species," stud; a *macho* was what you put in a pen to increase your stock.

I peeked over my comic book at my mother. She too was under Mamá's   9 spell, smiling conspiratorially at this little swipe at men. She was safe from Mamá's contempt in this area. Married at an early age, an unspotted lamb, she had been accepted by a good family of strict Spaniards whose name was old and respected, though their fortune had been lost long before my birth. In a rocker Papá had painted sky blue sat Mamá's oldest child, Aunt Nena. Mother of three children, stepmother of two more, she was a quiet woman who liked books but had married an ignorant and abusive widower whose main interest in life was accumulating wealth. He too was in the mainland working on his dream of returning home rich and triumphant to buy the *finca* of his dreams. She was waiting for him to send for her. She would leave her children with Mamá for several years while the two of them slaved away in factories. He would one day be a rich man, and she a sadder woman. Even now her life-light was dimming. She spoke little, an aberration in Mamá's house, and she read avidly, as if storing up spiritual food for the long winters that awaited her in Los Nueva Yores without her family. But even Aunt Nena came alive to Mamá's words, rocking gently, her hands over a thick book in her lap.

Her daughter, my cousin Sara, played jacks by herself on the tile porch   10 outside the room where we sat. She was a year older than I. We shared a bed and all our family's secrets. Collaborators in search of answers, Sara and I discussed everything we heard the women say, trying to fit it all together like a puzzle that, once assembled, would reveal life's mysteries to us. Though she and I still enjoyed taking part in boys' games—chase, volleyball, and even *vaqueros*, the island version of cowboys and Indians involving cap-gun battles and violent shoot-outs under the mango tree in Mamá's backyard—we loved best the quiet hours in the afternoon when the men were still at work, and the boys had gone to play serious baseball at the park. Then Mamá's house belonged only to us women. The aroma of coffee perking in the kitchen, the mesmerizing creaks and groans of the rockers, and the women telling their lives in *cuentos* are forever woven into the fabric of my imagination, braided like my hair that day I felt my grandmother's hands teaching me about strength, her voice convincing me of the power of storytelling.

11   That day Mamá told how the beautiful María had fallen prey to a man whose name was never the same in subsequent versions of the story; it was Juan one time, José, Rafael, Diego, another. We understood that neither the name nor any of the *facts* were important, only that a woman had allowed love to defeat her. Mamá put each of us in María's place by describing her wedding dress in loving detail: how she looked like a princess in her lace as she waited at the altar. Then, as Mamá approached the tragic denouement of her story, I was distracted by the sound of my Aunt Laura's violent rocking. She seemed on the verge of tears. She knew the fable was intended for her. That week she was going to have her wedding gown fitted, though no firm date had been set for the marriage. Mamá ignored Laura's obvious discomfort, digging out a ribbon from the sewing basket she kept by her rocker while describing María's long illness, "a fever that would not break for days." She spoke of a mother's despair: "that woman climbed the church steps on her knees every morning, wore only black as a *promesa* to the Holy Virgin in exchange for her daughter's health." By the time María returned from her honeymoon with death, she was ravished, no longer young or sane. "As you can see, she is almost as old as her mother already," Mamá lamented while tying the ribbon to the ends of my hair, pulling it back with such force that I just knew I would never be able to close my eyes completely again.

12   "That María's getting crazier every day." Mamá's voice would take a lighter tone now, expressing satisfaction, either for the perfection of my braid, or for a story well told—it was hard to tell. "You know that tune María is always humming?" Carried away by her enthusiasm, I tried to nod, but Mamá still had me pinned between her knees.

13   "Well, that's the wedding march." Surprising us all, Mamá sang out, "Da, da, dara . . . da, da, dara." Then lifting me off the floor by my skinny

shoulders, she would lead me around the room in an impromptu waltz—another session ending with the laughter of women, all of us caught up in the infectious joke of our lives.

Thinking Critically About Content

1. What happened to María La Loca after she was left at the altar?

2. Find at least one detail for each of the five senses. Does Cofer draw on any one sense more than the others?

3. Why does the narrator believe in "the power of storytelling" (paragraph 10)?

Thinking Critically About Purpose and Audience

4. What dominant impression does Cofer create in this essay?

5. Who do you think Cofer's primary audience is?

6. Explain your understanding of this essay's title.

Thinking Critically About Sentences

7. How does the addition of Spanish words to Cofer's sentences help you understand her main ideas?

8. Find a sentence that *shows* rather than *tells* her story. Explain your choice.

9. Write one or more complete sentences about the type of wedding you have had or hope to have.

Writing Topics: Describing

Before you begin to write, you might want to review the writing process in Part I.

1. In the first essay, Colette Russell draws on impressions from all the senses to show her readers what her life is like on the streets. Think of a tough situation that you have been through. Describe the situation, drawing on as many of the senses as possible—seeing, hearing, touching, smelling, and tasting—so that your reader can experience the problem as you did.

2. How much do you like rituals? Write a description of your favorite personal ritual with vivid details that make your readers feel as if they are participating in the activity with you.

40

NARRATING

Narration, or storytelling, is an interesting way of getting someone's attention and sharing thoughts and experiences. To understand how to write your own narrative essay, you may find it helpful to read some samples. The first essay, "A Giant Step" by Henry Louis Gates Jr., explains his disability and his coping skills for dealing with it. In the next essay, "The Struggle to Be an All-American Girl," Elizabeth Wong discusses her desire to become "more American."

Henry Louis Gates Jr.
A GIANT STEP

Focusing Your Attention

1. The world is full of people who are considered heroes. Whom in your life do you consider a hero? Explain your answer.

2. In the essay you are about to read, Henry Louis Gates Jr. tells a story about a pair of shoes that is very important in his life. Think of an object that is important to you and explain its role in your life.

Expanding Your Vocabulary

The following words are important to your understanding of this essay.

orthopedic: medically corrective (paragraph 7)

incurred: brought upon oneself (paragraph 8)

delinquent: troublemaker (paragraph 10)

psychosomatic: all in the mind (paragraph 27)

pathology: illness (paragraph 28)

immobilized: prevented from moving (paragraph 31)

orthotics: custom-designed shoes (paragraph 34)

amnesiac: forgetful (paragraph 40)

furtive: secret (paragraph 44)

Imelda Marcos: the wife of a former Philippine dictator, known for her large collection of shoes (paragraph 44)

"What's this?" the hospital janitor said to me as he stumbled over my   1
right shoe.

"My shoes," I said.   2

"That's not a shoe, brother," he replied, holding it to the light. "That's a   3
brick."

It *did* look like a brick, sort of.   4

"Well, we can throw these in the trash now," he said.   5

"I guess so."   6

We had been together since 1975, those shoes and I. They were ortho-   7
pedic shoes built around molds of my feet, and they had a 2¼-inch lift. I had
mixed feelings about them. On the one hand, they had given me a more or
less even gait for the first time in 10 years. On the other hand, they had
marked me as a "handicapped person," complete with cane and special
license plates. I went through a pair a year, but it was always the same
shoe, black, wide, weighing about four pounds.

It all started 26 years ago in Piedmont, West Virginia, a backwoods town   8
of 2,000 people. While playing a game of touch football at a Methodist summer camp, I incurred a hairline fracture. Thing is, I didn't know it yet. I was
14 and had finally lost the chubbiness of my youth. I was just learning
tennis and beginning to date, and who knew where that might lead?

Not too far. A few weeks later, I was returning to school from lunch   9
when, out of the blue, the ball-and-socket joint of my hip sheared apart. It
was instant agony, and from that time on nothing in my life would be quite
the same.

I propped myself against the brick wall of the schoolhouse, where the   10
school delinquent found me. He was black as slate, twice my size, mean as
the day was long and beat up kids just because he could. But the look on
my face told him something was seriously wrong, and—bless him—he
stayed by my side for the two hours it took to get me into a taxi.

"It's a torn ligament in your knee," the surgeon said. (One of the signs of   11
what I had—a "slipped epithysis"—is intense knee pain, I later learned.) So
he scheduled me for a walking cast.

12   I was wheeled into surgery and placed on the operating table. As the doctor wrapped my leg with wet plaster strips, he asked about my schoolwork.

13   "Boy," he said, "I understand you want to be a doctor."

14   I said, "Yessir." Where I came from, you always said "sir" to white people, unless you were trying to make a statement.

15   Had I taken a lot of science courses?

16   "Yessir. I enjoy science."

17   "Are you good at it?"

18   "Yessir, I believe so."

19   "Tell me, who was the father of sterilization?"

20   "Oh, that's easy, Joseph Lister."

21   Then he asked who discovered penicillin.

22   Alexander Fleming.

23   And what about DNA?

24   Watson and Crick.

25   The interview went on like this, and I thought my answers might get me a pat on the head. Actually, they just confirmed the diagnosis he'd come to.

26   He stood me on my feet and insisted that I walk. When I tried, the joint ripped apart and I fell on the floor. It hurt like nothing I'd ever known.

27   The doctor shook his head. "Pauline," he said to my mother, his voice kindly but amused, "there's not a thing wrong with that child. The problem's psychosomatic. Your son's an overachiever."

28   Back then, the term didn't mean what it usually means today. In Appalachia, in 1964, "overachiever" designated a sort of pathology: the overstraining of your natural capacity. A colored kid who thought he could be a doctor—just for instance—was headed for a breakdown.

29   What made the pain abate was my mother's reaction. I'd never, ever heard her talk back to a white person before. And doctors, well, their words were scripture.

30   Not this time. Pauline Gates stared at him for a moment. "Get his clothes, pack his bags—we're going to the University Medical Center," which was 60 miles away.

31   Not great news: the one thing I knew was that they only moved you to the University Medical Center when you were going to die. I had three operations that year. I gave my tennis racket to the delinquent, which he probably used to club little kids with. So I wasn't going to make it to Wimbledon. But at least I wasn't going to die, though sometimes I wanted to. Following the last operation, which fitted me for a metal ball, I was confined to bed, flat on my back, immobilized by a complex system of weights and pulleys. It was six weeks of bondage—and bedpans. I spent my time

reading James Baldwin, learning to play chess, and quarreling daily with my mother, who had rented a small room—which we could ill afford—in a motel just down the hill from the hospital.

I think we both came to realize that our quarreling was a sort of ritual. 32
We'd argue about everything—what time of day it was—but the arguments kept me from thinking about that traction system.

I limped through the next decade—through Yale and Cambridge . . . as 33
far away from Piedmont as I could get. But I couldn't escape the pain, which increased as the joint calcified and began to fuse over the next 15 years. My leg grew shorter, as the muscles atrophied and the ball of the ball-and-socket joint migrated into my pelvis. Aspirin, then Motrin, heating pads and massages, became my traveling companions.

Most frustrating was passing store windows full of fine shoes. I used to 34
dream about walking into one of those stores and buying a pair of shoes. "Give me two pairs, one black, one cordovan," I'd say. "Wrap 'em up." No six-week wait as with the orthotics in which I was confined. These would be real shoes. Not bricks.

In the meantime, hip-joint technology progressed dramatically. But no 35
surgeon wanted to operate on me until I was significantly older or until the pain was so great that surgery was unavoidable. After all, a new hip would last only for 15 years, and I'd already lost too much bone. It wasn't a procedure they were sure they'd be able to repeat.

This year, my 40th, the doctors decided the time had come. 36

I increased my life insurance and made the plunge. 37

The nights before my operations are the longest nights of my life—but 38
never long enough. Jerking awake, grabbing for my watch, I experience a delicious sense of relief as I discover that only a minute or two have passed. You never want 6 A.M. to come.

And then the door swings open. "Good morning, Mr. Gates," the nurse 39
says. "It's time."

The last thing I remember, just vaguely, was wondering where amne- 40
siac minutes go in one's consciousness, wondering if I experienced the pain and sounds, then forgot them, or if these were somehow blocked out, dividing the self on the operating table from the conscious self in the recovery room. I didn't like that idea very much. I was about to protest when I blinked.

"It's over, Mr. Gates," says a voice. But how could it be over? I had 41
merely blinked. "You talked to us several times," the surgeon had told me, and that was the scariest part of all.

Twenty-four hours later, they get me out of bed and help me into a 42
"walker." As they stand me on my feet, my wife bursts into tears. "Your foot

is touching the ground!" I am afraid to look, but it is true: the surgeon has lengthened my leg with that gleaming titanium and chrome-cobalt alloy ball-and-socket-joint.

43   "You'll need new shoes," the surgeon says. "Get a pair of Dock-Sides; they have a secure grip. You'll need a ¾-inch lift in the heel, which can be as discreet as you want."

44   I can't help thinking about those window displays of shoes, those elegant shoes that, suddenly, I will be able to wear. Dock-Sides and sneakers, boots and loafers, sandals and brogues. I feel, at last, a furtive sympathy for Imelda Marcos, the queen of soles.

45   The next day, I walk over to the trash can and take a long look at the brick. I don't want to seem ungracious or unappreciative. We have walked long miles together. I feel disloyal, as if I am abandoning an old friend. I take a second look.

46   Maybe I'll have them bronzed.

Thinking Critically About Content

1. What is Gates's injury? How did it happen?

2. Why do you think Gates tells the readers about the school delinquent? According to the essay, what is the significance of the delinquent's actions on the day Gates's hip comes out of its socket?

3. When referring to his shoes at the end of the essay, why do you think Gates says, "Maybe I'll have them bronzed" (paragraph 46)?

Thinking Critically About Purpose and Audience

4. Why do you think Gates calls this essay "A Giant Step"?

5. What do you think Gates's purpose is in this essay? Explain your answer.

6. Out of 46 paragraphs, Gates uses 20 of them to describe his medical examination by the first doctor. Why do you think Gates spends so much time on this aspect of the story?

Thinking Critically About Sentences

7. How do the sentences in paragraphs 15–24 help you understand the prejudice of the doctor treating Gates?

8. Find two sentences in the essay that contain dialogue, and explain what they add to Gates's essay.

9. Write one or more complete sentences that Gates's mother might have said to her son when his problem was finally diagnosed.

Elizabeth Wong

THE STRUGGLE TO BE AN ALL-AMERICAN GIRL

Focusing Your Attention

1. Imagine moving to a country where you don't know the language. Imagine going to school in a foreign country. How much of your heritage would you like to keep, and how much of your new culture would you like to adopt? Why?

2. The essay you are about to read talks about adopting the language and customs of a new country. How difficult do you think it would be to learn a new language? How difficult would understanding a new culture be? How are language and culture related?

Expanding Your Vocabulary

The following words are important to your understanding of this essay.

stoically: unemotionally (paragraph 1)

defiant: resistant (paragraph 3)

maniacal: insane (paragraph 3)

Nationalist Republic of China: Taiwan (paragraph 5)

kowtow: bow (paragraph 6)

ideographs: pictorial symbols (paragraph 7)

raunchy: crude (paragraph 8)

pedestrian: ordinary and dull (paragraph 8)

fanatical: intensely enthusiastic (paragraph 10)

pidgin speech: simplified speech that mixes languages (paragraph 10)

smatterings: pieces, bits (paragraph 10)

It's still there, the Chinese school on Yale Street where my brother and I   1
used to go. Despite the new coat of paint and the high wire fence, the school
I knew 10 years ago remains remarkably, stoically the same.

Every day at 5 P.M., instead of playing with our fourth- and fifth-grade   2
friends or sneaking out to the empty lot to hunt ghosts and animal bones,
my brother and I had to go to Chinese school. No amount of kicking,
screaming, or pleading could dissuade my mother, who was solidly determined to have us learn the language of our heritage.

3   Forcibly, she walked us the seven long, hilly blocks from our home to school, depositing our defiant tearful faces before the stern principal. My only memory of him is that he swayed on his heels like a palm tree, and he always clasped his impatient twitching hands behind his back. I recognized him as a repressed maniacal child killer and knew that if we ever saw his hands we'd be in big trouble.

4   We all sat in little chairs in an empty auditorium. The room smelled like Chinese medicine, an imported faraway mustiness. Like ancient mothballs or dirty closets. I hated that smell. I favored crisp new scents. Like the soft French perfume that my American teacher wore in public school.

5   There was a stage far to the right, flanked by an American flag and the flag of the Nationalist Republic of China, which was also red, white, and blue but not as pretty.

6   Although the emphasis at the school was mainly language—speaking, reading, writing—the lessons always began with an exercise in politeness. With the entrance of the teacher, the best student would tap a bell and everyone would get up, kowtow, and chant, "Sing san ho," the phonetic for "How are you, teacher?"

7   Being ten years old, I had better things to learn than ideographs copied painstakingly in lines that ran right to left from the tip of a *moc but*, a real ink pen that had to be held in an awkward way if blotches were to be avoided. After all, I could do the multiplication tables, name the satellites of Mars, and write reports on *Little Women* and *Black Beauty*. Nancy Drew, my favorite book heroine, never spoke Chinese.

8   The language was a source of embarrassment. More times than not, I had tried to disassociate myself from the nagging loud voice that followed me wherever I wandered in the nearby American supermarket outside Chinatown. The voice belonged to my grandmother, a fragile woman in her seventies who could outshout the best of the street vendors. Her humor was raunchy, her Chinese rhythmless, patternless. It was quick, it was loud, it was unbeautiful. It was not like the quiet, lilting romance of French or the gentle refinement of the American South. Chinese sounded pedestrian. Public.

9   In Chinatown, the comings and goings of hundreds of Chinese on their daily tasks sounded chaotic and frenzied. I did not want to be thought of as mad, as talking gibberish. When I spoke English, people nodded at me, smiled sweetly, said encouraging words. Even the people in my culture would cluck and say that I'd do well in life. "My, doesn't she move her lips fast," they would say, meaning that I'd be able to keep up with the world outside Chinatown.

My brother was even more fanatical than I about speaking English. He   10
was especially hard on my mother, criticizing her, often cruelly, for her
pidgin speech—smatterings of Chinese scattered like chop suey in her conversation. "It's not 'What it is,' Mom," he'd say in exasperation. "It's 'What *is*
it, what *is* it, what *is* it!'" Sometimes Mom might leave out an occasional
"the" or "a" or perhaps a verb of being. He would stop her in mid-sentence:
"Say it again, Mom. Say it right." When he tripped over his own tongue,
he'd blame it on her: "See, Mom, it's all your fault. You set a bad example."

What infuriated my mother most was when my brother cornered her on   11
her consonants, especially "r." My father had played a cruel joke on Mom
by assigning her an American name that her tongue wouldn't allow her
to say. No matter how hard she tried, "Ruth" always ended up "Luth" or
"Roof."

After two years of writing with a *moc but* and reciting words with multi-   12
ples of meanings, I finally was granted a cultural divorce. I was permitted
to stop Chinese school.

I thought of myself as multicultural. I preferred tacos to egg rolls; I   13
enjoyed Cinco de Mayo more than Chinese New Year.

At last, I was one of you; I wasn't one of them. Sadly, I still am.   14

Thinking Critically About Content

1. Wong includes many comparisons between American and Chinese
   cultures in her essay. Find two comparisons, and explain how they
   show Wong's desire to become "more American."

2. What do you think the time span is from the beginning to the end of
   this essay? Explain your answer.

3. In paragraph 12, Wong states, "I finally was granted a cultural
   divorce. I was permitted to stop Chinese school." Do these two
   sentences reflect a happy or sad moment in Wong's life? Explain your
   answer.

Thinking Critically About Purpose and Audience

4. Why do you think Wong wrote this essay? Who did she probably
   write it for?

5. Wong explains different Chinese customs in her essay. How do these
   explanations help the reader understand Wong's "struggle to be an
   all-American girl"?

6. Why do you think Wong included the information about her brother
   criticizing her mother? How does this section affect the entire essay?

Thinking Critically About Sentences

7. Wong focuses on her struggle to become an American girl. What does the last sentence of the essay—"Sadly, I still am"—suggest about this struggle?

8. Look at paragraph 9. What is the topic sentence? Do you think the remainder of the sentences in the paragraph support this topic sentence? Explain your answer.

9. Write one or more complete sentences describing how you think Wong now wishes she had felt about Chinese schooling.

Writing Topics: Narrating

Before you begin to write, you might want to review the writing process in Part I.

1. Gates's essay reminds us that we all have disabilities and problems in life—some more visible and obvious than others. Tell a story that summarizes one of your problems. Include in the story how you are dealing or have dealt with the problem.

2. Is culture always part of heritage? Can they be different? How ingrained is your culture in you? Write a narrative that highlights an important part of your cultural heritage.

ILLUSTRATING

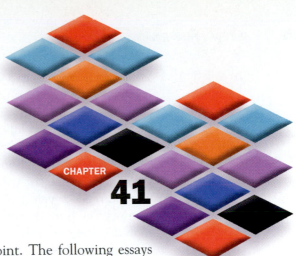

Illustrating is giving examples to make a point. The following essays develop their main ideas primarily through examples. The first, "A Question of Trust" by Sherry Hemman Hogan, uses a handkerchief to represent some special lessons she learned about trust. In "Mortality," author Bailey White demonstrates with many examples her love of an old car and her insistence on keeping it running.

Sherry Hemman Hogan
A QUESTION OF TRUST

Focusing Your Attention

1. Think of someone special in your life. Why does this person mean so much to you?

2. In the essay you are about to read, a father's handkerchief becomes an important symbol to his daughter. Think of an object that reminds you of someone special. Explain why this object is important and what your associations are with this object.

Expanding Your Vocabulary

The following words are important to your understanding of this essay.

treacherous: dangerous (paragraph 1)

mariner: sailor, navigator (paragraph 1)

waterworks: tears (paragraph 4)

admonition: warning (paragraph 4)

invariably: never changing (paragraph 9)

undaunted: fearless (paragraph 14)

1   When in treacherous waters, the mariner trusts the reliable beam of the lighthouse to guide his passage. My dependable beacon was my father's handkerchief. He didn't care for fancy French silk or Italian lace and had no need for those with elaborately embroidered initials. Dad preferred plain white cotton, the best buy from the local five-and-dime.

2   The uses of Dad's handkerchief were innumerable. It was a white flag hanging from the car window when the old station wagon overheated on vacation, filled with five squabbling kids, a dog, a cat, and two worn-out parents. The handkerchief, ever ready for back-seat disasters, sponged up melted Popsicles and oozing egg-salad sandwiches.

3   Amazing that a simple piece of cloth can evoke so many memories. It bound the wound of my favorite kitten after a close encounter with the neighbor's dog, then handled my sniffles too. It was Dad's amateur magician's prop for his disappearing-nickel trick. The first time I ever saw my dad cry, the crumpled cloth wiped his tears after he carried the lifeless body of his beloved German shepherd, Princess, out to her grave.

4   As a teen distraught over a crush on a boy, my waterworks ceased only when Dad offered me his handkerchief with the tender admonition "Here, take mine. You never seem to have one when you need it."

5   I remember going to him when I was 20 just before leaving on my first solo adventure, a trip to Europe. As the big moment arrived, I was scared, not so sure I was ready to be independent after all. The tears came as I confronted leaving everything I knew: my family, my home, my friends, and my boyfriend.

6   "You'll see; this is going to be one of the best experiences of your life," Dad said reassuringly as he handed me his familiar cotton square. "Trust me," he added with a wink.

7   Three years in France and Africa was, indeed, the greatest journey of my life. And upon returning, my first sight scanning through the throngs at Kennedy Airport was Dad's white handkerchief waving over the crowd.

8   It would make many appearances throughout my life—never more movingly than when my mom wept into it with joy at the triumphant birth of my daughter, Shannon, following two miscarriages.

9   Some 12 years later, and newly divorced, quite a few handkerchief sessions with Dad were in order as my daughter and I faced a whole new life together. After heart-wrenching discussions at Mom and Dad's, my search for a tissue invariably ended with my father's familiar offer. Then, concerned about my going home to a dark house, my parents established a routine for their peace of mind as well as mine. Within minutes of my arrival, I would always call to say, "Hi, Dad. It's me. I'm home."

10   My father was then fighting his own battle, a 12-year war with prostate cancer. By Christmas, 1997, the illness had taken over his body. Knowing

that we could lose him any time, we did our best to make it a joyous occasion. But when asked what he needed for presents, Dad could only say with a wry grin, "There's nothing I need where I'm going. Everything's provided for."

Still, we had to get him *something*. After a discussion with my sisters 11
and brother, I suggested handkerchiefs—he still kept a fresh one with him every day. I went to a boutique and bought some beautiful, expensive linen ones with the initial *R* for Robert, his first name, embroidered in brilliant black, red, and silver. Then, knowing my father, I ran to a discount store to purchase a few of the cheap variety. At home I placed them in three different gift boxes.

For the first time in 55 years, my parents were separated, living in two 12
constant-care rooms near each other in a retirement home. From his favorite chair, Dad opened the trio of gaily wrapped packages. "Well, what do you know!" he said each time, giving us the impish smile we cherished. "Just what I needed."

Setting aside the elegantly initialed linens, he chose a bargain hanky 13
and waved the familiar flag. "*This* is how I built that little nest egg for your mother," he said. "I'll only use the expensive ones for very important occasions."

Dad knew his time was short. As was his way, everything was pre- 14
pared, including his obituary. Undaunted, he and I spent several evenings writing it together. On a stormy night in January, I brought him the final draft. While he reclined in his favorite chair, I began to read aloud. Although strong during all our discussions, I could no longer suppress my emotions looking into the eyes that had seen me through 45 years. The tears just would not stop.

With tremendous effort, he squeezed my hand. "I'm ready to move on, 15
Sher. You know that. But look after your mother, okay?"

"You've . . . always been there for me, Dad," I barely choked out. 16

"And I always will be, just in a different way," he said. "Trust me." 17

I rooted in my purse for a tissue. Smiling, Dad said gently, "I've got lots 18
of these—thanks to you. Now dry your tears and blow your nose, okay? A good, hard one." He glanced out at the blustery weather. "You shouldn't have stayed so late. Driving may be tricky. Why don't you call me when you get in?"

During the ten-minute drive home, his words *trust me* echoed in my 19
heart. He was the most trustworthy person I knew. If he said something, he meant it. I felt far more peaceful now, but still found my voice catching when I phoned him as soon as I arrived. "Hi, Dad . . . I'm home." *Would this be the last time he would hear those words from me?*

It was. Dad passed away just ten days later. We knew he was ready. 20

21   In the weeks after the funeral, we did our best to stay strong for Mom. One of the most difficult chores was clearing out his room, which held so many reminders. My mom had no extra space in her room. So Dad's chair found a home in my living room, where Shannon, now 18, adopted it as her favorite spot to snuggle, nap, and do homework. Her grandfather had been her hero too.

22   Eight weeks after Dad's death, Friday, March 13, the permanence of such a major loss hit. This date, gloomy for the superstitious, was always one of optimism for our family. My father was born on the 13th day of September in 1919, and he assured us from childhood that it was a lucky day.

23   This Friday the 13th, however, provided no reason to celebrate; Dad was no longer with us. Yes, I knew that he was in a better place, but the father I could always rely on was gone.

24   Even the promise of spring, due to arrive in just seven days, seemed too much to hope for. Easter, the essence of rebirth, was only a month away, but I couldn't even bring myself to unpack the decorations. I felt lifeless, as I had during other crises. And to whom had I gone then? Dad.

25   In tears, I called my sister. "Dad always helped me through things like this. He had the answers."

26   "Talk to him, Sher," she said gently. "I do all the time."

27   I hung up, tears still streaming down my face. I wandered aimlessly around the living room and scrabbled in an empty box of Kleenex. Then I talked to him. "Oh, Dad. I know you're in a better place. I have that faith, mostly because of you. But I miss you so much. And I just wish I *knew* that you're all right."

28   Silence. Nothing. I felt worse. Sobbing uncontrollably, I could feel grief washing through my entire body. My hands turned icy cold, and I started to shake all over.

29   That's when I saw it. Out of the corner of my eye, a big square of white peeked from beneath Dad's chair. "What on earth is that?" I mumbled, impatient because I had just tidied the room that morning.

30   Stooping to pick it up, I stared through the fog of tears. It was one of Dad's new handkerchiefs with the embroidered design. I clutched it, stroking the elegant black letter *R*.

31   I took a few deep breaths and tried to calm myself. My mind worked. I clean this room every morning, I thought. I vacuum the entire rug, moving this chair, twice a week. Where on earth did this come from?

32   I felt pretty silly. But when we'd emptied Dad's room, I had carefully explored that chair, collecting pens and paper clips and other odds and ends that had slipped between the seat and armrests. Once in my living room, that chair had been lovingly cleaned. It had been bounced upon by my neighbors' grandkids and survived my daughter's slumber party with

seven teenage girls scrambling in and out of it throughout the night. So why had the handkerchief shown up now?

I paced through the house, shaking my head. This, I could not explain.   33

"All I have seen teaches me to trust the Creator for all I have not seen."   34 I could almost hear Dad quoting Emerson. And then his own words to me at Christmas came back: "I'll only use the expensive ones for very important occasions."

Gently tucking the embroidered cloth in my pocket with new resolve, I   35 retrieved the Easter decorations: the bunnies, eggs and butterflies—all symbols of creation, new life and rebirth, the very promise of spring.

Yes, I could trust that spring would arrive—it always does. And I could   36 trust the words of my father.

That handkerchief, which so mysteriously appeared, now has a trea-   37 sured place on my desk. It's a reminder that perhaps some things in life are better left unexplained. Leaps of faith can be very good exercise for the healing heart.

As far as I was concerned, it was Dad's way of sending me a message.   38 It was his way of saying, "Hi, Sher. It's me. I'm okay. I'm home."

Thinking Critically About Content

1. What does the handkerchief represent in this essay? Explain your answer.

2. Why does Hogan's father say, "Trust me," just before he dies (paragraph 17)?

3. Why does Hogan finally unpack the Easter decorations at the end of the essay?

Thinking Critically About Purpose and Audience

4. What do you think Hogan's purpose is in this essay?

5. What audience do you think Hogan had in mind when she wrote this essay?

6. What is important about the phone call to her father, saying, "Hi, Dad . . . I'm home" (paragraphs 9 and 19)? What other references to *home* are important in the essay?

Thinking Critically About Sentences

7. List the examples the author uses in paragraph 2. Does the paragraph's topic sentence introduce them adequately? Explain your answer.

8. In paragraph 28, Hogan uses very short sentences. How do these sentences help illustrate her mood in this paragraph?

9. Write one or more complete sentences from the father's point of view about the relationship he had with his daughter.

Bailey White

MORTALITY

Focusing Your Attention

1. Think of an item like an old shirt or pair of jeans that you want to keep forever, even though it might wear out. Explain why this item is important to you.

2. The essay you are about to read talks about a special relationship between a car and its owner. If you could have any car, what car would you choose? Why? Explain your answer.

Expanding Your Vocabulary

The following words are important to your understanding of this essay.

disintegrated: fell to pieces (paragraph 5)

odometer: distance gauge (paragraph 5)

fire wall: wall between the engine and the passenger compartment of a vehicle (paragraph 6)

slopped: poured (paragraph 10)

ominous: alarming (paragraph 11)

internal combustion: burning fuel inside an engine (paragraph 13)

hurtling: moving at a great speed (paragraph 13)

amble: walk (paragraph 22)

1   It really makes you feel your age when you get a letter from your insurance agent telling you that the car you bought, only slightly used, the year you got out of college, is now an antique. "Beginning with your next payment, your insurance premiums will reflect this change in classification," the letter said.

2   I went out and looked at the car. I thought back over the years. I could almost hear my uncle's disapproving voice. "You should never buy a used car," he had told me the day I brought it home. Ten years later I drove that used car to his funeral. I drove my sister, Louise, to the hospital in that car to have her first baby, and I drove to Atlanta in that car when the baby graduated from Georgia Tech with a degree in physics.

"When are you going to get a new car?" my friends asked me.   3

"I don't need a new car," I said. "This car runs fine."   4

I changed the oil often, and I kept good tires on it. It always got me   5
where I wanted to go. But the stuffing came out of the backseat and the
springs poked through, and the dashboard disintegrated. At 300,000 miles
the odometer quit turning, but I didn't really care to know how far I had
driven.

A hole wore in the floor where my heel rested in front of the accelerator,   6
and the insulation all peeled off the fire wall. "Old piece of junk," my friends
whispered. The seat-belt catch wore out, and I tied on a huge bronze hook
with a fireman's knot.

Big flashy cars would zoom past me. People would shake their fists out   7
the windows. "Get that clunker off the road!" they would shout.

Then one day on my way to work, the car coughed, sputtered, and   8
stopped. "This is it," I thought, and I gave it a pat. "It's been a good car."

I called the mechanic. "Tow it in," I said. "I'll have to decide what to do."   9
After work I went over there. I was feeling very glum. The mechanic
laughed at me. "It's not funny," I said. "I've had that car a long time."

"You know what's wrong with that car?" he said. "That car was out of   10
gas." So I slopped a gallon of gas in the tank and drove ten more years. The
gas gauge never worked again after that day, but I got to where I could tell
when the gas was low by the smell. I think it was the smell of the bottom of
the tank.

There was also a little smell of brake fluid, a little smell of exhaust, a   11
little smell of oil, and after all the years a little smell of me. Car smells. And
sounds. The wonderful sound when the engine finally catches on a cold
day, and an ominous *tick tick* in July when the radiator is working too
hard. The windshield wipers said, "Gracie Allen Gracie Allen Gracie
Allen." I didn't like a lot of conversation in the car because I had to keep
listening for a little skip that meant I needed to jump out and adjust the
carburetor.

I kept a screwdriver close at hand—and a pint of brake fluid and a new   12
rotor, just in case. "She's strange," my friends whispered. "And she drives
so slow."

I don't know how fast I drove. The speedometer had quit working years   13
ago. But when I would look down through the hole in the floor and see the
pavement, a gray blur, whizzing by just inches away from my feet, and feel
the tremendous heat of internal combustion pouring back through the fire
wall into my lap, and hear each barely contained explosion just as a heart
attack victim is able to hear his own heartbeat, it didn't feel like slow to me.
A whiff of brake fluid would remind me just what a tiny thing I was relying
on to stop myself from hurtling along the surface of the earth at an unnatural

speed, and when I finally arrived at my destination, I would slump back, unfasten the seat belt hook with trembling hands, and stagger out. I would gather up my things and give the car a last look. "Thank you, sir," I would say. "We got here one more time."

14   But after I got that letter, I began thinking about getting a new car. I read the newspaper every night. Finally I found one that sounded good. It was the same make as my car, but almost new. "Call Steve," the ad said.

15   I went to see the car. It was parked in Steve's driveway. It was a fashionable wheat color. There was carpet on the floor, and the seats were covered with a soft, velvety-feeling stuff. It smelled like acrylic and vinyl and Steve. The instrument panel looked like what you would need to run a jet plane. I turned a knob. Mozart's Concerto for Flute and Harp poured out of four speakers. "But how can you listen to the engine with music playing?" I asked Steve.

16   I turned the key. The car started instantly. No desperate pleadings, no wild hopes, no exquisitely paired maneuvers with the accelerator and the choke. Just instant ignition. I turned off the radio. I could barely hear the engine running, a low, steady hum. I fastened my seat belt. Nothing but a click.

17   Steve got in the passenger seat, and we went for a test drive. We floated down the road. I couldn't hear a sound, but I decided it must be time to shift gears. I stomped around on the floor and grabbed Steve's knee before I remembered it had automatic transmission. "You mean you just put it in 'Drive' and drive?" I asked.

18   Steve scrunched himself way over against his door and clamped his knees together. He tested his seat belt. "Have you ever driven a car before?" he asked.

19   I bought it for two thousand dollars. I rolled all the windows up by mashing a button beside my elbow, set the air-conditioning on "Recirc," and listened to Vivaldi all the way home.

20   So now I have two cars. I call them my new car and my real car. Most of the time I drive my new car. But on some days I go out to the barn and get in my real car. I shoo the rats out of the backseat and crank it up. Even without daily practice my hands and feet know just what to do. My ears perk up, and I sniff the air. I add a little brake fluid, a little water. I sniff again. It'll need gas next week and an oil change.

21   I back it out, and we roll down the road. People stop and look. They smile. "Neat car!" they say.

22   When I pull into the parking lot, my friends shake their heads and chuckle. They amble into the building. They're already thinking about their day's work. But I take one last look at the car and think what an amazing thing it is, internal combustion. And how wonderful to be still alive!

Thinking Critically About Content

1. Using examples from the essay, describe the kind of car White drove.

2. Why did White decide to buy a new car? Why do you think she drove the old one for so long?

3. Whom is White talking about when she says, "And how wonderful to be still alive!" (paragraph 22)—the car or herself? Explain your answer.

Thinking Critically About Purpose and Audience

4. Why do you think White calls her essay "Mortality"?

5. What type of reader do you think would most understand and appreciate this story?

6. What specific examples about the car were most interesting to you? In what ways do these examples help you understand White's attachment to the car?

Thinking Critically About Sentences

7. The topic sentence of paragraph 20 is "So now I have two cars." Do all of the other sentences in this paragraph explain this main idea? Explain your answer.

8. What do the sentences in dialogue form in paragraphs 12 and 13 add to the essay?

9. Write one or more complete sentences about how the car might feel about White's attachment to it.

Writing Topics: Illustrating

Before you begin to write, you might want to review the writing process in Part I.

1. Like the handkerchief in Hogan's essay, what objects carry special emotional value for you? Explain what one of these objects represents in your life.

2. After reading White's essay, what do you think are the main characteristics of the relationship between a car and its owner? How does this relationship develop? Do you have a similar relationship with your car, bike, motorcycle, feet, or bus pass? Explain your answer.

CHAPTER **42**

ANALYZING A PROCESS

Process analysis is a form of explaining. The essays you are about to read demonstrate both types of process analysis: how to do something and how something happened. They both tell what comes first, second, and so on. The first essay, "Ferrying Dreamers to the Other Side" by Tomás Robles, tells how illegal immigrants from Mexico are smuggled across the Texas border. In the second essay, "Stress Free in 10 Minutes," Peter Jaret explains how to control your reaction to stress in your life.

Tomás Robles

FERRYING DREAMERS TO THE OTHER SIDE

Focusing Your Attention

1. Think about the journey from your car or dorm room to the classroom you now sit in. In order, list every action you had to take to get to your seat. Don't forget to list small details like walking up stairs or opening doors.

2. The essay you are about to read describes the process of smuggling Mexican immigrants across the Texas border. Explain why you think people would risk their lives and leave their families and possessions behind to come to the United States.

Expanding Your Vocabulary

The following words are important to your understanding of this essay.

pateros: smugglers (paragraph 2)

coyote: smuggler (paragraph 8)

Matamoros: a city in Mexico (paragraph 8)

mordida: payoff (literally, bite) (paragraph 12)

La Migra: Immigration (paragraph 13)

wetback: illegal immigrant (paragraph 13)

gringos: Americans (paragraph 20)

First I look at you. I study you. Then I know whether or not you're going 1
to cross to the other side.

When people arrive, they're afraid. If I see that you've just stepped off 2
the bus and I ask if you want to get to the other side, you're not going to say
yes. You're uncertain. You'll think to yourself, "Who is this guy? Is he a criminal? A policeman?" So you'll tell me, "No, I am not going to cross. I'm just
here to visit some relatives." Now, when a lot of *pateros* hear this, they'll just
walk away. Not me. I say, "You know what? Whatever you want to do, my
job is to cross people over to the other side, and I won't charge you a nickel
until we get there."

I just keep talking. I don't stop. It's the *patero* who talks the best that gets 3
the most people. I say, "It doesn't matter to me if you've got no money. All
you need is a telephone number of someone over there, a relative or someone else who can pay your way. Here, I'll cover your food and lodging. I'll
give you a place to sleep and everything. I won't charge you a penny until
we've crossed over. Do you have the number of someone on the other
side?"

Then you'll look at me and say, "Okay, I want to cross. How much do you 4
charge?"

"Six hundred dollars from here to Houston. Everyone charges the same. 5
But listen, we can't talk here. It's dangerous with all these police. I live just
one block away. Let's go to my house. You can wash up. I'll buy you something to eat, and we can talk some more."

Then you follow me, see, and we keep talking. Once you're at my house, 6
you're mine. That's how it works. Before we cross the border, you give me
the telephone number of someone on the other side, and we call. If they
say, "We don't have any money" or "We don't know him," that's it, there's no
deal. That's how we arrange things.

We put you up in a hotel until we've gathered ten, twelve, or fifteen peo- 7
ple. Sometimes it takes two or three days. We won't carry just two or three
people across. It isn't worth it. We need at least eight, because we never
work alone. We usually cross over with three or four *pateros*. When we've
got everyone together, we tell them, "At four o'clock we're going to cross the
river. You'll have to leave your suitcases here. This isn't a vacation. You're
going to cross with just a shirt and a pair of pants. Okay?"

Then we say, "If they catch us, don't tell them who's carrying you across. 8
If they ask who helped you cross or which one's the coyote, you just say,

'Nobody's carrying us across. We're all just looking for work.' That way, if Immigration finds us, they'll just send us back across the border, back to Matamoros. They won't jail us, and we'll cross over again. If Immigration catches us, they'll ask for our names. We'll give them fake names, and if they catch us again, we'll give them different names. They never remember us."

9   Once we've talked this over and everyone understands, we take a taxi that drops us off close to the river. On the Mexican side, the police patrol the river on horseback. If they see us, they'll come over to check us out.

10   "Listen, we're just going over to Brownsville to earn a little money."

11   "Okay, just give us a little something so we can buy a drink."

12   So we give them a little money, and they let us pass. If we're caught by police who know we're *pateros*, we're screwed. They'll make us pay them one, two, maybe three hundred dollars. If we don't pay them, they'll arrest us for some crime we've never committed. They won't just charge us with being *pateros*. They'll charge us with assault and really screw us. . . . We have to work with them. After we give them their *mordida*, they'll let us pass.

13   Then we go on to the river. We take off our clothes and put them in a bag. We get in the water and cross the river naked. If we crossed wearing clothes, when we got to the other side we'd be wet and people would notice. If La Migra sees that, they'll say, "Look, there goes another wetback," and they'll nail you.

14   Sometimes we cross people who don't know how to swim. We buy inner tubes and put the people inside. They get nervous, but I tell them, "Don't worry if you can't swim. Just hold on tight to one of my feet." They'll grab on to my foot, and I'll swim across the river using my hands. It's about thirty feet across, but when the water's high, the current gets strong. If you know what you're doing, it's easy, but if not, it can be dangerous. Lots of people drown.

15   On the American side of the river, there are bandits who carry knives and guns. They'll wait for you and catch you as you get out of the water, naked. They'll tear open your bag looking for money. They'll check your socks and your shoes. They look everywhere. If you've got good boots, nice pants, or a decent shirt, they'll steal them. Sometimes they take everything. Other times they beat you up or threaten you with knives. That's happened to me many times. I've got a knife wound on my leg, another one over there, and another here. Look at all these scars. Look at how they've sliced me up.

16   Once we've crossed the river, we walk calmly into Brownsville. Then we call up some friends who drive taxis. We put five people in each taxi and carry them to a hotel. We get one room for everybody. The next day, around three or four in the morning, we wake everyone up. We divide the group between three cars. That way if the police or Immigration stop us on the way, they'll only catch one group and the other two will make it through to

Houston. We lose less money if we split up, because when they catch you, they arrest the driver, confiscate the car, and send everyone back to the other side.

Before we get to the immigration checkpoint, we get out of the car and let the driver continue north. The drivers have their papers, so they can pass through the checkpoint. Then we walk into the countryside. It's dark, but we know where we're going. There are power lines that we use to guide us. We go on together, walking and walking, for five or six hours. There are lots of rattlesnakes, and you can die if they bite you. We walk on through the brush until we get to a place to rest. Then one person—only one—goes out to the road to see if the drivers are there yet. When they arrive, we get back in the cars and off we go to Houston. 17

Then we drive to a special house. Our boss meets us there. We gather everyone into the house, park the cars, close the door, and then start calling the phone numbers, one by one. "Okay, we've got your nephew here"—or your son, your brother, whoever. "Come on over with the money." They come over and pay us. We give them the person, and off they go. There's times when they don't want to pay or when they only have three or four hundred dollars. Sometimes they'll give us rings, watches, or bracelets. If they don't have anyone who can pay and nothing to give us, we take the people back to Matamoros. If there's someone who'll buy the people off of us, we'll sell them. 18

Our boss collects the money, and when everyone's gone he divides it up. He takes his cut and everyone else gets a share. Then we go to the best bar in Houston and get drunk. We take a lot of chances on the road—the police might catch us, Immigration might send us back. Who knows? We might drown in the river or someone might kill us. So we celebrate to make up for everything we've gone through. We drink and drink until the table is covered with beer bottles. We have girls on all sides of us, sitting on our laps, dancing. We have a great time. Nothing but *pateros* and women. There in that bar, for one night, we're all kings. 19

I know that what I do is illegal, but it's man who invented these laws, not God. It's the American government that doesn't want us to pass people to the other side. They don't want us to be with you, the gringos. I'm not doing anything wrong. I'm not robbing, beating, or killing anyone. I'm not working against God. Where these people are from, they earn so little they can't even support their families. So even though what I do is illegal, in the end it's actually good. I'm helping people to better themselves, to realize their dreams. 20

I'm ready for whatever might happen. If today or tomorrow they kill me or a snake bites me or they crush the life out of me, my kids will have money in the bank. Every day, I risk my life for my family. It's an adventure being a 21 *patero*, a beautiful life—to know the road, to cross the river. If tomorrow something were to happen to me, who cares? In the end, every man suffers for the life he leads.

Thinking Critically About Content

1. List the steps of the process that Robles explains.

2. On the basis of the information given in this essay, do you think authorities can now catch *pateros* like Robles? Explain your answer.

3. Do you think Robles believes he is providing an honorable service to the Mexican people? Why or why not?

Thinking Critically About Purpose and Audience

4. Why do you think Robles tells readers how he illegally smuggles Mexicans across the border?

5. Who do you think would most appreciate reading Robles's story? Explain your answer.

6. Which step of this process is most interesting to you? Why? In what ways is this step important to the process?

Thinking Critically About Sentences

7. Find three sentences that contain specific numbers. What do these details add to your understanding of Robles's smuggling process?

8. Explain the meaning of the last sentence in the essay: "In the end, every man suffers for the life he leads." Do you think it is a good ending for this essay? Explain your answer.

9. In one or more complete sentences, write down what you think an immigration officer would say to Robles if they met.

Peter Jaret

STRESS FREE IN 10 MINUTES: SEVEN WAYS TO CHILL OUT AND RECHARGE

Focusing Your Attention

1. What causes stress in your life? Why do these particular issues cause stress for you?

2. In the excerpt you are about to read, Peter Jaret discusses seven strategies for controlling our reactions to stress in our lives. Have you

ever felt like you couldn't handle the stress in your life? What were the circumstances?

Expanding Your Vocabulary

The following words are important to your understanding of this essay.

oasis: something providing relief (paragraph 2)

susceptible: sensitive to (paragraph 2)

immune: free from disease (paragraph 2)

exacerbate: increase, worsen (paragraph 2)

beneficial: helpful, useful (paragraph 10)

synchronizing: making to agree in timing (paragraph 22)

progressive: something that is going forward (paragraph 26)

If the pace of life threatens to spin out of control, Shelley Wahle does more   1
than slow down. She stops completely. "I'll close my eyes and take a few
good long, deep breaths. A minute or two is often all it takes to calm down."
Wahle prepares medical reports for doctors—a job with tight deadlines—so
she has to manage stress or suffer. But the 53-year-old really began to
appreciate the power of stress relief after a nasty car accident left her struggling with back pain and emotional trauma. She went to the Stress Management Center of Marin, California, where she learned some simple
techniques. The turnaround in her health and mood was so dramatic that
her husband and two of their kids have followed her lead, making the Wahle
household one of the calmest in Marin County—no small feat.

With problems small or large, finding a quiet oasis from stress not only   2
preserves sanity, but can be a lifesaver. Constant stress can harm the heart
and even promote clogged arteries. New findings show it can cause a surge
of stress hormones in the bloodstream that can weaken the body's immune
defenses, making us more susceptible to infections like colds and flu. Everything from heartburn and cold sores to asthma and cancer are linked to
high stress levels—they can even exacerbate memory loss as we age.

But relax. There are proven ways to quell stress. At West Virginia Uni-   3
versity, scientists taught 59 adults a meditative approach to stress management. Afterward the volunteers not only felt less anxious, but also reported
fewer stress symptoms, such as headaches. When students at Murdoch
University in Australia learned easy ways to defuse pressure, they had
fewer sick days and faster recovery from colds. And a study at the University of Miami found that HIV-positive patients practicing stress reduction
could boost the number of immune cells circulating in their bloodstream.

4   You don't need to turn your life upside down to tame stress, says psychologist Frederic Luskin, a researcher at Stanford University. "A lot of people say they're too busy to stop and deal with stress. But things you can do anywhere, and that don't have to take more than a few minutes, can stop the stress response before it goes out of control. The truth is, by learning to calm down, you can actually feel less busy."

5   Try a different one of these techniques each day this coming week. Some will work better than others. What's important is finding two or three you can turn to whenever your stress meter climbs.

Do Nothing

6   Here's How: At least once during the day, take five or ten minutes to sit quietly and do nothing. Focus on the sounds around you, your emotions and any tension in your neck, shoulders, arms, chest, etc.

7   "It's one of the hardest things for many people to do," says Robin Gueth, founder and director of the Stress Management Center of Marin. "We're so used to thinking of our worth in terms of what we get done. Doing nothing can be a real struggle."

8   Just sitting quietly slows heart rate and reduces blood pressure, countering two of the most obvious effects of stress. It can also change your perspective and increase your sense of control over events. "Studies show that the most stressful situations are things we can't control," says psychologist James Carmody, research director of the Center for Mindfulness at the University of Massachusetts School of Medicine. "We can't change the past. We can't predict the future. The only thing any of us can control is the present moment," he explains. "When people in our program practice this technique, they regain a sense of control—and ease stress."

Laugh Out Loud

9   Here's How: Keep something handy that makes you laugh. It could be a collection of your favorite comic strips or a funny voice mail from, say, your child or a friend. You could even take a few moments to think about watching your favorite sitcom. Turn to this every so often during your day.

10   One of the most effective stress-busters occurs nightly, says researcher Lee Berk—when many Americans turn on their favorite sitcoms at the end of a long day. Berk's studies at Loma Linda University School of Public Health in California have shown that a good laugh reduces levels of the stress hormones cortisol and epinephrine and boosts immunity. What's more, the beneficial effects of a good belly laugh last up to 24 hours—just in time for the next rerun of *Friends*.

Even looking forward to laughing calms people. In results reported last 11
year, Berk and his colleagues found that telling volunteers they would participate in an experiment that involved watching a funny video created a
more positive mood and lowered their stress levels on the spot.

Tune In

Here's How: When you face a daunting task, play soothing music—be it 12
classical, country, or jazz. At work you can use the CD drive on your computer to keep the music at the ready.

In a study at Monash University in Victoria, Australia, two groups of stu- 13
dents were told to prepare an oral presentation. Some worked in silence;
others listened to Pachelbel's Canon in D major. Stress caused the silent
workers' blood pressure and heart rates to climb. Not so the volunteers in
the musical group, whose measurements remained steadier. They also
reported feeling much less stress.

Is there music you shouldn't listen to? "A lot of people find classical 14
music most relaxing, but not everyone," says psychologist Elise Labbe, who
has been testing the calming effects of music in experiments at the University of South Alabama. "Our volunteers select everything from concertos to
country music. Whatever music feels most calming to you is the one that's
most likely to help ease stress."

Think Happy

Here's How: Focus on someone or something you care deeply about for 15
anywhere from 15 seconds to five minutes. Or picture a scene from a
peaceful vacation. A phrase that makes you feel positive about yourself
and the world can also work.

It sounds like advice from a greeting card, but thinking happy, calming 16
thoughts can counteract the physiological changes that occur when we're
under stress. "A lot of the stress we experience comes from negative emotions we carry around with us—grudges, anger, hurt," says Luskin, who
studies the healing power of forgiveness (he's also the author of the book
Forgive for Good). "Just thinking about someone you're angry with—a boss
who's a jerk or a friend who hurt your feelings—can cause damaging stress
hormones to flood the system. Thinking of people and things you love can
have the opposite effect."

Hit the Road

Here's How: Get up from your desk, the couch—wherever you may be— 17
and take a ten-minute walk.

18   Most people have an intuitive sense that walking helps calm them down. Now scientists are finding proof. In a 2002 investigation by the Stanford University School of Medicine, researchers looked at people who were taking care of relatives with dementia—as stressful a situation as almost any of us will face. Those who began walking four times a week, the scientists found, reported feeling less distressed and sleeping better. Tests showed that their blood pressure was also more likely to hold steady when they were under stress.

19   Don't have half an hour to spare? Don't sweat it. Taking five- or ten-minute walks whenever you're under pressure may be just as effective. "Our research suggests that the best strategy is to take a few minutes—or even a few moments—to calm down whenever stress levels start to climb," says Stanford psychologist Luskin.

Breathe Easy

20   Here's How: For five minutes, slow your breathing down to about six deep-belly breaths a minute. In other words, inhale for about five seconds, exhale for about five.

21   We tend to take quick, shallow breaths, especially when we're feeling tense. Taking a few deep breaths forces you to stretch your shoulders and loosen up tight muscles.

22   Slow breathing has other unexpected benefits, according to an international study from 2001. Researchers found that when people practice yoga or recite a prayer, their breathing slows to the five-seconds-in, five-seconds-out rhythm, which, it turns out, matches a ten-second cycle fluctuation that naturally occurs in blood pressure. By synchronizing breathing to these underlying cardiovascular rhythms, people not only feel calmer, but may also improve the health of their cardiovascular systems.

23   If your day is full of small hassles and frustrations, Gueth recommends putting a dot of Wite-Out on your wristwatch or the clock on your desk. "Every time you see that white dot," she says, "take two or three long, deep breaths. You'll be amazed how quickly it calms you down."

Rise Relaxed

24   Here's How: Right before bed, and after the alarm goes off in the morning, take five minutes to relax your entire body. Start by tensing your toes; then consciously relax them. Move on to the muscles in your feet, and then your calves, upper legs, buttocks, moving upward until you end by scrunching up and then relaxing the muscles in your face.

If you start your day feeling tense, chances are you'll feel tense all day,   25
says stress expert Gueth. If you take your troubles to bed with you, they're
likely to disrupt your sleep. And that can mean even more tension. People
deprived of sleep, research shows, experience increased stress hormone
levels. Gueth's advice: Begin and end each day by taking a minute or two
to consciously relax.

One effective approach is called progressive relaxation, the technique   26
described above. In a 2002 study at the University of Southern Mississippi,
46 volunteers who were taught progressive relaxation experienced a
significant dip in heart rates, perceived stress, and levels of cortisol.

"Too much of my day is spent running around," says Shelley Wahle.   27
"I don't want to start it that way. So I take five minutes before the craziness
starts to quiet my mind. It's not always easy. But once it's part of your routine, you don't feel right without it."

Thinking Critically About Content

1. What can stress do to us physically?
2. What does psychologist Frederic Luskin claim are the main causes of
   stress in our daily lives?
3. Name the seven methods Jaret suggests for managing stress.

Thinking Critically About Purpose and Audience

4. In your opinion, what is Peter Jaret's purpose in this essay? Explain
   your answer.
5. Who do you think is the primary audience for the author? Explain
   your answer.
6. According to Jaret, why should we control the stress in our lives?

Thinking Critically About Sentences

7. Describe in a complete sentence the writer's point of view toward
   stress.
8. What is the topic sentence of paragraph 3? Do all the sentences in
   that paragraph support this topic sentence? Explain your answer.
9. After trying one or more of these methods, write several complete
   sentences explaining your reaction to the experience.

Writing Topics: Analyzing a Process

Before you begin to write, you might want to review the writing process in Part I.

1. Think of something in life that you want as much as the immigrants in Robles's essay want to come to the United States. Then explain your plan for achieving this goal or accomplishing this mission you have set for yourself.

2. What causes the most stress at this point in your life? Why is it stressful? How are you coping with it?

COMPARING AND CONTRASTING

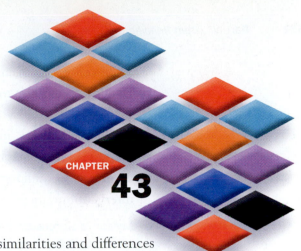

Comparing and contrasting involve finding similarities and differences between two or more items. The essays in this chapter demonstrate this type of thinking. The first example, "My Son, the Cross-Dresser," written by Lisen Stromberg compares her son, a 3-year-old "cross-dresser," with a neighborhood tomboy in order to question our stereotyping of young children. Then, in "The Ugly Truth About Beauty," Dave Barry humorously compares and contrasts the "beauty regimens" that men and women go through before they face the public.

Lisen Stromberg
MY SON, THE CROSS-DRESSER

Focusing Your Attention

1. Describe what you were like as a child. If you are a male, did you play baseball and collect bugs? If you are a female, did you wear dresses and play with dolls? Or did you do what you wanted and dress as you liked, regardless of your gender? Explain your answer.

2. The essay you are about to read talks about the criticism a young boy receives when he prefers dress-up and ballet to "boy activities." If you had a son who wanted to play dress-up or host tea parties as a child, would you try to discourage his behavior? If you had a daughter who wanted to play baseball and collect bugs, would you discourage her? Explain your answers.

Expanding Your Vocabulary

The following words are important to your understanding of this essay.

prances: dances around (paragraph 1)
repression: restrictions (paragraph 11)

adolescence: the teenage years (paragraph 11)

Ritalin: medication to treat hyperactivity in children (paragraph 12)

rambunctious: noisy, rowdy (paragraph 12)

docile: tame, meek, mild (paragraph 12)

reels: spins (paragraph 12)

taunting: scornful reproaches, sarcastic remarks (paragraph 13)

intervention: interference (paragraph 14)

1   My son is a cross-dresser. Most mornings he gets up, puts on a hand-me-down dress stolen from his sister, wraps an old white pillowcase around his head with a ribbon (his "long blond hair") and prances around singing, "The hills are alive with the sound of music." My son is 3-and-a-half years old.

2   At the toy store, he does not want Batman. "I want a Batgirl doll," he cries. When he begs to play with his friend Margo, it is not because he likes her better than his best friends Billy and Andrew; she just has more to offer—like an extensive collection of Barbie dolls and a whole wardrobe of little clothes he can dress them in.

3   He loves preschool—partly for the teachers, somewhat for the other children, but mostly for its wonderful selection of tutus, fancy party shoes, and pretend jewelry. His grandmother (my mother) received the shock of her life when she went to pick him up one day and he was wearing a blue tutu with beaded gold slippers. The other mothers laugh and tell me he is such a thespian. The teacher tells my husband and me that he is "highly in touch with his feminine side."

4   If we only had to worry about preschool, life would be fine—but his grandparents (on both sides), his aunts and uncles, his baby sitter and just about everybody else are up in arms. "Boys should be playing baseball, not Barbie," my mother-in-law exclaims. "I was so embarrassed," complains my mother after the harrowing tutu incident. "He keeps taking my daughter's Cinderella slippers!" my neighbor told my other neighbor who told me. The older siblings of his friends have called him an oddball, a weirdo and generally not normal. Adults tend to be more subtle with questions like: "So when do you think he will grow out of it?" or "How does your husband feel about it?"

5   I have tried to explain to each of them that my son approaches life with a unique flair. While he loves soccer, he often plays it wearing a silk cape that flutters in the wind when he runs. Playing with his cars takes on new dimensions when he acts out both the "damsel in distress" *and* the "sheriff to the rescue" role, alternating hats to represent each character. My husband can't wait for Little League to start because he sees a little slugger in our son

who can already hit the ball out of our relatively large backyard. Our son also can't wait to play baseball, but for a different reason: He says that cleats "are just like tap shoes."

Thankfully his preschool teacher has assured us that he is simply "evolved." "I wish all of my children were as well-balanced as your little boy," she told us at our first parent-teacher conference. "I love the way he plays cowboys and Indians wearing his favorite ballet slippers." She credits our "nonjudgmental and accepting parenting" for his creative expression. Frankly, I was a little relieved. So he is not a weirdo—he is "evolved." I wish I could take credit for this, but it is all of his own creation.   6

Interestingly, no one seems the least bit disturbed about our friend (I will call her Gillian). At 5-and-a-half years old, she refuses to wear dresses, plays T-ball and soccer and is proving quite skilled at climbing trees. She has more cuts and bruises as a result of roughhousing with her older brothers than my husband claims he ever received playing varsity college football. Gillian, I am told, is a tomboy. "Isn't she cute," a friend exclaimed to me when we were at Gillian's house for a Sunday barbecue. (My son was inside watching *Pocahontas* with two girls.) And my son is not cute when he dresses up and reenacts the glass slipper scene from *Cinderella*?   7

If Gillian is a tomboy because she likes to do boylike things, what then is my son who likes to do girl-like things—a janegirl? As far as I can tell there is no equivalent in the English language (at least there is not one in my Webster's dictionary). More important, there is no acceptable behavioral equivalent.   8

I have begun to ask myself what is normal? My son loves trucks, cars and trains. He plays for hours with his Brio train set while wearing his sister's striped dress. He is very affectionate and will frequently tell his friends he loves them with a hug. Last fall, during those terrible twos, he was accused of being a bully because he bit a girl at the playground. How can a child go from bully to sissy in a mere nine months?   9

I am coming to realize that while our sex-role stereotypes have expanded for girls, they have not for boys; there seems to be no acceptable cross-gender equivalent. A gay friend of mine claims all of the uproar is a homophobic response to my son's actions. "I remember loving to dress up and put on makeup, too," my friend tells me with a knowing glance. He is only 3-and-a-half years old, I remind my friend—a little early to be defining his sexual preferences.   10

The feminist revolution appears to have successfully helped foster an environment that makes it "cool" to be a girl. Much research is being done to ensure that girls are encouraged to excel in math and science, overcome the repression of adolescence and, with luck, one day be more than tokens on boards of directors across the land. I am thrilled. Trust me; I have a   11

1-year-old daughter. I want her to understand and respect her power, her opportunity, her femaleness. But what about my son? I would like him to be able to respect his power, his opportunity and his maleness even as he explores his feminine side.

12   It's not just in my house that the days of "boys will be boys" are over. A few months ago, the *Wall Street Journal* ran an article that claimed prescriptions for Ritalin were at an all-time high and increasingly, boys are expected to be less rambunctious and more docile (that is, more girl-like). And a guest commentator on an NPR program about youth violence expressed concern that the rise in the births of boys would result in a coming "deluge of testosterone-laden young men" creating havoc in our society. My mind reels: Is the conclusion that a 3-and-a-half-year-old should be more like a boy but a 12-year-old should be more like a girl?

13   I have to admit, sometimes I am embarrassed by my son's behavior. His declaration to my father-in-law that he wants to be a ballet dancer when he grows up almost created a family feud. When the father of one of his preschool classmates unintentionally called him a girl (he was wearing the favorite blue tutu, mind you), I cringed just a little. And I am often confused about the messages I'm sending him. I don't mind if he wants to wear lipstick to a birthday party—"Mom, you wear lipstick when you dress up!" he reminds me—but how do I protect him from the inevitable taunting that will occur as he ages?

14   I come back to my original question: what is normal? Sadly, my husband and I are learning all too early that the constraints of normality are very narrow indeed. Happily, my son, who at the moment is pretending to be Belle from *Beauty and the Beast*, adorned with his favorite pearl necklace and earring ensemble I gave him for his birthday, does not yet know this. With luck and a little parental intervention, he won't for a very long time.

Thinking Critically About Content

1. What is Stromberg comparing and contrasting in this essay?
2. Why does Stromberg feel that people should call her son a "janegirl"?
3. Why do you think Stromberg is not concerned with her son's behavior when everyone around her is?

Thinking Critically About Purpose and Audience

4. Although this essay was originally published in a parenting magazine, do you think readers who aren't parents can appreciate it? Explain your answer.

5. Why do you think Stromberg wrote an essay telling readers about her son's "cross-dressing"?

6. What attitude do you believe Stromberg wants readers to have toward people who assign stereotypes to young children? In what ways does the essay help you come to this conclusion?

Thinking Critically About Sentences

7. What new idea does the topic sentence of paragraph 5 introduce? How does the first sentence in paragraph 5 help Stromberg develop this comparison-and-contrast essay?

8. Describe in one sentence the writer's point of view toward stereotypes.

9. Write one or more complete sentences about the writer's son from the point of view of the writer's mother-in-law.

Dave Barry

THE UGLY TRUTH ABOUT BEAUTY

Focusing Your Attention

1. How much time do you spend getting ready in the morning? What is your daily routine?

2. The essay you are about to read compares males' and females' focus on their appearance. The media often feature actors and actresses who are too thin to be healthy. How much do you believe Hollywood is responsible for causing eating disorders in teenagers? Explain your answer.

Expanding Your Vocabulary

The following words are important to your understanding of this essay.

stud muffins: cute guys (paragraph 4)

regimen: routine (paragraph 5)

dispensed: distributed (paragraph 8)

genetic mutation: creature resulting from an unusual change in DNA (paragraph 8)

demeaning: degrading, insulting (paragraph 9)

bolster: boost, increase (paragraph 9)

1   If you're a man, at some point a woman will ask you how she looks.

2   "How do I look?" she'll ask.

3   You must be careful how you answer this question. The best technique is to form an honest yet sensitive opinion, then collapse on the floor with some kind of fatal seizure. Trust me, this is the easiest way out. Because you will never come up with the right answer.

4   The problem is that women generally do not think of their looks in the same way that men do. Most men form an opinion of how they look in seventh grade, and they stick to it for the rest of their lives. Some men form the opinion that they are irresistible stud muffins, and they do not change this opinion even when their faces sag and their noses bloat to the size of eggplants and their eyebrows grow together to form what appears to be a giant forehead-dwelling tropical caterpillar.

5   Most men, I believe, think of themselves as average-looking. Men will think this even if their faces cause heart failure in cattle at a range of 300 yards. Being average does not bother them; average is fine, for men. This is why men never ask anybody how they look. Their primary form of beauty care is to shave themselves, which is essentially the same form of beauty care that they give to their lawns. If, at the end of his four-minute daily beauty regimen, a man has managed to wipe most of the shaving cream out of his hair and is not bleeding too badly, he feels that he has done all he can, so he stops thinking about his appearance and devotes his mind to more critical issues, such as the Super Bowl.

6   Women do not look at themselves this way. If I had to express, in three words, what I believe most women think about their appearance, those words would be "not good enough." No matter how attractive a woman may appear to be to others, when she looks at herself in the mirror, she thinks: woof. She thinks that at any moment a municipal animal-control officer is going to throw a net over her and haul her off to the shelter.

7   Why do women have such low self-esteem? There are many complex psychological and societal reasons, by which I mean Barbie. Girls grow up playing with a doll proportioned such that, if it were a human, it would be seven feet tall and weigh 81 pounds, of which 53 pounds would be bosoms. This is a difficult appearance standard to live up to, especially when you contrast it with the standard set for little boys by their dolls . . . excuse me, by their action figures. Most of the action figures that my son played with when he was little were hideous-looking. For example, he was very fond of an action figure (part of the He-Man series) called "Buzz-Off," who was part human, part flying insect. Buzz-Off was not a looker. But he was extremely self-confident. You could not imagine Buzz-Off saying to the other action figures, "Do you think these wings make my hips look big?"

But women grow up thinking they need to look like Barbie, which for   8
most women is impossible, although there is a multibillion-dollar beauty industry devoted to convincing women that they must try. I once saw an
Oprah show wherein supermodel Cindy Crawford dispensed makeup tips
to the studio audience. Cindy had all these middle-aged women applying
beauty products to their faces; she stressed how important it was to apply
them in a certain way, using the tips of their fingers. All the women dutifully
did this, even though it was obvious to any sane observer that, no matter
how carefully they applied these products, they would never look remotely
like Cindy Crawford, who is some kind of genetic mutation.

I'm not saying that men are superior. I'm just saying that you're not   9
going to get a group of middle-aged men to sit in a room and apply cos-
metics to themselves under the instruction of Brad Pitt, in hopes of looking
more like him. Men would realize that this task was pointless and demeaning. They would find some way to bolster their self-esteem that did not require looking like Brad Pitt. They would say to Brad, "Oh *yeah?* Well what
do you know about *lawn care,* pretty boy?"

Of course, many women will argue that the reason they become   10
obsessed with trying to look like Cindy Crawford is that men, being as shallow as a drop of spit, *want* women to look that way, to which I have two
responses:

    1. Hey, just because we're idiots, that does not mean *you* have to be; and
    2. Men don't even notice 97 percent of the beauty efforts you make any-
way. Take fingernails. The average woman spends 5,000 hours per year
worrying about her fingernails; I have never once, in more than 40 years of
listening to men talk about women, heard a man say, "She has a nice set of
fingernails!" Many men would not notice if a woman had upward of four
hands.

Anyway, to get back to my original point: If you're a man and a woman   11
asks you how she looks, you're in big trouble. Obviously, you can't say she
looks bad. But you also can't say that she looks great, because she'll think
you're lying, because she has spent countless hours, with the help of the
multibillion-dollar beauty industry, obsessing about the differences between herself and Cindy Crawford. Also, she suspects that you're not qual-
ified to judge anybody's appearance. This is because you have shaving
cream in your hair.

Thinking Critically About Content

1. What are three comparisons or contrasts that Barry makes between
   men and women?

2. Why does Barry believe that "if you're a man and a woman asks you how she looks, you're in big trouble" (paragraph 11)?

3. Why do you think men care so little about their appearance?

Thinking Critically About Purpose and Audience

4. Why do you think Barry writes an essay comparing and contrasting men's and women's beauty regimens?

5. What type of audience do you think Barry had in mind when he wrote this essay? Explain your answer.

6. Why do you think Barry included in paragraph 10 his two responses to the issue that men want women to look like Cindy Crawford? What do you think he is trying to tell women in these responses?

Thinking Critically About Sentences

7. Look at the quotations in paragraphs 2, 6, and 7. How do these quotations help you understand what Barry is trying to say in this essay?

8. Describe in a complete sentence the writer's point of view.

9. Write one or more complete sentences that explain your opinion of some other problems men and women face today.

Writing Topics: Comparing and Contrasting

Before you begin to write, you might want to review the writing process in Part I.

1. In the first essay, Stromberg talks about the differences she sees in the upbringing of boys and girls in American society. Compare and contrast your upbringing with someone else's. What are the main differences between the two of you? What are the main similarities?

2. Expand on your ideas about other problems men and women face today (in response to question 9 after the Dave Barry essay).

DIVIDING AND CLASSIFYING

CHAPTER
44

Division refers to dividing a single category into many categories, whereas **classification** moves from many categories to one. They are mirror images of each other. The essays in this chapter demonstrate both division and classification. "Dads," the first essay in this chapter, divides today's fathers into categories that author Annie Murphy Paul feels represent the family today. In the second essay, titled "Why Do We Resist Learning?" John Roger and Peter McWilliams divide and classify students according to personality types that might resist learning in school.

Annie Murphy Paul
DADS

Focusing Your Attention

1. Describe your relationship with your father when you were a child. What aspects of your father's personality do you like the most? What traits do you wish you could change? Why?

2. The essay you are about to read discusses the common traits of the modern father. Before you read this essay, try to define for yourself what characterizes the perfect father. Do you think this perfect father exists? Explain your answer.

Expanding Your Vocabulary

The following words are important to your understanding of this essay.

gamut: range (paragraph 2)
unambiguous: clear, certain (paragraph 9)

Brothers Grimm: Jacob Ludwig Carl Grimm (1785–1863) and Wilhelm Carl Grimm (1786–1859), authors of *Grimm's Fairy Tales* (paragraph 14)

gleaned: collected, recovered (paragraph 18)

1   Once we all knew what a dad was: he was the guy who married mom, who gave you your eyes or your smile or your sense of humor, who made you eat your spinach and do your homework, who was always around somewhere, puttering in the basement or grilling burgers out back.

2   Not anymore. Today's fathers run the gamut, from sperm-bank donors to superdads—and there are a lot of men in the middle, trying to puzzle out the meaning of modern fatherhood. They're getting some help from psychologists, biologists and sociologists, whose research has something to tell us all about the ties that bind father to child. Here is a family portrait of today's fathers.

The Distant Dad

3   Throughout the 1980s, the deadbeat dad vied with the welfare queen and the tax-and-spend liberal for the prize of public enemy number one. Now his numbers are on the wane, thanks to stronger child-support enforcement efforts—and we're left with what may be a bigger problem. How do we ensure that these "nonresidential fathers" (the new, more neutral term) contribute time and care as well as money to their kids?

4   One of the keys lies in what would seem an unlikely place: the women these men have left or been left by. Even in intact families, research shows, mothers act as gatekeepers, supervising access to children. Their authority is further increased when they have primary custody of children, as is still the case in 87% of divorces. A friendly or at least civil relationship between ex-spouses can keep those gates from clanging shut. "Former partners don't have to be intimate or close," declares Constance Ahrons, Ph.D., a sociologist at the University of Southern California. "They just need to be mature enough to separate out marital issues from parenting issues and put the parenting issues on the front burner."

5   Some state and local governments are trying to make that effort easier, by requiring all divorcing couples with children to draw up a "parenting plan." "It's partly the outcome of the plan that's valuable, the set of decisions that are made about the children and how they will be cared for," says Ross Thompson, Ph.D., psychology professor at the University of Nebraska. "But just as important is the process. In the midst of negotiations to go their separate ways, the couple has to make plans for how they are going to continue to maintain contact."

The Disney Dad

Divorced fathers who do stay involved tend to "think that if they fill vis-   6
its with fun activities, the child will look forward to seeing him," says
Thompson. "But the fact is, those kinds of activities can be stressful. They're
nice on special occasions, but they're not the basis of an ongoing relationship." Psychologists blame the Disney Dad syndrome on the visitation system itself, with its rigid and unnatural limits on the noncustodial parent's
role. "Why should we be surprised when time passes and fewer and fewer
fathers maintain contact?" asks Thompson.

What's needed is an improved system of shared custody. One new   7
arrangement, now being experimented with by several states, grants responsibility for major decisions—where children go to school, what kind of
medical treatment they receive—to both parents, even if the child lives with
only one. "If parenting is about anything, it's about deep involvement and
intimate contact, being knit into the everyday experience of a child's life,"
Thompson says. "And how can you do that if you're only visiting?"

The Serial Dad

The serial dad is of the love-the-one-you're-with school: he has children   8
with one woman, then moves on to another and yet another, investing his
time and money in the family of the moment.

These men may never have come to see themselves as fathers in any   9
meaningful way, say sociologists. When fathers feel certain in their abilities
as parents, when their place in their children's lives is clear and unambiguous, and when they feel satisfied with their interactions with their
children, they are likely to stay involved with their offspring, according to
Randy Leite, program coordinator of human development and family
science at Ohio State University.

Some social scientists believe such confidence can be instilled by ac-   10
tively teaching parenting skills. Across the country, fathering programs like
"It's My Child, Too" at Purdue University and "Making Room for Daddies" at
the Center for Men in Cambridge, Massachusetts, are teaching men, especially those who are young and unmarried, how to be a father in full.

The Single Dad

Single fathers were once an amusing oddity: usually widowers, they were   11
portrayed in popular culture as hopelessly inept with diapers and blushingly
awkward with talks about the birds and the bees. But times have changed.
According to a report by the Census Bureau, the number of single fathers
jumped 25% in three years, from 1.7 million in 1995 to 2.1 million [in 1998].

12   Moreover, many of these men are taking on the role for new reasons: not because their wives have died but because judges have awarded them custody. That change reflects a larger one: Men are increasingly considered capable and effective single parents. "It appears that fathers raising children on their own are doing a better job than they were several decades ago," observes Doug Downey, Ph.D., a sociologist at Ohio State University. In fact, the care they provide is almost indistinguishable in its effect from that given by single mothers, as a recent study by Downey demonstrates: on measures of self-esteem, behavior and performance in school, relationships with others, and well-being later in life, children raised by single mothers and single fathers fared virtually the same.

13   There's a lesson here for fathers in intact familes: they only act like "Dad" because there's a "Mom" to play off of. "Faced with similar structural demands and without another adult with whom to 'do gender,'" notes Downey, "women and men in single-parent households act in less sex-stereotyped ways than their counterparts in mother–father households."

The Stepdad

14   Stepparents of both sexes are an increasingly familiar part of family life: more than 33% of U.S. children are expected to live in a stepfamily by age 18. While cultural fables abound about stepmothers, there are few featuring their male counterparts—but the social science research on them is straight out of the Brothers Grimm.

15   Stepfathers, it turns out, invest fewer resources in their charges, are less involved in their lives, and know less about their thoughts and opinions than biological fathers. Men find it more difficult to raise stepchildren than biological children and become less satisfied with stepfathering once they have had children of their own. Grimmest of all, the work of Martin Daly, Ph.D., and Margo Wilson, Ph.D., both psychology professors at McMaster University in Ontario, indicates that men are much more likely—on the order of 100 times—to abuse and even kill their stepchildren than their genetic offspring.

16   Blame nature for this bleak reality, the researchers say: such behavior is in an evolutionary sense "adaptive." A father looks after the well-being of his child, the theory goes, to ensure that his own genes will be reproduced in turn. A man has no such genetic investment in his stepchildren, who may even take resources from his own children or time from his partner, their mother.

17   Despite the harsh implications of such theories, Daly insists that looked at from another angle, they offer an impressive demonstration of the strength of the father–child bond. "Parental love is the most selfless love we know. You give and give to your kid and get nothing back and you're glad to do it," he says. "It would be very strange if people acted that way toward

just any old baby." The fact that the great majority of stepfathers are kind and loving toward their stepchildren is a testament to a bond of another sort: affection, freely chosen and generously given.

If there's any insight to be gleaned from this gathering of modern father   18 figures, perhaps it's just that: what makes a father may be genetic material, or a monthly check, or a legal document, but what makes a dad is love.

Thinking Critically About Content

1. What types does Paul divide "dads" into? What are the characteristics of each type?

2. What types of dads do you think Paul believes are the best? What types do you think she considers the worst? Explain your answer.

3. Do you agree with Paul's final statement that "what makes a father may be genetic material, or a monthly check, or a legal document, but what makes a dad is love" (paragraph 18)? Explain your answer.

Thinking Critically About Purpose and Audience

4. What do you think Paul's purpose is in this essay?

5. Who do you think is Paul's main audience for this essay? Explain your answer.

6. What do these categories of dads say about the problems facing fathers today? Explain your answer.

Thinking Critically About Sentences

7. Find two sentences that contain statistics. How do these sentences help you understand the problems those types of dads face?

8. Find a topic sentence that you think works well in its paragraph, and explain how the other sentences in that paragraph support this topic sentence.

9. Add another category to Paul's list. Why do you think this should be added? Explain your answer in one or more complete sentences.

John Roger and Peter McWilliams
WHY DO WE RESIST LEARNING?

Focusing Your Attention

1. How do you think your group of friends in high school was viewed by other people? If someone secretly watched you from a distance, how would your group of friends be described?

2. The essay you are about to read discusses various reactions to the process of learning. How important is learning in your life? What energy do you put into learning?

Expanding Your Vocabulary

The following words are important to your understanding of this essay.

tirade: outburst (paragraph 7)

Catch-22: no-win situation (paragraph 13)

reverse psychology: tricking someone into doing something by telling them to do the opposite (paragraph 17)

insinuating: trying to be accepted (paragraph 23)

homecoming floats: elaborately decorated vehicles used in parades during certain high school and college celebrations (paragraph 24)

1   If we're here to learn and if we have this seemingly in-built desire to learn (curiosity), why do we resist learning so much? The classic example is the argument that goes, "Listen to me!" "No, you listen to me!" "No, you listen to me!" Et cetera.

2   It seems that somewhere around the age of eighteen (give or take ten years), something in us decides, "That's it, I've had it, I'm done. I know all I need to know, and I'm not learning any more."

3   Why?

4   Let's return to the idea of the small child being taught about life by its parents. Parents are as gods to little children—the source of food, protection, comfort, love.

5   Also, parents are BIG! They're four to five times bigger than children. Imagine how much respect (awe? fear?) you'd have for someone twenty to thirty feet tall, weighing 800 to 1,000 pounds.

6   Let's imagine a child—two, three—playing in a room. The parents are reading, the child is playing, all is well. After an hour or so, CRASH! The child bumps a table and knocks over a lamp.

7   Where there once was almost no interaction with the parents, suddenly there is a lot—almost all of it negative. "How many times have we told you. . . ." "Can't you do anything right?" "What's the matter with you?" "That was my favorite lamp!" Shame, bad, nasty, no good, and so on. This verbal tirade might or might not be reinforced by physical punishment.

8   What does the child remember from an evening at home with the folks? Does the child remember the hours spent successfully (i.e., no broken anything) playing while mommy and daddy read, or does the child remember

the intense ten minutes of "bad boy," "nasty girl," "shame, shame, shame," after the fall?

The negative, of course. It was loud, and it was frightening (imagine a 9 pair of twenty- to thirty-foot, 1,000-pound gods yelling at you). It was, for the most part, the *only* interaction the child may have had with "the gods" all evening (especially if being put to bed early is part of the punishment).

When a child's primary memory of the communication from its parents 10 ("the gods") is no, don't, stop that, shouldn't, mustn't, shame, bad, bad, bad, what is the child being taught about itself? That it can do no good; that it must be alert for failure at every moment, and still it will fail; that it is a disappointment, a letdown, a failure.

In short, a child begins to believe that he or she is fundamentally not 11 good enough, destined for failure, and in the way. In a word, unworthy.

And there is very little in the traditional educational system to counter- 12 act this mistaken belief. If anything, school etches the image even deeper. (If we learned all we needed to know in kindergarten, it was promptly drummed out of us in first grade.) You are taught you must perform, keep up, and "make the grade," or you aren't worth much. If you *do* work hard at making the grades, some authority figure is bound to ask, "Why are you studying all the time? Why aren't you out playing with the other children? What's wrong with you? Don't you have any friends?"

Catch-22 never had it so good. 13

Naturally, we can't go around feeling unworthy all the time. It hurts too 14 much. So we invent defenses—behaviors that give the illusion of safety. Soon we notice that others have not only adopted similar defenses, but have taken their defenses to new and exotic levels. The school of limitation is in session.

We begin hanging out with other members of the same club. We are no 15 longer alone. In fact, we start to feel worthy. We have comrades, companions, cohorts, compatriots, confidants, confreres, counterparts, and chums.

The clubs? There are basically four main chapters of the Let's Hide 16 Away from All the Hurtful Unworthiness Clubs International.

The Rebels

The rebels like to think of themselves as "independent." They have, in 17 fact, merely adopted a knee-jerk reaction to whatever "law" is set before them. They are prime candidates for reverse psychology. ("The best way to keep children from putting beans in their ears is to tell them they *must* put beans in their ears.") They conform to nonconformity.

MOST FEARED FORTUNE COOKIE: "A youth should be respectful to his elders."

SLOGAN: "Authority, you tell us that we're no good. Well, authority, you're no good."

MOTTO (minus the first two words): ". . . and the horse you came in on!"

18   If the ones who tell you you're no good are no good, then, somehow, that makes you good. Somehow.

The Unconscious

19   These are the people who appear not all there because, for the most part, they're not all there. They're not dumb; they're just someplace else: a desert island, a rock concert, an ice cream parlor. They are masters of imagination. They are not stupid. They do their best, however, to *appear* dumb, drugged, or asleep to anyone they don't want to deal with. They want, simply, to be left alone by all authority figures.

FAVORITE FORTUNE COOKIE: "To know that you do not know is the best."

SLOGAN: "You can't expect much from me, so you can't criticize me because, uh, um, what was I saying?"

MOTTO: "Huh?"

20   The real world picks them apart, so they retreat to a fantasy world of which they can be a part.

The Comfort Junkies

21   These are the ones who hide in comfort. All that is (or might be) uncomfortable is avoided (unless avoiding it would be more uncomfortable), and all that might bring comfort (food, distractions, TV, portable tape players, drink, drugs) is sought after (unless the seeking after them would be uncomfortable).

MOST FEARED FORTUNE COOKIE: "The scholar who cherishes the love of comfort is not fit to be deemed a scholar."

SLOGAN: "Comfort at any cost! (Unless it's too expensive.)"

MOTTO (taken from Tolkien): "In a hole in the ground there lived a hobbit. Not a nasty, dirty, wet hole, filled with the ends of worms and an oozy smell, nor yet a dry, bare, sandy hole with nothing in it to sit down on or to eat: it was a hobbit-hole, and that means comfort."

22   They memorize as much of their motto as is comfortable.

The Approval Seekers

The best way to prove worthiness is to have lots of people telling you 23
how wonderful you are. These people work so hard for other people's approval (preferably) and acceptance (at the very least), they have little or no
time to seek their own. But their own doesn't matter. They, after all, are unworthy, and what's the worth of an unworthy person's opinion? These people take the opposite tack of the rebels: rebels deem the opinions of others
unworthy; acceptance seekers deem others' opinions *too* worthy. They
would run for class president, but they're afraid of a backlash, so they usually win treasurer by a landslide.

> MOST FEARED FORTUNE COOKIE: "Fine words and an insinuating
> appearance are seldom associated with true virtue."
>
> SLOGAN: "What can I do for you today?"
>
> MOTTO: "Nice sweater!"

Without such people, homecoming floats would never get built. 24

You've probably been able to place all your friends in their respective 25
clubhouses. If you're having trouble placing yourself, you might ask a few
friends. If their opinions tend to agree, you'll have your answer. You may
not like it, but you'll have your answer.

(NOTE: If you reject the idea that you could possibly fit into any category, 26
you're probably a rebel. If you accept your friend's evaluations too readily,
you may be looking for approval. If you forget to ask, maybe you're unconscious. If you're afraid to ask, you may be seeking comfort. If a friend says,
"You don't fit in any of these; you seem to transcend them all," that person
is probably looking for *your* approval.)

Most of us tend to pay some dues to each club at one time or another, 27
about one thing or another. We may, for example, be rebels when it comes
to speed limits, unconscious when it comes to income tax, comfort-junkies
when it comes to our favorite bad habit, and acceptance-seekers in intimate relationships.

These are also the four major ways people avoid learning. The rebels 28
don't need to learn; the unconscious don't remember why they should; the
comfortable find it too risky; and the acceptance-seekers don't want to rock
any boats. ("Leave well enough alone.") Most of us have our own personal
combination of the four—a little of this and a little of that—that have perhaps kept us from learning all we'd like to know.

Thinking Critically About Content

1. What are Roger and McWilliams dividing and classifying in this
   essay?

2. How do the fortune cookies, slogans, and mottoes help you understand the categories in this essay?

3. What do Roger and McWilliams say have "kept us from learning all we'd like to know" (paragraph 28)?

Thinking Critically About Purpose and Audience

4. What do you think Roger and McWilliams's purpose was in writing this essay?

5. What readers would find this essay most interesting? Who else would enjoy reading this essay? Explain your answer.

6. Why do you think Roger and McWilliams ask you to determine which group you fall into? In what way might this exercise benefit you?

Thinking Critically About Sentences

7. How do the four headings help you move through the essay?

8. Explain paragraph 12 in your own words. Does the first sentence state the main idea of the paragraph?

9. Identify which category in the essay describes your learning style. Explain your answer in one or more complete sentences.

Writing Topics: Dividing and Classifying

Before you begin to write, you might want to review the writing process in Part I.

1. In the first essay, Paul divides and classifies the behavior of contemporary dads. Using her essay as a reference, explain what category your dad fits into and why he fits there.

2. Using Roger and McWilliams's essay, place your personality in one of their categories, and explain your reasoning.

DEFINING

Definition explains a word, phrase, or idea so that the readers can understand clearly what it is. The essays in this chapter take several different approaches to definition. In the first essay, "The Perfect Trap," Monica Ramirez Basco defines "perfection" and examines its side effects. In the second essay, "Black and Latino," Roberto Santiago defines his ethnic identity as he discovers it through the eyes of others.

Monica Ramirez Basco

THE PERFECT TRAP

Focusing Your Attention

1. If you could design a perfect person, what physical, mental, and emotional qualities would this person have?

2. The essay you are about to read explains what it means to be a perfectionist: Their schoolwork must be perfect, their appearance must be flawless, and their job performance must be exemplary. What do you think drives them to these goals?

Expanding Your Vocabulary

The following words are important to your understanding of this essay.

agonizing: worrying (paragraph 2)

humiliation: embarrassment, shame (paragraph 3)

procrastination: postponing activities to avoid doing them (paragraph 6)

anorexia nervosa: an abnormal fear of gaining weight (paragraph 12)

bulimia: binge eating followed by vomiting to avoid gaining weight (paragraph 12)

relapse: return of the problem behavior (paragraph 12)

intolerant: unaccepting (paragraph 13)

flaunting: calling attention to (paragraph 13)

genetically: from birth (paragraph 14)

in flux: in a state of change (paragraph 17)

mundane: ordinary, unexciting (paragraph 19)

subordinates: employees (paragraph 19)

plagued: troubled (paragraph 23)

overanxious: very nervous (paragraph 23)

tyranny: oppression, cruelty (paragraph 24)

schemas: patterns (paragraph 25)

catastrophic: disastrous (paragraph 26)

existential: relating to one's experience (paragraph 29)

absolute: perfect, ideal (paragraph 30)

hypotheses: assumptions (paragraph 32)

1   Susan, an interior designer, had been working frantically for the last month trying to get her end-of-the-year books in order, keep the business running, and plan a New Year's Eve party for her friends and her clients. Susan's home is an advertisement of her talent as a designer, so she wanted to make some changes to the formal dining room before the party that would be particularly impressive. It all came together in time for the party and the evening seemed to be going well, until her assistant, Charles, asked her if Mrs. Beale, who owned a small antique shop and had referred Susan a lot of business, and Mr. Sandoval, a member of the local Chamber of Commerce and a supporter of Susan's, had arrived.

2   Susan felt like her head was about to explode when she realized that she had forgotten to invite them to the party. "Oh, no," she moaned. "How could I be so stupid? What am I going to do? They'll no doubt hear about it from someone and assume I omitted them on purpose. I may as well kiss the business good-bye." Though Charles suggested she might be overreacting a little, Susan spent the rest of the night agonizing over her mistake.

3   Susan is an inwardly focused perfectionist. Although it can help her in her work, it also hurts her when she is hard on herself and finds error completely unacceptable. Like many people, she worries about what others will think of her and her business. However, in Susan's case her errors lead to humiliation, distress, sleepless nights, and withdrawal from others. She has trouble letting go and forgiving herself because, in her mind, it is OK for others to make mistakes, but it is not OK for her to make mistakes.

Tom, on the other hand, is an outwardly focused perfectionist. He feels 4
OK about himself, but he is often disappointed in and frustrated with others
who seem to always let him down. Quality control is his line of work, but he
cannot always turn it off when he leaves the office.

Tom drove into his garage to find that there was still a mess on the work- 5
bench and floor that his son Tommy had left two days ago. Tom walked
through the door and said to his wife in an annoyed tone of voice, "I told
Tommy to clean up his mess in the garage before I got home." His wife
defended their son, saying, "He just got home himself a few minutes ago."
"Where is he now?" Tom demanded. "He better not be on the phone." Sure
enough, though, Tommy was on the phone, and Tom felt himself tensing up
and ordering, "Get off the phone, and go clean up that mess in the garage
like I told you." "Yes, sir," said Tommy, knowing that a lecture was coming.

For Tom, it seems like every day there is something new to complain 6
about. Tommy doesn't listen, his wife doesn't take care of things on time,
and there is always an excuse. And even when they do their parts, it usually isn't good enough, and they don't seem to care. It is so frustrating for
Tom sometimes that he does the job himself rather than ask for help, just so
he doesn't have to deal with their procrastination and excuses.

Tom's type of perfectionism causes him problems in his relationships 7
with others because he is frequently frustrated by their failure to meet his
expectations. When he tries to point this out in a gentle way, it still seems to
lead to tension and sometimes to conflict. He has tried to train himself to
expect nothing from others, but that strategy doesn't seem to work either.

The Personal Pain of Perfectionists

The reach for perfection can be painful because it is often driven by 8
both a desire to do well and a fear of the consequences of not doing well.
This is the double-edged sword of perfectionism.

It is a good thing to give the best effort, to go the extra mile, and to take 9
pride in one's performance, whether it is keeping a home looking nice, writing a report, repairing a car, or doing brain surgery. But when despite great
efforts you feel as though you keep falling short, never seem to get things
just right, never have enough time to do your best, are self-conscious, feel
criticized by others, or cannot get others to cooperate in doing the job right
the first time, you end up feeling bad.

The problem is not in having high standards or in working hard. 10
Perfectionism becomes a problem when it causes emotional wear and tear
or when it keeps you from succeeding or from being happy. The emotional
consequences of perfectionism include fear of making mistakes, stress
from the pressure to perform, and self-consciousness from feeling both

self-confidence and self-doubt. It can also include tension, frustration, disappointment, sadness, anger, or fear of humiliation. These are common experiences for inwardly focused perfectionists.

11   The emotional stress caused by the pursuit of perfection and the failure to achieve this goal can evolve into more severe psychological difficulties. Perfectionists are more vulnerable to depression when stressful events occur, particularly those that leave them feeling as though they are not good enough. In many ways, perfectionistic beliefs set a person up to be disappointed, given that achieving perfection consistently is impossible. What's more, perfectionists who have a family history of depression and may therefore be more biologically vulnerable to developing the psychological and physical symptoms of major depression may be particularly sensitive to events that stimulate their self-doubt and their fear of rejection or humiliation.

12   The same seems to be true for eating disorders, such as anorexia nervosa and bulimia. Several recent studies have found that even after treatment, where weight was restored in malnourished and underweight women with anorexia, their perfectionistic beliefs persisted and likely contributed to relapse. Perfectionism also seems to be one of the strongest risk factors for developing an eating disorder.

13   Sometimes the pain of perfectionism is felt in relationships with others. Perfectionists can sometimes put distance between themselves and others unintentionally by being intolerant of others' mistakes or by flaunting perfect behavior or accomplishments in front of those who are aware of being merely average. Although they feel justified in their beliefs about what is right and what is wrong, they still suffer the pain of loneliness. Research suggests that people who have more outwardly focused perfectionism are less likely than inwardly focused perfectionists to suffer from depression or anxiety when they are stressed. However, interpersonal difficulties at home or on the job may be more common.

How Did I Get This Way?

14   There is considerable scientific evidence that many personality traits are inherited genetically. Some people are probably born more perfectionistic than others. I saw this in my own children. My oldest son could sit in his high chair, happily playing with a mound of spaghetti, his face covered with sauce. My second son did not like being covered in goo. Instead, he would wipe his face and hands with a napkin as soon as he was old enough to figure out how to do it. As he got a little older, he kept his room cleaner than his brother. When he learned to write he would erase and rewrite his homework until it was "perfect."

Parental influences can influence the direction or shape that perfec- 15
tionism takes. Many perfectionists, especially inwardly focused perfectionists, grew up with parents who either directly or indirectly communicated
that they were not good enough. These were often confusing messages,
where praise and criticism were given simultaneously. For example, "That
was nice, but I bet you could do better." "Wow, six A's and one B on your
report card! You need to bring that B up to an A next time." "Your choir performance was lovely, but that sound system is really poor. We could hardly
hear you."

Unfortunately, with the intention of continuing to motivate their children, 16
these parents kept holding out the emotional carrot: "Just get it right this
time, and I will approve of you." Some psychological theories suggest over
time the child's need to please her parents becomes internalized, so that
she no longer needs to please her parents; she now demands perfection
from herself.

Some perfectionists tell stories of chaotic childhoods where they never 17
seemed to have control over their lives. Marital breakups, relocations,
financial crises, illnesses, and other hardships created an environment of
instability. One of the ways in which these people got some sense of order
in their otherwise disordered lives was to try to fix things over which they
had some control, such as keeping their rooms neat and tidy, working
exceptionally hard on schoolwork, or attempting to control their younger
brothers and sisters. As adults, however, when their lives were no longer in
flux, they may have continued to work hard to maintain control.

Are You a Perfectionist?

Perfectionists share some common characteristics. They are usually 18
neat in their appearance and are well organized. They seem to push themselves harder than most other people do. They also seem to push others as
hard as they push themselves. On the outside, perfectionists usually appear to be very competent and confident individuals. They are often envied
by others because they seem to "have it all together." Sometimes they seem
perfect. On the inside they do not feel perfect, nor do they feel like they
always have control over their own lives.

Let's look at some of these characteristics more closely and how they 19
interfere with personal and professional life. Terry, 34, a divorced working
mother of two, is a high achiever with high career ambitions. But she can
sometimes get hung up on the details of her work. She is not good with
figures but does not trust her staff enough to use their figures without checking them herself. She gets frustrated with this mundane work and makes

mistakes herself and then becomes angry with her subordinates for doing poor work.

20   Perfectionists also tend to think there is a right way and wrong way to do things. When Joe, a retired Marine Corps drill sergeant, takes his boys fishing, they have a routine for preparation, for fishing, and for cleanup. It is time-efficient, neat, organized. The boys think the "fishing ritual" is over-done, and they resent having to comply.

21   Expecting people to do their best is one thing. Expecting perfection from others often means setting goals that can be impossible to achieve. Brent, 32 and single, has been looking for Ms. Right for 12 years but cannot seem to find her. He does not have a well-defined set of characteristics in mind. He just has a general impression of an angel, a sexual goddess, a confi-dent, independent, yet thoroughly devoted partner. Blond is preferable, but he's not that picky.

22   Perfectionists can have trouble making decisions. They are so worried about making the wrong one that they fail to reach any conclusion. If the person is lucky, someone else will make the decision for them, thereby as-suming responsibility for the outcome. More often the decision is made by default. A simple example is not being able to choose whether to file in-come tax forms on time or apply for an extension. If you wait long enough, the only real alternative is to file for an extension.

23   Along with indecision, perfectionists are sometimes plagued by great difficulty in taking risks, particularly if their personal reputations are on the line. Brent is in a type of job where creativity can be an asset. But coming up with new ideas rather than relying on the tried and true ways of busi-ness means making yourself vulnerable to the criticism of others. Brent fears looking like an idiot should an idea he advances fail. And on the occasions when he has gone out on a limb with a new concept, he has been overanxious. Brent's perfectionism illustrates several aspects of the way that many perfectionists think about themselves. There can be low self-confidence, fear of humiliation and rejection, and an inability to attribute success to their own efforts.

Breaking Free

24   To escape the tyranny of perfectionism, you need to understand and challenge the underlying beliefs that drive you to get things "just right."

25   Each of us has a set of central beliefs about ourselves, about other peo-ple and the world in general, and about the future. We use these beliefs or schemas to interpret the experiences in our life, and they strongly influence our emotional reactions. Schemas can also have influence on our choice of actions.

Under every perfectionist schema is a hidden fantasy that some really 26
good thing will come from being perfect. For example, "If I do it perfectly,
then . . . I will finally be accepted . . . I can finally stop worrying . . . I will
get what I have been working toward . . . I can finally relax." The flip side of
this schema, also subscribed to by perfectionists, is that "If I make a
mistake," there will be a catastrophic outcome ("I will be humiliated . . . I am
a failure . . . I am stupid . . . I am worthless").

Changing these schemas means taking notice of the experiences you 27
have that are inconsistent with, are contrary to, or otherwise do not fit with
them. June, who prides herself on being a "perfect" homemaker and
mother, believed with 90% certainty that "If I do it perfectly, I will be
rewarded." Yet she does a number of things perfectly that others do not
even notice. June would tell herself that there would be a reward from her
husband or her children for taking the extra time to iron their clothes perfectly. Her son did not even realize his shirts had been ironed. When
Mother's Day came, she got the usual candy and flowers. No special treats
or special recognition for her extra efforts.

When June begins to notice the inaccuracy of her schema, she begins to 28
reevaluate how she spends her time. She decides that if it makes her feel
good, then she will do it. If it is just extra work that no one will notice, then
she may skip it. She is certain that there are some things she does, such as
iron the bedsheets, which no one really cares about. As a matter of fact,
June herself doesn't really care if the sheets are ironed. However, she does
like the feel of a freshly ironed pillow cover, so she will continue that chore.
June has modified her schema. Now she believes, "If you want a reward,
find a quicker and more direct way to get it."

If your schema centers around more existential goals, like self- 29
acceptance, fulfillment, or inner peace, then you must employ a different
strategy. If you believe that getting things just right in your life will lead to
acceptance, then you must not be feeling accepted right now. What are the
things you would like to change about yourself? What could you do differently
that would make you feel better about who you are? If you can figure out what
is missing or needs changing, you can focus your energies in that direction.

Or you may be motivated to take a different, less absolute, point of view. 30
Instead of "I must have perfection before I can have peace of mind," consider "I need to give myself credit for what I do well, even if it is not perfect."
Take inventory of your accomplishments or assets. Perhaps you are with-
holding approval from yourself.

If your schema is that other people's opinions of you are a mirror of your 31
self-worth, you must ask yourself if you know when you have done something well, if you are able to tell the difference between a good performance

and a poor performance. If you are capable of evaluating yourself, you do not really need approval from others to feel like you are a valuable worker or a good romantic partner.

32   In general, you must treat your perfectionistic schemas as hypotheses rather than facts. Maybe you are right or maybe you are wrong. Perhaps they apply in some situations, but not in others (e.g., at work, but not at home), or with some people, such as your uptight boss, but not with others, such as your new boyfriend. Rather than stating your schema as a fact, restate it as a suggestion. Gather evidence from your experiences in the past, from your observations from others, or by talking to other people. Do things always happen in a way that your schemas would predict? If not, it is time to try on a new basic belief.

33   One of my patients described the process as taking out her old eight-track tape that played the old negative schemas about herself and replacing it with a new compact disc that played her updated self-view. This takes some practice, but it is well worth the effort.

Thinking Critically About Content

1. What are the two types of perfectionists?

2. How does Basco think some people become perfectionists? What are some of the characteristics of a perfectionist?

3. Based on Basco's definition of a perfectionist, how much of a perfectionist do you believe you are? Explain your answer.

Thinking Critically About Purpose and Audience

4. What do you think is Basco's purpose in writing this essay?

5. What audience do you think would best understand and benefit from reading this essay?

6. Why do you think Basco compares perfectionism to eating disorders? In what ways are the two related?

Thinking Critically About Sentences

7. Describe in a complete sentence the author's point of view toward perfectionism.

8. Find two sentences that give examples of perfectionism in the essay. In what ways do these examples help you understand the definition of "perfectionism"?

9. Write one or two complete sentences explaining whether or not you are a perfectionist.

Roberto Santiago

BLACK AND LATINO

Focusing Your Attention

1. Think of a family member you have always gone to for answers to difficult questions about life. Who is this person, and why did you choose this person?

2. The essay you are about to read focuses on various advantages and disadvantages connected with ethnic identity. How many cultures make up your heritage? Are you fully aware of your ethnic background? What do you wish you knew about your family history?

Expanding Your Vocabulary

The following words are important to your understanding of this essay.

perplexes: confuses (paragraph 1)

East Harlem: a neighborhood of Manhattan, New York (paragraph 2)

boricua: slang for Puerto Rican (paragraph 3)

moreno: black (paragraph 3)

parody: humorous imitation (paragraph 4)

Indio: Mexican Indian (paragraph 6)

predominant: main, most important (paragraph 6)

determinant: conclusive (paragraph 6)

Piri Thomas: 1928–   , Puerto Rican author (paragraph 6)

bridle path: a path for saddled horses (paragraph 7)

Central Park: the largest park in Manhattan (paragraph 7)

whiffle ball: a ball game similar to baseball (paragraph 7)

solace: comfort (paragraph 9)

pegged: identified (paragraph 11)

iconoclast: a person who challenges others' beliefs (paragraph 11)

"There is no way that you can be black and Puerto Rican at the same   1
time." What? Despite the many times I've heard this over the years, that
statement still perplexes me. I *am* both and always have been. My color is

a blend of my mother's rich, dark skin tone and my father's white complexion. As they were both Puerto Rican, I spoke Spanish before English, but I am totally bilingual. My life has been shaped by my black and Latino heritages, and despite other people's confusion, I don't feel I have to choose one or the other. To do so would be to deny a part of myself.

2   There has not been a moment in my life when I did not know that I looked black—and I never thought that others did not see it too. But growing up in East Harlem, I was also aware that I did not "act black," according to the African-American boys on the block.

3   My lighter-skinned Puerto Rican friends were less of a help in this department. "You're not black," they would whine, shaking their heads. "You're a *boricua*, you ain't no *moreno*." If that was true, why did my mirror defy the rules of logic? And most of all, why did I feel that there was some serious unknown force trying to make me choose sides?

4   *Acting black. Looking black. Being a real black.* This debate among us is almost a parody. The fact is that I am black, so why do I need to prove it?

5   The island of Puerto Rico is only a stone's throw away from Haiti, and, no fooling, if you climb a palm tree, you can see Jamaica bobbing on the Atlantic. The slave trade ran through the Caribbean basin, and virtually all Puerto Rican citizens have some African blood in their veins. My grandparents on my mother's side were the classic *negro como carbón* (black as carbon) people, but despite the fact that they were as dark as can be, they are officially not considered black.

6   There is an explanation for this, but not one that makes much sense, or difference, to a working-class kid from Harlem. Puerto Ricans identify themselves as Hispanics—part of a worldwide race that originated from eons of white Spanish conquests—a mixture of white, African, and *Indio* blood, which, categorically, is apart from black. In other words, the culture is the predominant and determinant factor. But there are frustrations in being caught in a duo-culture, where your skin color does not necessarily dictate what you are. When I read Piri Thomas's searing autobiography, *Down These Mean Streets*, in my early teens, I saw that he couldn't figure out other people's attitudes toward his blackness, either.

7   My first encounter with this attitude about the race thing rode on horseback. I had just turned six years old and ran toward the bridle path in Central Park as I saw two horses about to trot past. "Yea! Horsie! Yea!" I yelled. Then I noticed one figure on horseback. She was white, and she shouted, "Shut up, you f—nigger! Shut up!" She pulled back on the reins and twisted the horse in my direction. I can still feel the spray of gravel that

the horse kicked at my chest. And suddenly she was gone. I looked back and, in the distance, saw my parents playing whiffle ball with my sister. They seemed miles away.

They still don't know about this incident. But I told my Aunt Aurelia   8 almost immediately. She explained what the words meant and why they were said. Ever since then I have been able to express my anger appropriately through words or actions in similar situations. Self-preservation, ego, and pride forbid me from ever ignoring, much less forgetting, a slur.

Aunt Aurelia became, unintentionally, my source for answers I needed   9 about color and race. I never sought her out. She just seemed to appear at my home during the points in my childhood when I most needed her for solace. "Puerto Ricans are different from American blacks," she told me once. "There is no racism between what you call white and black. Nobody even considers the marriages interracial." She then pointed out the difference in color between my father and mother. "You never noticed that," she said, "because you were not raised with that hang-up."

Aunt Aurelia passed away before I could follow up on her observation.   10 But she had made an important point. It's why I never liked the attitude that says I should be exclusive to one race.

My behavior toward this race thing pegged me as an iconoclast of sorts.   11 Children from mixed marriages, from my experience, also share this attitude. If I have to beat the label of iconoclast because the world wants people to be in set categories and I don't want to, then I will.

A month before Aunt Aurelia died, she saw I was a little down about the   12 whole race thing, and she said, "Roberto, don't worry. Even if—no matter what you do—black people in this country don't, you can always depend on white people to treat you like a black."

Thinking Critically About Content

1. What do you think Santiago is defining in this essay?

2. Why do Santiago's friends in the first part of the essay say that he isn't black?

3. What did Aunt Aurelia teach Santiago about his ethnicity?

Thinking Critically About Purpose and Audience

4. Why do you think Santiago wrote this essay?

5. Who do you think Santiago's primary audience is?

6. Does this essay help you understand your own identity? Explain your answer.

Thinking Critically About Sentences

7. How do the Spanish words sprinkled in some sentences help you appreciate what Santiago is saying? Explain your answer.

8. Explain how the topic sentence works in paragraph 7: "My first encounter with this attitude about the race thing rode on horseback." Do the other sentences in the paragraph support this topic sentence?

9. Write one or more complete sentences describing what you think Santiago's worst struggle has been.

Writing Topics: Defining

Before you begin to write, you might want to review the writing process in Part I.

1. In the first essay, Basco defines perfectionism. Write your own definition of another character trait, such as alcoholism, workaholism, procrastination, or optimism.

2. Using Santiago's method of development through examples, explain your identity.

ANALYZING CAUSES AND EFFECTS

Analyzing causes and effects is what we do to make sense out of the world around us. It involves searching for connections and reasons. The essays in this chapter discuss the causes and effects of certain actions or ideas. In the first essay, "How the Navy Changed My Life," Bryan Johnson explains how military discipline and education saved his life. The second essay, "For My Indian Daughter" by Lewis Sawaquat, discusses prejudice and heritage.

Bryan Johnson
HOW THE NAVY CHANGED MY LIFE

Focusing Your Attention

1. Describe a time when someone you know tried to talk you out of an important decision. Did you take his or her advice? Explain the issue and its effect on your life.

2. In the essay you are about to read, education was the beginning of a new life for the author. Describe how you think your college education will change your life. Where do you think you will be, and what do you think you will be doing after you graduate? How will your education help you reach your goals?

Expanding Your Vocabulary

The following words are important to your understanding of this essay.

sentiments: feelings (paragraph 2)

abysmal: awful (paragraph 3)

chaise longue: couchlike chair (paragraph 3)

canned: fired from a job (paragraph 3)

quintessential: purest, most perfect (paragraph 3)

Gen-Xer: member of Generation X, born between 1965 and 1985 (paragraph 3)

rack: bed (paragraph 6)

invigorating: exhilarating, stimulating (paragraph 9)

solitude: being alone (paragraph 9)

preconceived notion: preexisting opinion or assumption (paragraph 9)

1   I still remember a good friend's concern when I joined the Navy a year out of high school. "Dude, what are you doin'? You could die or sump'n. You're crazy, bro'."

2   I understood his sentiments. The thought of signing up for military service in post-Vietnam America evoked images of dope-smoking teenagers wandering the jungle. The "praise the Lord and pass the ammunition" days of World War II just didn't seem realistic in 1989. I thought of military enlistment as custom-made for boneheads not bright enough to further their education or talented enough to do anything else.

3   If that was the case, then I fit the mold at 19. I barely graduated from high school with an abysmal 1.8 GPA; my most formidable accomplishment was holding the senior-year record for skipping classes. After high school, I drove a patio-furniture delivery van. I had "quit" my other job as a cashier after being accused of fingering money from the register (truthfully, I just couldn't add or subtract). I could usually be found speeding through a retirement community en route to dropping off a *chaise longue*, giving old people in golf carts the bird when they yelled at me to slow down. Customer complaints were many, and if it weren't for a lack of available delivery boys, I would have been canned. I was the quintessential Gen-Xer, a prime example of why the world was going to pot.

4   Faced with a life of delivering windproof side tables, I decided to give the military a shot. When I bid farewell at the patio store and turned in my van keys, the manager laughed. "You'll be back," he said. I walked out thinking he was probably right.

5   My parents were more relieved than saddened when I left for boot camp. Mom knew those daily confrontations with Dad would end, and the old man thought a military hitch might straighten me out.

6   Pops couldn't have been more right. After naval boot camp, I was assigned as a "deck ape" on a destroyer, my days filled with backbreaking

hours of sanding and painting in a never-ending battle to preserve the ship's exterior. I learned the value of an honest day's work but soon began looking for a way out of a dull, weary routine. I found it that first Christmas home, when I spent my stocking money on remedial math and reading texts. I returned to the ship with a backpack full of scholarly spoils, and the tiny bulb over my rack burned every night for almost a year. My hard work paid off when I landed a position standing navigation watch.

As he showed me how to plot our destroyer's course, my new supervisor   7
said something that made a lasting impression. "If you don't do your job right, don't pay attention, people could die." Lives were at stake, and someone was trusting me to make good decisions. I was honored. What an odd yet wonderful feeling that was.

More important, a fire had ignited inside me. I now rose to challenges   8
instead of avoiding them and loved the sense of self-worth I felt at a job well done. I grabbed at every opportunity thrown my way. I won't soon forget the time I maneuvered the ship's wheel on a course through the Panama Canal or rescued a trapped dolphin in the Persian Gulf.

While life at sea had many invigorating moments, it could also be very   9
lonely. To fill in those empty hours of solitude, crew members talked with one another, and we often knew everything about the men we lived and labored with. I learned that a person's skin color or where he came from wasn't a very good indicator of his character. I also realized that my preconceived notion of a military consisting of losers was completely unfounded. I knew one sailor, for instance, who could have supported his wife and baby more easily by flipping burgers at McDonald's. He joined the Navy because he cherished his country's freedom and wanted to give his time and energy in return.

Despite a worthwhile four years, I decided not to re-enlist and to give   10
college a try. I diligently pursued a B.S. degree and graduated with honors and hopes of attending medical school.

Yet something was missing. I recalled the pride I had felt in my uniform,   11
a symbol of something greater than myself. I applied to the United States' only military school of medicine and started classes last fall.

Going home these days is a bit like winding back the clock 10 years—   12
old friends look bewildered when I mention that I've rejoined the service. Don't think I'm offended; I belong to an organization that defends the right of Americans to have their own opinions.

Although I've put the past behind me, I often wonder what that man-   13
ager would say if I dropped by the patio store. But then he'd be right; I would be back—but only to buy a ceramic yard frog.

Thinking Critically About Content

1. What caused Johnson to return to school after joining the Navy?

2. Why did Johnson first join the military? What values did he learn there? How did these values influence his future decisions?

3. How do you think Johnson's duties in the Navy will help him in his medical career?

Thinking Critically About Purpose and Audience

4. Why do you think Johnson wrote this essay?

5. What audience do you think would most understand and appreciate this essay?

6. Why do you think Johnson includes information about his "abysmal" school record and first two jobs? In what ways does this information help you understand the importance of the Navy in Johnson's life?

Thinking Critically About Sentences

7. Summarize this essay in a few sentences. Focus on the causes and effects that Johnson discusses.

8. What is Johnson's point of view toward education?

9. Write one or more complete sentences that Johnson might say to a group of seniors in high school about going to college.

Lewis Sawaquat

FOR MY INDIAN DAUGHTER

Focusing Your Attention

1. What do you know about your heritage? Have you or anyone you know ever gone through an identity crisis? If so, what was the situation?

2. The essay you are about to read is a personal memoir of the author's Native American roots. What do you know about Native American history in this country? What stories do you know about Native Americans that you can share with your class?

Expanding Your Vocabulary

The following words are important to your understanding of this essay.

guttural: throaty (paragraph 2)

affluent: rich (paragraph 5)

comeuppance: deserved punishment (paragraph 7)

irony: mockery, humor (paragraph 7)

lore: knowledge, teachings (paragraph 8)

powwow: ceremonial meeting (paragraph 9)

iridescent: shimmering, glistening (paragraph 9)

masquerade: disguise oneself (paragraph 10)

culminated: ended, peaked (paragraph 12)

discomfiting: disturbing, frustrating (paragraph 13)

solitude: being alone (paragraph 14)

My little girl is singing herself to sleep upstairs, her voice mingling with 1
the sounds of the birds outside in the old maple trees. She is two, and I am
nearly 50, and I am very taken with her. She came along late in my life, unexpected and unbidden, a startling gift.

Today at the beach my chubby-legged, brown-skinned daughter ran 2
laughing into the water as fast as she could. My wife and I laughed watching her, until we heard behind us a low guttural curse and then an un-
pleasant voice raised in an imitation war whoop.

I turned to see a fat man in a bathing suit, white and soft as a grub, as 3
he covered his mouth and prepared to make the Indian war cry again. He
was middle-aged, younger than I, and had three little children lined up
next to him, grinning foolishly. My wife suggested we leave the beach, and
I agreed.

I knew the man was not unusual in his feelings against Indians. His 4
beach behavior might have been socially unacceptable to more civilized
whites, but his basic view of Indians is expressed daily in our small town,
frequently on the editorial pages of the county newspaper, as white people
speak out against Indian fishing rights and land rights, saying in essence,
"Those Indians are taking our fish, our land." It doesn't matter to them that
we were here first, that the U.S. Supreme Court has ruled in our favor. It
matters to them that we have something they want, and they hate us for it.
Backlash is the common explanation of the attacks on Indians, the bumper
stickers that say, "Spear an Indian, Save a Fish," but I know better. The hatred of Indians goes back to the beginning when white people came to this
country. For me it goes back to my childhood in Harbor Springs, Michigan.

Theft

Harbor Springs is now a summer resort for the very affluent, but a hun- 5
dred years ago it was the Indian village of my Ottawa ancestors. My grandmother, Anna Showanessy, and other Indians like her had their land there

taken by treaty, by fraud, by violence, by theft. They remembered how whites had burned down the village at Burt Lake in 1900 and pushed the Indians out. These were the stories in my family.

6   When I was a boy, my mother told me to walk down the alleys in Harbor Springs and not to wear my orange football sweater out of the house. This way I would not stand out, not be noticed, and not be a target.

7   I wore my orange sweater anyway and deliberately avoided the alleys. I was the biggest person I knew and wasn't really afraid. But I met my comeuppance when I enlisted in the U.S. Army. One night all the men in my barracks gathered together and, gang-fashion, pulled me into the shower and scrubbed me down with rough brushes used for floors, saying, "We won't have any dirty Indians in our outfit." It is a point of irony that I was cleaner than any of them. Later in Korea I learned how to kill, how to bully, how to hate Koreans. I came out of the war tougher than ever and, strangely, white.

8   I went to college, got married, lived in La Porte, Indiana, worked as a surveyor, and raised three boys. I headed Boy Scout groups, never thinking it odd when the Scouts did imitation Indian dances, imitation Indian lore.

9   One day when I was 35 or thereabouts, I heard about an Indian pow-wow. My father used to attend them, and so with great curiosity and a strange joy at discovering a part of my heritage, I decided the thing to do to get ready for this big event was to have my friend make me a spear in his forge. The steel was fine and blue and iridescent. The feathers on the shaft were bright and proud.

10   In a dusty state fairground in southern Indiana, I found white people dressed as Indians. I learned they were "hobbyists"; that is, it was their hobby and leisure pastime to masquerade as Indians on weekends. I felt ridiculous with my spear, and I left.

11   It was years before I could tell anyone of the embarrassment of this weekend and see any humor in it. But in a way it was that weekend, for all its silliness, that was my awakening. I realized I didn't know who I was. I didn't have an Indian name. I didn't speak the Indian language. I didn't know the Indian customs. Dimly I remembered the Ottawa word for dog, but it was a baby word, *kahgee*, not the full word, *muhkahgee*, which I was later to learn. Even more hazily I remembered a naming ceremony (my own). I remembered legs dancing around me, dust. Where had that been? Who had I been? "Sawaquat," my mother told me when I asked, "where the tree begins to grow."

12   That was 1968, and I was not the only Indian in the country who was feeling the need to remember who he or she was. There were others. They had powwows, real ones, and eventually I found them. Together we researched

our past, a search that for me culminated in the Longest Walk, a march on Washington in 1978. Maybe because I now know what it means to be Indian, it surprises me that others don't. Of course, there aren't very many of us left. The chances of an average person knowing an average Indian in an average lifetime are pretty slim.

Circle

Still, I was amused one day when my small, four-year-old neighbor 13 looked at me as I was hoeing in my garden and said, "You aren't a real Indian, are you?" Scotty is little, talkative, likable. Finally I said, "I'm a real Indian." He looked at me for a moment and then said, squinting into the sun, "Then where's your horse and feathers?" The child was simply a smaller, whiter version of my own ignorant self years before. We'd both seen too much TV; that's all. He was not to be blamed. And so, in a way, the moronic man on the beach today is blameless. We come full circle to realize other people are like ourselves, as discomfiting as that may be sometimes.

As I sit in my old chair on my porch, in a light that is fading so the leaves 14 are barely distinguishable against the sky, I can picture my girl asleep upstairs. I would like to prepare her for what's to come, take her each step of the way saying, there's a place to avoid, here's what I know about this, but much of what's before her she must go through alone. She must pass through pain and joy and solitude and community to discover her own inner self that is unlike any other and come through that passage to the place where she sees all people are one and in so seeing may live her life in a brighter future.

Thinking Critically About Content

1. What does Sawaquat see as the origin of the hatred of Native Americans in the United States?

2. What does Sawaquat learn from his first powwow?

3. Why do you think Sawaquat says that his daughter "must pass through pain and joy and solitude and community to discover her own inner self" (paragraph 14)? To what extent do we all need to do this in our lives?

Thinking Critically About Purpose and Audience

4. Why does Sawaquat begin this essay with the story about his daughter on the beach? How does the story make you feel?

5. The author calls paragraphs 5–12 "Theft" and paragraphs 13–14 "Circle." Explain these two subtitles.

6. Who do you think would enjoy this essay the most? Who do you think would benefit most from this essay?

Thinking Critically About Sentences

7. Explain the significance of the sentence, "'Then where's your horse and feathers?'" (paragraph 13).

8. What is the topic sentence of paragraph 7? Do all the sentences in that paragraph support this topic sentence? Explain your answer.

9. Write one or more sentences that might represent how Sawaquat's two-year-old daughter felt when the fat man made whooping sounds on the beach.

Writing Topics: Analyzing Causes and Effects

Before you begin to write, you might want to review the writing process in Part I.

1. In the first essay, Johnson was motivated by a dead-end job to make a dramatic change in his life. Has anything motivated you to make an important change in your life? What were the circumstances?

2. In "For My Indian Daughter," Sawaquat says that his daughter must find her inner self on her own. Do you think you have found your inner self? How did you discover it? Was it painful? How does this discovery help you relate to others?

ARGUING

The purpose of **arguing** is to persuade people to take a certain action or to think or feel a specific way. The essays in this chapter show the power of argument. The first essay, titled "So That Nobody Has to Go to School If They Don't Want To," was written by Roger Sipher. In it, Sipher tries to persuade his readers that required attendance in high school lowers the quality of the education that is available and should be abolished. The second essay, "It's a Job for Parents, Not the Government" by John Romano, argues that parents rather than the government should take responsibility for protecting their children from violence in the media.

Roger Sipher

SO THAT NOBODY HAS TO GO TO SCHOOL IF THEY DON'T WANT TO

Focusing Your Attention

1. What role does education play in our society?
2. The essay you are about to read focuses on education as the key to living a good life. How important is education to you? How important is it to your family? Explain your answer.

Expanding Your Vocabulary

The following words are important to your understanding of this essay.

antagonistic: opposing, against (paragraph 2)

compulsory: required (paragraph 3)

mandatory: required (paragraph 4)

assertion: statement (paragraph 5)

repeal: to cancel (paragraph 5)

homage: respect (paragraph 7)

homily: words on moral behavior (paragraph 7)

recalcitrant: difficult to handle (paragraph 8)

1   A decline in standardized test scores is but the most recent indicator that American education is in trouble.

2   One reason for the crisis is that present mandatory-attendance laws force many to attend school who have no wish to be there. Such children have little desire to learn and are so antagonistic to school that neither they nor more highly motivated students receive the quality education that is the birthright of every American.

3   The solution to this problem is simple: Abolish compulsory-attendance laws and allow only those who are committed to getting an education to attend.

4   This will not end public education. Contrary to conventional belief, legislators enacted compulsory-attendance laws to legalize what already existed. William Landes and Lewis Solomon, economists, found little evidence that mandatory-attendance laws increased the number of children in school. They found, too, that school systems have never effectively enforced such laws, usually because of the expense involved.

5   There is no contradiction between the assertion that compulsory attendance has had little effect on the number of children attending school and the argument that repeal would be a positive step toward improving education. Most parents want a high school education for their children. Unfortunately, compulsory attendance hampers the ability of public school officials to enforce legitimate educational and disciplinary policies and thereby make the education a good one.

6   Private schools have no such problem. They can fail or dismiss students, knowing such students can attend public school. Without compulsory attendance, public schools would be freer to oust students whose academic or personal behavior undermines the educational mission of the institution.

7   Has not the noble experiment of a formal education for everyone failed? While we pay homage to the homily, "You can lead a horse to water, but you can't make him drink," we have pretended it is not true in education.

8   Ask high school teachers if recalcitrant students learn anything of value. Ask teachers if these students do any homework. Ask if the threat of low grades motivates them. Quite the contrary, these students know they will be passed from grade to grade until they are old enough to quit or until, as is more likely, they receive a high school diploma. At the point

when students could legally quit, most choose to remain since they know they are likely to be allowed to graduate whether they do acceptable work or not.

Abolition of archaic attendance laws would produce enormous dividends. 9

First, it would alert everyone that school is a serious place where one goes to learn. Schools are neither day-care centers nor indoor street corners. Young people who resist learning should stay away; indeed, an end to compulsory schooling would require them to stay away. 10

Second, students opposed to learning would not be able to pollute the educational atmosphere for those who want to learn. Teachers could stop policing recalcitrant students and start educating. 11

Third, grades would show what they are supposed to: how well a student is learning. Parents could again read report cards and know if their children were making progress. 12

Fourth, public esteem for schools would increase. People would stop regarding them as way stations for adolescents and start thinking of them as institutions for educating America's youth. 13

Fifth, elementary schools would change because students would find out early that they had better learn something or risk flunking out later. Elementary teachers would no longer have to pass their failures on to junior high and high school. 14

Sixth, the cost of enforcing compulsory education would be eliminated. Despite enforcement efforts, nearly 15 percent of the school-age children in our largest cities are almost permanently absent from school. 15

Communities could use these savings to support institutions to deal with young people not in school. If, in the long run, these institutions prove more costly, at least we would not confuse their mission with that of schools. 16

Schools should be for education. At present, they are only tangentially so. They have attempted to serve an all-encompassing social function, trying to be all things to all people. In the process, they have failed miserably at what they were originally formed to accomplish. 17

Thinking Critically About Content

1. What is one of the primary indicators that American schools are "in trouble" (paragraph 1)?

2. What is Sipher's suggested solution to the education crisis in the United States?

3. What does Sipher believe would be the dividends of ending compulsory attendance?

Thinking Critically About Purpose and Audience

4. What do you think Sipher's purpose is in this essay?

5. Who do you think is Sipher's primary audience for this essay? Explain your answer.

6. Why do you think Sipher suggests in paragraph 8 that we talk to teachers themselves? How does this reference further his argument?

Thinking Critically About Sentences

7. Write five sentences explaining Sipher's main arguments.

8. In paragraph 17, what does Sipher mean when he says, "Schools should be for education. At present, they are only tangentially so"? Why are these sentences important to his message?

9. Write one or more complete sentences in response to this essay. Address your remarks to Sipher himself.

John Romano

IT'S A JOB FOR PARENTS, NOT THE GOVERNMENT

Focusing Your Attention

1. At what age or in what situation do you think children can handle violence on TV or in movies?

2. In the essay you are about to read, the writer discusses issues connected with limiting or regulating violence on TV. What do you think some of these issues are?

Expanding Your Vocabulary

The following words are important to your understanding of this essay.

counterexperts: experts studying the opposing side (paragraph 3)

correlated, correlation: related, relationship (paragraph 3)

masquerading: disguised (paragraph 3)

impious: disrespectful (paragraph 4)

tainted: corrupt (paragraph 4)

purveyors: makers (paragraph 5)

foregone: predetermined (paragraph 5)

intervention: interruption (paragraph 6)

regrettable: sad (paragraph 6)

undifferentiated: not separated or distinguished (paragraph 7)

egregious: obviously bad (paragraph 7)

On an August day in 1993, a few hundred TV makers like myself, from writer-producers to network chiefs, gathered in the grand ballroom of a Beverly Hills, California, hotel for the less-than-grand experience of being pelted with statistics. Led by the then Sen. Paul Simon, experts presented the yield of a dozen years of university studies, showing or seeming to show that watching violence on TV made kids violent. From Saturday-morning cartoons to prime-time dramas and the news, the number of violent incidents per week approached four digits. American kids reached high school having "witnessed" some 8,000 murders. 1

Naturally, we TV folk squirmed. We'd ask, "Can our programs actually make a nonviolent kid violent? Will you settle for 'reinforce'?" They'd answer, "But why would you even want to reinforce violence in children?" Nice point. Or we'd say, "Where are the parents? Didn't they ever hear of flipping?" They'd shoot back, "What about latchkey kids, whose single parents have no choice but to use the TV as babysitter?" 2

But even on that day there were counterexperts pointing out that the studies were at best controversial and at worst unscientific because they showed correlation instead of cause. Remember your philosophy professor with his old saw about how the rise of alcoholism between 1885 and 1900 correlated with the rise in the number of Baptist ministers? He'd let you flounder for a while, then let you off the hook with the explanation: *population* rose between 1885 and 1900. But when the making of public policy is at stake, correlation masquerading as cause is not merely foolish; it's dangerous. Suppose a correlation could be shown, for instance, between certain ethnic groups and violent or criminal behavior: should ethnicity be cited as cause and targeted by Congress—or should deeper causes be looked for? 3

And as for the latchkey kid, some of the skeptics asked, aren't there other circumstances in their lives that we should be worried about? Circumstances of neglect or poverty that might bring violence into their lives in ways other than TV? But, on that August day, any questioning or criticism of the statistics went unanswered. The issue was our children's safety, and so even clear thinking seemed impious. By the time we collected our cars from valet parking, it was with a sense that we'd bought them with tainted money. Impressed by sessions such as this one, we in the industry imposed 4 a ratings system on ourselves in 1996, and the V-chip entered American life. Round One.

5   Enter 1999 and the 15 deaths at Littleton, Colorado, and an understandable sense of national urgency. The president summons to Washington, along with gunmakers, the purveyors of violence on TV and in movies. He orders up a study on the effects of TV—only this one, many in the media fear, is attended by the real threat of government regulation when the foregone conclusion is reached: TV causes violent behavior in youth. It's true that some social scientists continue to argue that the Littletons are not even the tip of the iceberg when measured against the vast majority of teenagers. But if such calm reasoning was uncomfortable before Littleton, it feels downright indecent now, when we can still remember seeing the bereaved friends and families. On TV.

6   And yet public panic never comes without a cost. The more seriously we take the possible dangers of TV watching, and the possible need for "tough" government intervention, the more important it is that we raise the IQ of the discussion. Of course, there are pointlessly violent shows not only available to children but aimed at them. They are a regrettable pollution of our popular culture, even if they cause not a single act of violence.

7   But it's also true that counting up the number of undifferentiated "incidents" of violence on TV is misleading. It lumps together egregious uses of TV violence with its (dare I say it) positive uses—for instance, the disturbingly graphic moments of bloodshed that give force to the morally edifying dramas of "NYPD Blue" or "Homicide."

8   The vigor of our nation's creativity must be protected. No government can spare its citizens the job of being good parents. If you don't want your kids watching, turn the darn thing off. Just as, if you don't want them reading the Iliad because it's violent or the Decameron because it's gloriously, openly erotic, you would put the books on a high shelf they can't reach. These days the public, goaded on by politicians, seems like it's warming up for a book burning, and the idea of holding a book burning in the halls of Congress is truly violent and obscene. And it's the most un-American thing anybody has thought of in a long time.

Thinking Critically About Content

1. Why do you think Romano starts his essay by referring to the official meeting on kids and TV violence that was conducted by Sen. Paul Simon? Is it an effective beginning to the essay? Explain your answer.

2. According to Romano, what makes violence on TV an issue for parents rather than for the government?

3. What does Romano mean in the last sentence when he implies that government control of violence on TV is like a book burning?

Thinking Critically About Purpose and Audience

4. What do you think Romano's purpose is in this essay?

5. Who do you think would be most interested in this essay?

6. What effect do you think this essay would have on parents?

Thinking Critically About Sentences

7. Describe in a complete sentence the writer's point of view.

8. Why do you think the writer refers to the 15 deaths in Littleton, Colorado, in 1999? What effect does it create in the essay?

9. This essay presents both sides of the issue on controlling violence on TV for kids but supports one side in the end. Rewrite the conclusion of this essay so that it recommends that the government (rather than the parents) regulate TV violence.

Writing Topics: Arguing

Before you begin to write, you might want to review the writing process in Part I.

1. In "So That Nobody Has to Go to School If They Don't Want To," Roger Sipher tries to persuade his readers that abolishing compulsory attendance in high school might raise the quality of education at that level. Think of another strategy that might improve the quality of education in our public schools, and try to convince a group of high school administrators to put your idea into practice.

2. Romano's essay argues that forcing parents to monitor their children's TV watching is necessary if we are going to remain a democratic society. Think of another strategy for controlling the violence that children are exposed to on TV, and write an argument that presents an alternate idea.

APPENDIX 1 Critical Thinking Log

Circle the critical thinking questions that you missed after each essay you read. Have your instructor explain the pattern of errors.

Reading	Content	Purpose and Audience	Sentences	Number Correct
Describing				
Collette Russell	1 2 3	4 5 6	7 8 9	
Judith Ortiz Cofer	1 2 3	4 5 6	7 8 9	
Narrating				
Henry Louis Gates Jr.	1 2 3	4 5 6	7 8 9	
Elizabeth Wong	1 2 3	4 5 6	7 8 9	
Illustrating				
Sherry Hemman Hogan	1 2 3	4 5 6	7 8 9	
Bailey White	1 2 3	4 5 6	7 8 9	
Analyzing a Process				
Peter Jaret	1 2 3	4 5 6	7 8 9	
Tomás Robles	1 2 3	4 5 6	7 8 9	
Comparing and Contrasting				
Lisen Stromberg	1 2 3	4 5 6	7 8 9	
Dave Barry	1 2 3	4 5 6	7 8 9	
Dividing and Classifying				
Annie Murphy Paul	1 2 3	4 5 6	7 8 9	
John Roger and Peter McWilliams	1 2 3	4 5 6	7 8 9	
Defining				
Monica Ramirez Basco	1 2 3	4 5 6	7 8 9	
Roberto Santiago	1 2 3	4 5 6	7 8 9	
Analyzing Causes and Effects				
Bryan Johnson	1 2 3	4 5 6	7 8 9	
Lewis Sawaquat	1 2 3	4 5 6	7 8 9	
Arguing				
Roger Sipher	1 2 3	4 5 6	7 8 9	
John Romano	1 2 3	4 5 6	7 8 9	

The legend on the reverse side will help you identify your strengths and weaknesses in critical thinking.

Legend for Critical Thinking Log

Questions	Skill
1–2	Literal and interpretive understanding
3–6	Critical thinking and analysis
7–8	Analyzing sentences
9	Writing paragraphs

APPENDIX 2A

Use the following questions to evaluate your partner's paragraph. Direct your comments to your partner.

Writer: _____ **Peer:** _____

Writing a Paragraph

1. Does the writer choose a subject that can be covered in a single paragraph? Explain your answer.

Topic Sentence

2. Does the topic sentence contain the paragraph's controlling idea and appear as the first or last sentence? Explain your answer.

Development

3. Does the paragraph contain enough specific details to develop the topic sentence? Explain your answer.

Unity

4. Do all the sentences in the paragraph support the topic sentence? Explain your answer.

Organization

5. Is the paragraph organized so readers can easily follow it? Explain your answer.

Coherence

6. Do the sentences move smoothly and logically from one to the next? Explain your answer.

APPENDIX 2B

Use the following questions to help you find editing errors in your partner's paragraph. Mark the errors directly on your partner's paper using the editing symbols on the inside back cover.

Writer: _____   **Peer:** _____

Sentences

1. Does each sentence have a subject and verb?

   Mark any fragments you find with *frag*.

   Mark any run-together sentences you find with a slash (/) between them.

2. Do all subjects and verbs agree?

   Mark any subject-verb agreement errors you find with *sv*.

3. Do all pronouns agree with their nouns?

   Mark any pronoun errors you find with *pro agr*.

4. Are all modifiers as close as possible to the words they modify?

   Mark any modifier errors you find with *ad* (adjective or adverb problem), *mm* (misplaced modifier), or *dm* (dangling modifier).

Punctuation and Mechanics

5. Are sentences punctuated correctly?

   Mark any punctuation errors you find with the appropriate symbol under Unit 5 of the editing symbols (inside back cover).

6. Are words capitalized properly?

   Mark any capitalization errors you find with *lc* (lowercase) or *cap* (capital).

Word Choice and Spelling

7. Are words used correctly?

   Mark any words that are used incorrectly with *wc* (word choice) or *ww* (wrong word).

8. Are words spelled correctly?

   Mark any misspelled words you find with *sp*.

APPENDIX 3 Editing Quotient Error Chart

Put an X in the square that corresponds to each question that you missed.

	a	b	c	d	e	f	g	h
1								
2								
3								
4								
5								
6								
7								
8								
9								
10								

Then record your errors in the following categories to find out where you might need help.

Fragments

1b _____ 1d _____ 2a _____ 3c _____ 4d _____

5c _____ 6d _____ 7b _____ 8g _____ 9e _____

10a _____

Run-togethers

1a _____ 1c _____ 2c _____ 3d _____ 4a _____

5d _____ 6c _____ 7c _____ 8c _____ 9f _____

10c _____

Subject-verb agreement   2b _____ 2d _____ 9a _____

Verb forms   3a _____ 3b _____

Pronoun reference	8b _____		
Pronoun agreement	4b _____	4c _____	4e _____
Modifiers	5a _____	5b _____	
End punctuation	6e _____		
Commas	6b _____	9d _____	10b _____
Capitalization	6a _____	9b _____	9c _____
Abbreviations	8a _____		
Numbers	7a _____		
Confused words	8d _____	8e _____	8f _____ 8h _____ 10d _____

APPENDIX 4 Error Log

List any grammar, punctuation, and mechanics errors you make in your writing on the following chart. Then, to the right of this label, record (1) the actual error from your writing, (2) the rule for correcting this error, and (3) your correction.

Error	
Comma	**Example** I went to the new seafood restaurant and I ordered the lobster.
	Rule Always use a comma before a coordinating conjunction when joining two independent clauses.
	Correction I went to the new seafood restaurant, and I ordered the lobster.
Error	**Example**
	Rule
	Correction
Error	**Example**
	Rule
	Correction
Error	**Example**
	Rule
	Correction
Error	**Example**
	Rule
	Correction
Error	**Example**
	Rule
	Correction
Error	**Example**
	Rule
	Correction
Error	**Example**
	Rule
	Correction

Error	Example
	Rule
	Correction
Error	Example
	Rule
	Correction
Error	Example
	Rule
	Correction
Error	Example
	Rule
	Correction
Error	Example
	Rule
	Correction
Error	Example
	Rule
	Correction
Error	Example
	Rule
	Correction
Error	Example
	Rule
	Correction
Error	Example
	Rule
	Correction
Error	Example
	Rule
	Correction

APPENDIX 5 Spelling Log

On this chart, record any words you misspell, and write the correct spelling in the space next to the misspelled word. In the right column, write a note to yourself to help you remember the correct spelling. (See the first line for an example.) Refer to this chart as often as necessary to avoid misspelling the same words again.

Misspelled Word	Correct Spelling	Definition/Notes
there	their	there = place; their = pronoun; they're = "they are"

CREDITS

UNIT **1** REVIEW
Photo: Ryan McVay/Getty Images, Inc./PhotoDisc, Inc.

UNIT **2** REVIEW
Photo: Nick Dolding/Getty Images, Inc./Stone Allstock

UNIT **3** REVIEW
Photo: Bill Bachmann/PhotoEdit.

UNIT **4** REVIEW
Photo: Tony Craddock/Getty Images, Inc./Stone Allstock

UNIT **5** REVIEW
Photo: Simon Bruty/Getty Images, Inc./Stone Allstock

UNIT **6** REVIEW
Photo: Getty Images, Inc./PhotoDisc, Inc.

UNIT **7** REVIEW
Photo: Tony Freeman/PhotoEdit.

UNIT **8** REVIEW
Photo: Myrleen Ferguson Cate/PhotoEdit.

CHAPTER **38**
Photo: Doug Menuez/Getty Images, Inc./PhotoDisc, Inc.

CHAPTER **39**
"A Day in the Homeless Life" by Collette Russell, originally appeared in *Street Magazine,* April 1989; *Utne Reader,* September/October 1990.

"Casa: A Partial Remembrance of a Puerto Rican Childhood" by Judith Ortiz Cofer, *Prairie Schooner.* Reprinted from *Prairie Schooner,* volume 63, number 3 (1989), reprinted by permission of the University of Nebraska Press. Copyright © 1989 University of Nebraska Press.

CHAPTER **40**
"A Giant Step" by Henry Louis Gates Jr., *The New York Times,* December 9, 1990. Copyright © 1990 The New York Times Co. Reprinted by permission.

"The Struggle to Be an All-American Girl" by Elizabeth Wong. Copyright © 1995 Elizabeth Wong. Reprinted by permission of the author.

CHAPTER **41**
"A Question of Trust" by Sherry Hemman Hogan, *Reader's Digest,* September 1999. Copyright © 1999 The Reader's Digest Association, Inc. Reprinted with permission from the September 1999 *Reader's Digest.* Copyright © 1999 by The Reader's Digest Association.

"Mortality" by Bailey White. From *Mama Makes Up Her Mind: And Other Dangers of Southern Living* by Bailey White. Copyright © 1993 Bailey White. Reprinted by permission of Perseus Books PLC, a member of Perseus Books, LLC.

INDEX ❖